JOURNEY INTO DIVINE INTIMACY WITH ST. TERESA OF AVILA:

A Retreat, Spiritual Direction Guide, and Study Resource

JOURNEY INTO DIVINE INTIMACY WITH ST. TERESA OF AVILA:

A Retreat, Spiritual Direction Guide, and Study Resource

Sister Leslie L. Lund, ocdh

Carmelite Sisters of Mary Publishers

Washington State

2019

Copyright © 2019 by Carmelite Sisters of Mary

All rights reserved.

Some quotations of St. Teresa of Avila are taken from the *Collected Works of St. Teresa of Avila*, translated by Kieran Kavanaugh and Otilio Rodriguez, Copyright © 1976, 1980, 1985; and *The Collected Letters of St. Teresa,* translated by Kieran Kavanaugh, Copyright © 2001, 2007 by the Washington Province of Discalced Carmelites ICS Publications, 2131 Lincoln Road, N.E. Washington, D.C. 20002-1199 U.S.A. www.icspublications.org Used with permission.

In addition to using the Kavanaugh/Rodriguez and Peers editions of St. Teresa's writings, many quotes are my own work based on one or another of the common translations of respected writers, and also the Spanish language edition: *Teresa de Jesus: Obras Completas,* Texto revisado y anotado por Fr. Tomas de la Cruz, c.d., © 1977.

ISBN: 978-0-578-53671-2

Copyright 2019

Cover art: by Patricia Shubeck
Other art by Sr. Nancy Casale, ocdh, Joni Dirks, and Patricia Shubeck

Printed in the United States of America

Lund, Leslie Lin, 1949-
    Journey into Divine Intimacy with St. Teresa of Avila : A Retreat, Spiritual Direction Guide, and Study Resource / Sister Leslie Lin Lund, ocdh.
   387 p. 25.5 cm.
   Includes bibliographical references and supplemental material.
   1. Teresa, of Avila, Saint, 1515-1582. 2. Prayer—Christianity. 3. Contemplation. 4. Spiritual Life—Catholic. 5. Mysticism—Catholic Church—History—16th century. 6. Spiritual Direction. I. Title.

Reader Reviews

"The author, Sr. Leslie Lund, ocdh, has done what very few have had the willingness to do, namely assemble a resource of information and answers to the many questions that readers, spiritual directors, and scholars encounter in their reflections on Teresa of Avila. It is a major undertaking, demanding extraordinary time, experience, and dedication. We are all grateful to Sr. Leslie for this gift. Lots of books of reflection and piety exist around Teresa's teaching, but nothing like this, and few as serious as this. However, not only has Sr. Leslie presented us a wonderful resource for questions on Teresa's life, theology, and spirituality, she has also shown us how to use Teresa's teaching on the "mansions" as a dynamic, transformational, and life-changing retreat that we can use individually or in groups. This book can be used by those in formation work, by novices in their training, by secular Carmelites as part of group development, by individuals in private retreats. It is a companion for spiritual directors in their ministry whatever their spiritual tradition. Anyone who reads this book will be drawn to deeper knowledge and dedication in their spiritual lives. May the book gain the wide-ranging audience it deserves."

Professor Leonard Doohan, PhD, Teresianum
Professor Emeritus, Gonzaga University; and Teresian and Sanjuanist Scholar

"I have to say I was very impressed by this book. It is something one could go back to again and again for help in prayer, in teaching, in study and for information—to mention a few things. It covers so many areas about prayer. Sr. Leslie rightly calls attention to the fact that besides the Jesuit way of praying, there is another prayer form lesser known and proclaimed: the Carmelite one. The Jesuits have many means of promoting their prayer and spirituality through their universities, parishes and retreat centers. Carmelites do not, although it is one of the church's most profound prayer and mystical traditions that has produced such saints as St. John of the Cross, St. Therese, St. Elizabeth of the Trinity, St. Edith Stein and others. Sr. Leslie knows St. Teresa well. And the book is a work of love that can only enrich all who read it. It belongs among the best works written about St. Teresa. May it be a best seller—it deserves to be!"

Sister Mary Teresa of the Sacred Passion, ocd
Carmelite Monastery of Boston

"*Journey into Divine Intimacy with St. Teresa* is a welcome and comprehensive guide to understanding St. Teresa of Avila's masterpiece, *The Interior Castle*. By means of guided meditations, reflection questions, scriptural references and personal insights Sr. Leslie invites the reader to journey more deeply into their own relationship of friendship with the Divine. Her rich trove of supplemental material on both St. Teresa and St. John of the Cross is a valuable resource for any seeking a deeper understanding of Carmelite spirituality."

Sister Claire Sokol, ocd
Carmelite Monastery of Reno

"This would certainly be an excellent book to use with formation in the novitiate and in retreats. I like the way the material was organized, and I especially liked the reflection questions. I found myself taking the questions to prayer, and found it incredibly helpful and thought provoking. I have certainly read *The Interior Castle* before, but the way the material is unpacked for the reader is so very helpful. The supplemental material is like a bonus feature—almost another book in itself! It has been a delight to read the book!"

Sister Susan Elizabeth of the Heart of Jesus, ocd
Carmelite Monastery of Seattle

"This is a book that calls us into a trusting relationship with God dwelling in us. It invites us to respond to Jesus' call to abide in his love. Here, the voice of St. Teresa still urges us to set forth on that journey within, proclaiming to us today how true and faithful a friend God is to us."

Sister Berenice of the Risen Christ
Carmelite Sister of Mary

"Thank you for allowing me to read, grow and have great hope and faith that I might be able to advance in my prayer life. This book is phenomenal. What an inspired and much needed guidance for all who want to experience even some of St. Teresa's prayer!"

Linda Dorrington
Retreat Director/Spiritual Director

"This is an extraordinary book and profound work that has something for everyone. *Journey into Divine Intimacy with St. Teresa of Avila* is a wonderful resource with practical tips and guidelines, and it also delves into the myriad types of prayer that Teresa of Avila describes in *The Interior Castle*. As a spiritual director and retreat leader I believe that Sister Leslie has provided a wealth of material in Carmelite spirituality that enriches me personally in my own life of prayer. I also see the book as being helpful with those I see for spiritual direction and/or work with on retreat."

Sister Patricia Novak, osf
Sisters of St. Francis of Philadelphia

"I have studied the writings of St. Teresa of Avila and St. John of the Cross, with associated commentaries, for 30 years. However, some of the language has always left me floundering. My wife got this for me at Father's Day 2022 – last June/July. She then put me on a 30-day retreat using my garden poustinia. My gosh!!!! Every day was a revelation. Every day was like walking with St. Teresa of Avila into the Interior Castle and discovering hidden treasures. The language is forthright (The ego must be dismantled, self-knowledge and humility are essential), but she also explains so much about the interior life, silence, solitude. Breathtaking. For anybody who takes their spiritual life seriously – and they are a bit of a rare breed at the moment – I tell you this is a MUST."

Reviewed in the United Kingdom on December 30, 2022

"This is the book I was looking for to help my prayer life as a novice lay Carmelite aspirant."

Reviewed in the United States on February 14, 2020

"This book breaks up the ideas in *The Interior Castle*, which is good news for those who struggle with archaic translations and the structure of the original book. Covering the stages of coming to know God as deeply as possible in this life, this analysis is a guide to the original. Since *The Interior Castle* holds ideas common at the time and a narrative written in an unfamiliar form, it can be hard for those without an academic background. This book makes the text more accessible. I can't tell you how many times I've heard Teresa misquoted and misunderstood – particularly in regard to meditation, which meant a different thing than what we mean today by meditation. Maybe this can act as a corrective. It is laid out with bullet points in Teresa's main points, which is useful in getting to what she wrote. It does make the book a bit scholastic, but in the right way. It allows the reader to understand Teresa's train of thought. The supplemental material also helps to understand the concepts and words used in the book. Of course, it's all words unless we actually practice what is taught. This examination is useful to both the experienced reader and the newcomer, because it begins with people at the very earliest stages and goes to union with God."

Reviewed in the United States on March 12, 2020

"One could spend hours reading, studying and contemplating the contents of this well-written, thought-provoking book. It is rich with insights and can guide on a meaningful."

Reviewed in the United States on December 17, 2019

This book is dedicated to friends who gave me a love for St. Teresa

To Dr. Leonard Doohan, PhD
who first introduced me to St. Teresa

To the nuns of the former Carmelite Monastery of Indianapolis, Indiana, and especially to my Novice Mistresses and mentors

Sister Jean Alice McGoff, ocd

Sister Elizabeth Meluch, ocd

Sister Rachel Salute, ocd

Sister Vilma Seelaus, ocd

TABLE OF CONTENTS

Foreword xiii
Abbreviations xv
Acknowledgements xvi
Introduction 1
How to Use this Book 5
How to Use this Book for Prayer 9
How To Use this Book for a Retreat 15

First Dwelling Places—Part 1 19
Description of the First Dwelling Places 19
Teresian Teachings for Prayer and Life 20
Internalizing the Teachings 23
    Reflection—The Riches of Prayer 23
    Reflection Questions 25
Guidance for Prayer and Prayer Period 25

First Dwelling Places—Part 2 29
Description of the First Dwelling Places 29
Teresian Teachings for Prayer and Life 30
Internalizing the Teachings 33
    Reflection—Human Maturation 33
    Reflection Questions 36
Guidance for Prayer and Prayer Period 36

Teresa de Ahumada (Childhood) 1515-1528 41

Second Dwelling Places—Part 1 43
Description of the Second Dwelling Places 43
Teresian Teachings for Prayer and Life 44
Internalizing the Teachings 47
    Reflection—Commit to a Serious Christian Life 48
    Reflection Questions 49
Guidance for Prayer and Prayer Period 50

Second Dwelling Places—Part 2 53
Description of the Second Dwelling Places 53

Teresian Teachings for Prayer and Life 54
Internalizing the Teachings..**57**
    Reflection—Failure and Growth 58
    Reflection Questions 59
Guidance for Prayer and Prayer Period 59

Teresa de Ahumada (Adolescence) 1528-1534 ....**63**

Third Dwelling Places—Part 1 ....**67**
Description of the Third Dwelling Places 67
Teresian Teachings for Prayer and Life 69
Internalizing the Teachings **73**
    Reflection—The Conventional Christian 73
    Reflection Questions 75
Guidance for Prayer and Prayer Period 76

Third Dwelling Places—Part 2 ....**81**
Description of the Third Dwelling Places 81
Teresian Teachings for Prayer and Life 83
Internalizing the Teachings **89**
    Reflection—St. Teresa and Prayer 89
    Reflection Questions 92
Examination of Conscience, Consciousness and Behavior 93
Guidance for Prayer and Prayer Period 96

Sister Teresa of Jesus (Young Adulthood) 1535-1553 ....**101**

Fourth Dwelling Places—Part 1 ....**105**
Description of the Fourth Dwellings Places 105
Teresian Teachings for Prayer and Life 111
Internalizing the Teachings **115**
    Reflection—Centering Prayer Observations...116
    Reflection Questions 119
Guidance for Prayer and Prayer Period 120

Fourth Dwelling Places—Part 2 ....**125**
Description of the Fourth Dwelling Places 125
Teresian Teachings for Prayer and Life 128
Internalizing the Teachings **131**
    Reflection—The Prayer of Quiet Experience 132
    Reflection Questions 137
Guidance for Prayer and Prayer Period 138

Sister Teresa of Jesus (Conversion Experiences) 1554-1555..................**143**

Fifth Dwelling Places 145
Description of the Fifth Dwelling Places 145
Teresian Teachings for Prayer and Life 153
Internalizing the Teachings 157
   Reflection—St. Teresa's Affective Life 159
   Reflection Questions 166
Guidance for Prayer and Prayer Periods 167

Sister Teresa of Jesus (Mid-Life Adulthood) 1555-1561 171

Sixth Dwelling Places 173
Description of the Sixth Dwelling Places 173
Teresian Teachings for Prayer and Life 181
Internalizing the Teachings 185
   Reflection—Christ, Our Mirror of Love—"Find Yourself in Me" 187
   Reflection Questions 189
Guidance for Prayer and Prayer Periods 190

Sister Teresa of Jesus (Mature Adulthood) 1562-1566 195

Seventh Dwelling Places 199
Description of the Seventh Dwelling Places 199
Teresian Teachings for Prayer and Life 212
Internalizing the Teachings 215
   Reflection—My Beloved Is Mine and I Am My Beloved's! 216
   Reflection Questions 217
Guidance for Prayer and Integration of Prayer and Life 218

Mother Teresa of Jesus, "La Madre" (Later Adulthood) 1567-1582 221

Supplemental Material 225

Absorption and False Mystical Prayer 227
Apophatic and Kataphatic Journeys to God 231
Centering Prayer 235
Consolations vs. Spiritual Delights 241
Dark Night and Purification Trials 243
   Passive Dark Night of Spirit Experience (Chart) 254
Discursive Meditation and Simple Meditation 255
Dispositions for Prayer 259
Distractions in Prayer 263
Faculties or Powers of the Soul 269
   Faculties of the Soul (Diagram) 274
Lectio Divina Recollection 275

Passive Recollection or Infused Recollection 279
Practical Preparations for Prayer 281
Prayer of Recollection—St. Teresa's Way of Praying 285
Prayer—Key Teresian Understandings 291
Prayer—Types and Categories 295
   Prayer- Stages of Active and Passive Prayer (Chart)................................308
Praying Through the Humanity of Christ 309
Soul and Spirit 311
   The Soul (Diagram) 318
Spiritual Direction According to St. Teresa 319
Spiritual Direction in the Passive Dark Nights 325
Union—Types Of 329
Various Mystical Favors—Introduction 333
Attribute or Quality of God Revealed 335
Delightful Wounds (Transverberation), Enkindlings 337
Locutions...341
Prayer of Jubilation or Prayer of Joy 345
Suspensions: Rapture, Ecstasy, Transport, Levitation, Flight of the Spirit ...347
Vehement Desires 357
Visions—Imaginative 361
Visions—Intellectual 365

St. Teresa of Avila, "La Santa" (Doctor of the Church) 1515-2015........369

Afterword...371

Bibliography 381

Song: "Nada Te Turbe" (Let Nothing Disturb You) 385

Mandala of the Interior Castle 386

FOREWORD

For some years I've been wanting someone in the Order of Carmel to design and offer a guided retreat based on the teachings of St. Teresa of Avila. And though I've been exposed to St. Ignatius' *Spiritual Exercises*, which are one good approach to prayer and a guided retreat, I was looking for something that better fit me and others who are looking for more teaching and guidance in contemplative prayer itself. The *Spiritual Exercises* with the emphasis on Discursive Meditation, or working with the mind and imagination moving from thought point to thought point in reflections about Christ Jesus, His attributes, or Gospel scenes, I find hard to do, unappealing to me personally, and not the way I pray or find intimacy with Christ. St. Teresa offers other ways of praying which are simpler, more approachable, perhaps go further, and are an answer to the needs and yearnings of men and women throughout the Church looking for more depth in prayer. This book is intended for any Christian seeking holiness and a closer relationship with the Lord through prayer, as well as for formation directors and those in formation, for members of various Lay Religious Institutes or Associates, Apostolic Religious, Contemplative Religious, clergy, religious educators and students, parish prayer groups, spiritual directors, and retreat directors. St. Teresa has wisdom, teaching and guidance for all when it comes to prayer.

I would have wanted this book when I was in formation as a Carmelite, but there is something to be said for having done all the work of study for myself—and St. Teresa does require explanation and study to gain the most benefits from her teaching. Since it kept coming to me that her teachings on prayer and the accompanying relational life of prayer are not as widely known as should be, it is an enormous loss for Christian formation in prayer. I thought I should, if I could, also offer something towards making her teaching on prayer more known. After forty years of reading and reflecting on her experience of passive prayer, it is my conviction that if her teachings were more widely shared, known and lived, it would be transformative for Christians, the Church and world. So I offer this spirituality, retreat and prayer guide from St. Teresa to deepen the prayer life of Christians and to share what St. Teresa discovered are the riches that are within our very own souls!

St. Teresa was not so much interested in thinking *about* the Lord, but in being *with* Him in a direct, personal and loving encounter with the One who is our Most Significant Other, God, through Christ Jesus. Prayer is relationship with Him, directly, intimately, personally and uniquely with each person. And this prayer relationship, seriously entered into, leads to transformation, expansion of being, and the revelation of the fullness of who we truly are as an image of Christ who dwells in our souls' innermost center. It will open anyone who is serious about prayer to the vast infinitude and beauty of their own inner being. The goal for this book is to enlarge horizons towards all the possibilities of passive contemplative prayer and life—prayer initiated and directed by God—and to help guide us on this journey to that transforming expansion of our real being and life in the love relationship with the Trinity.

As Christians we are asked to imitate Christ. Jesus was a contemplative as recounted in the scripture passages that refer to Him going off alone to pray, and as seen in His entire nights in prayer with His Father. Jesus was also a mystic as recorded at His baptism, temptations in the desert, the transfiguration, walking on water, healing, raising people from the dead, etc. So we, in imitation of Christ, are also called to be contemplatives and mystics. It was Father Karl Rahner, sj in his *Theological Investigations* (xvii) who said that: "The Christian of the future will be a mystic ... or will cease to be anything at all." Neither he, St. Teresa, nor I are referring to mysticism as esoteric prayer and experiences for the few, or mystical phenomena, but rather to a living and directly personal and intimate love relationship with the Divine. St. Teresa is certain that the Lord wants to grant favors of love, intimacy and fulfillment to us in this life just as He has for others in the past. And He is even more in need, and has a greater desire to give these favors than we have to receive them! How to surrender, be receptive and cooperate with these desires and gifts of God for us, beyond what we can imagine, is what St. Teresa par excellence has to share with the Church Universal. And this offering from St. Teresa of Avila, "The Teacher of Prayer"—as Pope Paul VI proclaimed her when he made her the first woman Doctor of the Church—is given to help further these desires of God which are also truly our own.

Sister Leslie L. Lund, ocdh
(Sister Joan Theresa Elizabeth of the Trinity, ocdh)

ABBREVIATIONS

IC	*The Interior Castle*	(*Moradas del Castillo Interior*)
L	*The Life*	(*Libro de la Vida*) [Autobiography of St. Teresa]
W	*The Way of Perfection*	(*Camino de Perfección*)
F	*The Foundations*	(*Las Fundaciones*)
ST	*Spiritual Testimonies*	(*Las Relaciones*)
S	*Soliloquies*	(*Exclamaciones del Alma a Dios*)
P	*Poetry*	(*Poesías*)
LT	*Letters*	(*Cartas de Santa Teresa de Ávila*)
SS	*Meditations on the Song of Songs*	(*Meditaciones sobre los Cantares*)

There are a few scattered references to St. John of the Cross' thought and writings which amplify and add to understanding something in St. Teresa's thought. (see: *The Collected Works of St. John of the Cross*. Translated by Kieran Kavanaugh, ocd and Otilio Rodriguez, ocd. **Revised Edition**. Washington, D.C.: ICS Publications, 1991.

A	*Ascent of Mt. Carmel*	(*Subida del Monte Carmelo*)
DN	*The Dark Night*	(*Noche Oscura*)
SC	*The Spiritual Canticle*	(*Cántico Espiritual*)
LF	*The Living Flame of Love*	*Llama de Amor Viva*)
SLL	*Sayings of Light and Love*	(*Dichos de Luz y Amor*)

AP Translation of the *Letters of St. Teresa* by E. Allison Peers
KK Translation of the *Letters of St. Teresa* by Fr. Kieran Kavanaugh, ocd

ACKNOWLEDGEMENTS

I'd like to acknowledge those who encouraged me to write this book—especially those two who said: "You have to do it!"—Sister Nancy Casale, ocdh and Professor Leonard Doohan, PhD. I thank Carmelite hermit Sister Patricia Morrison of the Institute of Carmelite Studies who also supported me and encouraged me to write this book as a needed contribution to Carmelite studies and teachings on prayer.

I'd like to express my gratitude to those who read the book with enthusiastic support and helpful comments and editing—especially Dr. Leonard Doohan, PhD, (the Teresianum), Carmelite Sister Nancy Casale. Sister Judith Ryan, snjm, and Sister Katherine Baltazar, mms both read and edited the book, used it for retreat, and have passed on the word to their Sisters in community about the riches of St. Teresa.

I am indebted to Angela Ruff for all manner of technical and computer expertise, and for her patience and kindness throughout bringing to completion this complex book.

I thank Marilu Chavez, an aspirant to the Carmelite life, who read over and approved my Spanish translations and is looking forward to reading the finished book.

I am grateful to Joni Dirks of our parish choir for notating with her Finale Song App the music I wrote for Teresa's Bookmark: *Nada Te Turbe,* and for her art work for the book's cover. It depicts one of St. Teresa's favorite ways of intimately being with Christ—comforting Him.

HOW TO USE THIS BOOK

St. Teresa is a teacher on prayer for the universal Church, and so this book was designed for a wide audience—for beginners in prayer, those stuck in their prayer life, for professors and students interested in St. Teresa's teachings, for formation directors, people in formation, prayer groups, for consecrated religious, priestly formation, various Secular Religious Institutes, Carmelites, spiritual directors, retreat directors, parish educators, and everyone in the pews called to holiness who desires "the more" in prayer and their spiritual life.

This book can be read both on an educational level as a pedagogical presentation of St. Teresa's mystical theology for those wishing to know more about her teachings on prayer and its connection to Christian life. But it can also be used on the spiritual level as a retreat and guide for growth in prayer and a relationship with Christ that is based on a living experience of prayer and intimacy with Him.

Because St. Teresa of Avila is a Doctor of the Church, her teaching on prayer is profound and substantive, yet meant to teach and inspire all the People of God without exception. Since she is a woman of the 16th century, some of her language and terminology require explanation. Though her goal is to deepen in her reader Christian friendship and intimacy with God through prayer and Christian life, to get the most out of St. Teresa's wisdom also requires some study and understanding of her terminology and teachings—the pedagogical level. So the two interconnected materials have been put together in this one book.

Though possibly a genuine neophyte might pick up this book, it is assumed that someone who has bought the book is probably a practicing Christian and beyond the first dwelling places—at least in some ways. However, there are extremely important teachings and insights in the earliest dwelling places that cannot be skipped or left behind. Most Christians are in and out of the various earlier dwelling places throughout their lives at one time or another.

The dwelling places one through four are divided into two parts, each with two sections containing the pedagogical offerings of **Description of the Dwelling Places** and **Teresian Teachings for Prayer and Life**. This is followed by the second section comprising **Internalizing the Teachings** and **Guidance for Prayer and Prayer Periods**. The first four dwelling places are divided into two parts because the material is foundational for understanding dwelling place four, as well as the last three dwelling places five through seven. I wanted to make the first four dwelling places easier to absorb and understand by putting the material into smaller increments. Dwelling places one through four are the dwellings where most people will find themselves. Dwelling places five through seven encompass other levels of prayer, that when explained, will be clearly seen as more remarkable and singular degrees of prayer and Christian living. The Prayer of Union dealt with in dwellings five through seven won't speak to as many readers as dwellings one through four, but should be read so as to discover what is possible in prayer, and because St. Teresa offers much inspiring guidance in these later dwellings, too. It is good to be aware that movement through the dwellings is not always chronological because God is free to do anything in a person at any time. The important aspect regarding any degree of union with God is that true union is the alignment of our will and desires with God's.

To delineate the two types of material, the pedagogical teachings of the **Description of the Dwelling Places** and **Teresian Teachings for Prayer and Life** will be in a different font type from the **Internalizing the Teachings** and **Guidance for Prayer and Prayer Period** materials.

Much of the material will be presented in bullet form which is intended to facilitate clarity and understanding of the major points of each dwelling place. In this format, any material that is significant for the reader can be indicated with a checkmark (✔) next to the bullet for emphasis and ease of locating it again.

The **Reflection** essay is offered for further insights into the material presented in each dwelling place.

Using the **Reflection Questions** should be an ongoing process and commitment that helps to further St. Teresa's fundamental insight that growth in self-knowledge underpins growth in prayer and a spiritual life. All are not necessarily meant to be pondered in any one retreat or prayer period, and may need further revisiting over time for deeper insight into the self.

The **Supplemental Material** provides expanded and additional information of various types and categories. Some of it is spiritual in nature in view of the self-guided retreat, and is spiritual guidance and direction. But some of it is more technical, pedagogical information, and *not suited to all*. Thus, this material is meant for different audiences with different purposes. Some of it is not geared to beginners and would only mire them in more complexity than they need to know. Some of it is meant for the proficient in prayer, or for students of St. Teresa, scholars, spiritual directors and Carmelites. Readers will have to decide for themselves which material is suitable for them. Any reading of recommended **Supplemental Material** should be read prior to, and outside of actual prayer periods.

ALWAYS READ from ST. TERESA HERSELF in conjunction with this book for the inspiration and encouragement of her experience and convictions. Since St. Teresa's writings are inspired, personal and engaging, her actual words are powerfully animating and encouraging. Thus, it is expected that any sections or citations given from *The Interior Castle* in Teresa's actual words will be read along with the study or retreat. Her writings are never exhausted for the spiritual guidance they provide!

HOW TO USE THIS BOOK FOR PRAYER

These suggestions for prayer are what St. Teresa would term Active Recollection—what you do yourself as preparation for prayer, and hopefully, also good preparation for your readiness for passive Infused Recollection and the subsequent depths of contemplative prayer of later dwellings.

Before you begin your retreat or prayer, it could be helpful to look over various topics on prayer in the **Supplemental Material**, especially: "Prayer—Types and Categories," "Praying through the Humanity of Christ," "Practical Preparations for Prayer," "Dispositions for Prayer," and "Distractions in Prayer." For some difficulties in prayer, the guidance given in these materials can be a great support for moving beyond blocks in prayer, and for fostering fidelity to prayer. The **Reflection Questions** underpin the important Teresian value of growth in self-knowledge. These can be profitably used at any time during or after retreat or prayer, or as part of a daily examination of behavior, conscience and consciousness. One or two questions may be sufficient to be pondered during a retreat or prayer period, and any of the questions may require revisiting for more depth of self-understanding at different stages of life or for subsequent retreats or prayer periods.

Pondering the emphasized **Theme** of each dwelling and reading the **Reflection** in advance can be helpful. Notice if any of St. Teresa's teachings internally stir up something in you that may need your attention. Make a check mark (✔) by any bullet that you sense may help you at this time. Give attention to the **Guidance for Prayer** suggestions. Choose any one of the **Scripture Passages** provided as desired. Use the **Guided Meditation** for your prayer if it fits for you.

There is no set amount of time that will fit everyone for the prayer periods. Busy people in active apostolates or lifestyles may only be able to manage 20 or 30 minutes for prayer a day. If the material is used for a self-guided retreat it is expected that more time would be given to prayer. However much time you give to prayer, the goal is to try to be mindful of the Lord as much as possible in all aspects of living—to become more aware of His friendship and nearness always.

However, it is traditional to give one-hour time periods to prayer—especially during a retreat—because it can take a while to become quieted for prayer (recollected), and one cannot really experience the aridity and dryness of prayer that is necessary for growth in prayer in shorter periods of prayer. Aridity, dryness, restlessness and resistance to prayer don't generally have enough time to take hold, become uncomfortable and an exercise in patience, or a sacrifice of time out of love for God. Others, experienced in prayer, find that the subtleties of God's presence aren't generally experienced in shorter spurts of prayer time, and prayer often doesn't deepen till near the end of longer periods of prayer. As the intimacy with the Lord intensifies through prayer, there is a greater need and desire for more time alone with Him which naturally grows over time. And lastly, it pleases God who loves and honors any time given to Him in prayer. According to St. Teresa: *"Just the raising of our eyes in remembrance of Him will have its reward."* (W23,3)

For **Dwelling Places 1-3** the following suggestions may be helpful:

- Before you begin, choose any favorite prayer, devotion, or spiritual book that you want to spend time with. Or, use a passage from any suggested **Scripture Passages** or the **Guided Meditation** provided in each dwelling place that you may want to use if you become too distracted or restless.
- Find a conducive place for prayer—a chapel, before the Blessed Sacrament, a place in your residence that is clean, uncluttered and peaceful with some meaningful sacred objects—a cross, icon, Bible, candle, etc.
- Do not have near you a phone or laptop, TV or anything that personally distracts you.
- When you come to your place of prayer make yourself aware of the sacred: bow, genuflect, take your shoes off, etc. Make any gesture that acknowledges your holy ground and holy space, as a special place of prayer and encounter with the Lord.
- On your prayer chair, bench, or cushion, sit up straight. A straight back is important. Get alertly comfortable, but not too comfortable so as to avoid falling asleep. Avoid long prayer periods after a heavy meal or before bedtime. Prayer may refresh you too much for sleep. Ideally, the temperature should be neither too hot, nor too cold.
- Determine in advance the amount of time you have to give to your prayer period, and set a gentle timer—one without a jarring ring. Set it for 20, 30, or 60 minutes—whatever time you are going to devote to your prayer period. Choose the amount of time that you are committed

and determined to give to being with God and do not cut it short if at all possible.
- Close your eyes and take a few relaxing breaths to signal to yourself the end of whatever you were doing or thinking before the prayer period began.
- Take a few minutes to set your *motivations* for your prayer. Ask yourself why you are coming to pray. Is it to give time to the Lord, to clear a space for Him, to listen to Him, to deepen your intimacy and friendship with the Lord, to express your love for Him and to receive His love in return? Be very clear with yourself about your motivations. Say them in your own words both to the Lord and yourself so that you know what it is you truly value and desire.
- Have your *intention*s for the prayer period also clearly in mind. These would include: "I will sit here and pray, no matter what, for these next 20/30/60 minutes." "When I become aware that my attention to the Lord has drifted, I will stop myself from daydreaming, making plans, arguing with myself or others, rehearsing, teaching, criticizing, worrying, etc." Or, "Whenever I find myself distracted or thinking about something else, I will return my attention, gaze and desire to Christ, with an image of Him in my mind, a favorite prayer, devotion, or sacred word/s or my breath."
- Enter within yourself—a space that is both contained and infinite. It is possible to pray outdoors, but it is distracting for many and generally distracting for beginners. The inner space you are seeking is a more hidden place of intimacy—the cave of your heart, a hermitage, or poustinia of prayer within. You could imagine entering through a door or veil into your inner sanctum, your interior castle, your Holy of Holies, the hidden garden of your soul, or your tabernacle of self where Christ awaits you.
- Make the sign of the cross and pray a doxology such as: "Praise God from whom all blessings flow," "Glory to the Father, Son and Holy Spirit," "All praise to you Source of all Being, Eternal Word and Holy Spirit," etc. In your own words acknowledge who you are and in *Whose* presence you are. "Here I am Lord, the one you love," "O God, come to my assistance, Lord make haste to help me," "Lord, open my lips and I will proclaim your praise." etc.
- When the period of prayer has ended and your timer goes off, in order to avoid a jarring experience for your body, spend a few more moments with your eyes closed as you come out of prayer, so as to readjust your external senses. End your recollection with a doxology, a favorite prayer,

or a spontaneous prayer of thanksgiving, adoration, or praise. Make another sacred gesture as you leave your sacred space.

For **Dwelling Places 4-7** the following suggestions may be helpful:

- Before you begin your prayer choose a sacred phrase or word/s (a monologistos) of one or two syllables to use during your prayer when distractions arise. It could be Father, Christ, love, Jesus, Savior, or Spirit. It could also be a sacred word from another language as: Abba, Kyrie, Sanctus, Fiat, Domine, Hosanna, etc. Or, you could choose a short meaningful aspiratory prayer as: "My Lord and my God," "Lord Jesus Christ, Son of God, have mercy on me," "Jesus my all," "Lord, I adore you," "I trust in you," etc. Do not change your sacred word/s or phrase during your prayer time.
- Begin to pay attention to your breath—either from your nose, or your rising falling stomach. If at first your mind is too busy to pay attention to your breath, you can count to 4 on your inhalation and to 8 on your exhalation for a little while. Sometimes this helps focus and calm the mind, just as counting to 10 can calm someone when they are upset. Recall that breath, or *ruah* in Hebrew, is sacred: "God breathed into Adam's nostrils the breath of life..." (Gen. 2:7) "Jesus breathed on the disciples and they received the Holy Spirit." (Jn. 20:22)
- Once you are calm and recollected, focus your gaze on Jesus—with a momentary image in your mind, or loving words said to Him. You can also focus on your breath, but don't continue counting it. If distractions start to come, you may gently introduce your sacred image or word/s again. From time to time, and only as needed against distractions, use about 5% of your inner voice energy to interiorly pray your sacred word/s, while leaving the other 95% of consciousness quiet to observe your breath, interiority and focus in loving *desire* for Jesus.
- In Active Recollection you may try any of several things to turn away from distracting thoughts and remain recollected: 1) observe your breath; 2) gently repeat a sacred word/s (a monologistos) *from time to time* when a distraction arises (not over and over as a mantra); 3) read a few passages from scripture or a spiritual book; 4) cast an interior gaze of love at Jesus who is with you in your inner sanctum. This image could be drawn from a scripture passage, but is not meant to be an involved reconstruction of a scene or the Discursive Meditation of involved thinking. If you pick an image or situation in Jesus' life, try to choose one that matches your own emotions or situation of the moment. St. Teresa used several of these ways for her prayer.

- Gently return your attention to your breath, or sacred word/s, or gaze at Jesus whenever you are aware of starting a thought or following thoughts from one to another.
- If your mind should become empty of anything—of attention to the breath, word/s, or thought—let it be so! Just remain in peaceful emptiness and non-conceptual attention with your *desire and energy of love towards God*, who is No-Thing.
- When the period of prayer has ended and your timer goes off, spend a few more moments with your eyes closed as you come out of prayer, so as to readjust your external senses. End your recollection with a doxology, a favorite prayer, or a spontaneous prayer of thanksgiving, adoration, or praise. Make another sacred gesture as you leave your sacred space.

HOW TO USE THIS BOOK FOR A RETREAT

Always read **St. Teresa herself** in conjunction with this book for inspiration and encouragement! Teresa is anxious to get everyone to the fourth dwelling places as soon as possible. But first, the material in the dwelling places one through three must also be understood and integrated into prayer and Christian life. Everything St. Teresa offers is helpful guidance.

The Seven to Ten-Day Retreat

- Time given to prayer should be at least in two periods a day—traditionally for a retreat that would be two one-hour periods.
- Time for study and reflection on the pedagogical teaching material should be incorporated and understood, *but outside of the time of prayer.*
- If the self-guided retreat is done as a seven, eight, or ten-day retreat, less time should be given to dwelling places one and two—perhaps only one day for both together.
- Dwelling places three is where many Christians are and become stuck. With proper guidance they could begin transitioning to dwelling places four. There is real need to understand the teaching material in dwelling places three in order to be prepared to be moved deeper into prayer.
- In dwelling places four St. Teresa is introducing whole new understandings and levels of prayer. So, devote the time needed to grasp well the material of the fourth dwelling places.
- More time may also be needed for understanding the fifth and sixth dwelling places. Study all the later dwelling places to understand the movement of prayer, what is possible in prayer, and what God desires to give.
- The **Guidance for Prayer and Prayer Period** material in each of the dwelling places underpins the retreat and is suited to, and appropriate for, each of the dwelling places where the suggestions are given.
- Expanded suggestions below follow for the six (or more) weekends retreat and can also be helpful for the shorter retreat.

A Six-Weekends Retreat

Basically, the same recommendations concerning which of the dwelling places are most important and deserve more time given to them in the seven to ten-day retreat are the same for a retreat made over six or more weekends. The first and second dwelling places can be moved through rather quickly. The third needs to be well understood for movement into the fourth. The fourth is particularly crucial to understand. The fifth, sixth, and seventh dwellings are also important and have helpful spiritual direction for prayer and life, even if God does not bring the retreatant into any of these dwellings during the retreat or life.

1. For the **First Weekend** of the six weekends retreat, reflect on the emphasized **Theme**, study any teaching material, and pray with the **Internalizing the Teachings** and **Guidance for Prayer and Prayer Period** offerings for the dwelling places one and two. Read the **Reflection** and explore one or two of the **Reflection Questions**, attending to any changes in attitudes or in your behavior as needed as you become aware of them.
    - During the weekdays pray as you usually do and put into practice some of the **Guidance for Prayer and Prayer Period** suggestions given for both dwellings places one and two. Review any material that stood out or personally spoke to you as necessary for your own growth in virtue and intimacy with God.

2. For the **Second Weekend** of retreat for dwelling places three, ponder the emphasized **Theme**, study the teaching material and keep in mind the **Internalizing the Teachings** and **Guidance for Prayer and Prayer Period** offerings for your prayer time. Continue working at identifying thoughts, attitudes or behavior in need of attention from the **Reflection Questions**. Read the **Reflection** and any **Supplemental Material** referred to. Make sure you understand these transitional third dwelling places well!
    - During the weekdays put into practice any new prayer suggestions given for dwelling places three, and again review any material that stirred within you as a personal call to growth in prayer and life-style changes.

3. For the **Third Weekend** of the retreat, ponder the **Theme**, study the extensive teaching material for dwelling places four, and begin to put into practice the **Internalizing the Teachings** and **Guidance for Prayer and Prayer Period** forms that may be new to you. Read the **Reflection**, and spend some time on any of the **Reflection Questions**. Make sure you understand well the ideas and terminology of St. Teresa given in the

fourth dwelling places as well as in any pertinent **Supplemental Material**.
- During the weekdays try or continue practicing the suggestions for prayer that may be new to you. As always, look for any parts of your life, attitudes and behavior that need change. During the week, try to begin to make a sincere inventory of your life choices using any of the Examination of Conscience, Consciousness, and Behavior material.

4. For the **Fourth Weekend** of the retreat, reflect on the **Theme**, study the teaching material, and have in mind the **Internalizing the Teachings** material and **Guidance for Prayer and Prayer Period** offerings as part of your prayer for dwelling places five. Refer to all needed explanatory material in the **Supplemental Material**.
   - During weekdays, as before, continue praying with the guidance that has been offered. Read the **Reflection** and begin looking more closely at your affective and relational, love-life in the **Reflection Questions** for any needed self-knowledge or changes in how you are loving God, self, and neighbor.

5. For the **Fifth Weekend** of retreat, reflect on the **Theme**, study the teaching material and pray using the **Internalizing the Teachings** and **Guidance for Prayer and Prayer Period** offerings for dwelling places six. Study or reflect on any **Supplemental Material** that enhances understanding of Teresian terminology and teaching. Read the **Reflection** and try to explore any of the **Refection Questions**.
   - During the weekdays continue trying to pray with the prayer guidance that has been offered all along. Reflect on significant trials or purifications in your past, or in your present, using the material given in both dwelling places five and six. Study especially the "Dark Night and Purification Trials" section in **Supplemental Material**.

6. For the **Sixth Weekend** of the six-weekend retreat, study the teaching material for the seventh dwelling places. The fifth, six and seventh dwellings of prayer and intimacy with Christ are more remarkable degrees of prayer, and good to know for inspiration and motivation. Read the **Reflection** and spend time on the **Reflection Questions**. Just continue praying in any of the ways suggested so far. Read all pertinent **Supplemental Material** for these dwellings, and continue striving to pattern your life on Christ's mind, heart and actions. Let the possibilities of both dwellings six and seven spur you to enthusiasm and fidelity for prayer.

Whether or not you have reached the stages of either Spiritual Betrothal or Spiritual Marriage of the sixth and seventh dwelling places in a mere six weekends or even in a life time (or that you may have and don't know it), hopefully you will have progressed in self-knowledge, prayer, virtuous Christian life and love, deepened your intimacy and friendship with Christ, and better aligned your will to His. And by the end of your retreat you may actually have made an integral habit of prayer and found a way to extend the length of your prayer periods.

At any time outside of your self-guided retreat, any one of the dwelling places can be reviewed and prayed with for help, support and growth in prayer and your Christian life.

1-1

FIRST DWELLING PLACES—Part 1

(*The Interior Castle* 1, Chapters 1-2)

Theme: *O soul, you are the Lord's dwelling place!*
And prayer is the door into this dwelling place.

Description of the First Dwelling Places:

"*I began to consider the soul as if it were a castle made of a single diamond or of very clear crystal, in which there are many rooms, just as in heaven there are many dwelling places. Now if we think carefully over this, Sisters, the soul of the righteous person is nothing but a paradise, in which, as God tells us, He delights. For what do you think a dwelling will be like which is the delight of a King so mighty, wise, pure and so full of all that is good? I find nothing to compare with the great beauty of a soul and its great capacity. In fact, however penetrating our intellects might be, they will no more be able to come to an understanding of this than to a comprehension of God; for as He Himself says, He has created us in His own image and likeness.*" (IC1,1,1)

o   A soul is described by Teresa in such images of dignity as a diamond or crystal castle, a pearl of the Orient, or a tree of life planted in living waters of life. (IC1,2,1)

o   Just inside the door of the first dwellings persons may converse with God occasionally—usually when in trouble or need—but they lack a habit of turning to God in prayer or of any prolonged prayer. (IC1,1,8)

o   Their prayer is distracted by many external things—as concern for reputation, possessions, health, business affairs, addictions, diversions

and escapes. Both the exterior and interior life in these dwelling places are full of distractions, confusion, busyness, chaos, and disturbances of many kinds. (IC1,2,14)
- However, Teresa says that just being inside one's interior castle at all, and praying even if only sporadically is already progress and a great blessing! Generally, when persons in these dwellings pray, they lack consciousness of who they are, to *Whom* they are speaking, and what they are really asking. (IC1,1,7) They do not have much self-knowledge—little on the conscious level, and definitely not on the unconscious level—and no one is able to truly know who they are without striving to know who God is, and who they are in God. Humble self-knowledge is essential in this journey to intimacy with God. There is much harm in not knowing who we truly are in God. (IC1,2,8-9)
- Spiritually speaking, those who do not pray are like people who are deaf, mute, crippled or paralyzed. (IC1,1,6) They do not know the tremendous capacities of the soul.
- Since persons in these dwelling places are careless in virtue, they are morally weak and easily led astray. (IC1,2,12)
- Persons here lack deep understanding of Christ's teachings, and have false understandings of God and perfection. They lack discretion, and make comparisons and judgments of others. (IC1,2,16-18)

Teresian Teachings for Prayer and Life:

- *"As far as I understand, the door of entry into this castle is prayer and reflection."* (IC1,1,7)
- If prayer is to be prayer at all, it must be accompanied by reflection. *"Prayer in which a person is unaware of who he is speaking to, what he is asking for, who is doing the asking, and of whom he is asking, I do not consider prayer, no matter how much the lips move."* (IC1,1,7)
- Because the interior space—the soul—is so infinite and sublime a dwelling place, one can only imagine it, but never understand or know it completely. (IC1,1,1) But each must strive to continue to explore the interiority of their soul, and know it as they can—and with gratitude—love its mystery, spaciousness and majesty. (IC1,2,8)
- In these first dwellings there is a need for deeper awareness of Christ's life and teachings, and a determined initial choice will need to be made to learn about His life, and to respond to Him in love in prayer.

- Any initial attraction and awareness of spiritual realities must also include the truthful self-knowledge of who one is as infinitely precious to God, as well as knowledge of who God is as the one who is in love with each person.
- God does not shower love and favors based on merit from any perceived "holiness," but because of God's own extravagant love, generosity, and desire to be known and loved in return. (IC1,1,3)
- Persons will have to start setting some initial boundaries over how they live, what they think, say and do. Difficult choices in keeping with Christ's mind and life, with *initial determination* to bring about needed changes in desires, instincts, and pretenses will need to be made. And this will begin to foster a fuller and richer relationship with the Lord. (IC1,2,14)
- In these dwellings, persons will find themselves pulled back into their primary sin situations and weaknesses. And, at the same time, outsiders may try to undermine any of their desires to change or pray. They must be aware that harmful peer pressure can slow or stop spiritual growth.
- Whoever does not trust, hope and believe in the Lord's favors and desires to love and be loved will have little experience of His love. They won't be looking for His activity or recognize it when it is there. It is more helpful for moving forward to reflect on the grandeur, love, mercy, and help of God, rather than on one's own weakness and misery. (IC1,2,8)

"As to the precious qualities there are in our souls, or who abides within them, or of what high value they are, these are things we seldom consider and so we make little effort about conserving the soul's beauty. All our concern is taken up with the plainness of the diamond's setting, the outer walls of the castle, our bodies." (IC1,1,2)

1-1

FIRST DWELLING PLACES—Part 1

Internalizing the Teachings: *Make a decision to be faithful to prayer!*

Here, prayer is not yet a faithful habit but only sporadic. And this is because you do not know who you most deeply are and what love and gifts God has for you if you would enter more intimately into relationship with God in prayer. Therefore, there is a great need to understand the truth about the beauty, dignity, grandeur, magnificence and infinite capacities of your own soul, made in the image of God, who delightfully dwells there, and that the door to your magnificent soul is prayer. Ask for the desire to pray, and act on that prayer of desire with determination. Do not limit God, and set no bounds for the Lord who abides in you!

Reflection:

The Riches of Prayer

When the disciples asked Jesus to teach them to pray He said: "When you pray, go to your private room, shut the door, pray to your Father who is in a secret place, and don't babble on like the pagans who think that if they use a lot of words they will be heard." (Mt. 6:5f)

St. Teresa does not disparage active, vocal prayer, adoration or devotions that are said with *mindfulness, loving desire and attention* to the Lord. However, she wants you to know about passive prayer that she will explain in later dwelling places, and which allows the Lord to enter more deeply into your prayer, or take over your prayer, and where you become open to receiving the gift of the Lord that is a deepening of the personal, more secret, intimate, love relationship with God.

From her own life St. Teresa was aware of stages, development and maturation in life and prayer. She knew that she had been wandering around in the first three dwelling places of her interior castle for some time before she was brought to the later dwelling places. Because she knows the abundant treasures of these later dwelling places, she is anxious to convince others of the riches of prayer and to get them to move as quickly as they can beyond the first three dwelling places in both prayer and lived Christian life. Your prayer life won't grow if you do not know deeply your own personal beauty and dignity, and who it is that dwells in you and loves you.

If the poem offered below raises any questions about prayer or uncomfortable feelings that you have been avoiding about your life, or if it names even vaguely sensed hopes and desires for a deeper relationship with God and more fullness of life, it is a beckoning for you to get moving to further dwelling places that are up ahead.

Prayer
(George Herbert)

Prayer the church's banquet, angel's age,
God's breath in man returning to his birth,
The soul in paraphrase, heart in pilgrimage,
The Christian plummet sounding heav'n and earth;
Engine against th' Almighty, sinner's tow'r
Reversed thunder, Christ-side-piercing spear,
The six-days world-transposing in an hour,
A kind of tune, which all things hear and fear;
Softness, and peace, and joy, and love, and bliss,
Exalted manna, gladness of the best,
Heaven in ordinary, man well dressed,
The Milky Way, the bird of Paradise,
Church-bells beyond the stars heard, the soul's blood,
The land of spices; something understood.

First Dwelling Places – Part 1

This poem is meant to help you reflect on how you have thought of prayer in your life. Have you ever thought of prayer as a banquet, breath, your soul in paraphrase, your heart in pilgrimage, or in plummet sounding depths, as engine, as tower, as reversed thunder directed at God Himself, as piercing spear, world-transposing, a tune, hearing and fearing, as both exalted and ordinary, as vast as the Milky Way, your very soul's blood, aroma and taste of spices, or something inchoately understood?

Reflection Questions: (Choose only one or two at a time to explore in depth.)

- Do you pray? If so, how often and in what context? Why do you pray?
- How do you think of prayer?
- Do the images of the poem open up new possibilities and understandings of prayer for you?
- Do any of these images surprise, attract or stir something in you to reflect upon?
- Do they raise up hidden assumptions or worn-out ideas of prayer for you?
- Can you reflect awhile on what each or any of the images might mean for your prayer life?
- What brings you to a sense of wonder, surprise, praise or reverence?
- Who is God/Christ for you? What are your images and names for the Lord? What do you think these names and images say about you and your relationship to the Lord?
- What are your images and names for yourself? What do these say about you?
- How do you see yourself before God?
- Are you at all interested in "the more" of prayer and Christian life? What are your true desires?
- Are you interested in God's desires or even interested to know what they are?
- Are you a friend of God, or would you like to be?

Guidance for Prayer and Prayer Period:

For this and each prayer period refer back to the "How to Use this Book for Prayer" section at the beginning of the book. Until you have internalized these suggestions for prayer and made a habit of them, you may need to consult them for these initial prayer periods.

- Spend some time reflecting on who the Lord is for you, and your favorite names or images for God/Christ. These names and images say much about you, God, and your relationship with God. This will help you enter into prayer with more awareness.
- Reflect also on yourself. Think about the names, images and descriptions you give about yourself. It is important that you seriously try to be humbly realistic and truthful. Some of your images of yourself may make you uncomfortable, and some should make you feel enlarged, broadened and comforted. You may want to write them down.
- As you are able, remain calmly in the reflections and any new insights you have had, in openness and awareness of your inner world. You can also turn your awareness to the sacredness of your breath that is giving you life in God. Or, you can use a favorite vocal prayer or psalm said slowly with attention to the meaning of the words.
- Make a conscious choice to leave behind your exterior self and any of its intruding cares, thoughts and feelings, as well as your outer world of external matters, concerns, and noise during your prayer period. Try to calm yourself with a few deep breaths and holy aspirations and short prayers.
- With an intentional mindfulness of courage and determination, enter through this door of your interior castle—the DOOR of PRAYER—in deeper inward awareness of what you are doing and saying, and of the meaning of your vocal prayer, petitions, contrition for failures, adoration, or reflection on a devotional thought or homily.
- Your prayer here may include cherished vocal prayers such as the Hail Mary, Our Father, the Memorare, the Acts of Faith, Hope and Love, the Angelus, the Apostles Creed, Act of Contrition, Stations of the Cross, psalms, litanies, or the rosary. Or you can also pray vocal prayers in your own words as petitions, adoration, contrition, praise and thanksgiving.
- Always and only, pray with attention any formulary vocal prayer or devotional practices that attract you and are helpful in fostering a deeper awareness of any awakening desires for God and of "the more" in Christian life. Be heartfelt in your prayer.

The following are scripture passages that can be used during the prayer period if desired. Choose one before you begin prayer.

Scripture Passages:
(God's Dwelling) Ps. 84; Jn. 14:23, 17:21-26; 1Jn. 4:13-16; Eph. 2:19-22, 3:14-21; Heb. 3:1-6; 1Cor. 3:16-17
(Determined Prayer) Mt.6:5f, 7:7-11; 1Jn. 5:14-15; 1Cor. 9:24-27; Eph. 6:10-18; Rom. 12:9-12, 15:4-6; Phil. 3:12-16, 4:6-9; Col. 4:2-3; Heb. 12:1-4; Is. 50:7-9; 1Chron. 16:11-15; Prov. 24:10

If it is helpful for prayer, you may also use the following meditation for your prayer period.

Guided Meditation:

See in your mind's eye your crystal diamond castle. . . . Walk towards your castle's door, and see over the entrance the engraved inscription: *"Set no bounds for the one who abides here."* To prepare to enter through the door, begin to leave behind your busy mind and outer world of modern life—the weight of possessions, reputation, burdens and cares, challenges and mistakes, the longing of unfulfilled desires. Take some deep breaths letting all that go in preparation for entering through the door and more deeply into your most sacred places. . . . Let your attention take note of the importance of the inscription over the door as wisdom for your life. Take a few moments to repeat this prayer of wisdom to yourself: *"Set no bounds for the one who abides here."* . . . Breathing deeply, with courage, turn the knob of the vaulted door and push it open and enter into your interior castle. Notice that the light is dim at first and you must adjust your eyes. Let your attention be arrested, absorbed and empowered by a preview of the vastness of your castle's interior. See the infinite caverns of your inner being. . . . Venture forth into a foyer space, where you can already see openings out to multiple possibilities to explore—to the sides, ahead and below—a succession of rooms, proliferating rooms—a revelation of uncountable rooms—nurseries, school rooms, music rooms, arboretums, dark rooms, holiday spaces, sacred rooms, love tryst chambers, waiting rooms, garden places that seem to bring the outside in, death rooms.

Notice that many of the rooms have a mirror. This is a mystical, unmasking mirror revealing hidden things about you. What do you see—

something amusing, sobering, unexpected, scary, exhilarating—perhaps something of your original face, or your glorious future?

Move into any room you feel drawn to. Wait in that room in stillness, just listening and looking intently. Try to hear the faraway sound of rushing water. Is it a spring, a fountain, a waterfall or a river? Try to see off in the distance an unusual and remote light. The light and sound make you believe that Someone Else is also dwelling inside your castle. What is happening within you at this realization?

Will the realization make you return to the foyer and exit the door of stillness, listening, reflection—prayer? Will you take the chance of returning again? Or, will you choose to go directly towards the light and water where the Someone Else waits for you? Will you dare to explore more closely more of the many chambers of yourself on the way to the innermost center? . . . You must make a decision for or against exploring your interior castle. You must make a new decision each time you open the door of prayer, of stillness, listening and reflection to receive what you find there.

No one else can tell you all that you will find in your interior castle of splendor. It would be too much for anyone to know or tell. But those who have made the journey before you know who you will find there.

How lovely is your dwelling place, O Lord! (Ps. 84)

"... If I had understood, as I do now, that in this little palace of my soul dwelt so great a King, I would not have left Him alone so often. I would have remained with Him at all times ..." (W28,11)

1-2

FIRST DWELLING PLACES—Part 2

Theme: *Set no limits on the Lord who dwells within you!*

Description of the First Dwelling Places: (continued)

Persons who find themselves in these dwelling places are immersed in the material life of the world, and rarely take time to reflect on anything spiritual, or to look deeply within. Their awareness, attention, consciousness and concerns are taken up with the outer, material world and the values of the culture around them. Persons here do not yet understand much about prayer, nor do they know the possibilities and blessings of the integration of prayer and life. (IC1,2,7)

- These persons are generally unconscious as regards a serious life of virtue, for their consciences are not well formed in the mind, values and teachings of Jesus. They are governed by their senses, and do not think of committedly following Jesus' example. (IC1,2,14-15)
- Though once in a while these persons have good desires, they don't always take them seriously or follow up on them. Their motivation for actions is generally based on the principle of seeking pleasure or avoiding pain—what feels good and what doesn't. (IC1,1,8)
- They may say an occasional prayer in need or in times of trouble, or try to bargain with God, but there is no solid personal relationship with Jesus.
- These persons lack self-knowledge, and live on the level of ego and persona that they have built up and created for themselves, without true knowledge of who they really are in God. (IC1,2,8-9)

- They have no perseverance in prayer, and little understanding of what they are actually saying or asking. There is no concept of aligning their desires with the desires and will of God. (IC1,1,7)
- These persons don't know who God is and generally have false or harmful ideas and images about God that get in the way of a deeper relationship with God and God's Son.

Teresian Teachings for Prayer and Life: (continued)

- In these dwelling places there can be an initial conversion experience, leading to a beginning desire to be a Christian or to know Christ. There is generally an intellectual acceptance of creeds, theological ideas, some Gospel values, or possibly even an experience of the love of God, which can be accompanied either with or without emotional consolation and joy, or dread and fear. More will be required!
- Persons in these dwellings have had little exposure to what the Lord can do supernaturally in a soul. Generally, what they have experienced has to do only with what they themselves can do or say in prayer, or achieve in following Christ.
- At this early stage, persons will be thinking that any spiritual progress is their own doing. They have not yet learned how to surrender. They are still in the grip of their own exteriorly, socially constructed, self-defined and self-controlled, small false self—persona and ego—and its self-centered desires. The more this ego and little false self is allowed to control and be resistant to trust and surrender to God, the more difficult it will be for the deeper interior self to receive the gift of the passive supernatural prayer of later dwelling places.
- It is necessary to move quickly out of these first dwelling places into the deeper awareness of the Lord's call in subsequent dwellings.
- *"A soul must not be compelled to remain a long time in one dwelling, except if it is in the room of self-knowledge! How necessary that is ... even to those whom the Lord has brought into the same dwelling in which He Himself is!"* (IC1,2,8)
    - Growth in accurate self-knowledge, which for St. Teresa is genuine humility—neither puffed up self-aggrandizement, nor doormat-self-deprecation—is a key element in forward movement.
- *"Without humility, all will be lost."* (IC1,2,8) The need for truthful self-knowledge—humility in recognizing the innate dignity, as well as human creatureliness and weakness—is crucial, along with compassionate understanding and forgiveness for the fallible self when it fails.

- Nothing is more important than the humility of truthful self-knowledge, which recognizes that without God's help we cannot know or choose the good, or become more fully like Jesus in imitation of His loving heart, consciousness and actions. (IC1,2,8-11)
- No good deeds have their source from the self, but from the Divine Fount in which we are grounded, and from which the Son gives life and warmth to all good works. (IC1,2,5)

○ Christian community, good Christian friends and mentors can help support perseverance in difficult times, and nurture truthful and realistic self-knowledge.

○ These persons must recognize that their determination to follow Christ is weak and vacillating—not yet a committed choice. To move further into their own interior castle they will need to make a resolution of "determined determination" to know, follow and imitate Jesus. And in humility they must ask in prayer for God's help. They will have to come to gradually accept and continually choose to make a habit of prayer, and stay in the struggle to pray and grow in virtue. This will be painful effort and struggle!

- There are few dwelling places in the castle in which a Christian will not have to wage a fierce battle with the Principalities of evil, and the false self as regards sin, selfishness, addiction, and inner darkness. (IC1,2,15)

They must "*set* [their] *eyes on Christ ... and on His saints.*" (IC1,2,11)

1-2

FIRST DWELLING PLACES—Part 2

Internalizing the Teachings: *Strive for progress in self-knowledge!*

In these first dwelling places you will need to begin to understand more about the state of your soul and interiority, and the benefits of truthful self-knowledge. You need to know about who you may have been in the past and have become up till the present, and how this has affected the state of your soul in its experience or lack of experience of the Divine Indwelling One—God. The interior life of your soul only becomes healthy by becoming more like the Divine image it is made in, by taking failings, addictions and sinfulness seriously, and by choosing to live in greater imitation of the mind, heart and integrity of Jesus. The shining Divine One is always present in your soul, and never leaves. Only you can block God's light, cover over the Divine beauty and stop the flow of fruitfulness and grace that comes through prayer. In *The Interior Castle* (IC1,2,10), Teresa suggests some of the ways you may block prayer and your relationship with God—by focusing on your misery, fear, faintheartedness, cowardice, concern about others' watching and judging you as "holier than thou," or on such ideas that extreme virtue is not good, that some prayer is too lofty for you, and that you are not only not special but such a sinner that it would be pride to dare hope for a deeper prayer life or intimacy with God.

Reflection:

Human Maturation

It may be that these dwelling places are mainly inhabited by younger Christians who are caught up in careers, experimenting in relationships and love, of being involved with starting a family and providing and caring for it, and of creating a self-made persona for themselves. Youth is a very busy time concerned with many externals, without as much thought given to mortality or more interior realities. As a natural part of human maturation, persons in their forties often start to reflect on deeper spiritual realities, and no longer find the same fulfillment in careers, social climbing, reputations, security, money, dream homes, and past successes. But older people are not immune to living a superficial Christian life, or of alienation from the true self. It just may take another form of avoidance concerning the meaning of their lives, of spiritual reality, and the inevitability of death which is getting closer. Habits may be so engrained with the achievements of success providing so much comfort that the older Christian may have become lazy or apathetic to growth, and so avoids change and approaching old age and death. This can take the form of escapes of travel, sports, working out, vacations, reading, face lifts, movies, new sexual partners, alcohol, drugs, games, time on-line with YouTube, pornography, Facebook, Twitter, etc. This is the life lived solely on the pleasure/pain principle, or seeking what is an escape, fun and pleasurable, while avoiding pain, discipline, challenge and change.

These people may still have their original childhood understanding of Christianity, go to church once in a while, or even assent to the basic Christian creed, and nominally consider themselves to be Christians. They may donate to charities once in a while, and they may pray in times of need. Generally, they think of prayer as grace before a meal or petitions for what they want or need in emergencies. They would not be making a habit of spending extended periods of time on prayer or scripture. They love their family and friends, but not always the "other" outside of their own class, experience or comfort zone. They are conventional in their approach to living, taking on the current values, fears and opinions of the society around them—especially as regards wealth, security, materialism and nationalism. They are not likely to know the demands of the extensive social justice teachings of the Catholic Church, read spiritual books, or follow teachings from the Magisterium. They generally think of God as "up there" somewhere distant in heaven, and haven't given thought to the magnificence of their own soul, what is contained in it and who abides there. It may be that some set-back, illness, disappointment or suffering may throw them more deeply back onto faith and exploration into prayer and spirituality. St. Teresa begs persons who are outside the first dwelling places to enter their soul's interior through prayer and reflection, and those who have put a foot through the door of interiority to take time to go deeper inward and explore and know about the riches within and to set no bounds for the one who abides there.

Set No Bounds For The One Who Abides Here

Sister Leslie Lund, ocd
Mansion 1—October 15, 1983 Indianapolis Carmel, reflection for a shared homily

In an unsettled season of the confining, narrow, commonplace,
weighed both by the slough of misery and desire's fascination,
I yearned to escape the hurly-burly, the dusty wind,
and the humdrum hucksters of carnival-spaces.
Travel-jaded I arrived at desolate limits—nominal perimeters
of distractions cushioning discord and delusion and altering awareness.

Glancing into denser darknesses
I discovered a derelict courtyard enclosure—
brittle weeds, naked trellis, forsaken fountain, tripping tiles—
and indistinctly beyond, an enormous castle edifice beckoning forward.
And over its solitary arched portal an engraved script:
"Set No Bounds For The One Who Abides Here."
Clumsy awkwardness unfastened a cumbersome knob of vaulted door,
pushed open to its width—a seepage of bats and beasts ensuing.
Arrested absorption from the menagerie menace
empowered a preview of a spacious castle interior.

In circumspection, I ventured from foyer space,
past multiple possibilities.
In Louvre-like sumptuous succession of rooms—proliferating rooms…
nurseries, school rooms, gardens, fountains,
music rooms, dark rooms, waiting rooms,
… rooms that seemed outside … death rooms …
And common to each chamber the provocative mirror—
unmasking mirror of the amusing, sobering, exhilarating,
awesome—and pre-existent.

A waiting room interlude
disclosed a crescendo of light tapering to vague remotenesses.
And far away, the sound of falling water—
fountain or waterfall?
Was someone home here?
And whose home is this? Is the resident truant?

> Subsequent re-visitings from antechamber to farther in
> seized attention to the spiraling stairway at the vestibule's distant end
> where hung above the circular case,
> embossed on tapestried banner, again the motto:
> "Set No Bounds For The One Who Abides Here."

Reflection Questions: (Choose only one or two at a time to explore in depth.)

- Has prayer been part of your life story? If so, how or when has it been part of your life?
- Are there special times or places that remind you to pray or help you to pray?
- What gets in the way of prayer for you?
- Is your prayer life the same as it was five or ten years ago? How has it changed, or not?
- Do you put any limits on God for your life? Do you have low expectations of the Lord?
- Who or what gets most of your time?
- Where do you find yourself blocked or challenged in your growth personally or spiritually?
- What aspects of your life are most in need of change?
- What do you really want from life right now? Where are you most alive?
- Do you take time to reflect on your life experiences or bring them to prayer?
- How would you describe your relationship with the Lord at this point in your life?
- Are you aware of a desire for the Lord, for more life, for more love?

Guidance for Prayer and Prayer Period:

You may need to refer again to the "How to Use this Book for Prayer" section at the beginning of the book. But before you begin this prayer period, consider some of the following attitudes and suggestions for your prayer. You may want to pick one or several to focus on.

- o It is profitable to spend some time making an examination of conscience, your actions, and of the contents of your consciousness, and of any of your most common failures, as well as virtues before you

begin prayer or sometime during the day, or perhaps before you fall asleep.
- Begin to strive to make progress in self-knowledge as a support to your prayer life. You cannot lie to God who knows your heart. And do not lie to yourself. In humility—neither in self-aggrandizement nor self-deprecation—enter and explore both the sinful and virtuous spaces of your interiority. You must walk through the various rooms of your castle—some very difficult—especially the poor, dark rooms in your soul. And though you must visit them and learn what you can in them, you must not stay indefinitely there nor beat up on yourself. Being focused on your misery will make you fearful, fainthearted, cowardly and trapped in your small, false self. Keep your eyes on Jesus instead!
- Explore also the dwelling places of your strengths, successes, and virtues. Ponder especially the love, grandeur and majesty of God dwelling within you. You will make more progress in prayer, virtue and your relationship with Christ if you are focused on the Lord's help and mercy, rather than on being tied down to your own failures and weakness. Looking truthfully at yourself, and then looking at God—back and forth—is the dialectic that helps move you more quickly towards your center.
- When you have done this for a time, ask for a true sorrow and even fear of creating anything that obscures from yourself the beauty of your soul and God's love and favors. Ask the Lord for a desire not to think, do, or say what blocks your relationship with Him, or His mind, love, and grace.
- Remind yourself that God is the one who knows best how to transform you. Self-sacrifice is important, while at the same time penances you create for yourself are ones you can manage and generally satisfy your ego pride in performance and self-reliance. They do not transform you as do the crosses and diminishments that you undergo that are out of your control—the crosses life sends you or God allows. If you are presently undergoing something difficult, ask for the grace of patience, surrender and trust that the Lord is with you in it and using it for your benefit.
- Be aware of and let go of any indiscreet zeal or scruples concerning how well or accurately you say your prayers or do devotions and penances. Focus more on loving desire, thoughts and acts towards Jesus and your neighbor.

- Worldly concerns, business affairs, daily concerns and problems will come into these first dwelling places and distract your prayer. As you are able, leave them at the door of prayer and take care of them after prayer. Your prayer will actually help you in dealing with them!
- It is important to keep your inner eye on Christ, and to ask the Holy Spirit, Mary and the saints for help with your prayer. Cultivate an expectation of a marvelous adventure as regards what the Lord does in prayer for those who are faithful to it!
- Whenever possible remain in calm quiet, focusing on your breath, and perhaps a simple vocal prayer or sacred word. Or, continue with attention, praying slowly, any favorite vocal prayer or pre-chosen psalm. Your prayer can also be in your own words and include adoration, sorrow for any failures, or praise and thanksgiving. It can comprise a reflection on your own life, or an inspirational thought, or a remembered homily. Always try to be aware of how Jesus has been part of your life, and ask Him for a deeper desire for a closer relationship with Him.

If desired for your prayer period, choose in advance any one of the scriptures below to ponder during your prayer.

Scripture Passages:
(God's Power) Mt. 19:26; Lk. 1:26-38; Rom. 4:20-25, 8:26-30, 38-39; Phil. 4:13; Eph. 3:16-21, 6:10-18; Is. 41:10-13; Jer. 32:17, 26-27
(Self-Knowledge) Heb. 4:12-14; Ps. 139; Lk. 16:15, 18:9-14; Mk. 5:25-34; 1Sam. 16:7; Is. 29:15; Jn. 8:1-11; Ps. 19, 51; Jer. 17:9-10; Prov. 5:21-23; Jb. 34:21-22

The meditation and images that follow can be part of your prayer if desired. The following scriptures particularly relate to the meditation: Mt. 13:44-46; Mt. 12:33-36; Mt. 6:19-21.

Guided Meditation:

Take some moments for some deep calming breaths. . . . Begin to imagine how you would feel discovering that your pearl of great price—your treasure and very soul—is misplaced or lost, or worse, that you have turned your back on it! . . . Or, imagine that your soul's Tree of Life at the center of your soul's inner garden is drying up, and its shading, cooling freshness is withering and no longer producing good fruit for your life. . . . Or, if you prefer, as Teresa also suggests, consider that the center dwelling of your crystal castle is covered in black pitch, or a heavy black cloth that blocks the shining sun—the Lord—who is deep within, so that His voice and brilliance cannot get to you. He *is* there, but you have stopped seriously listening to Him or looking for Him—the greatest treasure of all! If you do not pray you have misplaced your pearl and treasure, been letting your own Tree of Life wither, or have covered over your castle's center with a black cloth, so that the Light and Living Water of the Holy Spirit is blocked from flowing to you. Failure to enter your interior castle through the door of prayer, as well as any wrongful thoughts, choices and failures in love are keeping you from the pearl, the treasure, the Tree of Life and your Divine Guest. Stay with any of these images that most speak to you and pay attention to feelings, thoughts, memories or new images that arise from these. . . . Know well that there is no remedy but to seek this treasure—yourself in Him—to place yourself beside the Living Waters of the prayer relationship with Him, and move towards the Light in the center of your castle where He dwells waiting for you with love and blessings!

"In my opinion, we will never completely know ourselves if we don't strive to know God." (IC1,2,9)

Good books, along with the care my mother took to have us say our prayers and be devoted to Our Lady and some of the saints, began to awaken virtue in me when I was six or seven. When I played with other girls, I enjoyed pretending we were nuns in a monastery. It grieves me now to reflect how I was not constant in the good desires I had in my childhood. (L1,1,6,7)

TERESA de AHUMADA
Childhood—1515-1528

Teresa de Cepeda y Ahumada was born March 28, 1515 to Alonso Sanchez de Cepeda and his second wife, Beatriz Davila de Ahumada. She was born in Avila, Castile, during the Golden Age of Spain while King Ferdinand still reigned.

Teresa's father, Alonso, was charitable, compassionate and prayerful—a man of dignity and good morals. He was a merchant, and a widower when he married Teresa's mother, Beatriz. She was a child bride of thirteen who was beautiful and virtuous, and bore him ten children of which Teresa was third.

Teresa says both her parents were devout and God-fearing. She relates that she was the favorite of her father, that he doted on her, and wanted her and all his children to be well-educated and to read the inspirational books that he provided.

Her mother was gentle and intelligent and instilled in Teresa the importance of prayer, the practice of virtue, and a devotion to the Blessed Virgin Mary and to some of the saints. Teresa was aware of the importance of these things by the time she was six or seven.

Teresa was one of three girls, and nine brothers. She was closest to her brother, Rodrigo, and together they read the lives of the saints and martyrs. The two were so impressed by martyrs that when Teresa was seven, she and Rodrigo set off for the land of the Moors to beg them to cut off their heads for the love of Christ so they could go to heaven quickly. Luckily, their uncle got wind of this and caught up with them to bring them home.

With this failure to serve God, Teresa and her brother next made plans to be hermits and tried to make little hermitages in the family's garden. She and Rodrigo liked speaking together about God and eternity. She loved the thought of "forever," often repeating the words: *"forever and ever and ever."* She had an attraction, even in childhood, to truth.

Teresa's spirituality as a child included giving to the needy what little alms she had. Her prayer and devotions were many—especially the rosary and solitude.

Teresa writes that she had a good and pious beginning with desires to be a martyr, hermit, and nun, but she says it wasn't long before she lost, through her own fault, what God had given her in her childhood.

2-1

SECOND DWELLING PLACES—Part 1

(*The Interior Castle* 2, Chapter 1)

Theme: *Let the war within be ended!*

Description of the Second Dwelling Places:

Persons in the second dwellings are putting forth a little more behavioral effort with time given to prayer, and more attention to virtue, than they did in the first dwelling places. (IC2,1,2) And prayer is beginning to be more included in their Christian life, but it is still sporadic. There is some beginning fervor to practice devotions, penance, and some prayer, though it tends to be lukewarm or tentative.

- These persons still know very little about prayer—primarily only about the prayer that they do themselves—vocal prayer and devotions.
- Their spiritual life and prayer are generally based on vocal formulary prayer, petitions, some devotions, or short spiritual readings, occasional church attendance—with an occasional reflection on the sermon, or a short pondering on a scripture passage heard at church. (IC2,1,3)
- While persons in the second dwellings are "mute" they are not "deaf," and they do recognize the "voice" of God from time to time in their lives, from sermons, good books, through inspiring people, from prayer, trials and life experiences. These encounters begin to be internalized in deeper understandings of Jesus' teachings, and in a growing sense of His desire for a more personal relationship. (IC2,1,3)

- The determination to be faithful to prayer and virtue is weak in these second dwelling places—with many excuses from fear, laziness, cowardice, discouragement, and lack of perseverance.
- Rarely do individuals here see the dangers of their faults and sins, and their effects.
  - They aren't yet serious about avoiding occasions of sin and are lukewarm in virtue, which is not only disturbing the soul but soiling and defiling it. (IC2,1,2)
- These persons focus more on their miseries, than on God's care and strength, and are easily discouraged.
- These dwelling places encompass more spiritual warfare, with more doubt and questions. The soul undergoes great trials here from weakness and indecisiveness. (IC2,1,5-6, 9; W12)
  - The determination needed for virtuous choices or for imitating Jesus is much lacking.
- The doubt, resistance to needed change, indecision, and the prick of a developing conscience leave the troubled soul without peace!
  - *"Can there be a greater evil than the evil we find in our own house?"* (IC2,1,9)
- The nudge and voice of God can be felt as a nagging burden and resisted. (IC2,1,2-3)
  - There are nagging questions such as: "Should I continue or turn back?" "What's being asked of me?" "Can I do it?" "Do I really even want to?"
  - These persons may be thinking to themselves such things as: "I don't have time to pray." "I don't want people thinking I'm better than they are." "Extremes of virtue are naïve and not practical." Or, "I'm not worthy." "Praying a lot is for saints."
- Some initial conversion of the person's conscious life and powers is starting to emerge here.
  - Prestige, success, image, security, wealth, friends, health—the values and things of the culture and world—are little by little beginning to be seen in perspective against the backdrop of ultimate meaning, mortality, faith and a developing relationship with God.
- These persons are very much lacking in truthful self-knowledge.

Teresian Teachings for Prayer and Life:

- The continuing goal here in these dwellings is to try to align one's will and desire in conformity to God's will and desires.

- *"All that the beginner in prayer has to do—and it must not be forgotten, for it is very important—is to work and be determined with every possible effort to bring the will into conformity with the will of God. This encompasses the very greatest perfection which can be attained on the spiritual path."* (IC2,1,8)
- A more serious committed and determined choice for Christ is needed here because faith is still weak, and desire is focused more on the immediacy of what can be seen or felt than on what faith and Jesus promise.
- The ups and downs of feelings, emotions, or consolations are shifting sands that will not be a support in harsh struggles. Do not depend on them for information! Go by the way of imitation of Jesus in faith, hope and love.
  - The person here has to try to stop choices based solely on pleasure or pain motivations.
- Because trials are greater in the second dwelling places, and because of weakness in imitating Christ, greater determined determination and perseverance are needed to move more deeply into the interior castle of the soul. (IC2,1,2)
- God will support with mercy, enlightenment and strength any struggles with disordered desire, sacrificial choices, commitment and perseverance in prayer and virtue. (IC2,1,3,6)
  - And to help with this, St. Teresa points out that we also have within the soul faculties and powers of Intellect/mind, Memory/imagination and Will, with their corresponding work to do in deepening the virtues of faith, hope and love. (IC2,1,9) (see: "Faculties and Powers of the Soul" in **Supplemental Material**)
- With more determination and resoluteness in persevering in prayer and virtue, the less will evil desires, choices or spirits triumph.
- It takes courage to sustain the struggle while at the same time acknowledging its difficulties.
  - Do not give in to discouragement, which for progress is often worse than the original failure.
- Sometimes the Lord desires to exercise persons in their struggles with dryness in prayer, or with harmful or disordered thoughts and other afflictions that they can't rid themselves of. This helps them to recognize how committed—or not—they are to loving God and imitating Jesus. (IC2,1,8)
- Avoiding bad companions and seeking out the friends of God are great supports. (IC2,1,6)

- It is important to give up complaining of dryness or restlessness in the rooms of the second dwelling places, or of seeking consolations, or of trying to recapture the emotional pleasure of any earlier prayer or conversion. Persons should try to overcome any resistance to embracing the narrow way and the crosses of life. (IC2,1,7)
- Persons in these dwellings should not give in to discouragement or stop striving to deepen a prayer relationship with Christ. If allowed, God can, and will, draw good and profit from any falls. Failure can help growth in humility and reliance upon God.
  - Consciously choose a stance of trust and hope in God's activity for your good.
- Let the war from refusal to align the will with God's will, of indecision and vacillation—being ill at ease within one's own disordered interiority—be ended! (IC2,1,9)
  - Pray for this! Trust in God's mercy and grace for support in any efforts made. (IC2,1,10)

"Giving up prayer doesn't seem to me to be any other thing than to lose the way." (L19,12)

2-1

SECOND DWELLING PLACES—Part 1

<u>Internalizing the Teachings:</u> *Desire God's will for you!*

When you enter these second dwelling places you are beginning to include more prayer in your life, and are becoming aware of how, when you don't pray, or when your prayer is only sporadic, this adversely affects your choices, spiritual life, and your relationship with Christ. You are gradually learning that when you make more time for prayer you are more aware of God, and see and hear God in many more ways in your life—in homilies, spiritual books, trials, life events, and through other people. The pleasures of the world, the influence of friends and acquaintances, concern for health, status, financial attractions, and reputation still have a great pull in these dwelling places, but the tug of your conscience to put these in right order is beginning. There is a spiritual war growing in intensity between what you may be doing that is sinful, and what you are sensing you should be doing instead to be aligned with the desires and commandments of God. You aren't yet able to fully acknowledge and sustain a growing consciousness of what you are beginning to perceive. The struggle is to go forward in Christian living and prayer, or, to give up prayer and to turn back to the easy way, and the allurements of the world. There are great trials and inner wars in these dwelling places that call for your determination and perseverance to avoid the occasions of sin, and gradually move away from any former harmful ways of living. Being faithful to prayer, deepening self-knowledge, recalling what God has done for you in your life, what you owe God and the realization of the ever-present friendship and love of Christ are what will help keep you moving ever closer to Him. Desiring to know and become more sensitive to Christ's desires and will for you will give you more safety in your spiritual life and bring you closer in intimacy with Him in love.

Reflection:
Commit to a Serious Christian Life

There is the struggle in these dwelling places to truly commit to a serious Christian life and a lot of fence sitting, backsliding and avoidance of change. Decisions are still mainly on the level of what is comfortable and feels good and what doesn't. Internal arguments go on as to whether following Christ is reasonable, will lead to happiness or more suffering, or is even possible given your weakness, past mistakes and entrenched habits. The cost of discipleship seems steep and you can wonder if it is worth it. This should naturally lead to some examination of what God images you have, as well as the images you have of yourself. These greatly influence your love relationship with Christ and an authentic discipleship in following Him.

Is God a score keeper, out to get you, dangerous, capricious, violent and desirous that you suffer? Or, is God who Jesus describes as merciful, loving Father, who counts every hair on your head, who throws a banquet when you return from messing up your life, gives you the finest clothes and adornments, kisses you when you return, who promises eternal life and joy, and what eye has not seen nor ear heard for the absolute fulfillment of all your desires? Reflection on images of both God and self are very important as a base-line for a relationship between you and God, and they can be admitted to honestly with petitionary prayer that God change any that are destructive and false. A spiritual director can also help in this examination.

In these dwelling places there is a call to take more time to get serious about your spiritual life and practices. Often when you begin to have some occasional good desires and initial fervor for knowing and loving God and following Christ more closely, you become drawn to one or another of the various prayer devotions—attending church, confession, adoration, saying the rosary or Stations of the Cross, doing some penance or fasting, reading scripture daily, or doing a little reflection on the day's readings, or perhaps volunteering occasionally for something in the parish. This is a good start, but there must be awareness that "holier than thou" pride can creep in with newly added devotions, or complacency in thinking that devotions or Sunday attendance at church, and adherence to a set of theological doctrines and beliefs is all that is required for following Christ. No devotions, church attendance, or intellectual assent to theological ideas is sufficient for following Christ or intimacy with Him. Prayer, spiritual devotions, and good works are a must, but also have to be coupled with a more serious look at life and choices, sins and virtues, use of time, contents of consciousness, whether present friends are a support or not in living a Christian life—and above all—a deepening love relationship with the Lord and love of neighbor. Prayer and devotions should have the effect of influencing more seriousness about any change that is needed for virtue and service, and to a deepening relationship with Christ. If they don't, they are merely empty words, or a superstitious talisman, or perhaps a false idea that you are owed salvation for your religious practices. If so, you are avoiding a genuine, challenging and transformational relationship with God.

Sometimes in these dwelling places you may be ashamed of aspects of your life and try to remain anonymous in the sacrament of confession. But more growth comes by humbly being honest about your failures, by letting go of your ego's reputation, and by becoming more serious about avoiding sinful habits through going to confession more often and perhaps face to face. The accountability and discomfort of your ego pride in spiritual counseling and the challenge from a confessor or spiritual director is good for your soul. This can be a new element of your asceticism and determination to change and put your true self in charge over your persona and false self. Examinations of conscience and behavior are good practices to begin in these dwelling places for gaining some mindfulness of motivations, habits and choices that may need changing.

Reflection Questions: (Choose only one or two at a time to explore in depth.)

- How do you pray? What forms of prayer have you found helpful?
- What spiritual practices or devotions do you incorporate into your life?
- What are the greatest occasions of sin and failure for you?
- Is there anything in your life that you are ashamed of, that you don't even like to admit to yourself? Can you bring this to God for healing?
- Are you neighbor and friend to yourself? Do you love and accept yourself—your personality, your body, talents, your history?
- Do you know yourself as uniquely special to God? What do you think is your uniqueness as a person?
- What is most important in your life? What do you give your time to?

- What principles guide your life? What motives do you base your choices upon—the lure of pleasure and the avoidance of suffering, or something beyond these?
- How do you see the purpose and meaning of your life?
- What is God like for you? What is your operational God image—friend, dangerous, merciful, dominating, gentle, extravagant, caring, violent, providential, capricious, personal, non-personal, distant, close, or even a particular gender or racial color?
- Do you think you owe God anything that you are grateful for? If so, what is it?
- Where have you noticed any shifts in consciousness, intentionality and attitude?

Guidance for Prayer and Prayer Period:

- Reflect on whether you are being consistently faithful in your prayer and devotions—vocal prayer, church attendance, spiritual reading, reflection and meditation (spiritual thoughts and reflections about God), or devotions as the rosary, adoration, confession, Stations of the Cross, novenas, etc. Correct the situation if you have been negligent.
    - Are these practices and devotions still efficacious for you in fostering awareness of Christ and His Way, with a conscious and deeper commitment, perseverance, and desire for closer intimacy with the Lord? Are they heartfelt?
- Your prayer in these dwellings will still be vocal prayer, reflection and Discursive Meditation (thinking about Jesus and His life), adoration, supplication, and contrition. But when possible strive for a deeper attention to what you are saying, hearing, and reflecting upon in interior quietness and awareness in your prayer.
- You cannot calm or quiet yourself with force, but only with gentleness. (IC2,1,10) But have determination to begin the practice of calming yourself with a short, repeated prayer, with calming breaths, and by attention to these.
    - This will help you come to a deepening awareness of Christ's presence with you, and of His life and values, with a firmer choice and determination concerning them.

- Your aim is to develop a personal relationship with God through Jesus, and to desire what God desires. God alone knows what you need—not you!
- If you don't have the desire for God's will, pray even for the desire to desire what God wants and desires for you. (IC2,1,8)
  - Remind yourself of the great spiritual joys that are up ahead in later dwelling places if you continue to be faithful to prayer.

Refer to "How to Use this Book for Prayer" at the beginning of the book as needed.

The following are scriptures that relate to the teachings of the second dwelling places, and can be used if desired during your prayer period. Choose one before you begin.

Scripture Passages:
(Inner War) Gal. 5:13-26; Heb. 12:1-4; Eph. 4:17-20; Mt. 4:1-11, 6:1-34, 7:1-5, 10:28-31, 16:24-26; Lk. 4:1-13, 6:27-38, 11:24-26; Jn. 14:27, 16:33; Jm. 3:2-12, 4:1-12, 1:13-18; Ps. 51; 1Cor. 13:1-13; 2Cor. 12:9-10; 1Pt. 3:8-17, 2:11; 2Tim. 1:6-9; Rom. 8:5-11, 18-30
(God's Will) Mt. 7:21-27; Mk. 3:31-35; Heb. 10:8-10; Jn. 7:16-18; Eph. 1:3-14; Rom. 8:26-30, 12:1-2; 1Thess. 5:16-19; 1Pt. 3:13-17; 1Jn. 2:15-17

You may use the meditation and images below if they enhance your prayer period.

Guided Meditation:

Enter through the door of your interior castle through prayer and quiet, and begin to imagine moving further into your interior castle—your soul's interiority. . . . Become aware that some unwanted things have followed you in. You see that there is the mud on your shoes—perhaps the grime of fear, laziness, cowardice, faintheartedness and vacillation. From the outside world there are also poisonous things as negative thoughts, unwholesome tendencies or addictions, bad habits, entertained temptations, trivial distractions, and bad company. . . . But after observing these or any others for new insights, try to turn your attention and hear from time to time the voice of a most loving neighbor and friend—Jesus—

calling from deeper within, who seems to be there with you when you pay attention, and never stops promising more life and being. . . . Realize that you are not without His help, as well as the aid of your own inner faculties of the soul—your powers of Intellect/mind, Memory/imagination and Will—which are helpers in your dwellings for self-knowledge and wisdom for the journey. You have the help of your <u>Intellect</u> and reason that informs you through <u>FAITH</u> of the teachings of Christ and of His love for you. You have the good, the true and the beautiful in your life experiences and in creation. You have your <u>Memory</u>/imagination to recall and relive what has been helpful or unhelpful, life-giving or destructive, and is a source of <u>HOPE</u> for your journey. And you have your <u>Will</u> that moves and guides your Intellect and Memory and is the source for your choice to <u>LOVE</u> and imitate Christ.

"... in perfect conformity to God's will lies ALL your good ... the person who lives in more perfect conformity with God's will, will receive more from the Lord and make more progress on the spiritual path." (IC2,1,8)

2-2

SECOND DWELLING PLACES—Part 2

Theme: *Get up from a fall and begin again!*

Description of the Second Dwelling Places: (continued)

Teresa teaches about prayer throughout all her writings, and in these dwelling places she refers her readers to material for these dwellings that she previously wrote at length about in the book of her *Life* 11-13. She says the material there is very helpful for beginners. It would be beneficial to also read these chapters in the *Life* as guidance for these dwelling places.

- The labor required for drawing closer to Christ is greater for beginners in these early dwelling places than it will be in later ones. (IC2,1,8)
  - In these dwelling places it is like watering a garden with a bucket lowered and raised by hand from a well, rather than watering using an aqueduct, or canals that draw water from a stream, or by receiving abundant rain. (L11-22)
- Persons here are easily tired and expend more energy trying to recollect themselves for prayer.
  - They are easily distracted in prayer.
  - They aren't used to much solitude and silence.
  - They have not given much thought to how they have been living in the past.
  - They have rarely reflected on Christ's life, and when they do, it tends to weary them.

- Self-knowledge and the admission of weakness, sinfulness and selfishness are necessary here for genuine self-understanding and the recognition of the need for God's saving work.
- These persons may continue trying to detach from superfluous earthly concerns—as possessions, status and reputation—while putting in their place what matters more to Christ. This *work* helps move beginners in these dwelling places more quickly to a deeper relationship with God.
- These persons should not think that having desires for a closer relationship with God is brazen and presumptuous, and only for saints. This is false humility and a block to intimacy with God. (L13,4)
  - God loves and wants all mighty and holy desires and great confidence in Him! (L13,2)
  - God always knows for each person what is needed, when and how and will provide it.
- God is pleased with determination, perseverance and courage, and rewards these qualities.
  - Acts of determination, perseverance and courage for prayer and service with love are fundamental for moving deeper into the interior castle and for drawing closer to Christ. (L11,1)

Teresian Teachings for Prayer and Life: (continued)

- Teresa writes that: *"It is absurd to think that we can enter heaven* (the most interior and intimate love relationship with God) *without first entering our own souls, without getting to know ourselves, and reflecting on the wretchedness of our nature and what we owe to God, while continually imploring His mercy."* (IC2,1,11)
- Never stop striving for deeper knowledge and understanding of Christ's person, life and teachings. This work of understanding points to the deepest revelation of who the self actually is in Christ.
- Strength comes through determination and perseverance in prayer, and lessens the problems caused by temptations, and evil influences or spirits.
  - Do not be conquered by fear and faintheartedness. (IC2,1,6)
  - Courage and perseverance are strengthened by remembering that great spiritual joys are up ahead in later dwelling places. (IC2,1,2)
  - With greater desire, commitment, and perseverance, God's mercy, enlightenment, and guidance in struggles and difficulties increases. (IC2,1,10)

- If there is fidelity to prayer and the imitation of Christ, the Lord will guide everything for all benefit.
  - *"There is no remedy for the evil of giving up prayer than to begin to pray again, otherwise the soul will keep on losing a little more every day. Please God that it will understand this!"* (IC2,1,10)
- Give up any demands for former feelings or consolations in these second dwelling places, or of trying to regain or manufacture the emotional pleasure of earlier experiences. (IC2,1,7)
  - Don't fear any beginning dryness, aridity or restlessness in prayer. It's actually part of the movement of prayer and a helpful thing!
  - Depending on the continual and ephemeral comings and goings of feelings and emotions will not support hard choices to be made in difficulties.
  - The embrace of the cross is the only true strength and protection. (IC2,1,7)
- Seek the friends of God who inspire and support the life of faith. (IC2,1,6)
  - Consider having a wise mentor, or consulting a learned spiritual director with experience in prayer. (IC2,1,10)
- Always get up from a fall, and begin again. God loves any efforts to rise from falls. Do not let discouragement cause a relapse or stop progress. (IC2,1,9)
  - After a fall, make a rededicated, committed choice to eliminate any consciously known harmful habits, to develop a stronger love for Jesus, and never to give up prayer and the inner journey to the center.
  - With attention and reflection, learn from mistakes and their *impact* on inner peace, desire for God, and strength for following Jesus more closely in faith, hope and love. (IC2,1,9)
  - Home, rest, happiness, security and peace can never be found outside the self.
  - A relapse to an earlier dwelling, or leaving the interior castle altogether is worse than isolated sinful failures.

"His Majesty wants great determination, and He is a friend of courageous souls that do not put their confidence in themselves, but walk in humility ... the courageous soul can advance far in a few years." (L13,2)

2-2

SECOND DWELLING PLACES—Part 2

Internalizing the Teachings: *Persevere In prayer no matter what!*

When you come into these dwellings you have begun to pray more often, if still sporadically. If you have entered these dwellings you are beginning to get an uncomfortable sense that outside your castle there is no home, security, or peace to be found, and visiting foreign places isn't bringing the peace, blessings or happiness that you had expected. These cannot be found outside of your own castle. But you are still not convinced of this. You do not have a strong determination to pray, to escape the occasions of sin, or to avoid turning back from a deeper relationship with the Lord. There is still much weakness, doubt and faintheartedness, in these second dwelling places. Yet you are hearing more of the Lord's voice from deeper within. However, this is also putting pressure and the discomfort of indecision on you between addictive worldly pleasures and failures, and the growing desire to know, love and serve the Lord. It is crucial to set out on the right path of prayer and loving imitation of Christ to reach the innermost dwelling places. So, it requires a more resolute commitment to follow the path of the practice of prayer and imitation of Christ in virtue with greater perseverance and determination not to give up prayer and the inner journey no matter what! Here faith is becoming less an assent to theological ideas and more a chosen stance for your life in a deeper love relationship with Christ. But there is great fear of the demands of this commitment, causing struggle and affliction from the ambivalence between either continuing on, or to turning back.

Reflection:

Failure and Growth

Though the second dwelling places are already a greater favor than the first dwellings, do not fall into the traps of presumption about your progress, nor discouragement about your failures. Growth in the spiritual life is not a linear, straight line of self-made achievement. In humble truth, you will be in and out of these earlier dwellings most of your journey. But continue entering your interior castle and exploring it, mining it for deeper self-knowledge. Remember that there is no home, contentment or security in alien dwellings outside of yourself. The good Lord and His personal blessings for *you* are within *your own* castle. Continue to set out on the secure path of prayer—which is relationship with the Lord—and imitate Him so that one day you will be drawn into the innermost dwelling places for intimate meetings of love with Christ. You will be battling mightily with weakness, unconscious habits, faintheartedness and doubt in these second dwellings. But since you are already hearing more of the Lord's voice, let this attract you forward. The struggle with failures, the lures and accompanying afflictions of worldly attractions and cares, and the wars of indecision will be keenly felt. Even though spiritually you are only walking in baby steps, be determined to be faithful to pray as you can and to patterning your life on Jesus' example in the Gospels. Don't give up no matter how many times you fall! The Lord knows your human weakness and is greatly pleased whenever you get up from failures and try again—no matter how many times! Teresa said she always had to begin again. If you do this, your faith life and relationship with Christ will begin to grow and become a more spiritually healthy way of life for you. Though you may be troubled by worries of the demands and distance of the journey, with confidence in Christ, heed His command to "fear not." For He alone will always be your true strength and peace. Be determined to journey with Him and not to turn back no matter what!

Reflection Questions: (Choose only one or two at a time to explore in depth.)

- What in the present moment does a growing relationship with Christ mean and call for in terms of prayer and the way you live your life?
- Do you ever explore your interiority or reflect on various aspects of your feelings or life experiences?
- Have you compartmentalized prayer separate from the rest of your life? Do the sacred and secular have a connection for you?
- What do you think at this point is your greatest virtue and your greatest vice?
- What part have failings played in your life, and what do they mean to you? Have you ever brought them to prayer?
- Have you seen acceptance, growth and changes in your life that were the result of prayer?
- Have you ever experienced determination and perseverance in yourself for a goal you wanted to achieve? If you have, could you apply those qualities to your prayer, spiritual life and relationship with God?
- What is the Living Water that Jesus speaks of in the Gospel of John 4:1-30? What was the Samaritan woman really craving? What do you most deeply long for?

Guidance for Prayer and Prayer Period:

- Make decisions to pray regularly despite dryness, lack of felt interest or even distaste for prayer. Going against these feelings that prevent prayer greatly pleases the Lord. (L11,10)
    - Feelings are no indication of failure in prayer or of its efficaciousness.
- As it is true for progressing in anything worthwhile that "practice makes perfect," so is it also the case for the practice of prayer.
- Begin in your prayer to direct your love affectively towards Jesus as a way of looking at and keeping Him close to yourself. He is always looking at you. This inward gaze should not involve a lot of intellectual ideas *about* Him that tires you, but again, be more about loving desire and affection going out to Him as a way of being *with* Him in the present. (L12,2; 13,11)

- Just continue to keep your desire and eyes on Jesus. In an attitude of gratitude, recall what He has done for you as a spur to deeper love for Him.
- Use any prayer practices that are still helpful in fostering awareness of Christ and His life and teachings, or that stir up love, perseverance or a deeper commitment, and desire for God.
  - These can include vocal prayer, liturgical prayer, adoration, supplication, contrition, intercessions, examinations of conscience, spiritual reading, looking at the lives of the saints, praying with various devotions as the Way of the Cross, litanies, or the rosary, or reflecting on scripture or sermons.
  - Teresa suggests reflecting on the passion of Christ as a good place to begin to recall His great love for you and to stir up love for Him in return, though she wrote that it won't suit everyone. (L7,4; W26,6)
  - Reflections on God could also be about the magnificence of His creation, His power, or the teachings of Christ, His mercy and healings, or His miracles.
- If you are reluctant to pray, ask Jesus for the desire and perseverance needed to be faithful to prayer, to make any needed changes, to want what God desires, and to grow in love.
- If prayer has become extremely difficult, experiment and change something about it as needed. This could include when you pray, what devotions or prayers you have been using for prayer, how you have prepared for prayer, or what your physical and emotional state is as you come to prayer.
- Recognize a connection between failures and prayer. Do not have the attitude of: "I have failed, so how can this sinner—me—pray?" You will fail less, and will rise more quickly from failures if you remain faithful to prayer.
- If you are in a difficult period of life, or in adversity or discouragement, try praying with conviction: "God's will is welcome!" You can recall this prayer throughout your day.
- Try to have an attitude of: "I *get to* pray and spend time with the Lord," rather than "I *have to* pray."
- Make sure you are well rested, not hungry or cold, and have had the recreation and refreshment needed that gives energy for prayer.
- During the day outside of your prayer period, keep Christ present to yourself, and look for ways to offer Him service as an expression of your

love, even if the love isn't felt as an emotion. Do any acts that you have discovered that awaken love of Christ in you.
- Consider making a day of recollection at your parish or retreat center, or to joining a prayer group or scripture study group. Other Christians—the friends of God—will be a support to you on your faith journey, especially in weakness. Any of these spiritual activities can support you in prayer, and remind you of your desire to be faithful to your prayer life.
- Again, refer to "How to Use this Book for Prayer" at the beginning of the book, or to "Practical Preparations for Prayer" in **Supplemental Material**.

If you desire to use one of these scriptures for the prayer period that follows, choose one before you begin your prayer. If a word, phrase or sentence touches you, memorize it to use during the day or week.

Scripture Passages:
(Rise from Failure) Phil. 3:12-16, 1:6; 2Cor. 12:7-10, 4:7-12; Jer. 8:4-5; 1Cor. 10:11-13; 2Tim. 1:6-12; 1Jn. 1:8-10; Prov. 24:16, 3:5-6; Is. 41:10, 43:18-19; Dt. 31:8; Ps. 37; 40:2-3; 73:21-26; 145:14
(Perseverance) Sir. 2:1-11; Eph. 6:18; Lk. 18:1-8, 11:5-10; Rom. 5:3-5, 12:12; Jm. 1:12; Col. 1:11-12; 1Thess. 5:17; Mi. 7:7; Ps. 37:3-7; 116; 119:147-149; 88:1-18

If helpful, use the following meditation as a reflection for your time of prayer.

Water was St. Teresa's favorite element and she uses the image of water as a *symbol of prayer*. Can you see why? John 4:1-42 was St. Teresa's favorite scripture.

Guided Meditation:

Enter through the door of prayer and take time to acclimatize yourself to the stillness within. . . . Imagine a garden you have within your interior castle grounds. . . . See a fountain there whose splashing water refreshes you with spray and delicious water for drinking, and which could also be channeled with some effort to water your lovely garden. . . .

Already you are aware that water can flow to you with more or less effort. In Teresa's day, water could be laboriously hauled up from a well by hand with a bucket, or be supplied by a waterwheel, or by canals diverting water from a stream, or from blessed rain. Imagine yourself carrying water by hand, or digging canals from your fountain to channel water to your garden. . . . Then imagine how different it could be if an abundant rain always fell just at the right time for your garden and your own refreshment. . . .

Can you anticipate how these different ways of obtaining water might apply to various forms of prayer? At this stage of prayer, the Living Water has more difficulty flowing to you. You are like someone who has to walk a long distance over and over to gather the water in a bucket or jar and haul it to where you live. Visualize and feel the strain, time, and effort it takes for this water of prayer to satisfy your needs and saturate your interior garden. . . . Let the imagined effort spur you to more desire for fidelity to serious prayer and relationship with Jesus. Next begin to reflect on the Living Water Jesus speaks of in the Gospel of John 4. Begin to recall what in faith you have heard and know, of other ways of obtaining the Living Water of prayer—and how through fidelity, hope and desire for the Lord, one day you might live next to a river, or have your own pool or cistern, or blessed rain water bringing you to deeper union and love with Jesus—right where you are! . . . Through prayer, imitation of Christ, faith, hope and love you can envisage how one day you will no longer have the arduous work of prayer, of hauling your own water, but will arrive at an inner place that has its living spring or rain, right where you live, so that there is no longer arduous effort to drink there, wash, or be refreshed and satisfied.

o   Though you don't know all that this means at this point of the journey, pray to develop a desire for this Living Water right where you live. It will help in these early stages when you struggle mightily to grow in prayer and virtue so as to move closer to your center—to the Living Water that Christ gives.

"Even though they keep falling, there remains a sign that the Lord was present in them, and that is that they rise again quickly." (L15,14)

I began to dress in finery and try to attract others by my appearance, going to a lot of trouble with my hands, hair, perfumes and all the vanities I could indulge in, and there many, for I was vain. I used every effort to keep my actions secret. And these things did me harm, for I started to grow cold in my good desires. (L2,2,6)

TERESA de AHUMADA
Adolescence—1528-1534

When Teresa was about twelve, her mother died. This was a shattering experience and Teresa cried many tears, and missed her mother and her guidance very much. The death of Beatriz did not come without consequences for young Teresa as she was entering adolescence without her mother.

Teresa noticed that she was becoming a very pretty young woman, and others were aware of her beauty and attracted to her. She was attractive both in physical and in personality qualities. She relates that she began to have the fault of vanity. As many young women, she took an interest in her appearance. She was always careful about cleanliness. From feedback she could tell that others found her charming, witty, lively, fun, and a good conversationalist. This was all flattering to Teresa's ego. She was a typical teenager, experimenting with life and its possibilities and allurements.

She says she imitated her mother not in her most virtuous qualities, but in the frivolous waste of time in reading romance novels and books of chivalry. This certainly reveals her romantic nature and desire for love from an early age. Love and friendship were very important in Teresa's life. She became rather addicted to the books of romance and heroism that filled her imagination, and she admitted that she was so caught up in these books of romance that she wasn't happy unless she had a new one to read. Since her father wasn't pleased with her choice of books, she became secretly shrewd about hiding them from him. She writes that she had no bad intentions about her frivolities, and wouldn't have offended God knowingly, but she was rather unconscious of the effects of some of her attitudes and choices, and what she let captivate her.

More dangerous trouble began with the visits of her male first cousins, who often came to her house, and were attracted by Teresa's charm and beauty. Her mother was gone, and while her father was cautious about his beautiful daughter, and tried to guard her reputation, he couldn't supervise her every moment. Teresa says that these cousins liked her a lot, and she enjoyed talking with them and listening to their affections, flirtations and praise of her. Teresa does offer the excuse for her own carelessness with her cousins, that it was in view of a possible marriage. She offers the advice to parents of teenagers that they must be very careful about the friends and associates of their adolescent children because of the natural tendencies of the teenage years.

Teresa also had a frivolous female cousin who was a bad influence on her, but of course Teresa liked her the most. The two would get involved in their confidential girl-talk that Teresa enjoyed. Teresa certainly got caught up in vanity about her reputation as a charming beauty, but was not entirely careful about losing it in ways that would have ruined her honor. Both her father and her oldest sister became concerned for her reputation, and she admits that they were right to be worried because she was strikingly shrewd when it came to mischief and hiding what she was up to. These unguarded and superficial conversations with her cousin really changed her, so that she says she hardly had any virtue left from her early childhood. This later became a source of her understanding of the importance of having good friends of God for one's own friends.

Teresa wrote that she lost the fear of God, and only had a natural fear of losing her reputation by getting involved with her cousins in dishonorable ways. She said she dared to do many things, thinking that no one would find out, and that these were against her honor and against God. Even her maids colluded with her in hiding things from her father. But she says she was also never inclined to great evil or indecent things, but only to the pastime of some allusions to them in conversations. Her father, being aware that Teresa was going down the wrong path, and fearing for her reputation, and against her will, finally sent her to a convent school.

Teresa wrote that she was unhappy at the Augustinian convent school, but only for about a week before realizing that she was actually more contented and peaceful there. She was happy to see good nuns, and experienced being very loved there. Under the influence of the Sisters and with good companions, she gradually began to return to the virtuous habits she had in her early childhood. She especially enjoyed speaking with a nun who shared her faith and vocation story with Teresa. And though Teresa hadn't had any attraction to becoming a nun, that vocation became less unattractive than it had been. After about a year and a half Teresa began to recite many vocal prayers and to ask others to pray for her so that she would know what state in life she should take. She had no desire to be a nun, and asked God not to give her that vocation. But at the same time she also feared marriage because of the oppression she had seen within her own sister's marriage. By the end of her time at the convent school she was more favorable to the thought of becoming a nun, and was working on becoming more virtuous. She was not attracted to this Augustinian Order of nuns. At the time she thought some of the things they did were too extreme. She probably thought there were things she wouldn't be able to do herself, for she believed she had great hardness of heart. She realized later that God was preparing a place that was better for her. This better place for her true vocation was put in motion by an illness that caused Teresa to have to leave the convent school and return home to her father in 1532.

When Teresa became very sick, she spent some time convalescing at her uncle Pedro's home and also at her older sister, Maria's, home. Her uncle was good and virtuous and spoke to his niece about God and the superficiality of the world. He asked Teresa to read spiritual books to him, which she said she didn't really like, and only pretended to like. But Uncle Pedro was good company and his words to Teresa and the devotional words of the spiritual books influenced her heart. She began to understand what she knew as a child that all things come to an end, all the vanities of the world are futility and for the way she had been living, hell was a possibility for her. Teresa was struggling with what state in life she should choose. She saw that she had been living a superficial life and feared she didn't deserve heaven which had been her desire since she was little. The struggle of her reflections caused her so much strain and conflict that it affected her health. She wrote that it was a battle raging within herself. So she began to think that religious life was the safest state for her, and decided to force herself into it. Her inner turmoil caused fainting spells and fevers. She had doubts that she could live the hardships of religious life, but her present interior struggle was so terrible that she thought that convent life would be less suffering than her present anxiety and indecision. Blessedly, Teresa was reading spiritual books during this crisis which helped her to finally make a choice. She told her father of her decision to become a nun, but he would not give his permission. However, Teresa needed a remedy for her miserable soul, and though she said that nothing was harder than leaving her father, she made the decision to enter the Carmelite Monastery of the Incarnation in Avila.

3-1

THIRD DWELLING PLACES—Part 1

(*The Interior Castle* 3, Chapters 1-2)

Theme: *Beware of the dangers of the self-controlled, well-ordered Christian life!*

Description of the Third Dwelling Places:

This is where most practicing Christians are, and stop, in the development of their prayer life, and do not move on in preparation for the passive, supernatural prayer of contemplation. These dwellings surface the problem of the ordinary, typical and conventionally "good," adult Christian. And while there is certainly a continuum of degrees of commitment to following Christ in these dwelling places, and these persons are generally in step with requirements of institutionalized religion, they are not necessarily committed to the deeper love and engagement with Christ or the radical demands of the Gospel.

- o Here, ascetical practices, works for the Lord, and prayer are well-ordered and under the control of reason, or ego. Virtue is actually only still in baby steps, nothing that would wear out these persons, or compromise bodily comfort or health. "*Love is not yet ardent enough to overwhelm reason.*" (IC3,2,7)
- o Though these persons are beginning to feel drawn towards a deeper relationship with Jesus, they have *not yet surrendered and given themselves completely to God.* Their well-ordered lives and pious external efforts are not yet the *love that does not count the cost.* (IC3,2,7-9)

- Persons in the third dwelling places have built prayer into their lives, and regularly attend church services. For some, their prayer may also include such devotions as the Stations of the Cross, Eucharistic Adoration, litanies, fasting, pilgrimages, the Divine Office, or the rosary. For others, it may be reading and reflecting on scripture and various spiritual writings, joining a prayer group, or a lay religious or associate program, attending Christian workshops or retreats, or meeting regularly with a spiritual director. Good, conventional Christians generally give alms to their church and donations to charities. They may also do volunteer work at their parish or in their community, putting into practice love of neighbor, and the spiritual and corporal works of mercy. (IC3,1,5)
- Since these Christians are more conscientious about their Christian life and prayer, there is more security here in avoiding a sinful life, and more certainty of drawing closer to Christ, with less chance of giving up prayer and abandoning the Christian life altogether. (IC3,1,1-2)
- In these dwellings there is an expanding conversion on the *conscious* level, so there will be greater self-control and detachment from any *perceived* harmful externals, though these persons are still not completely convinced that the desires and distractions of the culture and world will never satisfy them, and that only God satisfies all longings.
- Deeper self-knowledge is lacking, with many *unconscious* faults and failings going completely unnoticed.
- People in these dwelling places are not as strong as those who have been tried through the struggle of more profound purifications of later dwellings—especially of difficult *unconscious* material. They can easily slip back into earlier dwelling places. (IC3,2,12)
- Though these persons are trying to pray, practice love of God and neighbor, avoid sin, and live a balanced Christian life, their well-ordered and secure spiritual life has become another attachment—and a block to progress in the spiritual life.
- Though their lives are conventionally Christian, when there is some setback, trial, or failure, they easily become discouraged and afflicted. Even minor trials can disturb these Christians. (IC3,2,1)
  - Disturbance about their failures, which does not pass quickly, is a revelation and painful bit of self-knowledge. (IC3,2,2)
  - This new self-knowledge of weakness often becomes more distressing than the faults committed, and can be beneficial for exercising humility.
    - Rather than focusing on failures and berating themselves, in true humility they should get up from their failures and try again.

They must not quit, or give up on themselves, or give in to discouragement.
- They have not yet found true humility and deep self-knowledge—especially of their unconscious, sinful, shadow side, which prevents them from moving forward. (IC3,2,8-9)
- Because of their well-ordered lives, persons in these dwellings tend to think they can teach others about virtue and the spiritual life. They may try to set others straight, and are easily shocked by others' faults. In fear and self-righteousness they can be standoffish from "sinners" or anything that might "contaminate" them. (IC3,2,1)
  - They are like the Pharisee to the Publican—prone to judge and compare themselves to others. (Lk. 18:9-14)
- There can be initial ease and joy in prayer and devotions in these dwellings, but after a time, despite fidelity to prayer and seriousness of devotion, **dryness, aridity and restlessness in prayer begin.** (IC3,2,10)
  - With this development prayer and devotional practices become laborious and burdensome.
  - Prayer may feel shallow, empty of meaning—like something is lacking or wrong.
  - It begins to feel more like a "have to" than a "want to."
- Because consolations or good feelings which used to come with prayer and devotions are drying up, these Christians begin to wonder what went wrong and what they should do next.
- God is inviting them to make a transitional leap to the next dwelling places, but they don't know what to do. They have not heard of the passive supernatural prayer of Infused Recollection or other stages of contemplative prayer which God wants to give them for closer intimacy with Him in prayer.
- Mature growth and freedom in these dwellings will call for surrender to the insecurity and loss of self-controlled Christian development into God-controlled development and maturation.

Teresian Teachings for Prayer and Life: (see: L11-13 & 23)

- *"In overcoming initial difficulties and entering the third dwelling places, the Lord has granted them no small favor, but a very great one!"* (IC3,1,5)
  - These persons have travelled a great distance into their interior castle and have begun earnestly to devote more time to prayer, to getting to know Christ better, and to paying more attention to imitating Him in virtue.

- And however much these persons may still stumble in these dwellings, they must not fear, turn back, or let any gains or virtue be lost.
- In living the spiritual life, Teresa teaches that **measured virtue is more wearisome than full out virtue.**
- In what is still a measured practice of virtue, these persons should strive to notice and abandon self-deceptive excuses for failures. They must leave behind fear, laziness and extreme concern for comfort and health.
- In loving trust and prayer, these persons must surrender into God's hands, caring only about moving quickly to know, love and serve God. (IC3,2,8)
- They must be vigilant about any occasions of sin which might be a particular downfall situation for them. They are still not strong enough in these dwellings and can fall back. (IC3,2,12)
- They must work at persevering in detachment (holy freedom) from addictions they have—whatever wearies, torments, darkens, defiles, or moves them away from God. (A1,6-13)
- These persons will discover that dryness and aridity in prayer begin to grow in these dwellings, and must be accepted with patience and without complaint.
  - Both consolation and aridity in prayer must be left to God's will and discretion for each person's life and ultimate good. (IC3,1,6-9)
- Aridity and dryness in prayer are part of the natural progression of a serious prayer life.
  - For the sake of advancing in prayer and life, one has to work up a good aridity in prayer!
  - Maturity in prayer and the relationship with God for the long haul includes being exercised in this aridity and dryness for endurance, determination and patience.
  - From persevering and patient acceptance of dryness in prayer one grows in humility (truthful self-knowledge), peace, and surrender to the will of God. (IC3,1,9)
  - Being faithful to praying even when it is empty and tasteless, when God withdraws the former joy and light, persons will more humbly and truthfully come to know themselves. (IC3,2,2)
- *"O humility, humility! Anyone who makes an issue of aridity in prayer is lacking in humility!"* (IC3,1,7)
  - One must not ask or oblige God to give consolations or graces that are not deserved. (IC3,1,6-7)

- God will always test persons to discover if they can love Him for His sake alone, without payment and reward. Remember, to whom more is given, more is asked! (Lk. 12:48)
  - *"If humility is lacking, we will remain here our whole life, and with a thousand troubles and miseries. For if we have not surrendered ourselves, this state will be very laborious and burdensome."* (IC3,2,9)
    - Without humility persons will remain in the first three dwellings. Any lack of humility prevents movement forward.
    - It is humility to recognize that no one *deserves* even to enter the third dwellings places, let alone later dwellings.
    - Where there is true humility God can bring healing. (IC3,2,6)
    - The humble live in gratitude, and make gratitude part of their prayer.
    - Persons should not look to the mistakes of others, but to their own failings. It is dangerous to make comparisons or be shocked by others.
    - Any Christian can learn both from those who are virtuous and those who are not. (IC3,2,13)
    - It's helpful to look at others in compassion, from the viewpoint of one's *own greatest weakness*. (W7,5)
  - Perfection lies not in spiritual delights but in the imitation of Christ, and in greater love and deeds of justice, truth and integrity.
    - Each must pass on from their puny works. Any commitment must not be mere words but include deeds. (IC3,1,6)
    - As the rich young man, do not turn and go away sad when the Lord has uniquely revealed what more must be done to become more perfected. (Lk. 18:18-23)
  - Those who think they have their spiritual life under control will feel greater inner distaste and restlessness when prayer seems empty and dry. Until they abandon themselves to God, everything will be hard and burdensome. (IC3,2,9-10)
  - *"Following our own will is usually what brings harm to us."* (IC3,2,12)
  - Know that God can, and does give consolations in prayer that are more compelling than any distractions that arise in prayer. (IC3,2,9)
  - The favors from God come brimming over with love and fortitude, with less labor needed for works of virtue. In the matter of either favors or aridity, God alone knows what is needed and when, and in what mode for every person. (IC3,2,11)
    - No matter how it seems, God ordains everything for each person's good. Praise His Majesty who never fails.

- It is very important for growth in prayer and the spiritual life to meet with a learned, experienced and knowledgeable spiritual director. (IC3,2,12)
- It is also helpful for persons to seek out friends of God, companions, models, and saints that are a support and help for seeing and discerning rightly the things of God.
- Know that any sensual desire for God or others is not the same as Divine spiritual love. The desire for the Lord here is still more on the level of sense than of spirit. But desire and love for Him is increasing in these third dwelling places and He is desiring to enkindle Divine Love.

"O Lord, test us, so that we may know ourselves. For you know the truth that we are fonder of spiritual sweetness, than we are of crosses." (IC3,1,9)

3-1

THIRD DWELLING PLACES—Part 1

Internalizing the Teachings: *Change my little water of prayer into your Living Water!*

Here the challenge in prayer and life is to rely less on yourself, to trust the unknown action of God in your life, and to align all of your life and choices more closely to the imitation of Christ with a serious perseverance and commitment to faith, hope and love. Above all, what is needed is a greater love and desire for a closer relationship with Christ than for anything else. It requires more changes concerning former sinful life choices along with some new spiritual attitudes and practices. These dwellings call for more quality time given to prayer and solitude, and to good works—the fruit of prayer. It is a time of going beyond conventional religion, and of discovering more painful self-knowledge and growth. There is a great need for genuine humility as truthful self-knowledge, and a recognition of the importance of discernment concerning what the Lord is asking, and how He is personally calling you in your deepening Christian life.

Reflection:
The Conventional Christian

As you walk through these rooms that are getting closer to where God dwells in you, the more you will experience and feel your own sinfulness. But the first thing that the Lord wants to do for your weaknesses is give you courage and make you unafraid of this and other trials. (W18,2) St. Teresa knows that you, and many practicing Christians remain living in the first three dwellings because you keep yourself tied to your sinfulness, and because no one has ever told you about contemplative prayer and the deeper relationship and union with Christ that is possible. She knows you are a sincere Christian, but stuck in the problematic state of the conventionally good Christian, who equates spirituality mainly with saying prayers and going to church on Sunday, but perhaps hasn't thought much lately about growth in virtue and love. You have probably assented to the Creed and the various Christian doctrines, and perhaps given alms to charities and engaged in some volunteering. You have possibly been practicing various devotions. You may have joined a prayer group, or attended retreats or workshops on Christian spirituality topics. It certainly isn't the case that these are insignificant or unimportant, but these can come with an unconscious belief that religion is a transactional "deal" or, "I do these religious things for God, and expect God to reward me in some way." You probably have not truly surrendered control of your life over to God, even if you think you have had some beginning desire to do so.

Generally, in the first three dwellings there is an unconscious attitude or belief that you are saving yourself by doing these religious things. This can bring a kind of self-satisfied, self-assured security—but not a true sense of God's saving power, mercy and love that cannot be earned or manipulated, and is a free gift. Yours is a beginning of a love relationship with the Lord, not yet for His sake alone, but more a transaction based on rewards and punishments, perhaps with a presumption that you have done enough, or all that is necessary to *earn* your reward. You may even be thinking that you have "played it safe" and appeased God.

This is a socially customary understanding of religion and relationship with God. It could reveal a lack in understanding Christ, an immature state of faith, and the radical demands of following Christ. Examine yourself to see if this could be something more serious and dangerous, as a chosen lack of desire to know and come closer to the Lord, lest He make more demands on you and require more change. Could you be hiding from yourself your reluctance to make a deeper commitment because you don't really want to do more? You might fool yourself about this, but you can't fool the Lord. If you don't want Him to disturb you, you may settle into these dwelling places until you make a determined choice to love Christ deeply and imitate Him more closely.

Even though you have some growing embers of love for God, and inhabit these third dwelling places as an "achievement," and more, a blessing, it is still a place of stumbling blocks and pitfalls and not yet the sparked and burning love of later dwellings. You still have little or no knowledge of what is possible in prayer and relationship with God beyond the "deal" or mere servant-hood. But Christ is desiring more—an intimate friendship and spousal relationship with you.

A great pitfall for you here is to judge others who, in your mind, have not even attained the well-ordered, conventional spiritual life that you have. Perhaps you both pity and fear any others who are not like you, even though you yourself have unconscious misconceptions about what "true religion" is. Like the Pharisee in his judgment of the Publican, you may need to check yourself for lack of compassion and empathy for others, and feelings of superiority in your religious practices. You dare not be smug that you will inherit eternal life while these other "lost souls" are in big trouble. Recall that of all groups and types of people, Jesus was hardest on the self-righteous. In careful reading and reflection of the Gospels it is clear that they do not show Jesus as one who puts an emphasis on keeping burdensome, man-made religious rules, devotions, or even theological ideas. Instead, Jesus primarily emphasized love, a life based in spirit and truth in following and imitating Him in thought and action. It may well be that there are people who do not go to church every Sunday, don't know how to pray the rosary or Stations of the Cross, haven't the faintest idea about creeds or what they mean, and may belong to an entirely different religious tradition, but they are very conscientiously living the Great Commandment of love of God and neighbor. Or, even lacking much of a belief in God, they are living truly and sacrificially in imitation of Christ, His "whatsoever you do to the least of my people, you do to me" love of neighbor that Jesus desires, and is pleasing to God. (Mt. 25:40)

Many persons, and perhaps you, are generally not comfortable with either silence or solitude—where God is heard and relationally experienced in new ways. And there is a lack of discipline to grow in virtue, pray or give more time to God. You won't progress in prayer if this is the case. Once the discomfort of dryness in prayer gets wearisome, you may also consider giving up prayer altogether. You have not known that aridity and dryness in prayer are a natural part of the development of prayer and underpin your need for growth in virtue, patience and fidelity in showing love for God.

Reflection Questions: (Choose only one or two at a time to explore in depth.)

- Do you have a favorite vocal prayer or psalm? What draws you to that prayer?

- What spiritual practices do you incorporate into your life?
- How attentive are you to what you are saying and asking during prayer?
- What assumptions do you have about effective, good or "successful" prayer?
- Do you continue to be faithful to prayer even when you feel restless, or your prayer feels joyless, unproductive or unsuccessful?
- What do you think you need in times of dryness and aridity in prayer to sustain fidelity to prayer?
- Can you identify your weaknesses and strengths? What do you hide about yourself from others, or from yourself? What do you want people to know or not know about you?
- Do you ever practice denying yourself something to see how free you are? Could it be time on the phone or computer; going shopping; getting in the last word in an argument; driving with patience for annoying drivers; letting go and stopping your mind from angry or critical thoughts; surrendering the need of setting someone straight; apologizing first; abstaining from that extra glass of wine; giving up the satisfaction of reaching your goal for the moment to allow more time for prayer; letting someone else take the credit instead of you?
- Are you looking for consoling or peak experiences during your prayer, or for whatever gift God chooses for you? How do you feel when your prayers seem not to be answered?
- What is your experience of Church and Christian community? Has it been a supportive teacher to you for a developing prayer life, or a disappointment in some way?

Guidance for Prayer and Prayer Period:

o Exploring one of the Church's major spiritual traditions—the Desert Fathers and Mothers, Benedictines, Franciscans, Dominicans, Carmelites, Jesuits, Vincentians, Salesians, etc.—can be an aid for providing more guidance and wisdom in the spiritual life.

o Make sure you have taken some moments before your practice of prayer to examine your life and responses to God in the past week or during the day. Make any needed intentions to correct a failing or to strengthen a virtue that you recognize.

o What you want to begin to arrive at is an awakening of your *affective desire and will to love Christ*. So try to keep Him ever present, interiorly gazing on and speaking with Him, asking for your needs, sharing your complaints, being glad with Him in your enjoyments—not only with formulary prayers, but even more with words that reflect your own desires and needs.

- Find some action, or an object, that you often do or see in your daily life that will remind you of Jesus' presence and His love for you whenever you come upon it (e.g. walking through a door, gazing at your garden, seeing your favorite tree, checking your watch, looking at yourself in the mirror, getting dressed, etc.).

o There is a progressive stage of simplification of prayer, which will in time move beyond words and the labor of Discursive Meditation—or thinking things about Christ.

o However, you must never stop considering the life of Christ in scripture as your example. Reflect especially on the love He bears you, of the glory He wants to share with you, and of the joy and fullness of life He promises you. This will help enkindle deeper love for Him.

o A practical suggestion, perhaps new to you, and a very good way of watering your inner garden and knowing Christ more deeply through scripture is the practice of **Lectio Divina**, or Divine Reading. This should become part of your prayer in some form by the third dwelling places. St. John of the Cross wrote: "Seek in reading and you will find in meditation; knock in prayer and it will be opened to you in contemplation." (SLL #158)

LECTIO DIVINA

o Lectio Divina is a profound way of getting to know Jesus the Christ better, and is a method of praying with scripture that includes: 1) *Lectio*—reading a scripture passage; 2) *Meditatio*—meditating on the scripture passage; 3) *Oratio*—praying over the scripture passage; 4) *Contemplatio*—hopefully being drawn into the quiet of contemplation and the presence of God with some insight into the scripture passage for your own lived-life.

Praying through Lectio Divina would be something like this:

1. Set aside at least ½ hour for Lectio Divina, in a quiet setting, with a comfortable chair, candle or low lighting, icon or statue, a hymn or whatever fosters an ambiance of prayer for you.

2. Choose a scripture passage—a favorite one, or a scripture from the daily readings of the Lectionary, or begin to slowly work through a particular book of the Bible. There is no set number of verses to have as a goal to get through, so let God be in charge of the length of the text.
3. Slowly and calmly read the text with a listening, attentive heart for any word or phrase that causes a stirring, attraction or movement within you. After recognizing any word or phrase that struck you in the first reading of the passage, sit in silent listening for a while.
4. Focus on and memorize the word or verse that struck you, and let it raise up in you anything that has to do with your present state of life, needs and desires. Ponder and reflect on the words and verse for some moments. Allow again a time of silent listening.
5. Using the word or verse and its connection to your life, pray with it in your own words saying anything you want to the Lord from it. Then leave words aside and listen in silence and receptivity, and just enjoy a still presence of God who is with you.
6. You may revisit the scripture passage in reading, meditating, praying and contemplative listening once or twice again, always in peaceful calm, and punctuated with silent listening.
7. End your prayer with thanksgiving and gratitude for God's presence to you and whatever word or verse or inspiration was raised for you in the prayer that you can take into your daily life.

o Refer to "Lectio Divina Recollection" in the **Supplemental Material** for more amplification of this type of prayer.

If desired, choose one of the following scriptures before your prayer period begins.

Scripture Passages:
(Love) Lk. 10:29f, 6:27-35, 14:25-33, 10:25-27; Mt. 7:1-5, 19:16-22, 22:37-39; Jn. 15:12-13; Col. 2:1-2, 3:14; Eph. 4:2-3; Rom. 12:9-21; 1Pt. 4:8-11
(Living Water) Jn. 4:1-42, 3:1-6, 6:35-37, 7:37-39; Is. 55:1-3, 41:17-20, 44:3-4, 12:2-3; Jer. 2:13; Ezek. 47:1-12, 36:25-28; Ps. 42:1-2, 36:8; Rev. 21:6-7; 1Cor. 10:1-4

You may use the following meditation during your prayer if desired.

Guided Meditation:

In quiet and stillness enter within your inner self and begin to imagine again the beautiful garden within your castle enclosure. . . . Start to notice the many kinds of colorful flowers, shrubs and fruit trees with their enchanting scents wafting in the air as you pass by. Also recognize a few places that require some weeding and more beautification. . . . Off to your right see a graveled narrow path with an arch of trellised vines leading to a special place with a wide-backed park bench in a cozy shaded cove facing a still, little pond. On your way to a rendezvous at this bench gather some beautiful scented flowers for a bouquet, and seat yourself quietly on the bench in anticipation of meeting your Beloved. While sitting there quietly scanning the various flowers and trees of your garden you discover that they represent the virtues and gifts that bring beauty and decoration to your garden, which you have chosen and carefully cultivated for the delight of your Beloved. . . . The setting that you have designed for your garden with love and careful choices and much labor reflects your growing desire to please the Lord and attract Him to take His delight in you and your interior garden (your soul)—a secret place where you both can meet and share loving gazes and words. You long to draw Him to yourself in this beauty. The flowers you have chosen say something about you and what you want to give to your Beloved. Begin to reflect on the flowers of the bouquet in your hand and why you have chosen these for Him so that you may tell Him when He arrives. . . . You have further realized how much work it is to water your garden and how this garden needs the Living Water of prayer for it to flourish and be the beautiful hidden place where lovers meet. Try to cast from your mind any thoughts of what the labor will cost, because the joy of intimacy with the Beloved is everything. You are aware that the garden can be watered in several ways. You know the hard work of drawing water from a well with merely a bucket (or a hand pump). You realize you could get more water by building canals or an aqueduct, which would take a lot of effort, too, but deliver more water over time. Then there is always the possibility of channeling water (or installing a water drip system) from a nearby spring. This would also be labor, but perhaps less than the other methods in the long run. Certainly, you know your Beloved would help you with any of these ways, so that you could experience more times of rest, joy and refreshment together in each other's company. On reflecting on these ways of watering your garden, realize now that primarily you have still been watering by the intensive work of drawing water from a well with only your own bucket—the prayer that you do yourself. You are beginning to recognize that prayer has been arduous in these first three dwelling places, and how different it could be in the future if you let your Beloved help you water the garden by other means of His design. Let this spur you to greater enthusiasm in your desire for the intimacy of communion, conversations and interchanges in prayer in your encounters with the Beloved in your garden. And even though in these earlier dwellings you don't yet know what depth is possible for your relationship with your Beloved and how He can help you water your garden, pray for the canals, springs, streams, and rain of the Living Water of prayer—the supernatural contemplative prayer He wants to provide, that can be yours and bring you closer to one another in intimacy.

"In my opinion there is no reason why entrance into later dwelling places should be denied these souls, nor will the Lord deny them entrance if they desire it; for such a desire is an excellent way to prepare oneself so that every favor may be granted." (IC3,1,5)

3-2

THIRD DWELLING PLACES—Part 2

Theme: *Trust! Be still and patient in the trials of prayer!*

Description of the Third Dwelling Places: (continued)

There begins to be changes in prayer in the third dwelling places—what seems like a breakdown or block in the usual, ordinary way of praying and relating to God. It is generally experienced as dryness, aridity, distaste or resistance, and restlessness in prayer. The value and usefulness of prayer may be questioned. It is often accompanied by a lack of feelings of consolation, with a temptation to give up prayer altogether. Aridity is actually an important and *necessary* stage for growth in prayer and to maturation in the Christian life.

ARIDITY/DRYNESS/RESTLESSNESS/LACK of CONSOLATION in PRAYER

o There are several causes and purposes for dryness and lack of consolation in prayer.
   - Dryness can be caused by not doing the one thing necessary—a "necessary" that is both universal and particular to each person. (IC3,1,6-7) (the Gospel of the rich young man—Mt. 19:16-22)
   - Dryness can be a revealing test from God to see whether persons are rulers of their passions, and free of what they assumed they had already accomplished or left behind. (IC3,2,6)
   - Dryness, aridity, boredom and restlessness can help foster humility, and surface unconscious faults and resentments. It can reveal an

attitude of presumption that God owes favors for virtue and good works. (IC3,1,6,8-9)
- Dryness must be accepted with patience and without complaint. It is a sign of lack of humility to make an issue of dryness in prayer. (IC3,1,6-7)
  - True humility leads to peace, compliance and resignation to God's will.
- God gives some persons dryness in prayer to build fortitude and perseverance, while others are given consolations to foster strength, gratitude and love. (IC3,2,9,11)
  - St. Teresa thought that consolations are often given to weaker souls. (IC3,1,9-10)
  - Consolations can be self-induced from our own brain chemicals, and can be misleading and bad guides. Consolations differ greatly from the spiritual delights of later dwelling places. Spiritual delights cannot be self-manufactured, but are supernatural gifts from God. (see: "Consolations vs. Spiritual Delights" in **Supplemental Material**)
- Prayer will still require much effort in the third dwelling places. Prayer here may be a mixture of vocal prayer and other forms of active recollection. These could include rosaries, novenas, pilgrimages, litanies, Mass, the Divine Office, Stations of the Cross, Eucharistic Adoration, Lectio Divina, or any recollection through Acquired Recollection or Discursive Meditation.
- Discursive Meditation, and Active or Acquired Recollection, are forms of active prayer, that is, prayer we do ourselves. (see: "Prayer—Types and Categories" in **Supplemental Material**)
  - <u>Discursive Meditation</u> or spiritual thinking, is working with the intellect and mind moving from point to point in a reflection *about* God, or attributes of Christ, a Gospel scene and its place, situation and characters, or a doctrine of Christianity, etc. Most Christians have been doing Discursive Meditation already, though they didn't know the technical name for it.
  - <u>Active or Acquired Recollection</u> is a natural way of calming and quieting the mind through reflection on the Gospel or other spiritual considerations, or through repetitive or short inspirational prayer forms. The calming and quieting of the mind can be achieved with practice, and often moves on to other thoughts and affections. The mind cannot be kept quiet for long in these dwellings.
  - Gradually the length of time of quiet mind will extend as one becomes accustomed to look at and love Christ in a simple gaze of

loving desire and faith, through the repetition of the rosary, through Centering Prayer, the Jesus Prayer ("Lord Jesus Christ, Son of God, have mercy on me"), a sacred word, or a few words from a short spiritual reading, or whatever prayer or devotion that helps quiet the mind.
- For prayer to deepen one must work at recollecting, that is, quieting the mind as well as the senses of seeing and hearing. This involves a new kind of work and effort.
- Active Acquired Recollection is different from the passive prayer of Infused Recollection or other stages of contemplative prayer which, if God chooses, will come later in subsequent dwellings.

o Again, the third dwelling places are where most practicing Christians are and stop, because of the new difficulties of prayer. And so they do not move on to the supernatural prayer that God initiates in the form of passive prayer that includes: Infused Recollection, and the various degrees of contemplative prayer that Teresa calls Prayer of Quiet, Prayer of the Sleep of the Faculties, and Prayer of Union. These will be explained in later chapters.
- People in these third dwellings are not yet strong enough in Christian virtue or a love that does not count the cost, and it may take some time for them to surrender to the new way of prayer that is more obscure, and out of their control and understanding, which begins in the fourth dwelling places.
- Until they surrender control of their prayer and life to God and respond more wholeheartedly in faith, hope and love to the sufferings of these dwellings, they will not be prepared for the even greater sufferings of purification in later dwelling places.

Teresian Teachings for Prayer and Life: (continued)

o St. Teresa speaks about the transition in prayer—the movement *from ordinary, natural, self-acquired* **Active Prayer** *to God directed, supernatural* **Passive Prayer**—from the prayer of the third dwelling places to that of the fourth dwelling places.

o **Transition Signs** of movement in prayer from the third dwelling places to the fourth dwelling places—or from active prayer to passive prayer—are scattered throughout St. Teresa's writings, and can be expressed in several ways which will be included in the following from both St. Teresa of Jesus and St. John of the Cross:

1. **Inability to do Discursive Meditation:** There is no desire to engage in complex thinking, or elaborate use of the imagination in prayer.
2. **Dryness—including the things of God, the spiritual life, and the world:** Initial enthusiasm and former consolations are gone.
3. **Growing desire for solitude:** Desire for simpler ways of praying develops.

1. **First Sign: Inability to do Discursive Meditation** (IC4,1,6-7; 4,3; L9,4; 11,10,15; 13,11,22)
   - There begins to be great disenchantment and dis-ease with the prayer of the first three dwelling places. It has changed, broken down and become difficult. It is experienced in an inability to practice the *work* of Discursive Meditation, imaginatively and intellectually constructed meditations, or other forms of active or Acquired Recollection and prayer.
     - There is a disinclination to fix the Intellect/mind, and Memory/imagination on any particular ideas or things. It has become tiresome and too much work.
   - Some begin to experience a new kind of prayer but don't recognize it, or aren't willing to surrender to it.
     - When the mind or Intellect ceases to function as it normally did before in prayer and meditation, many misinterpret this as their failure, and lack of fidelity to prayer.
     - Many cannot bear this, and give up prayer, or go back to earlier forms of prayer and piety, where they felt like they were "doing something."
   - Without a qualified spiritual director, and lacking understanding of what is happening, along with feelings of failure in prayer, the temptation is to quit and walk away from prayer, which has seemed to have reached some impassable limit.
     - The person of prayer has to muster the determination to battle the temptation to quit.

2. **Second Sign: Dryness—including the things of God, the spiritual life, and the world** (IC3,1,6-9; 4,3,3-14; L30,16; 8,2; 11,9-10; 14,9)
   - A certain dryness, lack of enthusiasm, boredom, disappointment and restlessness in the relationship with God, with the spiritual life, and the world is experienced in addition to the impasse, dryness and distaste for prayer.
     - There is a kind of dead-end experience to prayer in these dwelling places, with questions such as: "Now what?" "What's going on with

my prayer?" "Why can't I pray?" "How do I go forward in my spiritual life?"
- There is a *feeling* of less love for and from God, though this is actually a call to deeper understanding and experiences of Divine love beyond sensible feeling and emotion.
- This is a sign of development and new growth in love—from sensual love to spiritual love.
    - The desire for sensible consolation or gratification in prayer is a fault if the person won't pray, work or love without it. (L11,14)
- The darkness, dryness and hiddenness of God for St. Teresa and St. John of the Cross is not the actual absence of God, but a different experience and manifestation of God in God's transcendence.
- This experience of the brokenness, dryness, hiddenness, and darkness of the new stage of prayer is about the incomprehensibility of God—or the God who cannot be experienced through our natural faculties—and a correction to idolatrous projections, images and understandings of God.
    - It is experienced as a breakdown in communication, and requires new teachings on prayer and the letting go of attachment to former ways of praying.
    - This is a time of impasse in the relationship with God in prayer, and often everything else. But with fidelity, it will bring a new kind of presence and relationship to God and others, and to all things.
- There is a growing lack of attraction for former worldly values, interests, allurements and pursuits, with feelings of tedium, ennui and world-weariness that burden the soul and weigh on it with a heaviness.

3. **Third Sign: Growing desire for solitude and simpler forms of prayer** (IC4,3; L11-12)
- At the same time that the former way of praying has broken down, there is a recognized desire for solitude and remaining alone in loving attention, desire, and awareness of God without the labor of meditations, ideas, or words.
- Loving, serving, and being with God and others previously for the sake of consolation and gratification is beginning to change to loving, serving, and being with God and others out of loyalty and love solely for the sake of the other.
- In this new situation of the breakdown of prayer, the spiritual life and the former relationship with God, the person praying (or the directee) can't understand what is happening, and needs a spiritual director who is learned and knowledgeable in stages of prayer and the development of the spiritual life.

- Without guidance, persons will try to do what they have always done in prayer, but to no avail.

o The following **Transition Signs** of St. John of the Cross for recognizing the passage from active prayer to passive prayer are also scattered throughout his writings, and correspond to the teachings of St. Teresa. Both are being given here for further amplification.

1. **Inability to meditate:** There's no desire or ability to apply the imagination in images, stories, metaphors, or meditations in prayer. God isn't communicating through the senses anymore, but desires the person to move beyond them.
2. **Dryness in the things of God:** Former ideas about God are no longer viable or compelling. There is a lack of pleasure in the relationship with God, with accompanying feelings of sinfulness and personal failure on one's own part in relating to God.
3. **Weariness with the things of the world:** Life and its former pleasures seem dull and meaningless. Life is dissatisfying. The search for "the more" may lead to a developing desire to go deeper into solitude in loving desire and attention to God as a possible remedy.

2Ascent Ch. 13-15	**1Dark Night Ch. 9-10**	**3Flame Ch. 32-40**
1. There's a realization that one cannot make Discursive Meditation nor receive satisfaction from such prayer of the senses as before.	One no longer gets satisfaction or consolation from the things of God, or from created, worldly things.	The soul loses the satisfaction of Discursive Meditation and is placed in the state of infused Contemplation.
2. There's a lack of satisfaction in the things of God and things of the world, with the awareness of a disinclination to fix the imagination on these.	There's a painful solicitude concerning fear of not loving and serving God well.	The inclination is towards withdrawal from all things with an attraction to more solitude.

3. There's a loving general knowledge and awareness of God without acts, exercises or particular considerations in prayer. There's a preference to remain alone in quiet, loving awareness of God.	There's an inability to practice prayer of the senses as previously— viz. Discursive Meditation or the use of the imagination in prayer.	One experiences the grace, riches and gentle breathing of love and life in the Holy Spirit.

At this point in the spiritual journey—both in prayer and lived life—as part of a growing self-knowledge, it is helpful to EXAMINE, TEST and EXERCISE oneself before God does. (IC3,2,3)

- Persons should test their progress in humility when it comes to letting go of not looking good before others. (IC3,2,5) *"... if people lose their reputation, God often gives them the grace to bear this well, for He loves to help people to be virtuous in the presence of others, so that virtue itself will not undergo a loss of esteem."* (IC3,2,5)
    - Humiliation is hard on the ego, but good and profitable for the soul.
    - *"... true humility doesn't work in the soul with agitation or disturbance, nor does it darken it or bring it dryness. Rather, true humility consoles and acts in a completely opposite way: quietly, gently, and with light."* (L30,9)
- Persons need to recognize how slowly or quickly disturbances or humiliations hang on after failures.
- They can question themselves as to what they have truly let go of for love of God, and what they think they deserve from God.
- Persons can check to see if the way they face life's challenges and set-backs reveals that they are progressing in virtue, and in surrender to the Lord in everything that happens, and whether they trust Him beyond what feels good or bad to them. (IC3,2,6)
- They must be even more determined than ever to pray, serve with love, and earnestly imitate Christ.

❖ A thorough examination of conscience, consciousness, and behavior will follow in the next **Internalizing the Teachings** section.

"They must have a very earnest and determined resolve to persevere—whatever may come and however hard the labor ... to reach their goal or die on the road." (W21,2)

3-2

THIRD DWELLING PLACES—Part 2

Internalizing the Teachings: *Why can't I pray like I used to?*

When you have been faithful for some time to the practice of the types of prayer of the first three dwelling places (prayer that you do yourself—vocal, formulary prayer, devotions, and Acquired Recollection), prayer begins to change in significant ways, and seems problematic. It becomes generally more difficult to pray in former ways, with the loss of consolations and much aridity, dryness, and doubts about prayer. New questions arise about what appears to be a distaste for prayer, and questions about its usefulness, with thoughts that prayer is breaking down, and perhaps you aren't "successful" at it anymore. Strong doubts come about whether you should even try to continue with it. It is a time of restlessness and often a painful growing self-knowledge, with a need for more humility because of newly recognized uncomfortable revelations about yourself. You may wonder where to go with your questions of what to do now about prayer, and the confusion about what is happening, and if you are at fault. You need a spiritual director to help you learn about passive prayer and contemplation, and to aid you in your discernment about what God is doing in your life and asking of you. This uncomfortable loss of control, loss of direction and breakdown in prayer is really God calling you to a new stage of prayer and Christian commitment.

Reflection:

St. Teresa and Prayer

(see: "Prayer—Key Teresian Understandings" and the "Prayer of Recollection" in **Supplemental Material**)

Saint Teresa is a teacher of prayer par excellence, and is a Doctor of the Church for her teaching on prayer and the spiritual life. Though all the saints are only and always very human, St. Teresa is so candid in writing about herself that there is no mistaking it. Her very human characteristics are especially revealed in her autobiographical *Life* and in her *Letters*. She is revealed in her humanity as a person of weakness, failure, and struggle in prayer and virtue that anyone who is serious about prayer and following Christ, can identify with, understand, and draw comfort and encouragement from. She did not consider herself a saint, but saw for herself through her experience of the Lord in the light of her own weakness, how much He wants to love and give to everyone. Teresa writes of her life and prayer in a very personal, intimate and conversational way that is quite delightful and relatable. She is charming, witty, down to earth, and as many have said: "to know her is to love her."

What Teresa writes about prayer is not theoretical, but based on the power of her own lived experience. Her teachings on prayer permeate her writings. Her most mature and well thought-out understandings on prayer are in *The Interior Castle*. But excellent supplemental material to *The Interior Castle* are in chapters 10-22 of her autobiographical *Life* where she teaches about prayer from her earlier experiences. *The Way of Perfection*, especially chapters 19-38, have a great deal of teaching on prayer. *The Spiritual Testimonies*—also called *The Relations* (*Relaciones*)—include teachings on prayer, particularly ST 1, 12, 13, 14, 20, 22, 25, 29, 31, 34, 42, 46, 49, 51, 52, 53, 58, 59, and 65. Teresa also has an excellent section on prayer in chapters 4-8 of *The Foundations*.

Teresa asked her Carmelite nuns to spend two hours a day in mental (mindful) prayer but never prescribed a method for prayer, though she did suggest closing the eyes, or using a devotional picture or statue to help make Christ's presence real. She strongly recommended that it would be most helpful to inwardly focus on Christ and make Him present in His *humanity* during prayer so as to keep prayer grounded in relatable human experience. She had discovered for herself that it is easier to relate to Jesus Christ in His humanity, than to the No-thing-ness, or pure Spirit and Being-ness of the Godhead. Her desire was that her nuns would eventually move from keeping Christ present *with* them, to discovering Christ present and abiding *within* them.

Another practice St. Teresa used when she had difficulty praying was that she would try to discover her own feelings and moods and look for something in the Gospels that Jesus experienced that matched her own emotions and struggles. This was a support to her and united her to Him. She never insisted that anyone should pray her way or be concerned about "success" in prayer, which she knew could not ultimately be known, and should always be left in God's hands. She herself knew from her many and constant illnesses how hard it can be to pray when one is sick, depressed or discouraged, as when she wrote that there were days when she lacked courage and fortitude and couldn't *"step on an ant for the love of God."* (W38,6)

For St. Teresa, prayer was an intimate meeting between two lovers and friends, who know they love each other and want to be together to share their love. And relationships can't be manipulated by methods. Relationships involve a give and take of listening and sharing—not just throwing words out in the air at the other person. She didn't have the experience that she had to progress in prayer first with vocal prayer, then move to Discursive Meditation for some period of time before attempting Active Recollection, and lastly eventually be given contemplative prayer. St. Teresa was brought to contemplation without being able to do Discursive Meditation with the mind. And she knew that some of her nuns were drawn into passive contemplative prayer in a short period of time with attentive, heartfelt vocal prayer as their only form of prayer. She didn't see formulary, vocal prayer as a lesser form of prayer if it was prayed with loving attention to the words and to the One addressed. She wrote extensively on the riches of the Our Father and of how even just a few of Jesus' words in that prayer could lead her into contemplation.

In the beginning when she was young, St. Teresa found prayer a consolation, comfortable and easy. But in time she learned that prayer requires determination, patience and fidelity when it becomes arid and moves away from consolation, and comforting or pious feelings. When she came up against dryness in prayer, she said she watched the clock, longing for the time of prayer to be over. She had a struggle with prayer for almost 20 years. She tells us this so that we will not lose heart and give up. Her great desire is that we never give up prayer, and if we stop for a period of time, that we begin again. For prayer is the vehicle that fosters intimacy with Christ.

St. Teresa wasn't successful at Discursive Meditation—thinking or imagining things about Jesus and His life with the mind, and often she used a spiritual book or scripture to quiet her mind, which she said raced *"like wild horses."* For quite a while she doubted that she herself was called to sublime, mystical prayer. She understood the difficulties of prayer and all the things that can go on in the human mind—arguing, day dreaming, problem solving, rehearsing, counting, conversations, worries, songs, sensual temptations, replaying hurts and memories, nonsense thoughts, reliving triumphs, etc. All this is normal and with practice and fidelity can be quieted and loosened from the mind. But Teresa was certain that God wants to give the gift of contemplation to us, if we truly desire it and are faithful to the relationship in prayer with Christ.

Reflection Questions: (Choose only one or two at a time to explore in depth.)

- Have you felt dissatisfaction with your prayer or experienced any of the Transition Signs from active to passive prayer?
- Has your prayer felt dry and arid? Has it ever seemed like you can't pray anymore? Does your prayer feel like it has become blocked or come to a dead end?
- As the Pharisee judged the Publican, do you compare yourself to other Christians—as either better or worse?
- Can you identify and accept both your strengths and weaknesses?
- Who are your favorite saints? Why do you admire them? What qualities do they have that inspire you?
- Is your spirituality primarily a personal piety (viz. a "Jesus and me" cozy) or do you see your prayer and spirituality related to the needs of the wider world?
- What significant and meaningful things do you do with your life?
- What roads have you chosen? What have been the most significant decisions of your life?
- What place has God had in your life decisions?
- Perhaps you have been giving of yourself in ways that do not greatly cost you. Is there something the Lord is asking of you that you lack, or something you resist?

  o Development of prayer and the spiritual life in the third dwelling places demands an even more thorough scrutiny of attitudes, thoughts and behavior. Therefore, an extended section for a very thorough life examination follows here.
  o You might begin your examination with Ps. 51 or Ps. 139 asking for light on all your thoughts and behaviors, not just the ones you are conscious of, but even more of the ones that you are unconscious of, asking for a

sincere sorrow and desire to make needed changes of faults and sinfulness.

❖ **Do not try to examine yourself on everything all at once!** (W16,4) Just pick a couple of things from the following examination, to use as you can, for deepening self-knowledge and renewal. Remember that working on any one virtue helps strengthen other virtues.

Examination of Conscience, Consciousness and Behavior

o A humble and sincere examination of conscience, consciousness and behavior is a way of tackling the poisonous thoughts, actions and addictions that are part of your exterior life, which have infiltrated your interior castle.

o Once in a while this examination could be an overall life review, but afterwards a shorter examination that is done daily would generally be more helpful.

❖ The Examination of Conscience, Consciousness and Behavior can include any of the following:

1. Above all, examine yourself on the Great Commandment: "You shall love the Lord with all your heart, soul and mind, and your neighbor as yourself." (Mt. 22:34-40; Lk. 10:27) St. John of the Cross wrote: "In the evening of life you will be examined in love. Learn how to love as God desires to be loved. Leave behind your own ways." (SLL#60)
   - All examinations must be made from both of the standpoints of what you have committed or omitted as regards motivations, thoughts and acts.

2. See if you are at least observing the base line morality of the Ten Commandments (see: Exodus 20 and Deuteronomy 5), as well as the Church's Precepts (the absolute minimum required of Catholics): 1) Mass on Sundays and Holy Days; 2) Confession at least once a year; 3) Reception of the Eucharist during Easter Season; 4) Observance of the Church's regulations of fasting and abstinence; 5) Providing for any needs of the People of God. (see: *Catechism of the Catholic Church* #2041-3)
   - Give attention to prayer, fasting and almsgiving.

3. Reflect on, and go deeper into, Jesus' Beatitudes (see: Mt. 5; Lk. 6) and His challenge of: "You have heard it said, but I say ..." Reflect on the *minimum* and the *more* of virtue in your own life. The Beatitudes reflect Jesus' *interior attitudes* and stances for Christian living, and the *blessings these bestow*. They demand more and go beyond the Law of Moses in the Ten Commandments.

4. The three Theological Virtues—faith, hope and love—are interior Gospel stances of radical dependence on God. They underpin all other virtues, and are foundational attitudes and qualities necessary for an intimate relationship with God in Christ Jesus. Examine yourself on any attitudes and stances that are opposed to these three.
    - With respect to faith, watch for any ignoring, resisting or "cherry picking" of the teachings of Christ and scripture. Ask yourself if your faith is mostly on the level of belief and assent to doctrinal ideas and creeds about God, or if it is becoming a relationship of greater love, trust and confidence in the person, Christ.
    - As regards hope, guard against insolent presumption. Instead, have humble trust in God's mercy concerning your weakness and sinfulness. Pray about, and ask for the grace to root out any despair, lack of trust in God, inordinate self-reliance, and subtle forms of idolatry, that is, whatever you put your trust in that is not God.
    - For the sake of love, be alert for envy and jealousy of another's worldly and spiritual goods and holiness, and of any lack of compassion toward, or judgmentalness of, others. Be vigilant to look for and dismantle selfishness in yourself, with solicitous care for others.
    - Faith, hope and love are particularly foundational sources for living into divine life during trials, desolation and the dark nights of life.

5. Examine yourself on the Seven Capital (important) Sins and their corresponding virtues: 1) pride, hubris, arrogance—or truthful self-knowledge and humility; 2) greed, selfishness, avarice—or generosity and magnanimity; 3) disordered desire, lust—or modesty, balance, purity, restraint and chastity appropriate to your state of life; 4) anger, irritation, resentment—or reconciliation, meekness, patience, and restraint; 5) gluttony, self-indulgence, intemperance—or balance, moderation and temperance; 6) envy, covetousness, jealousy, rivalry, revenge—or generosity, peace-making, love of neighbor, and love of

enemies; 7) sloth, laziness, inertia, ennui—or diligence, perseverance and fidelity.

6. In your imitation of Christ who lived the Gifts of the Holy Spirit in fullness, sincerely ask in prayer for any gift of the Holy Spirit you feel you are particularly lacking in your daily life. The Gifts of the Holy Spirit are wisdom, knowledge, understanding, counsel, fortitude, reverence/piety/devotion, and awe/fear of the Lord. (see: *Catechism of the Catholic Church* #1831; Is. 11:1-3)

7. The Fruits of the Holy Spirit are the result of a Spirit lived-life. You can examine yourself on the work of the Holy Spirit in you by looking for the Fruits of the Holy Spirit that are flowing from your own *habits of virtue*. (Gal. 5:22-23) Look for those you observe that are ones you do more than others, and for the ones you really lack. The Fruits of the Holy Spirit are charity, joy, peace, patience, kindness, goodness, generosity, gentleness, faithfulness, modesty or humility, self-control and chastity. (see: *Catechism of the Catholic Church* #1832)

8. Be attentive to fulfilling any of the Corporal Works of Mercy that become present to you: 1) feeding the hungry; 2) giving drink to the thirsty; 3) clothing the naked and poor; 4) visiting prisoners; 5) providing shelter to the homeless; 6) visiting the sick; 7) attending funerals, and burying the dead with dignity; 8) caring for the earth and the environment.

9. Be attentive also to fulfilling any of the Spiritual Works of Mercy incumbent on you: 1) guiding and supporting the broken and sinners; 2) instructing those who do not understand or know the Good News; 3) counseling the doubtful, fearful, disturbed, lost; 4) comforting the sorrowing, mentally ill, depressed, mournful; 5) bearing misunderstandings and wrongs patiently; 6) forgiving injuries and misjudgments; 7) praying for the dead and the living.

o In making an examination of your attitudes, choices, behaviors, and growing conscious awareness, St. Teresa also recommends: (IC3,2,3-9)
   - Watch out for posturing and being attached to looking good before others. Catch yourself at it and let go of it. (IC3,2,5)

- Allow the discomfort of the ego without trying to save face or escape it. While humiliation is hard on the ego, it is healthy for the growth of the soul.
- See how slowly or quickly any disturbance or humiliation goes away after a failure.
- Test to see how detached you are from what you think you have done for God, or what God owes you for your service, or of what others think of you.
- Examine your choices—even in small matters—to discover if you are gaining control over your addictions and passions, as well as trying to surrender to God in all things that happen. (IC3,2,6)
- Pursue the path of truthful self-knowledge and never abandon it. Give time to pondering your past and present life, and how you try to imitate Jesus, His mind, heart, life and teachings. Desire earnestly to serve Him.

o End examinations of conscience, consciousness, and life reviews with an Act of Contrition—the formulary one, or one in your own words, with special recognition of the mercy of God and the absolute love that God has for you and desires from you. Always try to put the emphasis more on the Lord's love and mercy rather than on your own sinfulness and misery.

Guidance for Prayer and Prayer Period:

o In these dwellings if you sense the presence of God in ways you have not before, remain in quietude and acceptance. Do not let anything disquiet you or stop you from praying.

o You cannot judge what is happening in your prayer based on your feelings. By willed choice make acts of love—praising the Lord, rejoicing in His goodness, and desiring His honor and glory.

o Despite dryness and distaste for prayer, as you can, try to stir up loving and devout feeling and aspirations for Christ. Any awareness of Christ's sacred humanity is a good place to start.
- These will awaken affective love—strengthen your energy and will to love Him—and will move you more deeply into prayer.

o Keep Jesus ever present, interiorly gazing on and speaking with Him, asking for your needs, sharing your complaints, being glad with Him in

your enjoyments—not so much with formulary prayers—but with spontaneous words that reflect your own desires and needs.
- Pray any prayer of your own that awakens love of Jesus and causes resolutions to render God service. If drawn, express simple, loving, affective sentiments in your own words of prayer.
- If you cannot arouse in yourself your own loving prayer words, pray any formulary and vocal prayers you are drawn to, but *with deep attention* to each word. Stop and dwell on any words that stir up loving affection for Jesus.
  - Pray as you can, and don't be ashamed to return to "earlier" forms of prayer if needed.
- You must always strive to consider the life of Jesus in scripture as your touchstone, and especially think of the love He has for you, the joy and fullness of life He wants for you, and the glory He wants to share with you.
  - Generally, in these third dwelling places any meditations will be brief in duration and often move on to other thoughts and affections, since in these dwellings you still cannot calm and quiet your mind for long.
  - Gradually, simpler prayer with a quieter mind will extend as you practice becoming accustomed to just looking at and loving Christ Jesus in a simple gaze of faith and loving desire—as you would gaze on and desire any loved one.
- If you are stuck or distracted in prayer, read a few lines or paragraphs of scripture or a spiritual book. Or, review and practice Lectio Divina prayer.
- Read slowly. Stop at any words, or thoughts that catch your attention or cause a movement, stirring or feeling within.
- Prayer in these dwellings is not yet supernatural prayer (prayer that has been taken over and guided by God), but a progressive stage of simplification of prayer, advancing eventually beyond a lot of words or meditations that are based on thinking about Jesus and his life.
- Here, a self-willed and practiced quieting of the mind begins to be needed and practiced. Hold any inspirations or truths from reflections about Jesus in loving attentiveness and quiet.
  - This can be through Centering Prayer—a paying attention to breathing, with a holy word, or with a short, loving aspiratory prayer as: "My Lord and my God!" "I trust in you." "All praise and thanksgiving be to you, O Lord." "Lord, come to my assistance." Or,

as the Jesus Prayer: "Lord Jesus Christ, Son of God, have mercy on me." (see: "Centering Prayer" in **Supplemental Material**)
- During retreat, or in daily life, whenever possible try to incorporate deeper solitude and silence into your life, and begin setting aside and practicing longer periods of prayer.
  - Generally, an hour is a good rule of thumb for prayer periods during retreat for settling down and becoming recollected in prayer.
- Prayer involves not only time set aside, but work on your part, and you must make an effort at faithfully showing up for prayer and recollecting your exterior senses of seeing and hearing, and quieting your mind for listening and attentiveness to God.
  - This really is hard work, so pray for the will to do it, even when you may not want to.

As desired, use one of these scriptures for your prayer period. Choose one before you begin. Hold in your consciousness any word or phrase that has meaning for you.

Scripture Passages:
(Difficulty with Prayer) Rom. 8:26-27; Jb. 6:8-14, 42:2-6; Lam. 3:25-29; Mt. 6:7-27; Eph. 6:18-19; Phil. 4:6-8; Is. 55:6-11; 1Jn. 5:14-15; Ps. 116, 40:1, 42:5, 102:17, 145:17-18
(Perseverance in Prayer) Lk. 11:2-13, 6:12, 18:1-8; Mt. 6:7-13, 26:40-41; Ps. 116:1-4,16, 55:16-17, 141:1-2, 88:9-14; Eph. 6:18; Jer. 29:12-14; Phil. 4:6-7; Col. 4:2; Rom. 12:12; 1Thess. 5:1-18; Jm. 5:13

You may also use the following meditation for prayer as desired.

Guided Meditation: (Mt. 19:16-22; Lk. 18:18-23)

You have already been exploring some of the rooms of your interior castle in pondering scripture passages and reflection questions. You have looked at and spent some time recalling your personal faith journey, and where you first met Jesus. But now you are meeting Jesus in the present, further along into your journey. Take time to be quiet and enter into yourself where Jesus waits to meet you. Imagine Him here with you now. See what your imagination has constructed. Describe it to yourself. . . . Are you in a Gospel scene, at church, outside, in the Holy Land, nowhere, or in your own prayer space? Bring Jesus into your imagination. Pay special attention to the feelings you have in His presence. . . . Do you see yourself as indifferent, reluctant, shy, or afraid to approach Him, or do you run to Him with wide open arms in the comfort of a familiarity with Him? What is the distance between the two of you in your imagination? . . .

There must be something you would want to say or ask Him. He is eager to hear it. Ask Him now your most pressing question. . . . Or, tell Him about your most serious need. Has your deepening self-knowledge helped you name these for yourself before you put them to Him? How do you imagine yourself asking your question or putting forth your need? Are you kneeling, standing, bowed, holding His hand or sitting in His lap? . . . What is the affect and tone of your voice in the way you speak to Him? See and hear yourself for clues about your relationship. Would you risk asking the question of the rich young man? "Lord, what must I personally do to inherit eternal life and a deeper love relationship with you?" Take time to listen in silence. . . . Perhaps you are thinking you have kept the Ten Commandments well—better, at least, than earlier on your journey. Jesus is looking at you with a long, loving gaze and tells you: "But there is something you are lacking." Have you had a sense of that already—of something you have been trying to ignore, or something that gets in the way of a deeper love relationship with Christ? Take time to listen to any thoughts or feelings that arise. . . . Are you hearing within yourself the need for interior conversion concerning the quality of your faith, hope or love? Are there difficulties with forgiveness or judgments towards others, or a serious lack of love for yourself arising in need of attention? Or, do you sense Jesus is pointing to more exterior behaviors about aspects of your life that you hate to admit?   . . . Is He gently or sternly challenging you to one or more of the Beatitudes, or to a more serious attention to the Spiritual and Corporal Works of Mercy, or to fidelity to prayer? Is He hoping you will long for the pearl of great price—or the Living Water—fullness of the love relationship in prayer with Him? Can you sense His great love and desire for you? He is saying to you: "You have heard it said … but I say …" Are you desirous of His invitation, or will you also go away sad?

"When the Intellect ceases to work as it did before in prayer, many cannot bear it … (L11,15) But it has become clear to me that, even in this life, God does not fail to compensate our trials in prayer; and it is quite certain that a single one of those hours in which the Lord granted me a

taste of Himself made up for the afflictions I endured for all the years of keeping up with the practice of prayer. I believe the Lord gives us these trials in order to test His lovers, and discover if they can drink from His chalice and bear His cross before He trusts them with His great treasures ..." (L11,11)

My will did not completely incline to being a nun, but I saw that the religious life was the best and safest state for me, and so little by little I decided to force myself to accept it. (L3,5) But it would seem my God, as if I had promised to break all the promises I had made to You. All my resolutions profited me little. (L4,3,9)

SISTER TERESA of JESUS
Young Adulthood—1535-1553

Teresa's childhood, adolescence, and young adult years—with her good desires, vocal prayers and devotions, along with initial attempts to reform her life—is an example of someone moving in and out of the first three dwelling places of *The Interior Castle*. Except for a brief period in which she experienced some contemplative prayer (the Prayer of Quiet), the years before 1554 generally are also those of a conventional Christian who has only explored and known the first three dwelling places. Sister Teresa is not yet the person who is fully committed with a love for God that does not count the cost. She didn't like this about herself and felt uneasy and convicted, and knew she was weak and hypocritical.

In 1535, when Teresa was 20, she entered the Carmelite Monastery of the Incarnation in Avila. She didn't know a thing about this monastery, or the Carmelite Order, and she wrote that she wasn't in love with God. However, her good friend, Juana, was there and she said she would not have gone to the convent unless Juana was there. But God can use anything. So at first, she had to struggle against herself to accept this vocation. And it seems that God rewarded her sacrifice and she fairly quickly became happy with her choice in life.

Teresa made her profession of vows November 3, 1537 with great sincerity, resolve and happiness. But she writes that for almost twenty years she did not live an exemplary religious life, but instead, a superficial one.

A year later in 1538—perhaps due to a change in food, lifestyle, and scruples—her health collapsed with fevers, nausea, headaches, weakness and fainting spells. It was so serious that she had to leave the monastery and seek medical help. She was brought to her sister, Maria's, house for a cure after first stopping again at her Uncle Pedro's. He was living as a hermit and lent his spiritual books to Teresa which she read as she was convalescing. She was very impacted by the book, *The Third Spiritual Alphabet*, by the Franciscan friar—Francisco de Osuna. She devoured this book on mental prayer which deeply affected her soul. She began to practice this prayer and to experience the beginnings of passive contemplative prayer—the quiet, gentle presence of God within her.

The following year, 1539, she was able to start treatments from a medicine woman who bled her and gave her bitter herbs to drink, which only made her sicker and weaker. Her father was so concerned about her deteriorating health that he brought her back to the monastery. There she worsened, was given the last rites, and fell into a coma. She appeared dead for three days, and on the fourth day the nuns came to get her body for burial. But her father wouldn't let go of her yet, and luckily saw one of her fingers move. When Teresa finally opened her eyes, she was in terrible pain, and all her muscles had contracted up to her chin. For three years she crawled around the monastery's infirmary on her elbows and knees, gradually regaining better health which she attributed to her prayers to St. Joseph. She was finally able to rejoin the life of the Carmelite community in 1542, but never enjoyed robust, good health after that.

Because of her miraculous "rising from the dead" and also because she was charming, witty, and a good conversationalist, she was often called to the parlors to visit with guests and much needed benefactors. The monastery had too many nuns for its size and finances, and Teresa was a good money-raiser. With all this visiting, as well as her excessive attachments to her family, friends and social life, Teresa lived a very distracted life and gradually grew away from the quiet practice of mental (mindful) prayer and intimacy with the Lord. She grew to be disinterested in prayer, couldn't get herself recollected for it, watched the clock, forced herself to do it and couldn't wait for it to be over. Not even Teresa's father's reprimand of her, and the good example of his serious prayer life and holy death in 1543, were enough for her to get serious about her commitment as a consecrated nun. This bothered her conscience very much. She said she had begun to fear the practice of prayer and wasn't able to keep the good resolutions she made. She relates that she gave no attention to avoiding venial sins, and shed copious but fraudulent tears over her faults and inability to live as a committed nun.

During these years Teresa's brothers Hernando, Rodrigo, Lorenzo, Jeronimo, Antonio, and Augustin left for their military adventures in the New World of South America. And her youngest sister, Juana, left to marry. The sorrowful loss of her father's death and the separations from her siblings, as well as Teresa's weak health, surely were disheartening and had an effect on her spirit, energy and prayer life. Moreover, they may have made her vulnerable and better prepared for God to work a true conversion in her, the serious change of heart that was to come.

4-1

FOURTH DWELLING PLACES—Part 1

(*The Interior Castle* 4, Chapters 1-3)

Theme: *Focus your inner gaze on Jesus!*

Description of the Fourth Dwellings Places:

The fourth dwelling places mark a significant turning point in the life of prayer. These are the dwellings where passive, supernatural prayer begins in ever intensifying stages. (IC4,1,1) St. Teresa believed that if you don't know and weren't taught about the various levels of passive, supernatural prayer—contemplative prayer—which begin in these fourth dwelling places, you probably won't arrive at this prayer. (L11-22; W28-29)

o Passive prayer is a prayer of quiet, peace, gentle fervor, and a sense of God's presence, with lesser effort needed for the mind to remain quietly recollected. There is a sensed growing capacity for God in a kind of sweetness and an expansion in the interior of the soul, with a deepening confidence that one can truly enjoy God in new, unimagined ways—in intimate exchanges of love and gratitude.

o The **Transition Signs** and experiences of prayer in the third dwelling places have been preparation for movement from ordinary, natural prayer to the supernatural, passive prayer of the fourth dwelling places.
- It is ordinary to have been in the first three dwellings a long while, though there is no certain rule for length of time. (IC4,1,2)
- In each of the stages of prayer there are many gradations and levels. Persons may fluctuate among these stages and dwelling places as

long as they live, until they attain permanent transformation and union in God in the later dwelling places.
- In the transition from the active prayer of Acquired Recollection to the passive prayer of Infused Recollection the person contributes something to the prayer, and God contributes something. (see: "Prayer—Types and Categories" in **Supplemental Material**)
- Vocal prayer and Discursive Meditation will generally weary persons in this stage of prayer, and can be left aside.

o Many people use the word "contemplation," but what they are calling contemplative prayer is usually not what Teresa means by contemplative prayer. For example, Discursive Meditation or Centering Prayer (as taught by Fr. Thomas Keating, ocso) for Teresa would be the work of active Acquired Recollection only, though these are excellent preparations for passive or Infused Recollection, and could possibly lead to contemplative prayer, if God so chooses.

o Movement in the fourth dwelling places is from ordinary active prayer, prayer that persons do themselves, to the passive prayer that Teresa labels Infused Recollection or Passive Recollection, which can eventually become contemplative prayer—a generic name for the prayer that God guides and directs within the person. That is, it is supernatural prayer beyond the ordinary. Therefore, Teresa struggles to explain this prayer and what is happening. Her terminology will need some explanation, as well as reflection and perhaps some study. (see: "Prayer—Types and Categories" in **Supplemental Material**)

o Passive prayer seems to come from deep within the soul, not from the natural feeling or emotion centers. The developing surrender in allowing God to guide and direct passive prayer usually begins with Infused Recollection in which the senses and faculties of Intellect, Memory and Will start to become quieter, calmer, composed, engrossed, or fastened on God. This process can then further intensify into the contemplative prayer of the Prayer of Quiet, the Prayer of the Sleep of the Faculties, and finally to the Prayer of Union.

o Passive prayer is a more inwardly loving apprehension or contemplative gaze and presence to Someone there within—the Lord.

o The fourth dwelling places not only begin the *life* of prayer but the *contemplative life* of prayer.
- This is not to be equated with the expression of the contemplative life lived by monks and nuns. The term "contemplative life" can have many expressions, depending on each person's state and call in life.
- From the fourth dwelling places onward, Teresa speaks more about the life of prayer—beyond the natural and ordinary life of the culture

and its world systems and consciousness in which the first three dwellings are more immersed.
- As one progresses in prayer in the fourth dwellings, more negative aspects of the *unconscious* will begin to be released for integration in the spiritual life.
- Prayer and life from here on will become more subtle and delicate, and the rational mind will have more difficulty putting it into words. But sensitivity to God's subtle presence and action deeper within the person will be growing and recognized.
- Faithful responses to trusting God's care and love will begin to break the need for dependence on emotions and senses for "knowledge" of God who is, after all, unknowable.
- Here, God is conditioning the exterior and natural functioning of the senses, as well as the powers or faculties of the soul, to the person's interior life of the spirit, in order to eventually acclimatize these to God's Divine life of the Holy Spirit. This commences with the drawing of the five senses and the natural capacities of the faculties of Intellect/mind, Memory/imagination and Will into the soul's interior for the development of their latent spiritual capacities. This is brought about by God's activity in the person in and through passive, supernatural contemplative prayer. (IC4,3,1-2)
- The enlargement of the capacities of the soul is under the control, timing, means and mode of God, and uniquely so for each person. It is for transformation into Christ-likeness. (IC4,2,6; 4,3,3)
- The peaceful quiet and recollection of these fourth dwellings is clearly experienced—usually through a general feeling of satisfaction, well-being and peace bestowed on the soul, along with deep gratitude, contentment and calm, and a very gentle delight in the soul's faculties of Intellect, Memory and Will.
- In the fourth dwelling places St. Teresa labels *passive prayer*—or contemplative prayer—as:

1. **Infused Recollection** (also called **Passive Recollection**): This is a semi-contemplative prayer between active Acquired Recollection and the passive Prayer of Quiet.
2. **Prayer of Quiet:** This is the actual beginning of contemplative prayer.
3. **Prayer of the Sleep of the Faculties:** This is a form of contemplative prayer that is more intense than the Prayer of Quiet.

- Material for these three forms of passive prayer is expanded upon in "Prayer—Types and Categories" in **Supplemental Material**. But it is also needed here for more clarity in understanding these dwellings, and for the prayer period that follows. So, it requires some explanation here, also.

Prayer of Infused Recollection / Passive Recollection

- Recollection refers to the faculties or powers of the soul being rendered quieted, peaceful, withdrawn, taken out of use, stilled, calmed, composed, drawn inward, or engrossed. This calming recollection also includes the five senses, though they are still able to operate normally. (IC4,3; W28-29)
- In the fourth dwelling places the prayer of passive Infused Recollection (as opposed to the Acquired Recollection of Discursive Meditation, Lectio Divina, Centering Prayer, etc.) is a *semi-passive prayer*—somewhere between active Acquired Recollection, and the passive Prayer of Quiet, (also known as the Prayer of Spiritual Delight), which is properly true contemplative prayer. It is a touch by God at the threshold of passive, supernatural prayer, and is the prayer where ordinary, natural prayer and supernatural prayer mingle.
  - Since in Infused Recollection the person contributes something and God contributes something, this prayer cannot be attained by mere human effort—because here the soul begins to touch the supernatural. Active or Acquired Recollection can move to the passive prayer of Infused Recollection only if and when God desires. (IC4,3,8)
  - Acquired Recollection should be set aside if the passive prayer of Infused Recollection or the Prayer of Quiet begins to take place.
- There can be arid, dry beginnings to this prayer while the person is practicing such forms of Acquired Recollection as various devotions, or Discursive Meditation, Lectio Divina or Centering Prayer before it moves into a more passive, calm, Infused Recollection of God's drawing.
- The rational Intellect or mind may be surprised and stunned by these first touches of God which often darken, still or stop its normal and natural activity. The senses and faculties are drawn within through God's activity—and sometimes even before the person begins to try to become recollected.

- This prayer can last for a brief moment or for some length of time. (IC4,3,7)
- The distinguishing characteristic of Infused Recollection is that the Will—seat of affectivity and desire—(see: "Faculties and Powers of the Soul" in **Supplemental Material**) is quieted and fastened in love on the Lord, while the other faculties of Intellect/mind, Memory/imagination may or may not be calmed, recollected, or fastened on God, but free to wander. The senses are still operating freely and normally. Often the person hesitates even to physically move or stir lest this good be disturbed or lost.
- However, the powers and faculties of Intellect/mind, Memory/imagination and Will are not as captive, quieted, or "off-line" as they will be in more intense forms of contemplative prayer—that is, in the Prayer of Quiet, Prayer of the Sleep of the Faculties or the Prayer of Union, where the faculties and senses may become *more* still, absorbed or even suspended.

Prayer of Quiet

- The Prayer of Quiet is contemplative prayer, properly speaking, and is an intensification of the passive prayer of Infused Recollection. (IC4,3,8-9; W30-31)
    - Here the Will is subdued through being captive in love, and the faculties of the Intellect/mind, Memory/imagination are quietly recollected. In these dwelling places the Will (as restless desire, and unpurified love and decision) has an experience of deep rest, stillness or attraction to God. At the same time, the Intellect/mind or Memory/imagination can be quiet or wandering about, be a bother—or not—depending on the intensity of this prayer, or which prayer in these dwelling places the person is experiencing. (IC4,3,8; L14-15; ST59,3-4; A2,12,7-9)
    - The five senses and the Intellect/mind and Memory/imagination and emotions are generally quietly recollected, though free to operate normally. The body shares in this, but the person can still feel, see, hear, smell, etc. (IC4,2,6; 4,3,3; L14-15)
- In the Prayer of Quiet the human faculty of the Will is in some way united with God's Will, though the person doesn't know how, and can't really explain the experience. (IC4,2,8)

- St. John of the Cross explains this as God operating in the interior faculties of the soul beyond human ordinary understanding, in what he termed the Passive Intellect. (A2,10; C39,12)
- His thinking was that Intellect is gradually being subdued by God through the light of a dark, *unknowing faith* until it becomes captive and purified enough that it is free and ready for the Prayer of Union of the later dwellings.

o In this passive Prayer of Quiet, the person's Will (seat of desire, attraction and love) begins to warm to love of God and be enkindled with a holy love and desire for God and God's glory. A spark of Divine love is starting to light a fire of love in the soul. And in time, in later dwellings, the soul will be enflamed and even more captivated with love from within and without.

o The beginning of this passive, supernatural, contemplative prayer is a sign that the Lord wants to bestow on this soul even greater gifts, and possibly even spiritual delights and the Prayer of Union.

o When this prayer begins, a person should proceed with a simple loving attention to God without the work of specific prayer activities or devotions. (IC4,1,9; 4,3,4-5; A2,12,7)

o It is not necessary to know which type of prayer is occurring, but rather to simply lovingly gaze at Christ Jesus.

o If there are questions, doubts or confusion, persons should consult a learned spiritual director who knows the stages of prayer. Teresa writes that: *"...many people attain this prayer, but few pass beyond it."* (L15,2)

Prayer of the Sleep of the Faculties

o Prayer of the Sleep of the Faculties is a further intensification of passive prayer, deeper than the Prayer of Quiet, though the differences are subtle. It is similar to the Prayer of Union that occurs in the fifth dwelling places, but less intense than that prayer. (IC4,3,11-12)

o As its name implies, the experience is a kind of "sleep" but only as metaphor—and *not* actual natural sleep. It is a kind of deeper rest, stillness and quieting of the faculties and senses, though not languor or listlessness. In fact, the soul is *more wide awake* to God. It is hard to describe in words. The soul seems "asleep" to external things and the outer world, but alert to the Lord's presence and the inner world.

o In the Prayer of the Sleep of the Faculties the Intellect/mind and Will are captive, and the Memory/imagination is deeply quieted and recollected,

but free to operate normally if needed. The five senses are more intensely recollected and quiet, while also free for their normal operations if required.
- It is experienced as a very deep recollection, quiet and stillness, and though God is working in the soul, the person can't explain what God has been doing.
- Here persons become recollected almost without knowing when it has happened, how it has happened, where they have been, where their consciousness has been, or how long it has lasted.
- They can wonder if they have been asleep, though they haven't been, because sleep and grogginess act differently in the body. Instead, the person has been in a very deep kind of "off-line quiet" in God.
  - However, St. Teresa does speak of a period in her life when she never ceased from praying even when asleep. (L29,7)
  - Some people (like St. Therese of Lisieux who said she often slept through prayer) may think they also often sleep through prayer, but actually have been in the Prayer of the Sleep of the Faculties. They may think they have been asleep because this prayer was never explained to them. It requires discernment to know which is which, or, if the person has been in the false "prayer" and state of Absorption. (see: "Absorption and False Mystical Prayer" in **Supplemental Material**)
  - The Prayer of the Sleep of the Faculties is efficacious regardless of what is known about it. Though it isn't necessary to know which stage of prayer one is in, it is important not to get into the habit of going to sleep during prayer or of falling into Absorption.
- The Prayer of the Sleep of the Faculties (also called the Prayer of Inebriation by St. Teresa) is covered as the third degree of prayer or the third waters in the *Life*. This is the interior garden watered with less effort by a river or stream. (L16-17)

Teresian Teachings for Prayer and Life:

- St. Teresa doesn't teach that contemplative prayer only comes after years of ascetical practices or Discursive Meditation. She doesn't limit God to time lines. She writes that these gifts: "... *God gives when He wills and as He wills and they have nothing to do with either time or service. I do not mean that these things are unimportant, but often the contemplation the Lord doesn't give to one in twenty years, He gives to another in one. His Majesty knows the reason why.*" (L34,11)

- As a result of an ever-deepening life of prayer through contemplative prayer, there is also deeper spiritual growth.
  - Bad habits are rarer and there is improvement in all the virtues, with more inner freedom. Less self-centeredness, addiction and compulsion will be evident.
    - When temptations and falls occur here, they can be helpful so that persons will be on guard and conscious that they could be deceived and have a worse fall at any time if not vigilant. (IC4,3,10)
    - The sign that the Lord was present in these fourth dwelling places of prayer is that the person rises more quickly than ever before from failures.
  - There is growth in self-knowledge, self-control, self-mastery and choices for the Lord.
  - There is a strong desire to do more for God's honor and glory.
  - Faith, hope and trust in the Lord's love is becoming more alive than ever, and the soul is desirous of praising God!
  - Becoming more concerned with pleasing God alone starts to grow in these dwelling places.
  - There is a growing capacity for interiority and for being passively fascinated and engrossed with the Divine presence in prayer without a lot of effort.
  - In seeing something of the magnificence of God, one's own lowliness and need for God is known, and the attractions of the world will begin to pale for these persons.
    - Worldly concerns don't intrude on this prayer as much, though if they do, they can become an occasion of gain and strength in virtue, if the person can turn away from them as needed during prayer and in daily life.
  - Fear of God, as dangerous, capricious or frightening, is receding, though *awe* of God will always remain. There is loss of servile fear of God, along with growing care and solicitude for not offending the Lord. (IC4,3,9)
  - Avoidance and fear of the exertion of prayer, of difficult crosses and diminishments, of losing one's self-determination, of penances, of hard choices for virtue and imitation of Christ, or fears of loss of health or reputation are losing their hold.
- The contemplative life that accompanies this new stage of contemplative prayer is often a time of greater creativity.
- The solid pathway for movement from failures, error and the temptation to expect rewards in these dwellings is to follow the way of the cross: to

love the Lord for His sake alone, not counting the cost, rather than from the motives of self-seeking in the consolations or spiritual delights of contemplative prayer or from trying to *merit* God's favor.

o Persons may have difficulty understanding the teachings of what is termed Mystical Theology or Mystical Prayer, and would profit from a learned spiritual director. Though there are many spiritual directors, few are qualified or knowledgeable about later stages of prayer.

"However softly we speak, He is near enough to hear us. Neither is there any need for wings to go to find Him. All one need do is to go into one's inner solitude and look at Him within oneself. (W28,2) ... *Solitude is a great support for prayer."* (W4,9)

4-1

FOURTH DWELLING PLACES—Part 1

Internalizing the Teachings: *Allow God to bring you to passive prayer!*

In these fourth dwelling places (the second and third waters in Teresa's autobiographical *Life*) Teresa begins a description of the movement from active to passive prayer, that is, from active Discursive Meditation and reflection, to the passive prayer of Infused Recollection and by degrees into the Prayer of Quiet—the actual beginning of contemplative prayer—and then into its intensification in the Prayer of the Sleep of the Faculties. She describes characteristics of each intensification of passive prayer, and makes connections as to how they affect lived-life. She wants to teach us a less wearisome and simplified type of prayer that by degrees leads to deeper intimacy with Jesus.

She also refers to the differences between the exterior mind with its natural, rational capacities and tendencies to distractions and busyness, and to the faculty of Intellect with its passive supernatural *capacities* that can be calmed and expanded for supernatural delights, favors, revelations and experiences of God and His love.

Though St. Teresa didn't know the modern term and method for calming the mind called Centering Prayer, a brief summary of this form of active recollection will follow as prayer guidance, and as another possible suggestion of a form of active prayer for quieting the mind for recollection in preparation for contemplation if God desires to give it. It can be used for this prayer period if desired.

Reflection:
Centering Prayer Observations

St. Teresa never heard of Centering Prayer or the modern movement surrounding this type of prayer being taught today. But she did write that we can awaken affective emotions and the warmth of love for Christ in prayer by gently repeating a single loving word or phrase from time to time as needed to recall who it is we are present to and desiring to love. She writes in *The Way of Perfection* that we can enkindle desire for Christ and stir up a flame of love for Him in prayer by *"occasionally uttering a single gentle word, like a person giving a little puff to a candle."* (W31,7) So she herself did know the centering and calming effect on the mind of an occasionally repeated gentle word. She further wrote that one word or a single petition from the Our Father prayed with attention is more truly prayer than repeating the Our Father in its entirety over and over without attention. (W31,13)

For St. Teresa and for Carmelites, Centering Prayer is NOT the passive prayer of Infused Recollection and certainly NOT any of the various forms of contemplative prayer which are gifts of God that cannot be attained by human effort. Centering Prayer is only one possible form of active prayer or Acquired Recollection—a work or method of emptying the busy mind and restless self so as to be more available to whatever the Lord may want to do with the period of prayer that is given to God. The Lord may leave you on the natural level with your distractions, passing thoughts, images or feelings, or in restless aridity and dryness. Or, He can move your prayer to a semi-passive state of Infused Recollection that for some moments unites your human Will to God in loving attention, or even perhaps slows down the thoughts of your mind, or makes them quiet. Or, God may truly take over your prayer and bring you into the contemplative Prayer of Quiet, taking your Will into God's and quieting your Intellect/mind or even your Memory/imagination. If you happen to be given an experience of prayer that you never experienced before—of a new, sensed presence of the Lord in contemplative prayer—and think it is due to some technique or method of yours, as Centering Prayer, you are mistaken. In future attempts to make this experience of the Prayer of Quiet happen again, you will discover in short order that you cannot bring about contemplative prayer whenever you want to! This will teach you that God is in charge of passive prayer and gives it only according to God's desires and knowledge of what is best for you. It cannot be manipulated at will or by techniques.

These days the word "contemplation" has a wider, more general meaning than it did for St. Teresa, and sometimes the word "meditation" is used to mean contemplation. Many people who use the word contemplation in the context of prayer are referring to any quiet focused attention on God that could also include meditation, silence, few words, or, wordless prayer. This would be part of St. Teresa's understanding—the part that we do to make a deliberate connection to the Lord. But it is not the part that He contributes to the love relationship in a passive infused experience of Himself that we cannot bring about. Certainly, it is not always easy to know where our part leaves off and God's part begins.

Teresa was insistent that Christians pray through the humanity of Christ. So her prayer is not imageless, it's just not as much work or complex in the effort of imagining and setting up scenes as Ignatian meditations. Her prayer is more about intimacy and presence to Christ now in the present moment, than it is in constructing elaborate incidences from His life in the past. She wants to make Christ real to her readers right now. And she wants to stir up loving desire for Him. So, another way she has of praying in words is with passionate outbursts of love, which she termed "aspirations" that stir up the heart to love, as: *"O, Life of my life, and sustenance that sustains me!"* (IC7,2,6); *"O my delight…"* (S,VI,1); *"O compassion so measureless!"* (S,XIV,3); *"O true Lover!"* (S,XVI,2). Teresa's writings are full of such outbursts of loving words for the Lord. There is also a way in which the Simple Meditation of St. Teresa (see: "Simple Meditation" in "Prayer—Types and Categories" in **Supplemental Material**) could also be used in a Centering Prayer manner and call the mind back to loving attention on Jesus. Teresa's suggested momentarily imagined Gospel scenes could take the place of a sacred word, such that every time the mind wanders, the recall of this simple image of Jesus or a scene from His life would bring attention back to Him.

The Jesus Prayer from the time of the Desert Fathers and Mothers—"Lord Jesus Christ, Son of God, have mercy on me"—would be another ancient form of something like Centering Prayer, and is also tied to breath as the spiration or *ruah* of the Holy Spirit.

However, among some Christians there is criticism of Centering Prayer because of certain misunderstood "similarities" to the Transcendental Meditation of the Maharishi Mahesh Yogi, or other Eastern meditation forms. Transcendental Meditation using a neutral syllable for a mantra, can be "self-hypnotizing" for the mind—whether that is good or bad. But as a secular technique it can, and does, still and empty the mind. It is a peaceful experience, probably beneficial in some way for good health, and for all we know God can use this for His purposes. (I know about Transcendental Meditation because as an undergraduate I took a TM course that was offered at my secular university. TM is relaxing, calming and pleasurable. But though I was interested to learn about it, it didn't have a connection to my relationship with Christ, and I didn't pursue it.) The Christian use of a sacred Christian word is not a mantra, neutral or nonsense syllable, which is repeated over and over hypnotically merely to calm or void the mind of thoughts. It is instead a Christian monologistos—a sacred word/s connected to the name and actions of God, or of His Son and Spirit. It is not meant merely to calm the mind, but to call one back in *relationship* to the Divine One who is always looking upon us with love and desire. The Christian sacred word need only be repeated if attention has drifted away from the Lord.

St. Teresa would not support any so-called form of prayer that is centered on self rather than on Christ. This would not be Christian prayer. Christian Centering Prayer is not merely a practice to attain emptiness, peace, or to develop attention, or mindfulness in the sense of control over your thoughts or feelings as in the East. It is a practice to develop heart-fullness in the sense of loving presence and relationship to Someone—Christ. It requires circumspect vigilance in collecting all of your interiority and self in an affective, desiring and loving gaze, presence, and attention to the Lord. You know that when you are truly attentive to the presence of another you are alert, trying to listen well, to notice, to care, to be courteous and respectful, with an engrossed interest in the other person. Centering Prayer can help foster and focus a genuine attention and openness to Christ. It can help bring you to a space beyond your thoughts and emotions that is the hidden, secret place of contemplative prayer—even hidden from yourself—where you can intimately encounter Christ, the Beloved.

Concerning Centering Prayer, there is a sense in which St. Teresa's warning against the false prayer of Absorption would apply here. (see: "Absorption and False Mystical Prayer" in **Supplemental Material**) St. Teresa would not approve of any prayer that was a zoning out form of Absorption—a languishing spacing out, or a dreamy, possibly semi-sleepy mind state, which was merely a kind of relaxation or pleasurable hypnotizing of the mind. Christian Centering Prayer is not just for voiding the mind. It is leaving behind what is not God and a making space for Him to fill. Centering Prayer is a form of Acquired Recollection that can help make room for a deeper relationship with God—allowing space for God to enter the relationship more intimately One on one.

The whole intention of Christian Centering Prayer would be alert availability to the Lord. It would include awareness of any such false states of consciousness as self-hypnosis, spacing out, wasting time in a pleasurable emptiness, or any drifting away from the intention of being totally present and surrendered to the Lord. Spiritual directors need to discern true from false prayer when directees give an account of their prayer while using Centering Prayer. Directors need to be aware when descriptions of false prayer such as Absorption arise. If any do surface, the person should be steered away from Centering Prayer to vocal prayer, meditation, scripture, Lectio Divina or St. Teresa's momentary image in Simple Meditation prayer.

Reflection Questions: (Choose only one or two at a time to explore in depth.)

- Has your prayer changed in any way from what it was? Has it ever been out of your control, simplified, or different in any way?
- Do you ever reflect on your actual experience of prayer, how it has grown or changed, and affected your relationship with the Lord and your neighbor?
- Are you comfortable or uncomfortable with silence and solitude? Have you ever experienced long periods of silence? Have you ever sensed God's presence more deeply because you could be there in the silence and solitude just listening and attentive to God?
- Have you had any challenging or life transforming insights that have come to you through prayer?
- Have you ever brought highs and lows, successes and failures in your life to prayer?
- Did you take time to reflect on these and how you may have grown or been diminished by these events? Did you see them in a faith context? Did you think God cared about your concerns? Did prayer help you through them?
- Have you had experiences that God is absent or distant? How does this affect your prayer? How did you respond in faith?
- How do you relate Jesus to God, the Father and the Holy Spirit?
- When Jesus comes into your imagination how does He appear? Who is He for you? What names and images do you have for Him?

- What is your relationship with Jesus now? For deepening an affective love for Him can you use in your prayer and relationship with Him these names and images you have for Him? Are any of your thoughts or images of Jesus dangerous or destructive to your prayer?
- Have you considered joining a prayer group or attending retreats or talks on prayer?
- Where do you find a sense of Christian community? Do you have one that supports your faith life? Do you have many friends of God among your relationships?

Guidance for Prayer and Prayer Period:

A Christian Centering Prayer Practice
(For a fuller description see: "Centering Prayer" in **Supplemental Material**)

o Centering Prayer as a method of Acquired Recollection includes an attention to breath with an accompanying sacred word or short prayer. Though it is still only active recollection and not contemplation, it can be good preparation for receiving the gift of passive contemplative prayer if God chooses to bring you to passive recollection or contemplation.

1. Select a sacred word or prayer—as the Jesus Prayer ("Lord Jesus Christ, Son of God, have mercy on me"), another aspiratory prayer, or a word/s of one or two syllables to say if you become distracted. It can be a name of God or Christ, or a spiritual quality.
2. Set a timer with a quiet alerting ring or sound for the duration of 20, 30 or 60 minutes—or whatever length of time you choose for Centering Prayer.
3. Sit in a quiet space, in a comfortable chair, taking time to get settled by closing your eyes.
4. Begin by paying attention to your breathing, and continue doing this throughout the time you have set for yourself unless God draws you into a more passive prayer. Let go, as you can, of any thoughts, cares and concerns with the intention and desire to be present to the Lord. To do this it helps to focus your attention on your breath. When you have begun to settle down and be quiet, gently and calmly say your sacred word/s with attention, and try to align it to your peaceful breathing. You do not need to say your sacred word or prayer over and over, but

only when you notice your mind becoming distracted or busy with thoughts.
5. Whenever distracting thoughts arise, just quietly return your attention to your breath, sacred word, and desire for the Lord, letting bodily sensations, feelings, images, or reflections just arise and flow away gently as they come. You do not need to struggle with these distractions, but instead, positively return to your breath, sacred word/s and loving desire for God.
6. With the quiet ring or buzz of your timer at the end of prayer, and before opening your eyes, slowly bring your consciousness back to awareness of your body and surroundings, and in your own words make a prayer to Christ of love and thanksgiving. Then slowly stir, opening your eyes to end your prayer period.

- The two types of Acquired Recollection prayer that could be helpful in these dwellings are Lectio Divina and Centering Prayer. Both of these forms of Acquired Recollection can prepare you for being available and receptive to passive Infused Recollection or the Prayer of Quiet.
- The work of vocal prayer and Discursive Meditation will usually weary you at this stage of prayer in the fourth dwellings, and if you have first tried these and feel resistance, or find them tiring, you can set them aside for the time being. Though it may perhaps feel to you like you are doing nothing by focusing on your breath and repeating your sacred word/s from time to time, or that nothing is happening in these new prayer forms that have been suggested, try them anyway, and remain with open hands of surrender and receptivity to the Lord.
  - Former faithfulness to saying certain prayers and doing certain religious practices is not the goal. The goal is faithfulness to your *relationship* with Jesus and doing His will.
- Often prayer has dry, arid beginnings in these dwellings, so do not be surprised or disturbed by dryness, or restlessness in your attempts to become recollected. (see: Teresa's second water prayer L14-15) You are not wasting your time in saying a sacred word/s from time to time, or in focusing on your breath which is a sacred gift to you from God. You, your breath and word and time already belong to God who is always present.
  - A longer prayer period may bring you beyond these dry, restless beginnings.

- You may need to do a little bit of "work" of calling the Lord to mind with Lectio Divina or through your imagination by using St. Teresa's suggestion of Simple Meditation, by briefly recalling some image from Jesus' life to focus on in loving affection for Him—but NOT on the wearying work of extended, complicated ideas about God or Christ. (see: "Simple Meditation" in **Supplemental Material**)
- You could also try aspiratory prayer and make up your own loving outbursts to the Lord.
- Generally, in approaching prayer in these dwellings, it is most helpful to try to direct your inner gaze to Jesus. A simple, quiet, resting in Jesus with your gaze and *energy of love* directed at Him, or that simple momentary glance at Him using your imagination of a scene from His life is calming and recollecting. It makes your desire for Him explicit. Simply wait in trusting love for the deeper drawing inward by the Lord. Just be there with loving desire directed towards Jesus, expressing love and commitment.
    - *"... not with the noise of words but with longing He hears us."* (L15,7)
- Be disciplined in being aware of, and of choosing to stop all mind activities as they arise—rehearsing, lecturing, solving problems, day dreaming, planning, etc. (IC4,3,7)
    - Return your attention instead to Jesus—again, with a loving gaze, or sacred word or short prayer, or inner attention to the Spirit's breath in you. Returning over and over to Jesus after each distraction is good prayer, and pleasing to Him.
- You should let go of any work of prayer—even Centering Prayer, or Lectio Divina if you notice you have become captivated or pulled into a deep quiet and recollection. You needn't do anything but be still, aware and present to the quiet calm and loving presence of the Lord.
- If you think that your prayer is what you do for God, you will have problems, confusion, more dryness and discouragement. You cannot cause this passive prayer to happen, and you cannot manipulate or take the Lord by force—only by faithful love.
- The following are typical thoughts and experiences at this stage of prayer:
    - Once you have experienced this wonderful prayer, you may wonder why you can't make it happen again, or whenever you want it.
    - Or, you may try some former technique that you thought brought on this passive recollection or contemplation in the past—but it won't work.

- You may begin to think in the stillness that nothing is going on and you are just wasting time, or that God is absent, and be tempted to quit the prayer, or give up prayer entirely.
- You may doubt that you are really praying at all, and with compulsive scruples return to former ways of prayer, working at doubling-down on doing more Discursive Meditation, or saying more quantities of vocal prayer—as saying more rosaries, litanies, psalms, etc.
○ You must avoid this temptation and remain in the dryness, aridity, or empty quiet, if it is there. If it isn't, you may calm your mind with any Acquired Recollection practices such as Centering Prayer or Simple Meditation with attention to your breathing and a sacred word or short prayer.
- However, if a prayer disturbance is heading for harmful, destructive or negative feelings and thoughts about God, neighbor or yourself, you can start to read a good spiritual book, or get busy with some service and work of love for others, take a quiet walk in nature, or work in the garden, etc.
○ Even with the great gift of Infused Recollection, Prayer of Quiet, or Prayer of the Sleep of the Faculties your life will still have labor, suffering and adversity, but it will have a different quality, and not be as hard as before. There will be more peace in it, as well as acceptance of it and trust in God's love and care, and a sharing in the sufferings of Jesus.
○ Some persons in these dwellings may desire to extend their prayer time, and should during retreat.

For this prayer period refer to "How to Use this Book for Prayer" or "Centering Prayer" in **Supplemental Material**.

Use any of the following scriptures for prayer as desired, but choose one before prayer. Keep in mind any word, phrase or sentence that strikes you.

Scripture Passages:
(Silent Prayer) Mt. 6:5-13; Lk. 5:16, 11:1-4; 6:12; Mk. 1:35; Lam. 3:25-28; Rom. 8:26-28; Ps. 131, 139:1-4, 4:4; Ex. 14:14; Jb. 13:5

(Focus on the Lord) Mt. 14:23-33; Lk. 7:36-50, 9:28-36; Jn. 15:1-5, 15:7, 15:9-11, 21:15-17; Heb. 3:1, 12:2-4; 2Cor. 4:18; Phil. 4:6-7; Ps. 42, 27:1-5, 31:23-24, 84; Is. 41:10, 43:1-5; Prov. 3:5-12

You may also use the following meditation for a prayer period if desired.

Guided Meditation:

Take time to become quiet and still, and imagine your garden again. Teresa writes about a garden in her autobiographical *Life*. She says: *"Having now spoken of the labor and manual effort with which this garden is watered when one draws water from the well, let us now speak of the second way of drawing water which is carried out by the Lord of the garden."* (L14-15) In these fourth dwellings the Lord wants to draw you into a more passive prayer—a prayer of more Living Water with less labor to water your garden. You won't be using your bucket or a hand pump here. Sit back on your bench in the little cove by the still, small pool and just enjoy the stillness and quiet. . . . Your Beloved is helping with needed watering and beautification in your garden because He loves you and wants you to enjoy the peace, quiet and beauty of the garden you both care for. This lessening of labor and more help from your Beloved is like the passive prayer of Infused Recollection or the Prayer of Quiet. In the peace and stillness, notice how the trees of your garden are beginning to bud and blossom and give fruit, and also the variety of flowers are more fragrant than ever. . . . Whereas earlier it seemed your garden had more weeds and was drying up in areas for lack of water to sustain it (difficult laborious prayer), now it is more clear to you that the Lord is in the garden helping you, the poor gardener, by weeding out bad growth by the roots, and by helping you in bringing needed flowing water (easier flowing prayer) to your trees and flowers (virtues) which are beginning not only to grow again—but vibrantly and riotously so. . . . (L14,1,9) Recognize His hand all over your interior garden. Be thankful, and just love Him!

"The important thing is not to think much, but to love much, doing that which most stirs you to love." (IC4,1,7)

4-2

FOURTH DWELLING PLACES—Part 2

Theme: *Surrender your prayer into God's hands!*

Description of the Fourth Dwelling Places: (continued)

In the fourth dwelling places, the Lord often gives passive supernatural prayer to those who are faithful to the practice of prayer, and who are getting more serious about avoiding sin and are growing in virtue. These people are becoming more detached from addictions, compulsions and shackling forces within their lives, and are growing in self-knowledge and humility. They have more freedom in imitating Christ and seeking His will. There is much more self-mastery, consistency, perseverance, determination and commitment to live the Gospel, with a deep desire to know and love and surrender to God.

The stages of prayer that occur in the fourth dwellings, which St. Teresa calls the Prayer of Quiet (or Spiritual Delights), and the Prayer of the Sleep of the Faculties are fully contemplative prayer. Though these are deeper and more intense prayer stages than the passive prayer of Infused Recollection, they are still less intense than the Prayer of Union that begins in the fifth dwellings places, or the still deeper Prayer of Union that St. Teresa terms Intense Union, Ecstasy or Spiritual Betrothal in the sixth dwellings places, or finally, of Transforming Union and Spiritual Marriage of the seventh dwelling places. But contemplative prayer and contemplative life properly speaking begin here in the fourth.

- In the fourth dwelling places without a lot of the effort of earlier dwellings, persons become recollected through the activity of God, and no attempt should be made to return to any Acquired Recollection practices be they spiritual reading, vocal prayer, Discursive Meditation, or even Simple Meditation unless distractions start to intrude on the prayer. (IC4,3,3)
  - At this point, prayer is not about the ordinary natural faculty of the Intellect/mind trying to think about or imagine God within.
- There isn't generally a lot of work in getting quiet and recollected here through Lectio Divina or Centering Prayer, because God is beginning to give the quieting water of flowing prayer—the Living Water—without as much effort needed in prayer. (L14-15)
  - One sacred word, attention to breath, a loving gaze, or short outburst of a loving aspiratory prayer may be all the work needed to end any distraction should it arise.
- Passive prayer causes a kind of expansion, which swells the whole interior being, producing ineffable blessings and making more room for God. (IC4,2,5-6; 4,3,9)
- In the gentle drawing inward to stillness, peace, calm, and quiet in the interior part of the soul, persons enter into their interior self sooner and recognize God's presence more quickly. (IC4,3,1-3)
- Contemplative prayer cannot be manufactured or manipulated. The Lord alone gives passive supernatural prayer and is in charge of it. (IC4,3,3)
  - There are no methods or techniques that can bring one to passive prayer. Persons can only dispose themselves for it by fidelity to the imitation of Christ and through prayer—possibly by preparation to receive it through any of the various prayer forms of Active Recollection.
- In these dwellings the faculties of Intellect/mind, Memory/imagination and Will, as well as the five senses and exterior things of the world, are beginning to lose their hold during prayer.
  - In the Prayer of Quiet, the human faculty of Will (as the seat of desires, affections and love), is somehow connected and fastened to God's Will. It becomes fascinated, absorbed or captivated in love of God. (IC4,2,8)
  - At the same time the faculties of Intellect/mind and Memory/imagination are quietly recollected or are moved by desires and strong impulses to thanksgiving and praise of God.
  - The exterior senses of feeling, seeing, hearing, smelling, touching and tasting are also recollected but free for their normal operations.

- A person in contemplation can actually be united with God deeper within the soul's interiority, while the mind is busy on the outskirts of consciousness. (IC4,1,9)
  - The mind can be noisily distracting, or be a chatter off in the background or somewhere in the distance, while the soul is quiet and peacefully recollected and gazing in love at God.
  - While the soul is stilled and quiet, any suffering due to being disturbed by a noisy mind, is only completely quelled if the mind is brought into *suspension* in prayer. (IC4,3,7) (see: "Suspensions" in "Various Mystical Phenomena" in **Supplemental Material**)
  - Thoughts from the mind cannot be stopped if God does not do the work of absorbing or stilling the mind's thoughts.
  - In these fourth dwelling places the Holy Spirit is communicating more deeply with the human spirit. And in the work of spirit, the person who thinks less and has less desire for doing some kind of work of prayer, actually allows God to do more. (IC4,3,5)
- This prayer may be a sign that someone is being called to advance in prayer, and to more attentive listening, receptivity in prayer, and more serious attention to transformation of life in imitation of Christ.
- This prayer is not about *consolations* from exterior and natural feelings produced by brain chemicals which persons can manufacture themselves. Contemplative prayer may include both *consolations*, and more importantly, *spiritual delights* from God. (IC4,1,4-5)
  - Spiritual delights are supernatural and begin and end in God as their source.
  - Though God can have a hand in them, consolations are the "feel good" feelings and emotions in prayer that also proceed from our own nature, natural capacities, and brain chemicals. Consolations are more connected to meditation than contemplation. (see: "Consolations and Spiritual Delights" in **Supplemental Material**)
- There is less fear of injury or loss of health in serving God, less servile fear of God or of any possible coming trials, along with more confidence, that since one has begun to enjoy God's company, this will only deepen.
- The body and mind are not worn out by this kind of prayer. (IC4,3,11-14)
  - It doesn't produce languishing or inertia, as in Absorption, which is a waste of time, a kind of spacing and zoning out, and is not Christian prayer.

- The first time true contemplative prayer occurs, the person's faculties of Intellect and mind might be in confusion, wonder, and surprise as to what is happening.
- When contemplative prayer is newly experienced, there is more awareness *during* the Prayer of Quiet *of the prayer itself* and of any *spiritual delights* received, than there will be later as one becomes acclimatized to it, or in later stages of prayer to come in the fifth through seventh dwelling places where the faculties and senses become even more stilled.
- Contemplative prayer and contemplative life are the beginning of the Life of Resurrection.
- Here begins the knowledge, purification and conversion of the unconscious realms of the human person through the work of God in prayer. From the fourth dwelling places onwards, interior battles will intensify. (IC4,1,12)

Teresian Teachings for Prayer and Life: (continued)

- Beginning in these dwellings, contemplative prayer will be intimately tied to contemplative living. There will not be as big a separation between the sacred and secular.
- Be aware that contemplative prayer is NOT necessarily, or essentially an *experience* of God, but rather of being passively moved in greater love and virtue by God for transformation and the imitation of Christ through the Gifts of the Holy Spirit. (see: "Contemplative Prayer" in "Prayer—Types and Categories" in **Supplemental Material**)
- This supernatural prayer is not acquired by the human faculty of the Intellect striving to think about God within, or by the imagination imagining Him. It is truly the fascination of the love of the Lord, from Him, that stills, stops and captivates the mind.
- The soul here does not understand what is going on within it, or what it most deeply desires and needs, and certainly not what is possible in intimacy with the Divine.
  - How does one speak about these things? In a humorous passage, St. Teresa writes: *"The Intellect if it understands, doesn't understand how it understands, at least it can't comprehend anything of what it understands. It doesn't seem to me that it understands, because, as I say, it doesn't understand. I really can't understand this myself!"* (L18,14)

- St. Teresa gives guidance for being disposed for the gift of contemplation in the Prayer of Quiet. But she cautions: *"Do not try or even strive for contemplative prayer. Be surrendered to God's desire for you."* (IC4,2,9)
- St. Teresa's spiritual direction includes the following: (IC4,2,9)
  - Love God without self-interest, for God's sake alone despite lack of consolations or spiritual delights.
  - In true humility and detachment, or as much freedom as possible from the tyranny of the ego and false self, give up the thought that puny services *merit* such a blessing as contemplation, which cannot be earned and is a free gift at God's desire and discretion. This prayer is not about what persons do for God, but what God does in and for them—even if unknown and unexperienced on a conscious level.
  - Desire to follow the Way of Christ in self-emptying and the cross, rather than in spiritual delights.
  - Remember that ultimate human glory is keeping Christ's commandment to love, and imitating Him—not spiritual delights. So be detached from them.
  - Recall that this water of prayer does not come from any laboring or attempt to force it, but only comes as the Lord wills it, to whom He wills it, and often when least expected. It will not come just because one desires it, but only when His Majesty desires and grants it. And sometimes even before persons begin to think of Him, He will have already brought them deeper inside their interior castle—sometimes even outside the designated time for prayer.
  - Desire to let the Lord do as He pleases, whether exercised in the light of "Illuminative Contemplation" of wisdom or understanding, or the darker experience of "Purgative Contemplation" in fortitude, counsel and fear/awe of the Lord. (see: "Three States of Contemplation" in the section on "Prayer—Types and Categories" in **Supplemental Material**)

"... not all imaginations are by their nature capable of meditating, but all souls are capable of loving." (F5,2)

4-2

FOURTH DWELLING PLACES—Part 2

Internalizing the Teachings: *Make your prayer a longing for God!*

In the fourth dwellings St. Teresa begins a description of the movement from the active prayer of Acquired Recollection to the various levels of passive prayer—Infused Recollection, the Prayer of Quiet (Prayer of Spiritual Delights) and the Prayer of the Sleep of the Faculties. As one way of telling the difference between active and passive prayer, she describes the differences between the *consolations* (contentos) of earlier dwelling places that are natural and human-made in prayer—though God can also have a hand in them—and the solely God-given *spiritual delights* (gustos) that can accompany supernatural prayer. (see: "Consolations vs. Spiritual Delights" in **Supplemental Material**) St. Teresa continues to describe the growing supernatural effects of the Prayer of Quiet and the Prayer of the Sleep of the Faculties on the lived Christian life. Teresa's advice is to let God lead the way in prayer. She also speaks of some distractions to prayer. (see: "Distractions in Prayer" in **Supplemental Material**)

Reflection:
The Prayer of Quiet Experience

The beginnings of contemplative prayer—the Prayer of Quiet—can be described as a prayer of deep stillness, peace, calm and quiet recollection. However, it is not like a zoned-out, empty, absorption or blankness, for there is an alertness and attentiveness to it with a concentrated and arrested attention focused on God. It is more than a mere atmosphere of peace and quiet. Something tangible, or Someone's presence, is actually felt or sensed. The prayer, and experience, is not easy to describe. It is not always clear when the moment of God's presence is experienced and recognized. Neither, at first, is it easy to tell if it is the Lord's gifts of peace, quiet joy, and stillness, or if it is the Lord, Himself. Though it is a very gentle and subtle experience, it does not go unnoticed. Even if during this prayer there is some noise and thinking going on in the mind, this prayer can simultaneously be happening on another level in the soul. Though often this Prayer of Quiet can follow upon the attempt to be still, quiet and recollected, this is not always the case, and it can occur at any time in the midst of thinking, reasoning, imagining, and mind restlessness, when God breaks in and takes over the prayer.

After the first time the Prayer of Quiet occurs, there is the temptation to go over in your mind what you did to prepare or cause the prayer to happen, so as to bring it about again. There can be an accompanying skepticism that it was perhaps only a lovely feeling, or natural psychological state, and not anything supernatural at all. You will know the truth by its fruits.

Because it is a pleasant experience, you may try to duplicate the prayer by "doing" what you did the first time it happened. But you will soon make the discovery that the prayer cannot be brought on at will. Contemplation can follow after the work of some active Acquired Recollection technique for calming the mind—as attention to breath with the repetition of the Jesus Prayer or a sacred word, or a Simple Meditation. But other times you will be aware that you are already still, or have been given the gift of having a mind stilled of busy thoughts, which is fixed on God, and have done nothing yourself to cause the Prayer of Quiet. At still other times, you may consciously or unconsciously have the desire for this prayer but not be able to be quiet or calm—to stop thinking or imagining or feeling—yet the Prayer of Quiet has nonetheless been given to you.

The Lord's presence can come gradually and slowly, deepening almost imperceptibly, such that you aren't sure when it actually happened. At other times you can have a sense of almost being invaded by His presence—and quickly. Or, you can have the sense of having dropped suddenly to a new depth—or if you prefer—risen to a new level of some new kind of consciousness or place in the soul. At other times it is as though the Presence is there, or has been there all along, but you had not discovered it or focused your attention on it, and so did not know it was there until you turned your interiority more deeply inward.

While in the Prayer of Quiet you will lose a sense of time. It is difficult to say how long the prayer has lasted. Sometimes it may be only a few minutes, and at other times an hour or more.

Because the experience of this prayer is pleasant, you naturally try to hold on to it. Since you cannot in the first place cause this prayer by techniques or anything you do, so too, you cannot control the duration of the prayer. Within the prayer there are moments not of unconsciousness, but of a more empty or simplified consciousness, or a captivation to Someone that obscures consciousness to other things. When you become aware of yourself in this state, you sometimes realize that you have stopped breathing for a few moments, or have fewer respirations. Sometimes there is the temptation to leap up and shout and move about to see if the state will end, but you never do this. In fact, even if you find yourself in a cramped position you may be unwilling to move a muscle for fear the wonderful experience will slip away. There is a sense that it is fragile, and that if you are clumsy, it could just evaporate. It is almost as if you think the Lord has accidently visited you, and you know it, but wonder if He might not realize He has come to you, and that if He did, He would realize His mistake and depart immediately from sinful you. So, you try to be still and hidden. But of course, all these doubt-filled thoughts are far from the truth, and in a short time change to feelings of deep gratitude and love, along with perhaps some awkwardness and amazement at being visited by the Lord Himself. You wonder what it could mean.

During the Prayer of Quiet nothing else matters—not your pain or worries about attachments, or your spiritual progress, or anything. It puts things into perspective and creates a proper hierarchy of values with the Lord and His values at the center. It is not a time when all thinking, imagining, self-talk or restlessness ends, but all that does slow down, and is much less bothersome and distracting. Sometimes you can hear your mind, but it is as if it is a voice muted or far away off in the distance. You still feel and know that even with some background commotion, your basic desire, inclination, intention and the faculty of your Will are united to the Lord. And His presence is so compelling that you cannot deliberately go chasing after other lesser thoughts or interests. You do not even consciously examine thoughts or images that come to mind for fear that if you follow them this could break the fragile awareness of the Lord's subtle presence. There is generally a sense of deep gratitude and joyful thanksgiving for the gift of this prayer.

Because of the special quality of this prayer, you will often have the temptation to judge all other prayer by it, and count anything else as of a lesser value or not even prayer at all. You like this prayer because of the immediacy of it and the real awareness that the Lord is dealing directly with you—as opposed to the more seemingly indirect dealings with you through others, or scripture, or events of your life. However, the Lord knows when to give this prayer and when not to—all for your own unique good. Even the alternation of having this prayer and not having it can be a dialectic of growth for you, though you may not understand how and find this frustrating or difficult.

Often there is a mistaken belief that once this level of prayer has been reached it is continuous. It is not. It is not due you. You do not earn it, and there are frequent dry times when the qualitative difference and specialness of this prayer are not experienced.

This can cause anxiety or disappointment, for you desire God's direct presence always. You have experienced that you have more love and fervor and great resolutions because of this prayer. You experience joy and consolation in it. You also may have the gift of tears from seeing how much you are loved and how little you deserve it. The prayer returns you to basics and helps you to grow in becoming more like Christ. Some of your former pains and troubles seem lighter, and you sense you are truly growing. You have a certain exuberance and desire to talk about the Lord and His gifts and mercy and His action in your life. You want everyone to know Him, love Him, and receive His blessings, too. You recognize an increased desire to be alone with Him, to spend more time in prayer and solitude, and to be generous with yourself for His service. You experience Him working in your life and all around you. You feel you would like to do more and to love Him more deeply. So it is natural, after having experienced so much benefit to be troubled when you have periods when you cannot experience this prayer, and wonder if you ever did. You fear that because of all you have seen it work in you, nothing can happen without it. But this is not really a time to worry. Teresa uses images of the Lord weeding His garden—you—and cutting and pruning back buds so as to make the new buds even healthier and more fragrant. It is a time to trust, which is the primary attitude necessary here. It does no good to try to force the prayer mechanically. Without God's activity all the effort and strain will not bring about the prayer. It will only exhaust you, and often bring the opposite effect from what you desire. St. Teresa is clear in saying God cannot be dealt with by force.

During dry times of this stage of prayer, do not think the favors of the Lord are over, and fall back into old habits and faults. Sometimes there is the temptation to discouragement and to giving up, or to concluding that the Lord does not care about you anymore. And you might begin to think that you may as well do whatever you want. But employ here some determination to keep out of serious sin and occasions of sin. Even if you fail, no matter what happens, do not give up this resolution to set aside the usual time and attention for the practice of prayer. It is only a temporary weakness and discouragement. Your failures may be more carelessness and ignorance than lack of love for God. Do not be too harsh on yourself. But if you quit praying because you think you are being a hypocrite you are off track and it is more difficult for God to get through to you. Sometimes when your prayer is dark or arid, you will fear you have quit praying, and think you are not even capable of recollection or your usual manner of praying. But your prayer is in a new guise and form, and your relationship with God is still very much alive. It is like a relationship with a friend that you are separated from. On a feeling level, it is experienced as a less close form of relationship, though it isn't necessarily the case. There are rhythms to relationships. They have their ebb and flow. Try not to be overly concerned. Human beings cannot keep up any one particular emotion indefinitely. But whatever happens, do not give up praying! Prayer will help you understand your situation more clearly. It will keep you more aware of your failings and help you avoid them. It will open you to the Lord, and strengthen your sincere attempt to build the relationship. The Lord will favor you with more fortitude to enable you to be open to more dryness, purification, uncertainty or suffering, if He desires to bring you closer to Himself that way.

Continue to be faithful to prayer times. Come with simplicity. Leave behind abstract reasoning and argumentation. Avoid any mental or spiritual gymnastics and self-talk, or even eloquent words. Place yourself in the Lord's presence. He desires that you just be in His presence. Surrender gently, without struggle or violence to the Prayer of Quiet. You cannot browbeat the mind, imagination or feelings into order. Also, you can expect to have trouble achieving calmness if you have had a hectic day, are all keyed-up, are having difficulty in a relationship, or if something emotionally or psychologically upsetting has just happened. You need to be attuned to the factors in your life that contribute noise, commotion and disturbance. There are different interior movements that affect mood, and therefore prayer. All you can do is prepare yourself as best you can, realizing that your own effort is not all that is required, and that God's free gift is involved here. Do not employ force in prayer. Doing so often distracts and makes prayer impossible, and can even cause worse effects and disturbances. Watch for the trap of spiritual ambitiousness, or "spiritual climbing"—something analogous to "social climbing."

It is wise to prepare yourself for prayer as you are able, at a particular time of your choosing. But have the attitude always of openness and acceptance to whatever happens or doesn't happen during that time, in trust that the Lord is leading you the way best for you. It is possible to cultivate (or at least pray for) the desire to want what the Lord wants for you.

All this that involves the Prayer of Quiet, including any dryness, is part of this degree of prayer. It is good to remember that your interiority, your soul and spiritual life has its ups and downs, and does not grow as other things in one unbroken straight line. But there are ways to ascertain growth that is of the Lord, even within the periods of failure and dryness. It is helpful to remind yourself that you have been given the Prayer of Quiet and that this is a tremendous gift and favor of God's love, and you should respond appropriately as to a friend who has given you a special gift reflecting a great friendship. Those who have much experience in the spiritual life claim it is the pledge of even more wonderful favors to come, and that God has chosen you for greater things, and to be a benefit for others.

During the dry times of prayer, precisely because of past experiences of the Prayer of Quiet, things can look worse than they are. To paraphrase St. Teresa—the situation is that the greater the favors to you, the greater your trials may be, as well as a deeper experience of your brokenness and selfishness. But this is a step forward in wisdom and understanding. Both the dry times of this prayer and your remembrance of your own failings serve to further your humility better than any ascetical program of humbling yourself that you could devise. That is to say, this is a process of truthful humility that genuinely reveals you to yourself, and also reveals something of the Lord, and His hidden realities and designs for you. This humbling truth makes you realize that God is with you and at work in you and desirous of a deeper relationship with you. You begin to develop a mistrust of yourself and your power to know or save yourself. You come to the realization that you don't even know what is best for yourself. This allows you to transfer trust to God. You are leaving behind the fears that you had when you failed again, or moved into dryness, as well as any concerns that you have lost the Prayer of Quiet, or lost your way to God. Instead, you are maturing into a confident belief that no matter how you see yourself, the Lord is merciful and faithful, and at work in transforming you.

As a spur to keep you from giving up prayer, St. Teresa reminds you that all things will come to an end, and you are accountable for what you do with your life. But despite these cautions to help keep you praying, she instructs that it is better to persevere in love than in fear. She reminds you that your true home is in God. Beyond the dire consequences from giving up prayer, Teresa speaks even more of the great marvels, delight, glory, gifts and fulfilling love deriving from contemplative prayer that can reach an unimaginable tremendous love-union with the Lord. The Prayer of Quiet is the beginning of a new life, of a deeper love relationship with God, and is accompanied by growth in the imitation of Christ's mind and life. The results of this gift of the Prayer of Quiet are fruitful good works.

Reflection Questions: (Choose only one or two at a time to explore in depth.)

- Have you had any of the experiences like those described in the reflection above?
- What is prayer like for you at this moment in your life? Do you experience it as sometimes easier than at other times, a struggle, out of your control, consoling or not?
- Have you experienced a prayer that was momentarily taken out of your hands, away from your doing and usual way of praying—perhaps without words and with some loss of thoughts and time? Did this surprise you? What were your thoughts and feelings about it? Because you weren't saying words did you think you had stopped praying?
- Do you experience any rhythms of prayer in your life? If so, are they connected to any particular situations in your life?

- Have you made the decision to pray no matter how you feel, how dry or arid your prayer, or how absent you may experience the Lord?
- If your prayer has changed from what it once was, how do you feel about that? How has it affected your relationship with God?
- How do you presently see your prayer and its connection to your faith life?
- Is your faith moving away from an assent to theological beliefs to a faith more centered on the person of Jesus?

Guidance for Prayer and Prayer Period:

- When you begin to recollect yourself for prayer, recall what debt of gratitude you owe God, and in humility reflect on who you are in your littleness before His great mercy and loving kindness. Come to prayer as one poor in spirit asking for transformation and a deeper relationship with Jesus. Wait with humility for God's activity and desires for your prayer.
- Less striving or thinking about how you can bring about enjoyment in your prayer, and more desiring for God is what is most helpful. Desire is energy for love.
- Forceful striving in trying not to think will rouse anxiety, and more thoughts in your mind.
- When contemplation doesn't come following your own work of prayer in active Acquired Recollection, or you are restless and distracted, do not ask yourself such questions as: "What did I do wrong?" "Why aren't my techniques working today?" "Why is God absent?" "Is God avoiding me because I've fallen again?"
  - Do not become troubled over your so-called "performance" at prayer. This is a trap.
  - Don't give prayer a rating of success or failure.
  - Do some work of recollection and quieting of your mind however that may be possible in this present moment and circumstance. This can be a short aspiratory loving prayer, a momentary image of Jesus from the Gospels, a slowly repeated sacred word or two of love with attention to your breathing. Focus your energy of desiring love in an inner gaze towards Jesus in His humanity.
  - Every time your attention is brought back from distractions during prayer to a loving prayer or gaze at Jesus, this is a good prayer and

pleasing to the Lord. Even if you have to do this many times during your whole prayer period, this is good prayer!
- It pleases the Lord that you continue to try to love Him more deeply, be grateful and mindful of His honor, glory and goodness. God also welcomes your attempts to forget yourself, your own benefits, comforts and delights, as well as your self-made struggles to progress in prayer.

o You will not understand what is happening and what God is doing during the deep calm and quiet that is contemplation. Just be there in love, listening with open alertness and attentiveness to God. Do not give in to the temptation of thinking that you are wasting time and need to do something else when the stillness and quiet mind of contemplation comes, or when what *feels* like nothing is happening occurs.

o Leave your soul surrendered into the Lord's hands. Let Him do whatever He wants with you, with the greatest disinterest about your own benefit, and with the greatest trust and resignation to God's will and work in you during prayer. Surrender in trust as a child into the arms of love.

o When His Majesty desires your Intellect/mind to stop its busyness, He will quiet, still it and absorb it in Himself. He will occupy it in ways that give it favors so far above what you can attain on your own, that it will remain calm.
- You have no choice but to let your mind, imagination, feelings and faculties of Intellect, Memory and Will perform their natural functions until God quiets them and appoints them to something different and greater.

o Once your Will and gaze have become fastened on the Lord in contemplative prayer, be surrendered to Him, doing nothing except loving Him in return. Do not try to meditate or do any active work of prayer of your own—not even a sacred word.

o When the moments of contemplation end, and your mind becomes busy again, then once more you can work at some form of active Acquired Recollection with Simple Meditation, Centering Prayer, a short scripture passage, or an aspiratory prayer, etc.

o For this prayer period look again as needed at the "How to Use this Book for Prayer" section, or refer to the suggestions for the prayer of

Lectio Divina, Centering Prayer, and Simple Meditation as described in **Supplemental Material**.

If desired, you may use one of these scripture passages that follows for your prayer. Some phrase from a scripture might suggest an outburst of love in an aspiratory prayer for you.

Scripture Passages:
(Longing) Sg. 1:1-4, 3:1-4; Lk. 7:36-50; Jn. 21:15-17; Ps. 42, 63, 27:7-14, 73:23-26, 84, 143:5-8; Is. 55:1-3; Mk. 12:28-34
(Surrender) Prov. 3:5-8; Jn. 15:1-7, 14:1-7; 1Pt. 5:6-10; Phil. 2:5-8; Lk.9:23-24; Heb. 12:1-2; Jb. 11:13-19; Rom. 12:2; Mt. 11:28-30; Ps. 139

You may use the following meditation for reflection if you prefer.

Guided Meditation:

Enter again into the quiet of your interior garden and take some moments to survey it. As the co-helper gardener of the interior garden of your soul, notice the progress of the continuing beautification of your garden, and how you have come a long way in making it beautiful with and for the Lord. Recall that with His help you have pulled up by the roots many invasive, poisonous and dangerous plants. . . . Think of how you have fertilized your garden with prayer, loving thoughts and words, and virtuous actions. . . . See, too, that you have protected your garden from creatures that would trample or destroy it by putting in some needed fencing. . . . It has become an ever-safer place for a rendezvous of love with the Lord. Now you have much less work to do than when you first started and more time to rest and enjoy the peace, calm and beauty. Just take some time to enjoy this for some moments. . . .

Bring your attention to how the water coming to your garden by springs and channels is more dependable and costing you less labor than when you had to use your own arms to draw water up from the well with only a bucket, or, when you had to do the work of digging the channels to bring the water. See that because of this more reliable water source, the trees and edibles of your garden are budding and blossoming and giving more bountiful fruit. The many new flowers you have planted are blooming and giving forth marvelous color and fragrances for you and the Lord to enjoy. . . . Notice how the Lord Himself has planted some exotic and special ones just for you, and taste the honey from the bee hives the Lord has gathered for you! . . . Think back on so many times the Lord has come unexpectedly and with delight on His own to nurture your garden helping you plant, cultivate, prune, harvest and tend to the honey bees. . . .

Do you recognize your Lord's own delight as He surprises you with many intricate bouquets of flowers, baskets of fruit and tasty treats from your garden that you can both enjoy together? Offer Him praise and gratitude for these gifts and for the refreshment of the artesian spring—the Living Water of flowing prayer—that is now abundantly flowing where needed in your garden. (L14,9)

"O my Lord and my good God! ... How you desire, Lord, to be with us ... You say that your delight is to be with the children of men. ... What is this? As often as I hear these words, they bring me great consolation, and they did so even when I was very lost. Is it possible, Lord, that there be a soul that reaches the point where you grant such mercies and gifts, and understands that you are with it, and then returns to offending you after so many favors and after such great expressions of love that you have for it which cannot be doubted because of the clear effects of your work? ... How many are the reasons I can sing of your mercies forever!" (L14,10)

As I read The Confessions, *I saw myself in them ... when I came to the passage where St. Augustine speaks about his conversion and how he heard that voice in the garden, it seemed exactly as if the Lord were speaking that way to me, or so my heart felt. I remained a long time dissolved in tears with affliction and weariness ... It seemed my soul gained great strength from His Divine Majesty, and that He heard my cries and had compassion on all my tears. His Majesty was only awaiting some preparedness in me for His spiritual graces ... (L 9, 8-9)*

SISTER TERESA of JESUS
Conversion Experiences—1554-1555

Sister Teresa was never comfortable or at peace with her years of poor responses to the Lord. But in her weakness, she still went along in her conflicted and dissipated life of busyness at the monastery, visiting friends and benefactors in the parlor, clinging to friendships that she later came to see as harmful, and living a prayer life that was merely going through the motions. Her hypocritical, vacillating life went on this way until the life-changing experience of 1554, when Teresa was thirty-nine. In that year during Lent, Teresa was deeply moved and experienced a profound conversion while praying before an image of the wounded Christ, which softened her heart to desire changes in her life. (L9) She had been desiring and praying to finally be true and not offend the Lord with her pretense of being a good nun. Before Christ's sufferings and tremendous love for her, she dissolved in genuine tears over her weak response to His great love. It marked the beginning of a change in her spiritual life.

Building upon this conversion experience of the wounded Christ, the following year Teresa read St. Augustine's *Confessions* and found him to be a kindred spirit because of his years of living with a divided heart and conflicted relationships. His struggle and conversion so moved her that she again wept for her failures. This further awakened her and strengthened her resolve to turn from her mediocre religious life, and her continual fainthearted, indecisive wandering around within what she would later know as the first three dwelling places.

Sister Teresa began to return to prayer in earnest determination, with a desire to spend more time in solitude with the Lord who loved her. She began to gain strength and to get serious about avoiding what were occasions of sin, and any interferences to living her religious life with integrity. From here on she began to move forward in her prayer relationship with the Lord and to be given the many graces and favors of the later dwelling places.

5

FIFTH DWELLING PLACES

(*The Interior Castle* 5, Chapters 1-4)

Theme: *Enjoy deepening intimacy with God in the dwelling of transformation!*

Description of the Fifth Dwelling Places:

While many people will not be able to relate to all the contemplative prayer experiences of the fifth, sixth and seventh dwelling places, the descriptions should nonetheless be read for an understanding of what can lie ahead and is possible in the life of prayer. For some it will be an attractive, alluring and encouraging spur to keep them moving forward in prayer. St. Teresa actually believed that many were called to the fifth dwelling places, even if they didn't have all the experiences in prayer that she had. Always remember that true union for St. Teresa is having one's will totally aligned and conformed to God's will. Although none of the outward forms of the Prayer of Union itself may ever be experienced, dedication to seeking the will of God, desiring it and trying to be surrendered to it must be the concern of every Christian. Even if persons do not relate to the descriptions and material on prayer itself in these last three dwellings, there is helpful and inspiring Teresian teaching for life in these dwellings—especially on purification and deepening love of God and neighbor. St. Teresa uses the human terminology of the progression of the relationship of lovers in the fourth through seventh dwelling places. While the fourth dwelling places is where the lovers meet, the fifth is the place of falling in love, holding hands and courtship. The sixth will be the stage of Spiritual Betrothal, and the seventh the state of Spiritual Marriage.

- St. Teresa gives notice right from the beginning of the fifth dwellings that it will be difficult to explain these dwellings. *"How can I ever explain to you the riches, treasures and delights that are found in these fifth dwelling places?"* (IC5,1,1)
- Here, God's very own Self comes to be known as the dwelling place of the soul! (IC5,2,5) God is joined and united with the essence of the person's whole soul—spirit to Holy Spirit. (IC5,1,5)
- The fifth dwelling places are also the fourth waters in St. Teresa's autobiography, *Life* (L18f), and an intensification of the contemplative prayer of the fourth dwelling places—the Prayer of Quiet and the Prayer of the Sleep of the Faculties.
- Persons in the fifth dwelling places have a long history of relationship with God, which comes with great confidence in the relationship—particularly in both understanding and experiencing that God abides in the soul, and the soul abides in God.
  - Souls must be strong—especially in faith, hope, love and virtue for the Prayer of Union.
  - This prayer carries the absolute certitude of being joined and united with God—Essence to essence, and not only by grace. The person has absolutely no doubt about it. (IC5,1,9-11)
- The Prayer of Union itself—in contrast to a *life* of union—is of short duration, and seems shorter than it probably is.
  - Teresa isn't certain of the length of time of this prayer—perhaps a little while—the length of a Hail Mary—or maybe as much as half an hour. (IC5,2,7; L18,12)
- True union in God is primarily a *way of living* in God in imitation of Christ, with the will in complete alignment with God's will in the Beatitudes, commandments, virtues, and the mind and actions of Jesus.
  - This union of imitation and likeness to Christ is the safest and clearest union in God, and it does not necessarily or usually include the more extraordinary experiences that St. Teresa experienced. No one can reach union without being in union with the mind and actions of Christ.
- Though great delights don't necessarily come with this union, peace and joy are experienced beyond natural, earthly pleasure and joy. (IC5,1,6)
  - The experience of deep rest and joy in God—of spiritual delights—makes other things less significant.
- The Prayer of Union is not a dreamy state, (not zoned-out languishing absorption) and it only seems to others like the person is asleep. Persons don't experience that they are asleep nor do they exactly feel awake as

Fifth Dwelling Places   147

they would ordinarily experience wakefulness. (IC5,1,4-5) (see: *Review for Religious,* "Praying through Sleep," July/August 2000.)
- In the Prayer of Union, the soul is experienced as something separate from the body.
- Depending on the intensity of the union, various operations of the soul within the body are suspended, uprooted from their natural operations, and put on hold by God. (IC5,1,4)
  - God suspends all the faculties of Intellect/mind, Memory/imagination and Will, so there is no need in these dwellings, nor is it possible, for anyone to use a method to do this for themselves. There *is no* human technique to suspend the faculties. In the Prayer of Union, the Lord alone can suspend them, and only if or when He chooses.
  - Intellect/mind cannot impede this union, and neither can Memory or imagination.
  - When God suspends the Intellect/mind, the person can't think and doesn't even want to use any energy to think, though there is the desire to understand something about the experience.
  - The faculty of the Will is captivated and loving, and the person does experience the self as loving, but doesn't understand how, or who or what it loves, or what it even desires.
    - Consciousness is as though stunned, and is nearly lost, or can be completely lost.
  - Though the operations of the soul are uprooted from their natural operations, this is generally a delightful experience.
  - During the time of union, the soul is left as though without the functioning exterior five senses. (IC5,1,9) Usually, the person is not even aware of breathing, and wouldn't notice what is happening outside of their soul. *"...neither a hand nor foot stirs."* (IC5,1,4)
  - In the *full* Prayer of Union all the faculties are suspended and asleep to the things of the world and asleep even to the person. The experience is that one is even without the five senses. It is as if dead to the world.
- God and the soul are more alone together in these dwellings than ever. There is no room for anything poisonous or destructive to intrude on the intimacy of the Prayer of Union.
  - Even the tiny "lizards" that entered in the fourth dwellings—those little thoughts and doubts which proceed from the Memory or imagination—cannot impede the Prayer of Union with God. (IC5,1,5)
- As wondrous as this Prayer of Union is, it does not yet reach the fuller intimacy of Spiritual Betrothal. (IC5,4,4)

o The PURPOSE of this Prayer of Union is not about staying in a state of suspended consciousness or spiritual delight, but for the strengthening of love for the birth of **GOOD WORKS** that the Lord desires. (IC5,3,11; 7,4,6)

Prayer of Union: Three Degrees of Deepening Intensity

1. In **Simple Union** the faculty of the Will and Intellect/mind are quietly recollected, while Memory/imagination may wander or also be recollected. The five senses are quiet, but still operate in their natural functions. Physical sensation would be felt and recognized, but the faculties of Will, Intellect/mind are suspended and without distractions. Memory/imagination may be functioning as normal, or could also be fastened on God.
   - The person at prayer would hear the doorbell and be able to leave the prayer to answer it. But in general, the sense perceptions though received, are not registered or paid attention to by the Intellect/mind, since it is all intent on Someone else—God.
   - At first, this prayer may be very brief and come only after years of less intense forms of passive recollection and contemplation, or longer periods of mental prayer. (L18,9)
2. In **Full Union** the Intellect/mind, Will, and Memory/imagination are all three captive and "off line." The exterior senses are very still, but operative as in Simple Union.
   - During the time that this intensification of the Prayer of Union lasts, the soul is left as though without its interior senses or understanding. (IC5,1,4; 5,1,9)
   - This is not an out of the body experience, but the soul is experienced in some way as separate and distinct from the body. (IC5,1,4)
   - The person should not worry about how they do or do not understand this union. It cannot be intellectually grasped by the human mind, and God does not allow it. (IC5,1,5)
3. In the **Prayer of Intense Union** (Suspensions: Ecstasy, Rapture or Transport)—an even more intense experience within the fifth dwelling places—all interior senses are so suspended that any sense perceptions may not even be perceived enough to be noticed or remembered later, and so it seems to the soul that it feels and experiences nothing external during this prayer.
   - Few people ever experience the Prayer of Intense Union or Suspension: Ecstasy, Rapture, Transport, Levitation or Flight of the

Spirit. (see: "Various Mystical Phenomena" in **Supplemental Material**)

Characteristics of the Prayer of Simple Union, Full Union, Intense Union

1. **Certitude is a hallmark of the Prayer of Union.**
   - It is an undoubtable experience of the soul in God and God in the soul in a secret and intimate meeting and exchange. (IC5,1,9-11)
   - Certitude is present even after the experience of union has ended. (IC5,1,10) The certitude is not lost even when recalling the experience years later. (IC5,1,9)
   - The certitude doesn't have to do with any bodily forms of the presence of Christ Jesus—seen or unseen—but only with supernatural union in His Divinity.
   - If certitude is not part of this prayer, the Prayer of Union has not been experienced within the whole and deepest center of the soul where God dwells. (IC5,1,11)
2. **Distractions are absent.**
   - Here the soul is meeting God in its center where God dwells, and nothing else can go there.
   - God doesn't even entrust this secret loving meeting to the person's own conscious mind, and nothing can disturb it. (IC5,1,5)
   - Since all the faculties are suspended and "off line," the interior and exterior faculties are not free to operate as they normally do. (L18,1)
     - Except for the Will, the faculties of Intellect/mind, and Memory/imagination *can come out of union*, and wander about, operating in their normal functions.
     - If this occurs, the person will be in a lesser intense form of the Prayer of Union. That is, prayer here could alternate between Prayer of Union, and Prayer of the Sleep of the Faculties, or Prayer of Quiet, and one could experience distractions again.
   - Lack of distractions applies only to the actual moments of the Prayer of Union.
   - The soul knows that God is working in it by the effects of the prayer, not by understanding the actual activity of God in the soul, or the prayer itself.
3. **Fatigue is absent.**
   - Personal effort at prayer is reduced to a minimum due to God's work alone.

- There's a feeling of powerlessness out of which comes a new kind of dependence and strength in God.
- There is generally an extraordinary abundance of joy in the Prayer of Union, though great delights—as Suspensions: Ecstasy, Raptures, or Transports—don't necessarily come with this union. (IC5,1,1-2; L18,1)
- Any rejoicing often comes without the soul understanding what it is rejoicing in, or how.
- In this blissful state of prayer, the soul is unable to express what the experience is that it is having. (L18,1)
- Throughout the day, the person may experience the Prayer of Quiet, or Infused Recollection (a kataphatic experience), or instead, a habitual, dark, or arid contemplation (an apophatic non-experience of God). (see: "Apophatic and Kataphatic Journeys to God" in **Supplemental Material**)

4. **Prayer of Union is not always or necessarily experienced during the hours set aside for prayer.**
    - It may or may not be experienced during the time set aside for prayer, for God could break in and give this Prayer of Union at any time—even while the person is at some other occupation than prayer.
    - At first, the prayer may be very brief and come only after much time given to mental or contemplative prayer. (L18,9)

Effects of the Prayer of Simple Union, Full Union or Intense Union

- The effects of the Prayer of Union are many and wonderful. In the fifth and sixth dwelling places they are nearly identical, but the *force or intensity* of the effects differs.
- In general, the effects of the Prayer of Union include the following:
    - There is delight and satisfaction above all delights and consolations known before, that can't be put into words. The peace and joy are above all earthly joys that have ever been experienced. (IC5,1,6)
    - There is an immense desire to continually praise the Lord. (IC5,2,7)
    - Anything the person does for God seems little in comparison to the gift of this union, and souls will have a willingness and desire to suffer penance and great trials or even a thousand deaths for God. It is as though they can't do enough for God. (IC5,2,8)
    - The works of penance are easier and not felt as difficult, but rather are a joy to do for God. There is even a kind of delight in suffering in doing the will of God. (IC5,2,14)

- - There is growing pain at seeing God disregarded or offended, as well as painful concern for others if they are separated from God. (IC5,2,10) There is a tremendous desire that everyone know and love God. (IC5,2,7)
  - More and more the lures of the world are losing their appeal. Though calmer than ever, there is still a restlessness for even more fullness and intimacy with God. The person has the desire to leave this world to be with God in the next. (IC5,2,10)
  - There is a deepening desire for solitude, which comes easily now. (IC5,2,7-8)
  - God is putting love in order within the soul. (IC5,2,12; 5,3,7-12) The person will make great efforts to advance in love and virtue.
  - New trials begin. But trials are undergone with peace. There is an intensification of spiritual purification deeper within the soul itself—a purification that breaks the ego, and grinds and transforms the soul anew—a dark night experience. (IC5,2,11)
- Persons know the difference between other forms of prayer and the Prayer of Union once it is experienced, for the favors of earlier dwellings seem coarse by comparison. It is analogous to something superficial on the body, "... *like a freckle, compared to something in the very marrow of the bones.*" (IC5,1,6)
- After a person has been placed within the greatness of God for a little while, and so closely joined with God, the soul is **transformed** when it comes out of this prayer. (IC5,2,7)
  - Teresa uses the image of the changes of the silkworm caterpillar into a butterfly to illustrate the astounding transformation that begins to take place in these dwellings.
    - In this transformation the soul doesn't even recognize itself anymore! (IC5,2,7-8)
- In the midst of the deep peace of these fifth dwelling places, **TRIALS** and **SUFFERINGS** (the Dark Night) begin to increase, and will intensify even more in the sixth dwelling places.

There are **VARIOUS KINDS OF SUFFERINGS** in these fifth dwellings:
 (see: "Dark Night and Purification Trials" in **Supplemental Material**)

1. **<u>Physical Sufferings</u>**
- External and physical *life failures, set-backs and sufferings* are certainly present and purifying, but are not as radically purifying and transforming as spiritual sufferings.

- These external sufferings do not reach or touch the soul's innermost depth for transformation, and thus do not cause as great a suffering or disturbance as spiritual sufferings. (IC5,3,4)
- These do not afflict in the same way in the fifth dwelling places as they did previously in earlier dwelling places, because the growth in faith, trust, hope and the profound experiential love of God, causes them to pass more quickly.
- There will always be the ordinary sufferings or consolations that affect *human nature* that never go away.
- St. Teresa wrote: *"Don't think, for example, that if my father or brother dies I ought to be in such close conformity with the will of God that I won't grieve at their loss, or that, if I have trials or illness, I must enjoy bearing them."* (IC5,3,7)

2. **Spiritual Sufferings**
   - These sufferings have a more intense experiential quality which begin to break and grind the soul into pieces and to remake it in the image of Christ. (IC5,2,11) Courage is needed here more than ever!
   - Spiritual things afflict the person in this stage of prayer much more severely than the physical, external, day to day ordinary set-backs and sufferings of life events.
     - In the fifth dwellings the ego self—the little, self-centered, false self—will begin to get dismantled, and painfully so.
     - The sufferings are more in the senses and faculties of the soul, but not the center of the soul where true peace resides. (IC5,3,4)
     - There is a new restlessness for more of God, though the soul has never been quieter or calmer in other ways. Since it has experienced true rest and joy in God, everything else pales. Everything but God is wearisome. (IC5,2,8)
     - There is powerlessness to cause the Prayer of Union at will, for the person cannot bring about another experience of union with God, who is now ALL they desire. (IC5,2,9)
     - There is a sense of exile in living in the ordinary, natural world. Persons feel estranged from earthly values and concerns and even from themselves and others. (IC5,2,8-9)
     - There is pain that they may not be entirely surrendered to God's will—not knowing for sure if they are. Any sense that the person could possibly lose God again is a complete torment. (IC5,2,10)
     - There is distress for all the ways that God is offended and not well-loved in the world.

Fifth Dwelling Places   153

- Persons cease to worry about themselves but are instead full of painful concern for others and their good. (IC5,2,10-11)
- The person can't return to their former life in the same way.
- The sufferings in these fifth dwelling places can be compared to the interior sufferings of Jesus at the Last Supper.

Teresian Teachings for Prayer and Life:

o St. Teresa says that while many are called to enter these dwelling places, few will experience some of the things that are possible in these rooms, which she experienced. (IC5,1,2)
- But St. Teresa asserts: *"How prepared God is to grant us favors now just as God has granted them to others in the past."* (IC5,4,6)

o Persons must be disposed and prepared by God, so that God can communicate this prayer to them. (IC5,1,2) It is an unmerited and inestimable gift.

o There is much to be gained or lost in these fifth dwelling places for one's self and others.
- This Prayer of Union benefits others who "catch fire" from the influence and fire of the person who has been brought to these fifth dwelling places. (IC5,3,1)
- Often God allows a person to be tested here because this person will be a light and have great influence over others. It is crucial to know of any possible weak points needing attention.

o The powers of evil are particularly operative here in trying to get a person off the path of this prayer.
- Evil can confuse a soul in little things, get the person distracted with apparent goods, or darken the Intellect/mind as to what is the good and true mind of Christ, and cool the faculty of Will's ardor to love God.

o An extraordinarily careful practice of virtue—especially love—is needed in these dwellings. (IC5,1,2)
- In the spiritual life persons are either advancing or going backwards. Vigilance is needed to avoid backsliding. There is no static Christian life!
- Any thought of offending God or of any danger of losing the Lord's company, is a complete torment. In humble fear of the Lord, persons in these dwellings must fervently petition that God sustain them, lest they should stumble again. (IC5,3,6-9)

- Here, persons cannot afford to be careless in either great or small things, otherwise they will only be crawling along, in the minimum obligation of avoiding sin, but not advancing in deeper imitation of Christ and intimacy with Him.
  - There is good attention paid to the performance of ordinary tasks.
- These people do frequent examinations of conscience and consciousness to determine if they are becoming more like Christ, or not—especially in love.
  - Self-examination can come with the pain of not knowing if they are entirely surrendered to God's will.
- There is more growth in the diminishments that God allows or sends in these dwellings than there is in the asceticism or sacrifices that persons invent and choose for themselves, and which their ego self, heretofore, had taken much false pride.
- The ego self is getting dismantled and removed as the central controller of the self.
  - Spiritual setbacks afflict the true self more than the ego or persona. The person will be exercised in practices and situations that shame and discomfort the ego self.
  - Growth in humility here can be gauged by the loosening of a propensity to try to hide faults.
  - There is an increasing ability to live with being misjudged or seen in unflattering ways, with a letting go of the need to explain or justify behavior.
  - The person becomes more uncomfortable with praise from others.
  - Instead, they will try to hide the faults of others, and to rejoice when others' virtues are known.
  - They are able to bend their will to others, even though they may lose their so-called "rights."
  - Even though human nature and the ego self still put up much resistance, persons are becoming more able to forget the self-centered attitudes of: "What's in it for me?" "How am I coming across to others?"
- Persons here feel estranged from earthly material reality and things, including themselves, and can't return in the same way to their more outwardly day-to-day worldly life that they knew before.
- Because of overwhelming joy and delight, there is desire to praise God and to endure trials for God, and they generally feel they can't do enough for God.
  - There is great desire that everyone know God and God's love for them.

- But at the same time, purification trials (the Dark Night of Spirit) are beginning to deepen. (see: "Dark Night and Purification Trials" in **Supplemental Material**) The great dismantling of unrecognized unconscious material and purification of spirit are underway.
- Though sufferings and purification in the faculties and senses continue, those sufferings don't disturb, discourage or disquiet in the same way as in earlier dwelling places. However, the purification of spirit is becoming the most intense form of suffering in the soul and these sufferings are much more agonizing and painful!
- St. Teresa suggests the silkworm's development within the secrecy of the little cocoon into a butterfly, as the metaphor for the great transformation.
  - The cocoon—the house of transformation—is Christ Himself! (IC5,2,4-7)
  - God is united with the essence of the soul *in this secret transformation.*
  - For the greater life of the butterfly one should: *"Let the silkworm die!"* (IC5,2,6)
  - Due to the effects of the life and Prayer of Union the soul will scarcely recognize itself for the changes that have occurred. It's much more even than the difference between an ugly worm and a beautiful butterfly. (IC5,2,7)
  - The person should not worry about how they do or do not understand this transformation and union. (IC5,1,11)
  - The Great Commandment, love of God and love of neighbor, must more radically be lived in greatest perfection. Love in these dwellings is costly!
- **God is putting love in order within the person here for Divine Intimacy and the birth of good works!**

"We will not reach perfection in love of neighbor if that love doesn't rise from love of God as the root." (IC5,3,8-9)

5

FIFTH DWELLING PLACES

Internalizing the Teachings: *Love, without counting the cost!*

In the fifth dwelling places St. Teresa has begun to try to explain how a soul is united more deeply in love and intimacy with God in the Prayer of Union, and to describe the demanding *life* of love that accompanies it. Though she admits that it is not possible to explain the mystery of the intimate encounter in the soul with God or what the experience is like, she is clear that it is for transformation of love of the Lord and neighbor. What she can speak about is the effects of this union. She is also very clear that suffering for the sake of love is increasing in an ever-deeper purification and transformation of the understanding and cost of love—that one must enter the dark cocoon—the abode who is Christ for this metamorphosis.

The Prayer of Union in the fifth dwelling places cannot be achieved by human effort, but those desiring to enter these dwellings can find inspiration and guidance for their spiritual life through these teachings of St. Teresa along with the help of a knowledgeable spiritual director.

Poem Reflection: (Poem #8)

Buscando A Dios	**Seeking God**
St. Teresa de Jesús	St. Teresa of Jesus

Alma, buscarte has en Mí
Y a Mí buscarme has en ti.

Soul, seek yourself in Me
And in yourself seek Me.

De tal suerte pudo amor,
Alma, en Mí te retratar,
Que ningún sabio pintor
Supiera con tal primor
Tal imagen estampar.

From such surpassing worth I may love,
Soul, to have you engraved in Me,
But not even the sagest painter
Could ever know how to so exquisitely
Imprint such an image.

Fuiste por amor criada
Hermosa, bella, y así
En Mis entrañas pintada,
Si te perdieres, mi amada,
Alma, buscarte has en Mí.

You were created for love,
Lovely, beautiful, and as that,
Imprinted in the heart of Me,
If I should lose you, my beloved,
Soul, seek yourself in Me.

Que yo sé que te hallaras
En Mi pecho retratada
Y tan al vivo sacada
Que si te ves te holgaras
 Viéndote tan bien pintada.

I know that you will find yourself
In My heart portrayed
And in such living likeness drawn
When you see yourself you will delight
To encounter yourself so well painted.

Y si acaso no supieres
Donde me hallarás a Mí,
No andes de aquí para allí,
Sino, si hallarme quisieres
A Mí buscarme has en ti.

And if by chance you do not know
Where to find Me,
Do not go here and there,
Instead, if you desire to find Me
In yourself seek Me.

Porque tú eres Mi aposento,
Eres Mi casa y morada,
Y así llamo en cualquier tiempo,
Si hallo en tu pensamiento
Estar la puerta cerrada.

Since you are My abode,
And My home and dwelling place,
I can call on you anytime whatsoever
Even if I find your thoughts
To be a closed door.

Fuera de ti no hay buscarme,
Porque para hallarme a Mí,
Bastará solo llamarme,
Que a ti iré sin tardarme
Y a Mí buscarme has en ti.

Do not seek Me outside yourself,
Because in order to find Me,
It will be enough only to call Me,
Then I will come to you without delay
And in yourself seek Me.

Reflection:
St. Teresa's Affective Life

St. Teresa was not a great poet by literary standards, and she even said she was no poet, but rather wrote some of her poems from an outpouring of feeling and passion. (L16,4) However, some of her poems will be offered in these last three dwellings because they do shed light on her affective experiences of intimacy with the Lord in these later dwelling places. The poem above was written to describe a locution she had from the Lord: "Find yourself in Me!" (Poem #8) It seemed like such a significant communication to her that she asked for some reflections from others about what they thought the words meant. (see: ST14 and Satirical Critique) Teresa's Poem #8 reveals that she came to some understanding herself of the words of the locution. And her interpretation may also have come from her mirror experience where she saw herself imprinted on Jesus. (L40,5-6)

The longing for union with others and with God is the deepest desire of every human being. At times, this fundamental longing of our restless hearts for God, is directed, symbolized and lived out in desire for union and completion with another human being, though not always in healthy ways or selflessly. No one loves perfectly—not even St. Teresa—nor without the desire to be loved in return—love for love. God also desires to be loved, Love for love—Beloved to beloved. The affective journey of love is the most important learning and development in the spiritual life. Coming to love all things, and one's neighbor in God, is the ultimate joy, freedom and fulfillment of love. All along the journey, but with special seriousness in these fifth dwelling places in which the Prayer of Union takes place, examinations of growth, maturation and deepening of love must be made more seriously.

The love-journey of prayer—the life of the friendship and intimacy with God—is for putting love in order, that is, for bringing about the conversion and transformation of all one's loves, passions and affections. It is the main work of every human being to come to love and be loved truly. It is to fulfill the Great Commandment of love of God and love of neighbor. All love is only well-ordered and life-giving if all things are loved in God—not outside of God. All along the journey, but perhaps even more seriously beginning here in these fifth dwelling places, it would be profitable to reflect on one's love-life and how it is connected to Christ's commandment to St. Teresa: "Find yourself in Me."

St. Teresa—passionate and insatiable for love—also traveled the journey of the conversion, retraining and transformation of her emotional and affective life of love—both for God and neighbor. She writes in her autobiographical *Life* that she had a very serious fault which gave her a lot of trouble. It was that if she came to realize that someone liked her, and found her attractive and loveable, she became so attached to them that she couldn't get them out of her mind. (L37,4) For a long time she experienced her own love-life as a conflict between her love of God and her love and attachments to her friends, family and social life. She finally received a locution in a Rapture that carried a grace that began to effect and resolve this conflict she had. The locution was: "I no longer want you to converse with men, but with angels." (L24,5-6) It had a profound effect on Teresa and began to free her from her dependence on the love of others. Like most human beings, she had been seeking herself in others and looking for that complete affirmation and fulfilling love from them that comes only from God. Jesus' later words to her that she find herself in Him was a further remedy for her, and the remedy for all of us.

In chapter 4 of *The Way of Perfection*, Teresa writes about love and friendship. Since Teresa was devoted to Mary Magdalene and felt a kinship with her and with St. Augustine, it seems safe to say that she must have related to them particularly on the level of their affectivity and relationships. She writes a lot about her struggles between love of God and love for "the world." She is strong in her advice that spiritual friendships with true friends of God are a necessary support for anyone wanting to live a good Christian life. Teresa had a great need to be pleasing to others, presumably to attain their love. She did have a great need to love and be loved and her *Letters* especially reveal her struggles to be freer in her relationships. And she doesn't seem to always be conscious that she herself hasn't attained the ideal that she prescribes for her nuns. She could be jealous and lament to her friends if they didn't respond as often to her letters or in the way she was hoping—love for love. She missed her friends terribly in her absences from them. The context of Teresa's charism is the love between Lover and beloved, and friendship was extremely important for Teresa. The conversion and education of desires, loves and affections is a key element of Carmelite spirituality for Teresa. She did fail at times in not following her own advice in *The Way of Perfection*, but this shows her humanity and puts her in the mix of ordinary human needs and emotions with everybody else. However, Jesus never let go of Teresa and she discovered that there was no friend or lover as helpful, desirable, loving and fulfilling as Christ.

St. Teresa knew very well the joy and "hair shirt" of love, and this is evident from her collection of *Letters*. A primary example of this struggle is her relationship with Sister Maria de San Jose, prioress of Seville Carmel. Maria was probably Teresa's most loved friend, and their relationship is quite revealing in Teresa's letters. Teresa wrote Maria that she felt that they were very close friends, and that there were few women that she enjoyed speaking and discussing things with more than Maria. (LT AP159/KK173) Teresa did love several of her friends with a special love but none more than Sr. Maria to whom she was so drawn that she wrote many times of her great love and affection: *"I love you so much more now that it amazes me, and I so long to see you and embrace you again and again."* (LT AP284/KK304) She wrote Maria: *"I really love you more than you think. I love you tenderly and want everything you do to be a success."* (LT AP309/KK331) Teresa said she just couldn't help but love Maria, and sometimes she had such longings to see her that it seemed she *"could think of nothing else, and that that is the truth."* (LT AP107/KK120) Even though Teresa had written about the danger of particular friendships (W4) it doesn't seem that Teresa herself let knowing and loving God preclude loving her friends deeply. She thought that loving her friends in God was a greater, more beneficial and more genuine love, and this didn't exclude passionate, devoted friendship for them and their well-being.

Sr. Maria de San Jose was thirty-three years younger than Teresa, but there was a continual exchange of letters between them, especially from Teresa who told Maria that her letters to Maria were the longest—four times longer—and most personal. (LT AP307/KK330) Teresa really worked at developing and strengthening their friendship and it did cost her. She wrote Maria that despite the displeasure Maria sometimes caused her, she couldn't help but love her. (LT AP307/KK330) She often complained that she wrote more letters to Maria than Maria wrote to her (LT AP143/KK158,114), and that her loneliness at missing Maria was perhaps greater than Maria's. *"I assure you I very much appreciate what you say about feeling lonely without me ... I was so delighted that I felt quite touched and forgave you on the spot. Provided you love me as much as I love you, I forgive you everything, whether in the past or the future."* (LT AP99/KK112) While Teresa was visiting Maria in Seville, it didn't seem to Teresa that Maria wanted to be with her as much as Teresa wanted to be with her. (LT AP99/KK112) *"I was treating you as one of my dearest daughters and it hurt me terribly not to find the same frankness and love in you."* (LT AP99/KK112) Because Maria saved Teresa's letters, we can see every aspect of their friendship—the affection, gifts sent, advice, humor, union in prayer, trust, complaints, reproach, teasing, and even envy, possessiveness and jealousy in Teresa! When Teresa left the nuns in Seville, but especially Maria, she needed support and consolation in her loneliness. She hoped they missed her when she left, but wrote that their grief was nothing compared to hers! (LT AP97/KK110, 237) Separation from Sr. Maria was especially difficult for Teresa and she fretted that Maria did not seem to return Teresa's love, measure for measure. (LT AP99/KK112) One wonders who could compete with the passion, strength of desire and affection of Teresa. To be fair to Maria, wouldn't she be in an awkward position being younger and a daughter—not a peer—of the famous foundress? And wouldn't she have known Teresa's thoughts and warnings about particular friendships? (W4) But Teresa didn't seem to be thinking of that as regards Maria, and let her know how delighted she was when Maria did seem to love her as much as Teresa loved her. It is a wonderment that Teresa would pick someone thirty-three years her junior for her special friend. Though perhaps because of their shared values, and Teresa's transcendent experiences, Teresa had a sense that, in God, age and gender were inconsequential in relationships. And in all fairness to St. Teresa, who was a peer of this spiritual genius?

Maria's returned love relieved Teresa and she said she enjoyed hearing of Maria's love for her in letters. She wrote that human nature wants love for love, and reminded Maria that even the Lord wanted to be well loved in return. (LT AP385/KK412; Jn. 21:15-17) There's hardly a letter to Maria in which Teresa is not concerned about Maria's health, and she said she would feel the loss of Maria the most of any of her prioresses. (LT AP369/KK395) Teresa lavished overflowing words of love on Maria, and hungered for them to be returned. She was always wanting more letters from Maria. (LT AP336/KK357,455) And the longer Maria's letters were, the happier Teresa was. (LT AP131/KK148) And Teresa found pleasure in writing to Maria even if she was very busy. (LT AP159/KK173) Teresa's complaints about the seeming inequality of their love, and her great preference for Maria may be a surprise to anyone who might think of Teresa only as a saint, and therefore, as totally different from other human beings. Her very human need for love is witness to her ordinary humanity that is like our own. She didn't really have an explanation for herself as to the mystery of her attraction for Maria. She wrote: *"I don't know why I love you so dearly."*

(LT AP369/KK395,180) Despite any disappointments in the equality and strength of Maria's love for her, Teresa's love never wavered. It seems she couldn't help herself. She did know that all relationships on this earth are imperfect, and only God's love will completely satisfy.

In her letters, Teresa used code names and nicknames for herself and her friends, and certainly pet names are a sign of special affection and intimacy. Her writings are full of the importance of friends for her. And friendship among her nuns was a hallmark of her charism where *"all must be friends, all must be loved, all must be held dear, all must be helped."* (W4,7) Teresa was very frank, spontaneous, and uninhibited in her declarations of love, though she probably never expected anyone else would be reading her letters. Teresa even reveals envy when others are seeing much more of her friends and enjoying them when she can't. After she broke her arm, Teresa was concerned that she wasn't expressing her love as well as when she wrote her letters herself, rather than by dictating them to her friend, nurse and secretary, Sr. Ann of St. Bartholomew.

Another friendship that was of utmost importance to Teresa was with the charming, if flawed, Father Jeronimo Gracian, ocd—Teresa's junior by thirty years. It was an unusual and complicated relationship. Sometimes she was mother to Gracian and sometimes daughter or sister. And he was sometimes her son (LT AP147/KK162) and sometimes Rev. Father to her, as well as her confessor and Religious Superior. Teresa's maternal instincts led her to a constant and solicitous concern for Gracian's health, safety, sleep, and moods. (LT KK254,291,213,256,272,307) And she seemed to be envious of Gracian's mother, asking him whom he loved more—his mother or her! Teresa, writing of herself in third person using a code name, Laurencia, reminded him that his mother has *"... a husband and her other children to love her... but poor Laurencia* (Teresa) *has no one else in the world, but you, Father."* (LT AP111/KK124) His absences from her were a suffering (LT AP229/KK334) and brought her loneliness, (LT AP229/KK334,390,410,465) while his visits were a joy. (LT AP269,319,397/KK290,340,426) Some of the best days of her life were being with him, and she considered him perfect for the Order and a saint. (LT AP72,78a/KK81,88) Of her friendships with other priests she described them as a *"bond only of the soul, a friendship based on the spirit!"* (LT AP78a/KK88) In another letter referring to herself in the third person with the nickname, Angela, she wrote about how her mind was still not entirely at rest about the suspicion she was entertaining that: *"... it is not to be wondered at, for she has nothing else to console her but your friendship, and she wants no other consolation than that. And she has so many trials and is so weak by nature, that she becomes distressed when she thinks her affection is not repaid. You must not be careless with her; for where there is love, it cannot slumber so long."* (LT AP290/KK311) Teresa seems not to have been disturbed or embarrassed by her affection for Father Gracian, though Father Gracian had some concern that Teresa might love him too much. But no matter what anyone thought, Teresa was not giving up her relationship with him. For her, the relationship was a *"holy of holies."* (LT AP366/KK390; see also: ST#36) She wrote to him: *"Let me have this one* [attachment] *then, for no amount of talk will ever change the way I am with you ... The knot is so tightly tied that only death will break it; and after death it will be firmer than before..."* (LT AP160/KK174) After Gracian was imprisoned and forbidden to write or speak to Teresa, she became despondent, and in her grief cried many tears. Later she shared with him the sorrow of those days: *"How well I remember last Christmas Eve and what suffering this caused me during those days just a year ago. That letter* [informing me that you could not communicate with me], *however long I live, I shall never forget it."* (LT AP296/KK317) Because of Teresa's deep love and the intimacy of her letters, she reproached him for reading some of them aloud to others. They were private, intimate, and sacred to her. He was proud that he was so well loved by the great Mother Teresa. Gracian did love Teresa more than anyone and it is reported that his dying word was: "Teresa."

It appears that Teresa was in a sort of "love triangle" with Sr. Maria and Fr. Gracian that caused her suffering. She would have wanted both Sr. Maria and Fr. Gracian to prefer and love her most. And it distressed her or caused her doubt that they may have been closer friends to each other than to her. Sr. Maria and Fr. Gracian were peers and nearer in age, and Teresa was still the foundress and "La Madre" and not a peer in the same way. So it is natural that Maria and Gracian would be drawn to each other. But Teresa always had both of them in her thoughts, and wrote Maria that: *"You will not have failed to notice that every time I write to our Fr. Gracian, I write to you, though so busy. I am astonished at it myself."* (LT AP159/KK173)

Teresa is conversational in her writings, and even more so in her letters, and she was a prolific letter writer. Since we don't have every response to St. Teresa's letters from Sr. Maria and Fr. Gracian, it is not easy to know the extent of the mutuality of these friendships. Nevertheless, from Teresa's side, the depth of her love for Maria and Gracian comes through clearly, and it wasn't merely an infatuation, but lasted for her whole life. Teresa's good friends—Sr. Maria, Fr. Gracian, (F23-24) Sr. Ann of Jesus, Fr. John of the Cross, and Sr. Ann of St. Bartholomew remained devoted to Teresa even after her death.

Probably most people who come to know of Teresa's deep and passionate love for a few friends will wonder how it fits together with her experiences of the heights of contemplation and mystical marriage with the Lord. Teresa in her relationships should dispel any ideas people have that mystics are somehow less human than they are, or different from everyone else in their struggle to love, and in their desire for union with God and others. Teresa would not have done any inappropriate activity with her friends, and allowances can also be made for her Spanish temperament and the emotive and passionate qualities of the Spanish language itself. What seems like an enigma in Teresa's affective life, or why these two people gave her the emotional, psychological, and above all, spiritual support she felt she needed, situates her as all of us, in the mystery of human attraction and affinity, that isn't totally explainable.

In her deep intimacy with Christ, Teresa also needed to "put skin" on Him, and so she always prayed through His humanity, which she could relate to and tangibly love. Teresa did enjoy deeply the gift of the human love of her friends—needed to love them present in the flesh—also with skin on. But her relationships never included any sensual carnality, but rather her deepest relationships were always founded in a spiritual relationship based in their mutual love of God. She wrote: *"I have never been able to form a deep friendship, nor find true solace, or any particular love, unless I deem them to love God and to strive to serve God."* (L24,6) Teresa's freedom and ability to both love God and her friends passionately may be pointing to what is delightfully and joyfully possible when one lives in union with God and loves from within that union of love—even if the love is sometimes humanly flawed or needy in some ways. A quote from St. John of the Cross that is focusing in Carmelite spirituality is: "In the evening of life you will be examined in love" (SLL#60), which relates to the Great Commandment that Jesus quoted: "You must love the Lord your God with all your heart, with all your soul, and with all your mind, and your neighbor as yourself." (Mt. 22:37-40)

Reflection Questions: (Choose only one or two at a time to explore in depth.)

- To move forward in union with Christ has most to do with how you love and serve. The development and retraining of desires, emotions, eros, affectivity, and learning how to love truly as Christ loves—not from self-centeredness but from other-centeredness—is the fundamental transformation, goal and end of the spiritual journey in God. It is important here with genuine candor to reflect for yourself—before God—on the history of your affectivity, love relationships and deepest desires. What have they been, and what are they now?
- What are your most important relationships? Who are these people for you? Why do you love them? How are they part of your school of learning to love?
- Do you regularly review and examine your affective life, your relationships and how you are growing in love? Take time to reflect on some aspect of your past or present affective love life that was significant for you.
- How do you define love? Are you aware of any manipulation or elements of seductiveness in your behavior?
- Have you rejected or polarized either male or female qualities in yourself?
- Do you think God understands love very differently from you?
- How do you love yourself? Do you see yourself as one of the "neighbors" to love? Do you love and respect yourself enough?
- Have you found a conflict in your love for God and your love for someone else? Have you, or do you love anyone too much? Were you ever in an unhealthy relationship?
- Were you ever in a love triangle? Have you experienced envy or jealousy in any of your relationships? Are you addicted to any relationship, or to "love" as you define it?
- Did you grow in love, or spiritually, from any such experiences, or did they adversely affect your ability to love or to trust others, or to trust in God's love for you?
- Were you ever betrayed by someone you love? How did you handle it? What were your feelings? What did you learn about yourself?
- Have you ever demanded of anyone a love they cannot give, but only God can give? Has anyone ever demanded that from you? What effect did it have on you?

- Do you have any unequal or broken relationships? If so, do these affect your trust in God's love for you? Do you bring your relationships to prayer and ask God for help with them?
- What qualities of loving do you personally bring to a relationship?
- If you were meditating on 1Cor. 13:1-8, which quality of loving would best describe you? Which would you need to better develop?
- How have any of your relational situations affected your relationship with God and your prayer life?
- What is your sense of your affective integration at this point in your life? How can you intentionally grow in love at this present time?
- Do you have a growing sense that God is your "Most Significant Other?" Do you think God desires this? Do you find any desire in yourself for this level of intimacy? Why or why not? If yes, what attracts you to this, if no, what repels?
- In these fifth dwelling places Teresa begins to use as a transformation symbol the silkworm that when perfected and transformed in the mysterious darkness of the cocoon, dies to become a butterfly. What do you think this transformation and death includes for you?

Guidance for Prayer and Prayer Periods:

- Usually this Prayer of Union only comes, if at all, after years of fidelity to prayer, to substantial time given to friendship with God in prayer, and to serious imitation of Christ.
- What has already been offered in the "Guidance for Prayer and Prayer Period" sections of the fourth dwelling places is generally what you can still use by way of being prepared and disposed for the gift of supernatural prayer in the fifth dwelling places should God desire to give this tremendous gift.
- So for your prayer periods in these dwelling places, proceed as in the fourth dwelling places, trying to quiet and recollect your senses and mind choosing from any of the following suggestions for prayer: Lectio Divina, Centering Prayer, a loving aspiratory prayer, short spiritual reading, keeping Jesus present by Simple Meditation, or any favorite vocal prayers.
- There will only be one offering of prayer guidance for the fifth dwelling places, though you may well be adding extra prayer time at this point in your prayer journey.

- Once you have entered the fourth dwelling places, and have been given contemplative prayer, generally you will already be setting aside more time for prayer, or extending the length of time in prayer and solitude, to be alone with the Lord in loving friendship.
- Though the most active and busiest among us won't be able to follow Jesus' example of going off to pray alone in solitude, or for a whole night, Jesus was a contemplative and this is an aspect of His life that must also be imitated—a true seriousness about prayer.
- As preparation for prayer, or afterwards, consider reflecting on Teresa's locution: "Find yourself in Me" and how it relates to your affective relational life of love for yourself, God and others.
- If it takes a long time to become quieted and recollected, just remain in the dryness, aridity, restlessness, or empty quiet, if it is there. If it isn't, try to calm your mind with any of the Active Recollection practices: spiritual reading, Lectio Divina, Simple Meditation with momentary loving glances at Jesus, with an aspiratory prayer of love, or with Centering Prayer in attention to your breath and a sacred word/s, or short prayer.
- What pleases God is that you be mindful of His honor and glory and forget yourself, your comfort, needs or consolations, and that you surrender any struggles in prayer into His hands.
- All the teachings so far that St. Teresa gives for the serious authentic Christian contemplative *life* that must accompany contemplative *prayer* can always be reviewed for inspiration and encouragement as needed before you enter into prayer proper.
- Wait in trusting love for the deeper drawing inward of Infused Recollection, or the Prayer of Quiet, if God desires to give it. Perhaps God will one day lead you further and deeper into the passive, supernatural, and more intense contemplation that Teresa calls the Prayer of Union.
- You can simply rest in Jesus in a loving gaze with affective energy directed at Him from a Simple Meditation, or stir up your love with a prayer that is an aspiratory outburst of love. Try to match these to feelings or circumstances in your own life at present.
- If your gaze has become fastened on the Lord in contemplative prayer—during that time—be surrendered there, and leave your soul in His hands. Let Him do whatever He wants with it, with the greatest disinterest about your own benefit, and with the greatest trust and resignation to God's will and working in you.

If needed before you begin to pray, review material on Centering Prayer, Lectio Divina, or Simple Meditation, and "How to Use this Book for Prayer."

If you decide to use one of the scriptures below, choose it before you begin prayer.

Scripture Passages:
(Life in Christ) Acts 17:28; Gal. 2:20-21, 3:26-28; 2Cor. 3:18, 5:16-20; 1Cor. 6:17-20, 12:27, 3:16-17, 12:12-13; Phil. 2:5; Eph. 2:4-10, 4:17-24; Col. 2:9-10, 3:1-4; Jn. 15:10-17, 17:13-26

(Transformation) Rom. 12:9-13, 6:8-11; Jn. 12:24-27; 1Jn. 3:2, 3:24; 2Cor. 5:16-17, 3:18; Col. 3:1-4, 9-10; Lk. 9:28-36, 15:11-32; Gal. 2:19-21; 2Tim. 2:11-13; Ezek. 36:24-29, 37:1-14

You can also use the following meditation as a recollecting reflection.

Guided Meditation:

Enter into yourself, breathe and become calm and recollected. . . . Imagine yourself going through the amazing metamorphosis of a beautiful silkworm butterfly. See yourself the size of the tiny silkworm larva—the size of a grain of pepper or of a period on this page. You don't look like much from the outside, and don't even appear as something alive. . . . But somehow by a mysterious Hand you are deposited in a safe place where a mulberry tree grows. This Someone knows exactly what you need to grow. When the leaves on the mulberry trees of your garden begin to appear in the spring, you are provided with the very food that sustains your life. Now, though you have been dormant, even apparently dead, you start to notice the mulberry leaves. You begin to come alive, eat, and grow! . . . Your special Gardener sees you—the little spec come alive and begin to grow in size, move and attach yourself securely to a branch from the mulberry tree. . . . You begin eating the mulberry leaves voraciously and growing bigger day by day. . . . To appearances you, the little larva speck, are now forming into a brown and tan stripped accordion-like caterpillar worm, actually not that attractive, but rather hairy and ugly. That is, until your first molting, where you shed your outer covering and replace it with new growth. After this first shedding you gain a smooth skin and are somewhat better looking.

More sheddings and moltings of outer skins are in store for you as you go through your life as a mere caterpillar.

One day you seem to know that it is time as a caterpillar to attach yourself with cords of silk to a twig or branch. With your inner resources, through your little mouth swaying from side to side, you begin your work of spinning out almost a mile of a continuous strand of silk, shaping it into a little brilliant yellow cave-cocoon that you encase yourself in. In the cocoon, you have put yourself into a defenseless, precarious and uncertain condition, and you can only hope that it will protect you from predator enemies during your hidden time of transformation. From the outside all now appears lifeless and still. . . .

But in this mysterious concealment within your cocoon, the great metamorphosis is happening which is completely disintegrating your former self—entirely dissolving your caterpillar body into a fluid. This occurs through a process unknown to you, secretly happening to you within the darkness of your cave-cocoon. To all appearances it seems that you, the caterpillar, have lost your former life as a worm and died! But in time, amazingly instead, you are reconfigured and emerge as a beautiful white butterfly, with a fluffy feathered-like body and wings, large dark eyes and with lovely filigreed antennae on either side of your head that expand and enrich your experience of a vaster world. From this amazing transformation process that appears like annihilation and death, you have made precious silk thread and become a beautiful butterfly. Instead of being earthbound, you can now soar and find your longed-for Mate! (IC5,2,2-9)

"... build the house wherein you will die ... I would like to point out that the house is Christ where your life is hidden with Him ... Courage! ... Be quick to do the work of weaving the little cocoon by getting rid of self-love, self-will, and attachments, instead performing deeds of penance, prayer ... and the other good works. Would to heaven that we would do what we know we must! ... Let it die; let this silkworm die ... and we will see God, and ourselves as completely hidden inside His greatness ..." (IC5,2,4-6)

Although for more than 18 years of the 28 years since I began prayer, I suffered this battle and conflict between friendship with God and friendship with the world, the Lord began to grant more spiritual riches, than I even knew how to desire. (L8,3; 10,5)

SISTER TERESA of JESUS
Mid-Life Adulthood—1555-1561

Once Sister Teresa returned in seriousness to mindful, mental prayer, and also sought spiritual direction, making herself accountable and resolutely determined to live her vocation with integrity, the Lord began to favor her with love, graces, tender delights and various gifts of mystical prayer. Within a short period of time, she was given the Prayer of Union, and by 1556 she was brought to the stage of what she terms, Spiritual Betrothal. In subsequent years, the intellectual visions and the imaginative visions of Christ were given, as well as the "transverberation" (the wounding of her heart by love), and a frightening vision of hell in 1560.

Teresa was also helped by great spiritual friends who became her directors and also later her disciples. These included Jesuits, Dominicans and Franciscans—even some who later were made saints as St. John of Avila, St. Peter of Alcantara, ofm and St. Francis Borgia, sj. Their support helped free Teresa from doubts about the source of the favors she was receiving in prayer—whether the cause was God, the devil or herself.

Before she was led to holy and learned directors and confessors, she had been suffering greatly from her first two inexperienced and youthful spiritual directors who were frightened of her experiences in prayer. That they were frightened was understandable, since it was not a good time in Church history for women to be having visions and mystical experiences, or trying to teach *men* about passive, supernatural prayer. The Spanish Inquisition was in full force and operation during Teresa's life. The Church with its enforcement arm of the Inquisition was worried about heresy and was suspicious of personal piety, devotions, and mystical experiences taking the place of the sacraments. False mystics did seem to abound and it was thought that foolish women were susceptible to the devil, to illusions, and to tempting men. Teresa was denounced to the Spanish Inquisition a couple of times, but fortunately, had the support of some of her well-respected spiritual directors and theologians who believed in the validity of her experiences and her sincerity in living her religious vocation. Had they not, she could have gone up in flames by being burned at the stake.

During the early 1560's Teresa, and a little group of relatives and friends who shared her mind, met in the Monastery of the Incarnation and spoke of their spiritual hopes and dreams. They spoke of Elijah, the man of prayer and spiritual inspiration for Carmel, and of the saints of the desert, and how, even though they couldn't go to the desert, they could found a little monastery. There, fewer nuns could live together in deeper prayer, detachment, freedom, solitude and community. Teresa had learned that the original Carmelite Rule had been relaxed and she became interested in the former, more primitive expression of the Carmelite Rule, and the first 13th century Carmelite hermits on Mt. Carmel in the Holy Land, who also lived a simplified community life. The eremitical spirit had a great appeal to her. The lifestyle she aimed at was not just that of nuns but also of hermits. (W13,6) In 1561 St. Clare appeared to Teresa and promised to help her with her undertaking of starting a smaller Carmelite monastery where Teresa and her friends could live their vocation more deeply, in less busyness and distractions, with more solitude and time for prayer, and a more intimate community life of true friendship.

6

SIXTH DWELLING PLACES

(*The Interior Castle* 6, Chapters 1-11)

Theme: *Courage! The darkness purifies for light, life and love!*

Description of the Sixth Dwelling Places:

Some aspects of the sixth dwelling places become even harder for St. Teresa to explain, not only because of the many spiritual delights and personal mystical experiences she had in prayer in these dwellings, but also because of the deepening relationship of union with God that is ultimately impossible for anyone to put into words. This includes as well God's unknowable activity in the purification trials that bring about human transformation. (see: "Dark Night and Purification Trials" and "Various Mystical Phenomena" in **Supplemental Material**) Those entering the sixth dwelling places must be forewarned that these dwellings are for those with intrepid courage! Persons here must proceed at great risk and cost—the cost of the death of the false self—a place of no self—or the end to an understanding of what was formerly thought to be the self. A new self is evolving—a Christ self that is replacing the old: "I live now not with my own life, but with the life of Christ who lives in me." (Gal. 2:20) If the following seventh dwelling places are an experience of fuller life—the Life of Resurrection on earth—the sixth dwelling places have many experiences of death—not physical death—but a dismantling of the ego, persona and small, false self. Physical death or martyrdom would actually be less painful, and easier. For the sixth dwelling places agonizingly involve the loss of everything that is not God.

Spiritual Betrothal

- There are more chapters in the sixth dwelling places than in any of the other dwellings.
- There is an open door between the fifth and sixth dwelling places. There is not a great difference in the experience of union between the two dwellings, except for the actual moment (recognized or not) of the particular mystical favor of Betrothal, and also in the *growing intensification* of the union with the ever-expanding longing and desire for deeper union with God. (IC6,4,4)
- Continuing with Teresa's correlation of the evolution of the relationship of lovers from meeting and falling in love in the fourth dwellings, to holding hands and courting in the fifth, she now arrives in the sixth dwelling places to the more serious commitment of an engagement—Spiritual Betrothal. (See also material on the fourth waters of prayer in *Life* 18-22.)
- St. Teresa uses the betrothal and marriage metaphors for describing the intimacy and deepening mutual love commitment between God and the soul. The language of Lover and beloved is the closest analogy she can think of to describe the relationship between God and the soul in the fourth, fifth, sixth and seventh dwelling places. The human understandings of betrothal and marriage—what it is to be in the relationship of bride and bridegroom—best characterizes what she means concerning the union of the soul with God in the last two dwelling places.
- A marriage proposal and agreement of betrothal is more than just the moment of "popping the question," with such questions as: "Do you love me?" "Do you have a desire to join your life and love to mine?" "Would you discern with me sharing and committing our lives together?" (And these are questions God also asks!) Thus, saying "yes" to a proposal of engagement is more than this verbal assent, and includes the *whole period of the engagement* and deepening of the relationship prior to the marriage.
  - This *state of life* following a "yes" to engagement questions, *tests the strength* of the mutual commitment for some *period of time* before the finalization and consummation of the stable and irrevocable relationship of marriage.
  - Likewise, Spiritual Betrothal is more than the moment of any intense supernatural mystical favor of betrothal within the Prayer of Union. Betrothal is a stage and period in the spiritual *life* that is an ever-

deepening friendship, intimacy and committed relationship with Christ in preparation for the permanent state of Spiritual Marriage.
- Teresa's betrothal language is very suggestive of a kind of passionate courtship, seduction and wooing of the soul by God in these later dwelling places. Her description of her own courtship and actual Spiritual Betrothal is of a kind of Divine "foreplay," and enticement of the Lord to build desire for the Spiritual Marriage union with Him.
  - This fits with Teresa's passionate and romantic nature. For her, God's love was experienced as a *fire of passionate love*, and the burning heat of it touched her soul with a *spark* of God's fire of love that was a delectable pain.
  - Teresa's own personal experience was that the actual favor of Spiritual Betrothal comes about when God *"gives the soul raptures that draw it out of its senses."* (IC6,4,2) She wrote that the precise moment of the Betrothal isn't known, though afterwards the soul is certain it has occurred.
  - She was also aware from experience that God's fire of love could overwhelm and kill a person if it continued unabated.
- During the betrothal period of the Lord's seduction and wooing of the soul, He uses delay to build passionate desire for Himself before the full union of Spiritual Marriage. (IC6,2,4)
  - This is often through the alternation of moments of union with God, as the present and passionate Lover, who then becomes the longed for, unfelt, "absent" Lover.
  - This is painful but a necessary part of the purification process. The suffering stirs in the soul an extreme desire to love the Lord in return as He loves, and in a lovesick desire and longing for total and permanent union.
- Teresa is strong in declaring that God's love is a passionate fire of love for every person and God's great desire is for union with everyone. But God's relationship will be different for each person, depending on the capacities of the person and what that soul is ready to receive. How God builds desire in attracting a person to deeper union and love is very individual, and depends on what God knows of each unique soul. Yet, God will continually be working in them to increase desire for Himself.
  - In these sixth dwellings not everyone will have Teresa's experience of the manifested and recognized moment of Spiritual Betrothal. There are souls deeply in love with God who do not have the same marked or noticed betrothal *event* and *mystical favor*, but are nonetheless brought to these dwelling places for further preparation for the habitual and permanent union of Spiritual Marriage.

- The actual mystical favor of Betrothal passes quickly and afterwards the soul remains without the same awareness of God's company. In the sixth dwellings the soul does not have the *constant awareness* of God's company that it will have in the seventh dwelling places.
  - The length of time of the betrothal period *depends on the depth of purification* the person still needs before final permanent union with God in Spiritual Marriage.
- Teresa thought that the length of time of the betrothal period before the union of Spiritual Marriage was generally shorter in duration than periods in other earlier dwelling places.
- There is an even greater integration in the sixth dwelling places between the intensification of the Prayer of Union and the *lived-life* of union in Christ. The Prayer of Union becomes a way of life. The effects of the Prayer of Union are not just experienced during the time set aside for prayer proper, but carry over into all of life.
  - Since prayer is friendship with Christ, the friendship is less about some amount of allotted time set aside for prayer, and more and more about the friendship and love that is experienced and permeates all of life.
  - The soul and Christ seek one another continually, and are united and with one another more and more, and not just during prayer.
  - This deep union will be known by its effects: the conformity of the person's will with God's, and a very serious living out of love and virtue.
- In the sixth dwelling places Teresa writes of many of the mystical phenomena—or favors—that happened to her and that are possible, though these will not necessarily or even probably happen for very many persons.
  - *"There are many holy persons who have never* [and will never] *receive one of these* [extraordinary] *favors; and others who receive them but are not holy. And do not think the favors are given continually; rather, for each time the Lord grants them there are many trials. Thus, the soul doesn't think about receiving more favors but about how to serve for what it has received."* (IC6,9,16)
  - Some of the mystical phenomena that God can give in these dwellings includes: Delightful Wounds, Enkindlings and Transverberation, as well as Suspensions of Rapture, Ecstasy, or Transport; Prayer of Jubilation and Joy (being slain in the Spirit); Flight of the Spirit (out of the body type experiences), Levitations, Locutions, Intellectual Visions, Imaginative Visions, Showings of a Truth, a Quality or Attribute that is within God and Favors of

Vehement Desires for God. (see: "Various Mystical Phenomena" in **Supplemental Material**)
- o Though the sixth dwelling places can be the dwellings of possibly greater *favors*, it is definitely the dwelling of greater *interior trials* and *purification*—the Dark Night. (see: "Dark Night and Purification Trials" in **Supplemental Material**)
  - If what trials lay ahead were fully known, many would lack determination to go forward, though the Prayer of Union of the fifth dwelling places is a support for fortitude during the betrothal period. (IC6,1,2)
- o God greatly tests the beloved before bringing her to the complete union of Spiritual Marriage. (IC6,1,1)
  - God can communicate and bring about transformation in the interior castle of the soul by many modes—either by *favors* or *trials*. (IC6,1,1)
- o Spiritual Betrothal could be experienced temporally in two different ways:
  1. Spiritual Betrothal can occur *towards the end* of God's inner work of transformation in the soul through the trials of extreme suffering and purification—the passive Dark Night of Sense and Spirit.
     - The passive Dark Night of Sense and Spirit is an ineffable Divine gift, but it will be experienced as a terrible and excruciating interior pain. (see: DN 1 & 2)
     - This process would be the purifying and testing trials *with few or no accompanying favors, consolations, or spiritual delights*, which is more intense and painful. This would be an apophatic experience of God. (see: "Apophatic and Kataphatic Journeys to God" in **Supplemental Material**)
  2. Betrothal can occur *simultaneously* (as for St. Teresa) with the interior purification of sense and spirit accompanied by occasional favors.
     - This transformation process would be experienced somewhat less painfully due to some relief in the trials because of mystical favors received. This would be the kataphatic experience.
- o To be brought into the sixth dwelling places is a gift beyond telling. Not many enter these dwelling places, nor are many intrepid enough to accept this tremendous gift, which on a feeling level will not generally be experienced as a gift at all, but rather as a possibly non-survivable trial. The person is left hanging between two excruciatingly difficult choices. It is both unimaginably hard to assent to the loss and death of self, as it is to free one's self from the overwhelming desire for union

with God that includes that dying to self. This is a dilemma, and the person is in extreme straits, with no discernable way back and no way forward. The person can only surrender in faith, trusting hope and love, with careful attention to the practice of virtue, and a total dependence on God who alone can steer the soul on the way through the death of the false self to transformation in Christ and the full permanent union of love in the Trinity.

- The betrothal experiences of union in the sixth dwelling places are still transitory and not yet permanent. The person has an awareness that the soul and God can still separate and often do. Only in the seventh dwelling places will union be experienced as permanent. (IC6,2,4)
- Between the sixth dwelling places, the rooms of Spiritual Betrothal, and the seventh dwelling places of Spiritual Marriage, the difference is as great as between those on earth who are only engaged to be married, and those two spouses who are married and can no longer be separated. (IC5,4,3-5)
- The journey will be unique for each one who enters these dwellings.

PERIOD of INTENSIFYING TRIALS (IC6,1; L20,9-16)
(see: "Dark Night and Purification Trials" in **Supplemental Material**)
(see also: *The Dark Night,* by St. John of the Cross)

- What St. John of the Cross calls the Dark Night of purification—interior trials of the soul—are also in St. Teresa's works, but not as well-developed. Some of the wisdom of St. John of the Cross regarding Dark Night purification will be included in the **Supplemental Material** because it describes in more depth other possible experiences of purification, and significantly adds to the topic of transformation.

1. The SMALLER TRIALS—EXTERIOR TRIALS—of the sixth dwellings are lesser sufferings when compared to the interior sufferings of the soul.
   - These are primarily the difficult things that happen in lived-life—losses, set-backs, failures, betrayals, deaths and disappointments of every kind.
   - Teresa mentions some of these trials that include the following: (IC6,1,3-6)
     - There are betrayals, or abandonment by friends and loved ones.
     - Many humiliations for the ego-self occur here.

- There is often gossip and judgments that one is trying to be better than others.
- There can be criticism that one is mistaken, has gone astray, and will come to a bad end.
- Both ridicule as well as the trial of unmerited praise, can occur and cause suffering.
- Certainly, the death of loved ones and worry concerning them is a trial.
- Disillusionments, failures of all kinds, serious illnesses, and bad health can be part of passive purification.

2. The <u>GREATER TRIALS</u>—**INTERIOR TRIALS**—of the sixth dwellings are those of the soul especially in the Dark Night of Spirit purification. (DN 1 & 2) Severe purification trials come as preparation to enter the seventh dwelling places. (IC6,1,15)

- These are the *interior sufferings* of the soul that are indescribable and unnamable afflictions. (IC6,1,9-15) In the midst of these trials and sufferings it seems that everything is lost. (IC6,1,3)
  - The sufferings of the sixth dwelling places can be compared to the sufferings of hell, and in the midst of them there is no consolation from anywhere. No confessor, spiritual director, friend, spiritual book or former devotions can end or ease the suffering. (IC6,1,9-10)
  - The sufferings, that are a purification in these dwelling places, are so intense that persons can feel like they are losing their minds. (IC6,1,14)
  - This Dark Night is a different darkness than depression or other sorrows which can lead to escapes, fantasizing, addiction, crutch behaviors, and various backsliding in sinful pleasures to alleviate the suffering. (IC6,1,11)
    - Dark Night trials are known to be authentic and genuine in these dwellings when there is refusal in any manner to offend God with sin.
  - Persons are not in control, and God wants this to be completely known. God is in charge of transformation. (IC6,1,12) *"... O Lord, what a great comfort to me that you did not want the fulfillment of your will to depend on a will as miserable as mine ... What a state I would be in, Lord, if it were left up to me as to whether or not your will were to be done!"* (W32,4)
  - In this Spiritual Betrothal period of trials God uses delay of the Spiritual Marriage to build desire for God. (IC6,2,1) The suffering

also greatly consists of extreme desire to love God as God loves, and in the excruciating desire for total union with God.
- In trials or favors the soul is wounded with love for the Lord—lovesick and smitten. Desire is intensified almost beyond what the person can live with. (IC6,1,1)
- Generally, it is hard to disguise the depressive affectivity, gloom, ill-temper, or low energy that afflicts these persons. (IC6,1,13)

o Teresa mentions some of these trials that include the following: (IC6,1,8-15)
- The person is totally off balance, off center, and unable to see the truth about themselves or God clearly. The mind and imagination turn against them in condemnation, critical thoughts and harshness.
- There is torment that causes doubts that one has ever been mindful of God or ever will be again. Persons question if they have ever loved God at all! (IC6,1,11)
  - Past favors, consolations or the closeness of God seem like a dream or made up. Grace is so hidden it seems not present at all.
- The interior suffering is so oppressive that the soul thinks God has rejected it. The soul feels forsaken by God.
  - For what lies ahead, the Lord wants them to know their misery and powerlessness that can only be remedied by God.
- More unconscious levels of selfishness and failings are revealed, and persons believe they are worse than ever. In the exposure of unconscious materials, they see in themselves even more sinfulness and ingratitude towards God. (IC6,7,1)
- There is heightened concern about the consequences past sins and bad choices have caused.
  - The person has a new and stronger realization of past and present sinfulness and faults which causes disturbances concerning self-worth, feelings that one is lost, with a sense of failure, meaninglessness and nothingness.
- The person feels they have not been praying, and can't pray. (IC6,1,13)
- This purification is outside the person's control, though God may unexpectedly send words or spontaneous, graced happenings that will momentarily calm the person or awaken more love with a wound of love, but these don't last. (IC6,2,2)
- There is darkened understanding that doesn't perceive the truth, but is prone to negativity and darkness.
- Ignorant spiritual directors or confessors, who misjudge the person's situation and soul, can cause doubt about God and the self, causing

fear and disorientation. They can level accusations that the person is being deceptive in confession or spiritual direction. (IC6,1,9)
    - It is a great trial for persons to be unable to adequately describe to a spiritual director, confessor, or counselor their inner state, with the worry that they may be deceiving them and being dishonest.
- There is a perception of inner war, chaos and oppression, often with strong, painful experiences of evil—especially temptations to impurity/fornication, blasphemy and all manner of spiritual questions, doubts and disorientation. (DN1,14)
- Both being with others and alone is hard to bear.
- Being in solitude is difficult, and feels more like only being alone with the miserable self. There is much difficulty with prayer. The mind is generally incapable of staying with vocal or mental prayer, or making sense of it. The person feels helpless and impotent in being able to pray, and the attempts to pray seem to cause more darkness. (IC6,1,13)
- With foreboding the person senses that there may be even deeper sufferings to come. The prolonged period of suffering with no end in sight adds to a further suffering in hopelessness and near despair.
- The trials of the Dark Night have duration, and the experience may last for one year, to ten years or even for most of a lifetime (as for St. Therese of Lisieux or St. Teresa of Calcutta).

Teresian Teachings for Prayer and Life:

o Any who are in these sixth dwelling places must realize in humility that they have not deserved the holy favors or holy trials of these extraordinary dwelling places. The graces of these dwellings are freely given to them from the Lord's extravagant mercy and love. They must trust that He knows what they need, when and how, and all is for their good and benefit—*no matter how it seems or feels.*
  - Human feelings are no indications of God's hidden presence or workings in the soul.
o As best they can, disregarding feelings as guides, each must continue to faithfully set aside time for the Lord in solitude and prayer even if these are a suffering. These persons must be faithful to pray as they can, detached from both understanding their prayer or what is going on.

- In dealing with particularly destructive feelings and dark afflictions, or resistance in prayer, one can choose to engage in some external works of charity instead. (IC6,1,13)
  - They can also pray for the strength to endure and to cooperate with their own God-guided purification and transformation journey.
  - For encouragement and support, they should try to recall past favors and signs of love from the Lord and His past fidelity that can be counted on always.
  - They can remind themselves that in these dwellings, persecution or false blame need not disturb, because these can provide an opportunity for the soul to grow in strength and humility.
    - They can choose to ignore both the stinging gossip of others or their praise, and pay no more attention to good comments than to the bad. (IC6,1,4) "… *What would it matter, when you are in the arms of God if the whole world blames you!*" (W16,10)
    - Persons can try to accept with humility and allow God to use whatever others say of them—including glowing praise. God can use that to inspire or benefit others.
  - God is the only one who knows the full truth concerning the soul of every person. Trials and persecutions benefit the soul and help it gain. (IC6,1,5)
    - If these persons are intent to look only after the honor and glory of God, rather than their own, it will lessen the pain and misunderstanding.
  - Everyone is provided with occasions to grow in love of enemies and persecutors. One should even try to cultivate a special and tender love for all persecutors. They are often greater friends and more advantageous than those who speak well of us. (IC6,1,5) Love your enemies!
  - In these times of trial and darkness there is no remedy but to wait for the mercy of God, who alone saves, transforms, and heals all sufferings and hurts. (IC6,1,10)
  - The call is to strive to surrender in a dark faith, hope and love whenever possible.
  - In this Dark Night state, grace is so hidden it seems not present at all, but continue to trust it is there, and do not in discouragement backslide and offend God. (IC6,1,11)
  - Change any unhelpful spiritual directors or confessors for more knowledgeable and experienced ones. "… *a good means for having God is to speak with His friends.*" (L23,4) "… *For a sick person it is a great help to find another stricken by it, too. It is a great comfort to know that*

one is not alone. ... The two are a help to one another in their sufferings ..." (L34,16)

o Remember that when things seem out of control, the Lord may unexpectedly send words or graced happenings that will restore peace and calm, with an experience of the closeness of God again. God does not abandon. He is *closer than ever*, though His closeness can feel like blinding darkness. (LF1,20-22)

"*O, how everything that is suffered with love is healed again!* (W16,7)
"*... God will not abandon you if you do not leave Him.*" (W26,10)

6

SIXTH DWELLING PLACES

<u>Internalizing the Teachings:</u> *Let the transformation be done to me!*

The sixth dwelling places deal with the great purification for transformation that God works in the soul, with the exterior trials, and particularly, the interior trials that accompany the purification. This is a time of testing the seriousness of the Spiritual Betrothal relationship in preparation for the union of Spiritual Marriage of the seventh dwelling places. Direction is given for how to respond to living through these great sufferings. In these eleven chapters, St. Teresa also describes some of the mystical favors that awaken the soul to deeper and more vehement love, which can also occur in these dwellings, though most people would not necessarily experience many or even any of them. The longing and desire for God is so great that those in these dwellings will feel they are dying of love, and the discomfort makes them want to get out of their own skin to be united and one with God in fulfillment and complete satisfaction of love and desire. But no one can remedy the situation themselves, and no one else has a cure for their lovesickness either. They can only wait for God to complete the work that needs to be done in them for the fuller union of Spiritual Marriage of the seventh dwelling places.

Poem Reflection: (Poem #1)

Vivo Sin Vivir En Mí	**I Live Without Living in Myself**
St. Teresa de Jesús	St. Teresa of Jesus

Vivo sin vivir en mí,
Y de tal manera espero,
Que muero porque no muero.
Vivo ya fuera de mí,
Después que muero de amor,
Porque vivo en el Señor,
Que me quiso para sí.
Cuando el corazón le di
Puso en él este letrero:
Que muero porque no muero.

Esta divina prisión,
Del amor con que yo vivo,
Ha hecho a Dios me cautivo.
Y libre mi corazón
Y causa en mí tal pasión,
Ver a Dios mi prisionero,
Que muero porque no muero.

¡Ay, que larga es esta vida!
¡Que duros estos destierros
Esta cárcel y estos hierros
En que el alma está metida!
Sólo esperar la salida
Me causa un dolor tan fiero,
Que muero porque no muero.

¡Ay, qué vida tan amarga
Do no se goza el Señor!
Porque si es dulce el amor,
No lo es la esperanza larga.
Quíteme Dios esta carga,
Más pesada que el acero,
Que muero porque no muero.

Sólo con la confianza
Vivo de que he de morir,

I live without living in myself,
And in such a manner do I hope,
For I am dying because I do not die.
I still live outside of myself,
Since I am dying of love,
Because I live in the Lord,
Who wants me for Himself.
When I gave my heart to Him
I put to Him this notice:
For I am dying because I do not die.

This divine prison,
Of love wherein I live,
Has made God captive to me.
And frees my heart
And causes in me such a passion,
To see God my prisoner,
For I am dying because I do not die.

Oh, how long this life is!
How hard these banishments!
This prison and these iron chains
In which my soul is fastened!
Longing only for a way out
Causing me a pain so fierce,
For I am dying because I do not die.

Oh, how bitter is this life
Without enjoyment of the Lord!
Because His love is so sweet,
Lengthy waiting for it is not.
Deliver me, God, from this burden,
More heavy than steel,
For I am dying because I do not die.

Only with confidence
That I will die, do I live,

Porque muriendo el vivir	Because dying is to live
Me asegura mi esperanza.	And hope assures me of this.
Muerte do el vivir se alcanza,	Death is the attainment of life,
No te tardes, que te espero,	Do not delay, since I hope in you,
Que muero porque no muero.	*For I am dying because I do not die.*
Mira que el amor es fuerte.	See how strong love is.
Vida, no me seas molesta.	Life, do not disturb me anymore.
Mira que sólo me resta	See only what it leaves to me
Para ganarte perderte.	In order to gain yourself lose yourself.
Venga ya la dulce muerte,	Come now sweet death,
El morir venga ligero.	Let death come swiftly.
Que muero porque no muero.	*For I am dying because I do not die.*
Aquella vida de arriba,	That life from above,
Que es la vida verdadera,	That is true life,
Hasta que esta vida muera,	Until this life dies,
No se goza estando viva.	One cannot enjoy living.
Muerte, no me seas esquiva;	Death, do not be elusive to me;
Viva muriendo primero,	In first dying, may life come to be,
Que muero porque no muero.	*For I am dying because I do not die.*
Vida, ¿que puedo yo darte	Life, what can I give to you,
A mi Dios, que vive en mí,	To my God, who lives in me,
Si no es el perderte a ti,	If it is not to lose you,
Para merecer ganarte?	In order to deserve to gain you?
Quiero muriendo alcanzarte,	I want dying so as to reach you,
Pues tanto a mi amado quiero:	Because I want you so much my love:
Que muero porque no muero.	*For I am dying because I do not die.*

Reflection:

Christ, Our Mirror of Love—"Find yourself in Me"

St. Teresa's poetry is not of the caliber of St. John of the Cross'. It is not as elegant or artistic, but it is also not doggerel in conveying her passionate longing desire for complete union with God. There is no mistaking the lovesick pain of love and desire in this poem.

Much of the suffering of these sixth dwelling places can be likened to the betrothal of engaged couples who are experiencing the intensity of their love in the desire to consummate their relationship and join their lives together permanently so that they are never without the enjoyment of each other's company, love and support. St. Teresa does speak of this dying from unconsummated, unfulfilled love in her poem: *Vivo Sin Vivir En Mi* (*I Live Without Living In Myself*). She refers to her dying of love as a prison— as an isolation and confinement away from the love she passionately desires that continues to well up in her heart, with a terrible and unbearable longing that feels like dying from wanting the Beloved so intensely. Though the love of God is ultimate satisfaction and sweetness, waiting for its completion is not, and life is so burdensome that it seems it would be a relief just to die and finally be united fully to God.

Regarding deepening intimacy with the Lord in these dwellings, Teresa writes that she thinks it is most beneficial for recollection and union to imagine and ponder the Lord as very deep within your soul. Such a thought is much more alluring and efficacious than thinking of Him as outside of yourself. She taught, and it is in agreement with what Jesus desires, that we find Him within. (Jn. 14:17; 15:4) Jesus desires the deepest form of co-mingling—His interiority and Spirit with our interiority and spirit. And so Christ dwelling within yourself, is very clearly the best place to look for Him. And in prayer, look for Him in His humanity. Teresa was adamant that Christians pray through the humanity of Christ! (see: "Praying through the Humanity of Christ" in **Supplemental Material**) It's not necessary to go to heaven or anywhere else than your own self to find Him. To look for Him outside of yourself is tiring for your spirit, distracts your soul, isn't as much support, and doesn't yield as much fruit. (L40,5-6)

St. Teresa did at one point hear the locution from Jesus saying: "Find yourself in Me." (Poem #8; ST14) And the mirror experience of seeing herself in Christ must have been something like how we describe the bonding and mirroring between a baby and its mother. The baby learns about itself, its beauty and loveableness, from the love that is mirrored to it in its mother's loving face. This is analogous to how Teresa came to see who she really was, how beautiful her interior was, and how loveable she was as loved by Christ. Finding our true identity, beauty, worth, dignity and loveableness is the desire of God who also longs to be gazed at in love in the mutual gaze of Lover and beloved. Jesus longs to be loved. Jesus asked Peter three times if he loved Him. Peter answered that he loved Jesus with the Greek word for friendship love. But Jesus asked the question with a Greek word for love that means more than friendship. (Jn. 21:15-17) Jesus wants to be even more than a friend.

Reflection Questions: (Choose only one or two at a time to explore in depth.)

- How truly can you pray, "Let it be done to me—Your will, not mine?" (W32)
- If you daily consciously tried to incorporate the will of God into your decisions and choices how would this change your life?
- What aspects of your choices and behavior indicate to you that you are doing God's will?
- How do you experience trials, purifications, setbacks, failures, or humiliations in your life?
- How obedient are you to the purifications and sufferings in your life? How do you view the pattern of Christ's life of dying and rising in relation to your own story? Is one aspect or another of the Paschal Mystery—either the death or the resurrection aspect—out of balance for you? Do you value, practice, or emphasize one more than the other?
- Do you tend to resist and fight against setbacks and trials, or do you surrender in faith to them, and to the Lord's work in you through them?
- Have you ever felt abandoned or forsaken by God? What has been your greatest anguish and suffering in life? How did you respond to God in these situations?
- What sorts of experiences can trip you up and pull you off center into discouragement or questioning of your faith or God's love for you?
- Though you may be conscious of faults you are working on to change, are there unconscious and dark aspects of yourself that you sense are there, but refuse to bring to consciousness and admit?
- Has anyone pointed out something to you about yourself that felt threatening, that you reacted to with strong emotion?
- How do you view asceticism? Is it only denying yourself something—as fasting from critical thinking, judgments, complaining, food, alcohol, or entertainment? Or, do you ascetically also add something positive to do in your life—as engaging in the corporal or spiritual works of mercy, or adding more solitude and prayer time to your life, or keeping a peaceful, accepting, gentle and positive attitude around other people?
- Do you tend to think of purification trials as a gift, punishment, bad luck, or fate? Do any of them feel like your fault, while others seem to be fastened on you from outside of yourself? Do you have a faith stance towards dark times that sustains you? Have you ever thought of these trials as a gift?

- Have you ever felt you were dying of love and desire to be completely united with the Lord?
- Which emotions are most uncomfortable for you and give you the most trouble? What do you do with feelings like anger, fear, envy, lust, jealousy, discouragement, or alienation? Can you accept them and honor them for the information they are giving you about yourself and your situation, without necessarily acting them out?
- What is your worst-case scenario? In faith do you think you could live serenely and acceptingly through it? What would be, or are now, your deepest sorrows or joys? Do you think you have experienced the peak of either sorrow or of joy?
- What do you think Jesus' "peace beyond understanding" means?
- If you use the **Guided Meditation** at the end of this section, when you look in the mirror what do you see? Do you see yourself in the image and likeness of Christ? Do you see Him imprinted in you? Do you see yourself imprinted in Him? Can you look in the mirror and say "I love you" to yourself?

Guidance for Prayer and Prayer Periods:

- At this stage of the journey through the dwelling places, more of your prayer and life will be outside of your control. However, you do have control over your choice to surrender and let the Lord direct your prayer and life as He desires.
- Obviously for betrothal union there are no techniques or methods of prayer that can bring about this tremendous union of Spiritual Betrothal or the Prayer of Union. Nor are there any methods you can use to bring relief from the purification and death of your false self. It is God's sovereign will alone how this needs to come about for you. Your part is to agree to the purification, and to surrender to it. It is God's work which you have to undergo without control over it.
  - However, you could still backslide and refuse to cooperate in the purification and lose all the good that has been gained. But this would be foolish, and would not take away the pain of the purification, or the desires for God's total love. You will also not find peace or be happy if you refuse God's work in you.
- When you do try to pray, you may well feel as though you haven't been praying at all, or that your prayer seems meaningless as well as not

particularly well-understood. This is not the time for Discursive Meditation prayer, which will feel wearisome. And because the faculties are generally incapable of that practice from being so near to the Lord, you may not recognize that you are praying or that He is near. (IC6,1,13)

- By now you have a strong habit of praying, and a life of prayer. Jesus has always been with you, and you speak with Him throughout the day. Now you may wonder if you are speaking only to yourself. As Jesus comes to be recognized more and more as your true self, it *is* both He and you that are in communion and communication. There is little separation. You are coming to know more deeply that your true self has always been in His image and likeness.
- Even though you may be low in energy, as best as you can, pay even greater attention to virtue and to the living out of the theological virtues of faith, hope and love. No matter what, do not give up prayer!
- Patiently wait for God who is secretly working in your soul for transformation. Unexpectedly with one word alone, or a chance happening, God can calm the storm within you. (IC6,1,10)
- Too much solitude in Dark Night experiences can cause greater harm. (IC6,1,13) Sometimes the best and only response is to involve yourself in external works of love.
- In radical hope and trust, throw yourself on the mercy of God. The great purification and transformation of the Dark Night is God's mercy, though a "hell of mercy" (Isaac of Stella), and generally experienced more as absence, anger or punishment from an incomprehensible God.
- Remind yourself that these trials are for your transformation and preparation for entering the seventh dwelling places—the life of the Spirit and the Life of Resurrection on earth.
- **Pray always through the humanity of Christ Jesus!** (IC6,7,5; L22; W29,4-8) (see and review: "Praying through the Humanity of Christ" in **Supplemental Material**)
- There is nothing more to add as a suggestion for your times of prayer. All that has been offered thus far for prayer is at your disposal now to use to deepen your intimacy with God.
- Pray as you can, and make your responses to the Lord and to your life situation a stance in trusting faith, hope and love, and dependence on Him.

The following scriptures can be a support in darkness and trials. If you want to use one as part of your prayer period choose one before you start.

Scripture Passages:
(In Suffering) Rom. 8:18-27, 12:12; 2Cor. 12:9-10; Lk. 9:23-26; Jn. 16:20-22, 15:1-7, 14:1-3; Mk. 8:34-37, 15:29-39; Mt. 27:45-50; Phil. 3:7-13; Heb. 4:12-13; Ps. 3, 16, 22, 23, 25, 42, 43, 51, 62, 77, 88, 140; 1Kgs. 19:1-8; Lam. 3; Sir. 2; Jb. 3:3,20-26; Ecc. 3:1-8; Eph. 6:10-20; 1Pt. 5:5-11
(Let it be Done) Mt. 12:46-50, 26:36-46, 6:10; Mk. 3:31-35, 14:32-42; Lk. 1:26-38, 22:41-46, 11:1-4; Jn. 4:34-38, 5:30, 6:38-39; 1Pt. 4:1-2; Ps. 143:10
(Mirror/Image of Christ) 1Cor. 13:12; Jm. 1:22-25; 2Cor. 3:7-18; Col. 3:5-11; 1Jn. 3:2
(Mystical Experiences) Lk. 9:28-36, 24:13-35, 24:36-43; Mt. 14:22-33, 28:1-10, 17:1-8; Mk. 16:9-14; Jn. 20:11-18, 20:19-29, 21:1-14; Acts 1:6-12, 9:1-19; 1Cor. 15:3-8; 2Cor. 12:1-10

You can use the meditation below for self-knowledge, recollection, or for pondering if helpful. It is connected to some of the **Reflection Questions** above.

Guided Meditation:

Reflect on the following based on an experience St. Teresa had when she saw herself imprinted in Christ. Recollect yourself as you are able by calming breaths and presence to yourself. . . . Enter into your interiority and begin to imagine your soul to be like a brightly polished mirror, but without back or sides or top or bottom—everywhere you look is an infinite, sparkling clear mirror. As you begin looking up, down, and to the sides which recede into infinite horizons, realize that you are looking at your very soul and at the same time at Christ! Imagine Him looking out from within the unsubstantial mirror that is your interior—is your soul. Within this "place," see both Christ and yourself *within* each other as well as *distinct* from one another—somehow indwelling one another. See yourself and Him clearly in every part and space of your crystal-clear mirrored soul. . . . And then recognize that the mirror is somehow also completely impressed upon the Lord Himself—where He dwells. He and you are both there where you are and where He is! (L40,5) You are within one another! . . . Listen to Him for any loving communications, especially an understanding that there is no space or time where He does not indwell you always. . . . He is always present, giving you being, living your life with you, and loving you. . . . Recognize with new understanding that it is only any failings to love and imperfections on your part that *obscures* your vision, and prevents you from seeing this reality.

"With these trials and all the rest that were mentioned, what peace can the poor little butterfly have? All of these are meant to increase the desire to enjoy the Spouse, and His Majesty, as one who knows our weakness, is enabling the soul through these trials and many others to have the courageous intention to be joined with so great a Lord and take Him for its Spouse." (IC6,4,1)

One day, after communion, His Majesty earnestly commanded me to work with all my might for this new monastery, and made me wonderful promises that it would be founded, and that He would be highly served in it. He said it should be called St. Joseph's, and that the saint would watch over us at one door, Our Lady at the other, that Christ would remain with us, and that it would be a star shining with great splendor. (L32,11)

SISTER TERESA OF JESUS
Mature Adulthood—1562-1566

Even though the desire was there among Sister Teresa and her friends concerning their inspiration for a more serious form of religious life, with more time for the solitary prayer, it wasn't coming to fruition. Teresa was living a comfortable and settled life at her Monastery of the Incarnation and realized that if she tried to bring about her vision, she would be facing ridicule, outcry, derision and resistance. But one day after communion the

Lord appeared to her and commanded her to move forward as best she could with the new monastery. Teresa quietly bypassed her Provincial and Bishop and obtained a Patent from Rome for the new foundation. She had her brother-in-law secretly handle getting the building for the monastery. Teresa had to resort to subterfuge quite often in founding her monasteries. She was right about the trouble to ensue from her ideas for a more serious Carmelite life. Teresa was 47, when on August 24, 1562, she established the Monastery of San Jose. When it was discovered, there was a riot in the town of Avila with lawsuits against Teresa and her community. But in a few years these ended as the townspeople became devoted to Sister Teresa of Jesus and her nuns.

At this time, it was Teresa's Dominican spiritual directors who ordered and supported her in writing an account of her life, prayer and experiences. Providentially in 1561, and for two years afterwards, Teresa had had an uninterrupted experience of the humanity of Christ which deepened her love relationship with Him, energized her, and inspired her with confidence for the writing of her autobiographical *Life* despite the shadow of the Inquisition. The first edition of her *Life* was written in 1562 and later redacted by 1565. The book was confessional, with the struggles of her life, and thus was semi-secret, and not meant to be published. It also contained much valuable teaching on mystical prayer. During Teresa's lifetime the book was always in the hands of the Inquisition!

The five years Teresa lived at her reformed Monastery of San Jose were some of the happiest of her life. She and her little band of nuns lived the evangelical counsels of poverty, chastity and obedience, as well as a balance of solitude and community, work and recreation, and vocal and contemplative prayer. Following the Carmelite Rule, they tried to live in deep friendship and allegiance to Christ. Teresa wanted her daughters to live in smaller communities where Sisters were friends and equals—where each would be loved, held dear and helped. She did not want her nuns to be caught up in concerns for reputation, honor, or the Spanish value of "purity of blood." She wanted a less complicated life—poorer, simpler, freer and detached from what was not necessary—but never austerity for itself. She simplified the Divine Office for more personal prayer time with the Lord. She sought a joyful life of affability, gentleness and celebrations. Her nuns engaged in spiritual combat with the darkness of their own hearts for the sake of opposing evil in the world. They earnestly sought continual renewal, transformation, and the intimate union of love with the Lord. They looked for God's desire in all things. Everything they did, and all their prayer, which was their apostolate, was for the sake of the Church and world. As the foundation for prayer and relationship, Teresa emphasized only three things for her daughters: love of God and neighbor, humility as truth about themselves, and detachment from both themselves and from whatever left them enslaved and unfree for love of God and neighbor.

Because Sister Teresa now had Carmelite daughters to form in her conception of Carmelite life, she needed material they could refer to for their formation. In 1563 she wrote her *Constitutions* laying out her vision of Carmelite life, and in 1566 she wrote her first redaction of *The Way of Perfection*. It was her nuns at San Jose who wanted to have in writing the counsels, spiritual wisdom, and teachings that Mother Teresa had often spoken about with them. Again, it was her Dominican confessor who ordered a resistant Teresa to undertake the task of writing this book

7

SEVENTH DWELLING PLACES

(*The Interior Castle* 7, Chapters 1-4)

Theme: *Intimacy and Union with God!*

Description of the Seventh Dwelling Places:

These dwellings are the center of the soul where Christ alone dwells. They are the dwelling places of the prayer and *life* of intimacy of the Spiritual Marriage union between the soul and God, (IC7; ST31 & 46) where the Lord brings the soul to His own home and dwelling place within the center of the soul, and where He joins the soul to Himself—spirit to Spirit. (IC7,1,5) Here the two are permanently joined together. Teresa uses the analogy, imagery and language of the intimacy of human marriage as the best way to describe and understand the state of transforming union—of Spiritual Marriage. It is a tremendous favor that the Lord has revealed to anyone, as He has to St. Teresa, what depth of loving intimacy and union with God is possible in this life—which is a true taste of heaven on earth. (IC7,2,3) These dwelling places, though very interior, are not some small, remote corner of the soul, but a whole interior world where there is infinite space with many compelling, attractive and beautiful rooms for delighting in God.

- At a time the Lord knows best, He takes pity on the soul for what it has suffered in its painful desires of love in previous dwelling places. And before the union of Spiritual Marriage is consummated and made

permanent, He brings the soul into *His own dwelling place* within the soul's *center*. (IC7,1,5; 7,2,9)
- Here the soul is given greater favors—a taste of the glory of heaven itself. And even though it seems that the merciful favors and union the soul has already been given are vast, God is without limit, and desiring to give in these dwelling places more than can even be imagined! (IC7,2,3)
- Truly persons now come to know and rightly value their own souls and the deep secrets that lie within them! (IC7,1,1)
- The Spiritual Marriage union is a harmony, likeness and fusion between God, and God's qualities, with the soul.
- In the center and substance of the soul—in the intimate complexity of spiritual and psychological being—the person is brought into union with God. The soul somehow experiences great delight, and feels and "sees" itself so near and intimate with God. (IC7,1,5)
- Spiritual Marriage is both an *event and state* of accomplished union, and a *process* of developing union that never ends. Spiritual Marriage is not completed in this life. It is a growing relationship going on into Eternal Life in the Beatific Vision. (IC7,2,1-3)
  - Between Spiritual Betrothal and Spiritual Marriage, the difference is as great as between those who are merely betrothed, and those who are married on earth and can no longer be separated. (IC7,2,2)
  - The union and favors of Spiritual Marriage are very different from Spiritual Betrothal, which for Teresa included many mystical experiences such as the Suspensions of Rapture, Ecstasy, Transport, etc. It is also different from other less intense Prayer of Unions or spiritual favors. (IC7,1,5; 7,2,3) But the doorway is open between the sixth and seventh dwelling places, and the Lord can give any favors He chooses.
- The whole person—body, interior faculties, and senses—share in the comfort of this union. (IC7,2,6) But when the actual Spiritual Marriage union occurs, the soul is made blind and deaf to the perception of the nature and kind of favor the joining is. That is, all faculties and senses are lost in the actual moment of joining in Spiritual Marriage.
- Spiritual Marriage can include the experience of a kind of consummation or intense period of spiritual delights—Suspensions as Ecstasy or Rapture—that are felt both in the body and the spirit.
  - This is not universally experienced by mystics, and *not necessary* for full Spiritual Marriage union.
- As earthly marriage is more than the activity of sexual consummation, so is Spiritual Marriage more than Raptures or other spiritual delights.

- The life of Spiritual Marriage is not about spiritual delights, Rapture or Ecstasy, but is a union of the human spirit to the Holy Spirit in the substance of the soul.
- In these dwellings, for the most part, Raptures and Transports are taken away and don't occur in public. (IC7,3,12)
- In these dwellings the person is indifferent and detached from spiritual delights, and consolations, or rewards.

o Though these dwellings are not necessarily a state of extraordinary, visible mystical favors, it is a state of lofty contemplation and some understanding of God's perfections.

o There are almost never any experiences of dryness or interior disturbances as were present in other dwelling places. The soul is almost always in quietude. (IC7,3,10) And the soul and God rejoice together in the deepest silence. (IC7,3,11)

- The silence experienced in the interior faculties has permeated the person's whole being with peace, serenity and stillness.
- The soul rests continually in God's embrace all day long, and the Divine Presence radiates from the center of the soul, but without the interior and exterior faculties and senses being distracting, noisy or absorbed.
- Christ is the Word, but God the Father is known and experienced primarily in silence.
- Previously, the Prayer of Union was experienced only when God granted it, but now when the time for formal prayer comes—presupposing a life of fidelity to virtue—the person can enter into the silence of the interior faculties at will.

o When the soul is brought to God's Dwelling Place, there is first a enkindling of love in the spirit in a magnificent splendor, in which Christ, and the Three Persons of the Blessed Trinity are revealed to the soul! (IC7,1,6) Union in this dwelling comes differently than in other unions. It is more like scales being removed from the soul's eyes, so that in a strange way the favors and revelations of heavenly things that are being granted are seen and experienced. (IC7,1,6)

o The first time the *mystical favor* of Spiritual Marriage is granted, the Lord usually shows Himself to the soul through an Imaginative Vision of His most Sacred Humanity. (IC7,2,1)

- This Imaginative Vision is making it clear to the soul *Who* the union is with—the Lord, Jesus Christ. (IC7,2,1) (see: "Imaginative Visions" in **Supplemental Material**)

- The vision may be of the Risen Christ in splendor, beauty, and majesty which confirms the favor. (IC7,2,1) Here, the Lord also spoke words to Teresa along with the vision. (IC7,2,2)
- Christ is seen here in the *interior* of the soul where other visions do not occur—except the Intellectual Vision of the Trinity. (IC7,1,6) (see: "Intellectual Visions" in **Supplemental Material**)
- It is an experience that conveys that what belongs to Christ now belongs to the soul also, and that Christ will take care of what belongs to the person. (IC7,2,1)
- This vision, though similar to past visions of the Lord, is so different that it leaves the soul stupefied and frightened, for this vision comes with greater force. (IC7,2,2)

o Once the Imaginative Vision of Christ in His humanity in the center of the soul has made clear to the faculties and senses of the body Who is uniting to the soul, it is followed by an Intellectual Vision of the Lord in the center of the soul that is much more delicate, secret and sublime, giving heavenly delight to the soul to which nothing can compare. (IC7,2,3)
- The marriage union is accomplished secretly as a mystery to human understanding, and also secretly in that no one knows exactly when it happened.

o It isn't possible to explain much about this sublime experience. All St. Teresa can say is: "*The soul, I mean the spirit, is somehow made one with God.*" (IC7,2,3)

o It causes a likeness between the Lord and the person, and the very love with which the person loves is like the love of God, and flows from participation in God's own love.
- "Anyone who is joined to the Lord is one spirit with Him." (1Cor. 6:17) The soul's life is now Christ's. Here, even the little butterfly has died and taken on Christ as its life. (IC7,2,5)

o There is the greatest difference between all previous visions and those of these dwelling places.
- Intellectual Visions in these dwelling places are more delicate and sublime than those mentioned in the sixth dwelling places.
- In the fifth and sixth dwelling places it doesn't seem to the soul that it is called to enter into its center, as in the seventh dwellings, but rather to enter into something more like "the superior part" of the soul. (see: "Soul and Spirit" in **Supplemental Material**)
- In the fifth and sixth dwellings the person is joined to God in ways that aren't understood, because the faculties are becoming lost, and

Seventh Dwelling Places **203**

perception of the nature and kind of favors being enjoyed aren't understood as in the seventh dwelling places. (IC7,1,5-6)
- o In the seventh dwelling places the Trinity, itself, is revealed in an Intellectual Vision. (IC7,1,6)
- o In these dwellings all three Persons of the Trinity communicate themselves, speak to the soul, and explain the assurances of Christ that He, the Father, and the Holy Spirit will come to dwell with the soul that loves Him and keeps the commandments. What has been held in creed and faith, is now understood through spiritual "sight!" (IC7,1,6)
  - Of this union Teresa says: *"What a difference there is from hearing and believing the contents of faith from knowing how true these are!"* (IC7,1,7)
- o The soul understands some things about the Trinity itself *"by a representation of truth in a particular way"*—through an Intellectual Vision! (IC7,1,6)
  - The soul understands that there are three distinct Persons in the Trinity, and that the Three Persons are one Substance, one Power, one Knowledge—One God alone.
    - In this state there is no more thought of the body than if the soul were not in the body.
    - Thoughts are only concerning the spirit and union within the very interior center of the soul, where God dwells. (IC7,2,3)
  - The presence of the Trinity is *felt most fully* when it is revealed the first time, but also at other times when God grants the soul this favor.
    - If the Divine Presence were felt clearly all the time, the soul would find it impossible to be engaged in service or to live among other people in an earthly manner. (IC7,1,9)
  - Every day the soul becomes more amazed since the Trinity never leaves it anymore, and the person clearly beholds that the Trinity is within the soul in its extreme interior—some place very deep within. (IC7,1,7)
  - Up to this point, everything that took place had come by means of the senses and faculties—including the appearance of the humanity of Christ. (IC7,2,3)
- o Since the Presence of God and the perception of the Presence of God—the Trinity—*never departs* from the soul, the soul finds itself in the company of the Trinity every time it chooses to take notice! (IC7,1,9)
  - If the soul doesn't fail in being present to the Lord, He will never fail to make His presence clearly known to the soul. (IC7,1,8)
    - It is not in a person's power to "see" the Trinity whenever desired, but only when the Lord desires that the window of the

interior faculty of the Intellect be opened to "see." It is something like being with someone in the light and then having the light taken away. One knows the person is still there. (IC7,1,9)
- Through this wonderful company of Christ, the soul is prepared for more favors and growing likeness to Christ. (IC7,1,10)

o In these dwellings there is the TRANSFORMATION of the whole person into the likeness of Christ. The old false self has died and there is a new life in Christ.

o The soul's life is Christ in these dwellings, and the effects of this are better understood as time passes. (IC7,2,5-6)
- Death of the small false self and *self-forgetfulness* is the new mode of being and loving.
- To make the silk, both the worm and butterfly had to die. The butterfly died because its life is now Christ's.
- The experience conveys that what belongs to Christ now belongs to the person. The will and desires of God, and the will and desires of the soul are one and the same, and united in love, purpose, desire and action.
- Teresa's actual experience was that what she wanted was what God wanted, and what God wanted was what she wanted! Their wills were completely aligned.

o In these dwellings the soul is divinized and becomes like God through likeness and participation in God.
- Faculties and actions become divine-like and are centered in God. God and the person move together simultaneously as one.
- Teresa became aware of God loving through her.

o Teresa also says that she experienced a kind of delicate division that was hard to explain between the soul and its faculties on the one hand, and her spirit on the other. It seemed to her that the soul and its faculties, though joined and one with the soul's spirit, were somehow *"divided" in their functions*. It was as though the soul and faculties were doing the good works of Martha, while the spirit at the same time, like Mary, was quietly savoring the presence of God. (Lk.10:38-42)

o The seventh dwelling places have continual thrusts and impelling energies of love from God that are like love letters from the Lord. These bring the joyful realization that God desires that the soul remain with Him always.

o One might think that the soul would be outside itself and so absorbed in God that it wouldn't be able to be occupied with anything else. But on the contrary, the soul is more occupied than ever with the service of God and neighbor. (IC7,1,8)

- - The person has more energy and desire for apostolic service, with fortitude strengthening it for love.
  - Once the person's duties are over, the person remains with the enjoyable company of the Trinity.
- Sufferings may increase in this dwelling, but they don't disturb the soul's center or take away peace.
  - The only distress comes from thoughts that one could ever lose God again, or about past sins and ingratitude.
  - Any slavish fear is gone as is any fear about evil, the devil, hell or death.
  - There is great concern for the honor and glory of God.
- The soul is also fed and expanded by God who gives life to the soul through secret aspiratory prayer. (IC7,2,6)
  - These aspirations are loving expressions that are spontaneous, cannot be doubted, and come very often.
  - These are vehemently forceful utterances, which cannot be described, and cause the soul to cry out in outbursts such as: *"O Life of my life."* (IC7,2,6)
- God also wants to bring comfort and joy to all the *"people of the castle,"* that is, to the *interior senses and faculties.* (IC7,2,6) The *exterior senses and faculties* have nothing to do with what goes on in the center of the soul in the seventh dwelling places, though they can share in the peace and joy that overflows from the center. (IC7,3,10)
  - Nothing disturbs the soul's peace. There are none of those movements or shocks that usually take place in the senses, faculties, and imagination of other dwelling places. (IC7,2,9)
  - Faculties and senses are not lost here but remain in delightful amazement at the intimacy of the relationship with God. (IC7,3,11)
  - In this experience, the soul sees with spiritual understanding that there is Someone in the interior depths who sends life-giving water to the faculties and senses.
- The soul experiences a deep peace and repose in these dwellings.
  - The soul has seen so much and been through so much, that nothing frightens it anymore.
  - Since it enjoys the company of God, it doesn't experience the former *lonely* solitude it once did. (IC7,3,12)
- However, as long as a person lives, their humanity does not disappear, and they must be vigilant against backsliding, sin and offending God. One must also trust and depend on Christ to keep the soul in His hands. (IC7,2,9)

- The more that persons are favored by the Lord, the more they are afraid and mistrustful of themselves. They also become more aware of their misery and sinfulness. At the same time, they have a profound gratitude for God's mercy, and a desire to please Him. (IC7,3,14)
o The cross never leaves life, but in these dwelling places it does not disquiet, and any storms pass quickly. (IC7,3,15)
o In the seventh dwelling places persons alternate on the one hand between the desire to die and be completely united to God, and on the other, a desire to live in order to serve God as much as possible. (IC7,3,14) (Phil. 1:20-26)

CHARACTERISTICS OF SPIRITUAL MARRIAGE

1. INTIMACY
   - God penetrates the bride's very being and soul, and is the co-principle of her life and actions. The marriage fusion is accomplished secretly as a mystery to human understanding, and secretly in that no one knows exactly when this intimacy happened.
   - Just as between married persons there is a blending and uniting of two lives and a desire to share fully of one's inner self, this is even more so between God and the soul.
   - The soul's aim has been to love God as much as she has been loved. The soul and God live as it were—face to Face.
   - A kind of equality of giving and receiving love is reached in Spiritual Marriage union.
   - The soul's least hopes and desires have power over God's heart, because all of the soul's energies and actions are in God's heart in their mutuality of union.

2. PERMANENCE OF THE UNION
   - In previous stages, union was transitory. This union is now a permanent bond that cannot be dissolved. In fact, fear of infidelity towards the Lord strengthens through faithful vigilance to the love relationship. (see: "Unions—Types of" in **Supplemental Material**)
   - The soul is conscious that it now possesses God, as God possesses the soul.

3. TRANSFORMATION

- Even on earth this is what is possible for the transformation, wholeness, integration, and perfection of a human person—in sense, personality, psyche and faculties.
- There is likeness of qualities between the soul and God.
- The natural and supernatural faculties are integrated and work together perfectly and instinctively.
- Transforming Union causes a transformation of the higher faculties of Intellect, Memory and Will as regards their manner of operation. The faculties become divine in their operation by participating in the union with God's life.

4. AN ABIDING NEW DIVINIZED CONSCIOUSNESS
   - The state of Spiritual Marriage, or Transforming Union, is often accompanied by an Intellectual Vision—either an experience of Christ, the Trinity, or of a Divine attribute or quality of God. (see: "Attribute or Quality of God Revealed" in **Supplemental Material**)
   - The Intellectual Vision is not necessary for union, and all do not experience it. But persons are habitually conscious of the Divine underpinning and cooperation in all their higher operations.
   - The transformed human consciousness is immersed in the mind and consciousness of Christ.

5. SERENITY, PEACE, SECURITY AND JUBILATION
   - There is no more bodily fainting or weakness due to Rapture or Ecstasy overcoming the senses or faculties.
   - Any disordered passions, emotions and temptations are easily conquered from the increased determination and strength God gives to the soul.
   - The soul's center is steeped in the peace of God, as ideally, married persons are sure of each other's love.
   - There is serenity for the Intellect in the silent, simple perception of Truth itself.
   - There is serenity for the Will in the silent, continual embrace of Love.
   - There is serenity for the Memory and imagination in that unwanted memories, images and emotions do not disturb as before.
   - The soul lives in an ongoing state of refreshment, joy, and celebration!

6. STABILITY

- The stable union of God and the soul persists even during external occupations. Spiritual Marriage and apostolic good works do not interfere with each other.
- The seventh dwelling places are stable as regards remaining always in union with God, but these dwelling places are not a static state of life. The love for the Lord and His people continually grows, as do virtuous choices and actions.

7. SELF-FORGETFULNESS
    - There is a complete letting go of one's own will and abandoning of the self to the will of God.
    - The person is indifferent and content to live or die as God desires.
    - There is zealous eagerness that the will of God be done in all things, as well as loving concern and action for the good and salvation of the neighbor, no matter the cost to oneself.

8. INTEGRATION AND HARMONY OF THE CONTEMPLATIVE AND APOSTOLIC LIFE—CONTEMPLATION IN ACTION
    - The person is more desirous than ever to serve God and others in "good works." (IC7,4,6,12) There is an integrated unity between the apostolic life and the contemplative life.

9. INCREASED VIRTUE
    - The foundation of life in Christ in these seventh dwelling places is more than the practice of prayer, and must include striving for all the virtues—especially humility (truthful self-knowledge), love and detachment (holy freedom)—and practicing them as perfectly as possible. (IC7,4,9)
    - Growth in holiness, virtue and likeness to Christ is accelerated in these dwellings.
    - Generally, the person is "confirmed in grace" (free of serious or mortal sin) though there can be inadvertent errors, faults or venial imperfections.

EFFECTS of SPIRITUAL MARRIAGE

o Not all effects listed below are always present in the seventh dwelling places, but ordinarily they are present. (IC7,4,1)

1. There is TRANSFORMATION of the whole person into the Christ self.

- The old false self is transcended—has died. Self-forgetfulness is the new manner of living. (IC7,3,1-2)
- There is a radical experience of a kind of "nothingness" as regards the former false or ego self, which is now seen as an illusion.
- The concern is only to look after what belongs to God, and what is for God's honor and glory. (IC7,3,2)
- The person is detached from rewards, consolations and spiritual delights. (IC7,3,8)
- The soul is always in its peaceful center, though the senses, passions or faculties may or may not be. (IC7,2,10-11)
- The passions—the emotions, ego, and self-centered systems—are now conquered and do not dare enter the soul's *interior* activities and domain because they, too, have become subdued by interaction with the soul's center abiding in God. (IC7,2,11)
- However, the passions and emotions are more alive and integrated than ever in the most helpful sense.
- Though in the other dwelling places there is much tumult, noise and many poisonous allurements, none enter these center dwelling places to disturb, or move the soul to leave it. (IC7,2,11)

2. There is a great DESIRE FOR SACRIFICES and for enduring any suffering for the love and will of God. The desire for the will of God is total and extreme. (IC7,3,4)
    - The faculties, senses and passions are not always in peace, but the soul is. (IC7,2,10-11)
    - The person has deep interior joy, even when persecuted. (IC7,3,5)
    - Hostile feelings towards persecutors or difficult persons are gone and there is a particular love and thanksgiving for them. (IC7,3,5)
    - All aspects of love and non-violence are alive in the person—empathy, compassion, benevolence, understanding and forgiveness. Any judgmentalness or fear of others is gone.

3. There is LOSS OF SERVILE FEAR—of stress, fear and anxiety, which is accompanied by the true peace and tranquility that only God can give. (IC7,3,10 & 13)
    - There is loss of a fear of death. There is no more fear of death than of a Rapture. (IC7,3,7)
    - There is no fear of meddling by the devil or evil spirits. (IC7,3,10)
    - The person loses the fear they sometimes had of the previous disruptive favors. (IC7,3,10)

- Fear of aridity is gone, and rare are periods of dryness or interior disturbance. (IC7,3,10)

4. There is a ZEALOUS CONCERN ABOUT COMMITTING ANY IMPERFECTIONS including venial sins, and the person is generally free of serious sin, though not immune to it if careless.
    - The soul doesn't trust itself or consider itself safe from losing salvation. The person has greater concern than ever over faults and sins, and guards against even small sins. (IC7,2,9)
    - There is deep concern about any hidden sins the person doesn't yet know about. (IC7,4,3)
    - Their greatest security is in begging God that they not offend Him. (IC7,4,3)
    - There is a kind of habitual pain and confusion when the person sees the little they can do, and the great deal they should do and want to do for God—this is a great cross and penance. (IC7,2,9)
    - The person experiences happiness in doing penance, particularly the penance that comes when God brings bad health or diminishments. (IC7,2,9)

5. SUFFERING CAN BE INTENSE here, but not so as to disturb the soul's center and take away peace. (IC7,2,9)
    - The seventh dwelling places do not preclude suffering over any sins or fear of separation from God. (IC7,2,9-10)
    - There is distress whenever the soul imagines it could lose God through its own fault. (IC7,4,3)
    - There is suffering in remembering past ingratitude, foolishness, lack of respect, or any abandoning of God during the person's life. Even the thought of God's forgiveness of ingratitude or sinfulness is not much relief.
    - At times the person is left more on their own in a "natural state" for a short while—a day or so—to undergo some disturbance for growth in humility, determination, stability, good resolutions, or recognition of dependence on God. (IC7,4,1-2)
    - God leaves some old wounds for the sake of the soul's humility.

6. There is GREAT DETACHMENT.
    - There is a kind of holy indifference and lack of importance attached to anything or everything that happens, with a focus to be alone with God, or helping others. (IC7,3,8)

- The Lord may wish to reveal to others what He secretly has done for this soul for reasons He alone knows. And while this could be humiliating in the past, it isn't so here. (IC7,3,12)

7. Much WEAKNESS IS REMOVED.
   - The Lord's favors fortify, enlarge and make the soul capable of more virtuous activity. (IC7,3,12)
   - Strength and fortitude come from drinking the wine from the inner wine cellar of the Holy Spirit, and strength flows back to the body for service from the fortified soul. (IC7,4,11)
   - The impelling energies of love from God to the soul dispose it to do the will of God with a resolute will. (IC7,3,9)
   - The "tree" is now beside the living water and is fresher and gives more fruit. (IC7,2,9)
   - In unseen quiet, God helps the soul in every way to advance in Christ-like perfection. (IC7,3,11)
   - The soul finds herself improved in everything. (IC7,1,10)

8. The SERVICE OF GOD AND NEIGHBOR becomes the great desire. (IC7,4,9; 7,3,6)
   - There is great desire to do "good works" so as to benefit others. (IC7,3,6)
   - Despite trials, business affairs needing attention, and loving service for others, the essential part of the soul never leaves God. (IC7,1,10)

9. JUBILEE, DELIGHT, REFRESHMENT, JOY AND PRAISE of God is the default state of the soul.
   - God and soul delight in one another, and rejoice alone together in the deepest silence, not in a lonely solitude. (IC7,3,11-12)
   - In these dwellings, persons need not remain continually with their faculties in silence, but may enjoy, praise and speak lovingly to the Lord any time, and ponder something about Him, or be instructed by Him either in prayer or the events of their lives.
   - Generally, Raptures are taken away, but if they are given, they are without Transport or Flight of the Spirit. (IC7,3,12)
   - Usually there are no interior trials or feelings of dryness, but rather a continual remembrance and tender love for the Lord in the center of the soul. (IC7,3,8)

10. FAITH, HOPE and LOVE are lived out as perfectly as possible.

Teresian Teachings for Prayer and Life:

- Spiritual Marriage is a state of human integration and wholeness, encompassing the union of the contemplative and apostolic life working in complementarity and harmony together. It is the joining together of the activities of Martha and Mary. (Lk.10:38-42)
    - Though it may seem like a division between the *interior and passive* part of the soul (Mary) and the *exterior and active* part of the soul and person (Martha), the exterior and active part is totally in union with the interior passive part, which is completely directing the active exterior part for service and good works.
    - *"... believe me, Martha and Mary must work together when they give the Lord lodging, and must have Him ever with them, and they must not entertain Him badly and offer Him nothing to eat. And how can Mary give Him anything, if she is seated as she is at His feet, unless her sister helps her?"* (IC7,4,12)
    - Obviously, no one can sit always in the delight of contemplation at the feet of the Lord. (IC7,4,13)
    - Prayer and contemplation cannot be the sole activity of Christians, for unless they strive after the virtues and practice them, they will be stunted in virtue. (IC7,4,9)
    - If persons don't move forward in love, service and virtue they will begin to fall backwards. There is no stasis in the spiritual life. Actions and works must reflect what is said in prayer. (IC7,4,7-9)
    - Being truly spiritual means becoming a servant of God. There is no progress in the spiritual life without this attitude of generous service. (IC7,4,6-8)
- The aim of contemplative prayer in the Prayer of Union—the purpose of Spiritual Marriage is for *"the birth of good works, good works."* (IC7,4,6)
- Prayer should be engaged in, not merely for enjoyment, but for the sake of gaining strength for service. (IC7,4,12)
    - Souls must not build towers or *"castles in the air"* (IC7,4,15) without foundations—with wishful ambitious fantasies of heroic deeds.
    - Beware of the ego's ambitious desires to do great or impossible things, while avoiding the needs and works nearest at hand. Serve God in ways that are possible. Be content with great desires. No one

can nor needs to serve everybody in the whole world, but must serve those nearest, to whom they have a greater obligation. (IC7,4,14)
- However, through prayer itself, anyone, anywhere can be greatly helped. (IC7,4,14)
  - Humility, self-denial, service, virtue and great love towards others is of great benefit, and enlivens and awakens and inspires these qualities in others, as well as builds the possibility for energies of love throughout the whole world.
  - Any person can influence the whole world, for whatever they imagine, think, feel, say or do affects the whole world—either impeding or furthering the Kingdom of God. (IC7,4,14)

"The Lord doesn't look so much at the greatness of anything we do as much as at the love in which it is done." (IC7,4,15)

7

SEVENTH DWELLING PLACES

Internalizing the Teachings: *My Beloved is mine!*

In these dwelling places St. Teresa describes the great favors God grants souls who are brought into permanent union with God in Spiritual Marriage or Mystical Marriage—also called Transforming Union by St. John of the Cross. Teresa explains the difference between Spiritual Marriage and other spiritual unions, and she writes of the effects and purposes of the Spiritual Marriage between the soul and God. What Teresa shares of her experience of the life of Spiritual Marriage with God is meant to encourage and entice you to desire and cooperate with God in the work of transformation for the sake of Mystical Marriage for you, also. Spiritual Marriage is the most profound level of human life possible—heaven on earth—and Teresa can't say enough about its wonders, and the extraordinary fulfilling love, goodness, truth and beauty of this state of union. The description recalls St. Paul's compelling hint of the heavenly delights that "eye has not seen, nor ear heard, nor has it entered the human mind what God has for those who love Him." (1Cor. 2:9) St. Teresa writes in these dwelling places of the glories of life and love in God!

Poem and Reflection: (Poem #3)

Sobre Aquellas Palabras	**On Those Words**
"Dilectus Meus Mihi"	*"My Beloved Is Mine"*
St. Teresa de Jesús	St. Teresa of Jesus

Yo toda me entregué y di,	I've surrendered and given all of myself,
Y de tal suerte he trocado,	And my fortune is so changed,
Que mi Amado para mí,	*that my Beloved is for me,*
Y yo soy para mi Amado.	*and I am for my Beloved.*
Cuando el dulce Cazador	When the sweet Divine Hunter
Me tiró y dejó rendida	wounded and left me surrendered
En los brazos del amor	into His arms of love,
Mi alma quedó caída;	my soul was overthrown;
Y cobrando nueva vida,	and began receiving new life,
De tal manera he trocado	In such manner have I so changed
Que mi Amado para mí,	*That my Beloved is for me,*
Y yo soy para me Amado.	*and I am for my Beloved.*
Tiróme con una fleche	He launched a dart at me
Enerbolada de amor,	of quickening love,
Y mi alma quedó hecha	and so my soul has come to remain
Una con su Criador.	one with her Creator.
Ya yo no quiero otro amor,	There is no other love I desire,
Pues a mi Dios me he entregado,	since I have surrendered myself to God,
Y mi Amado para mí,	*and my Beloved is for me,*
Y yo soy para mi Amado.	*and I am for my Beloved.*

My Beloved is Mine and I am my Beloved's!

St. Teresa's passionately outpoured words in this poem of spiritual ecstasy well describe her enraptured experience of Spiritual Marriage of the seventh dwelling places. A poem can better evoke the emotions and sense of an experience than a prose explanation of it.

It was in a cooperating surrender to God that Teresa discovered that what she most desired could only be given to her as the gift and work of God. God is the Divine Wooer and Searcher for our love, and our wounds from God are only for healing to later become the delectable wounds—as of a Cupid's dart—of longing and love. It is only when our illusory, false self is overthrown and dies that we begin to know who we are and what it is we truly desire—to be one with our Beloved Creator. What Teresa knows and tries to capture in her poem can't adequately be conveyed in words. Only those who have been brought to the union of Spiritual Marriage can truly understand her. But the Good News given to us in Jesus Christ, and confirmed in the experience of St. Teresa of Jesus, is that the One we desire, also desires us, and even more than we can imagine! In the seventh dwelling places St. Teresa conveys her joyful experience, enthusiasm and certainty that God, the Beloved is ours, and we are the Beloved's.

Reflection Questions: (Choose only one or two at a time to explore in depth.)

- Do the outpoured feelings of Teresa in this poem touch you in any particular way? Do you have an attraction or desire for the union she speaks of, or is there something that feels fearful or resistant in you about it? Would you endure the cost of dying to your false self for such a Soul Mate's tremendous love?
- What aspects about Teresa's experience of life lived in union with the Trinity do you find attracts you, and would these keep you faithful to prayer, and deepen your desire for this favor of union?
- Do you believe that the Lord wants this union of love with you much more than you do? Do you care enough that God has this desire for your love?
- Have you had any favors from the Lord that you cherish, that you have never forgotten and that affect your life in God? Or, have you set them aside, rarely bring them to mind, and take them for granted?
- What have been the peak moments of your spiritual life?
- How integrated is your life of prayer and apostolic ministry for others? Does your prayer life support and contribute to your ministry in some way? How?
- How is the Lord making His loving presence known to you at this time?
- Is your life, including how you undergo sufferings or setbacks of your life, a compelling and attractive witness to your love relationship with Christ and the power of His love in your life? Would it enhance an openness to the experience of the Lord's love in others? Would they see and experience God's love through you?

Guidance for Prayer and Integration of Prayer and Life:

- Even though few may reach these dwelling places, you should still continue to live as virtuous a life as you are able, and pray as you can with the guidance for prayer and the spiritual life that has been recommended and presented in the previous dwellings—especially the fourth through the sixth dwelling places. This is what you can do, and what the Lord can use to deepen your friendship and intimacy with Him.
- But remember, the Lord is free in His Divine autonomy and choice to "knock anyone off their horse" at any time, and bring them closer to Himself! (Acts 9:1-19)
- Generally, there is not a break in these seventh dwelling places between periods of time set aside for formal prayer, and a life of constant prayerful interconnection, communication and union with the Lord. Whenever attention is towards Him, it comes with the sense of His continual abiding presence that is ongoing within all life experiences. Contemplative *life* is interwoven with contemplative *prayer* in the seventh dwelling places. But you also can work to form a habit and practice of turning your attention to the Lord's abiding presence in every circumstance of your life.
- However, as lovers need to be alone to enjoy one another in solitary intimacy, time for formal prayer will still need to be set aside for being alone with the Beloved, and generally this is through more time given to prayer than earlier dwellings.
- There is always some preparation or activity required for entering into periods set aside for prayer, even here, just as some planning or preparation is involved for a special celebration and encounter of love between any two spouses. From time to time look for ways to give gifts to the Lord and make your time together special.
- Refresh your memory and spirit as needed by reviewing the section on "How to Use this Book for Prayer" as well as the articles in the **Supplemental Material**: "Practical Preparations for Prayer," "Dispositions for Prayer," "Distractions in Prayer," and "Praying through the Humanity of Christ." You can also review the material on "Centering Prayer," "Lectio Divina," and the "Prayer of Recollection."
- Primarily prayer in the later dwelling places will come naturally by placing no obstacles in its way, by letting the Lord take the lead, by abandoning concerns and surrendering totally to Him during the time set aside for Him alone. The Lord has first loved you and is the initiator

of the loving Prayer of Union and Spiritual Marriage. These suggestions apply to your prayer, also, no matter which of the dwellings you are in.
- In these seventh dwelling places there may still be some occasional distractions, but they come and go without distress. Recall the advice for "Distraction in Prayer" in the **Supplemental Material** and do not give in to distress or discouragement.
- Generally, souls in these dwelling places will rest continually in the Lord's embrace all day long, with the Divine Presence radiating from the center of the soul working in harmony with His desires however they are engaged. Keep practicing mindfulness of Christ's presence with you so that you can also be at peace and rest in His loving presence.
  - You can whisper loving expressions to Jesus throughout your day keeping Him close in your heart and thoughts.
- Any contemplative Prayer of Union must encompass a life of love, and the service of good works. Your prayer must lead to bearing fruit in loving service. Check for this in yourself.
- In the contemplative prayer of the seventh dwelling places persons always *experience* being with the Lord when they turn their attention to Him. And when they leave that encounter of relationship, they return to another experience of Him in lived contemplative *life* among others in the world. In both contemplative prayer and contemplative life there is the going from the Lord, to the Lord. There is only God "in whom we live, and move and have our being." (Acts 17:28)
- Persons in the seventh dwelling places *know* they go from the Lord in prayer to the Lord in life. He is known to be always present and abiding in these dwellings (F5), with a continual, and known loving presence between the person and Himself as the Divine Spouse.
- During any times when you do *not consciously know* this, you can still do whatever you personally need to do to *remind yourself* that no matter which dwelling place you find yourself in, you also go from God in prayer to God in life.
- At any time, in a single act of intense, silent love you can offer perfect praise, adoration, reparation, thanksgiving and petition as extensive and infinite in power as is the One *who is praying within you.*

If you want to use one of the scriptures below for your prayer period, select one before you begin.

Scripture Passages:

(Spousal Union Intimacy) Jn. 3:29-30; 4:5-21; Gal. 2:19-21; Sir. 24:19-22; Is. 62:2-5, 54:4-6; Hos. 2:14-20; Jer. 2:2, 31:3-4; Zep. 3:14-17; Lk. 10:38-42; Mt. 6:25-34; Phil. 4:4-9; Eph. 3:14-21, 1:15-23; 2Cor. 5:16-20, 6:16-18; Rom. 8:38-39, 8:18-30; Jn. 17:21-26; Ps. 63, 42, 16, 84; Jn. 21:15-18

(My Beloved) Sg. 1-8; Ps. 43, 63; Jn. 11:1-27; Lk. 7:36-50; Jn. 3:16-17; 4:5-26; Rom. 8:38-39; Mt. 17:1-8, 12:18-21, 3:13-17; Eph. 1:3-14; Is. 43:3-7

The following meditation may help you recognize that there is only God in whom you live.

Guided Meditation:

Recollect yourself in quiet as you are able, and imagine your soul to be like a brightly polished mirror, without back or sides or top or bottom—everywhere you look there is a sparkling clear mirror. . . . See yourself filling up every space in the mirror as you look up and down and to the sides which recede into the infinite horizon that is your soul. . . . See uncountable images in the mirror of yourself from the past, present and into the future. . . . Now look more closely and recognize that this mirror of yourself is also completely overlaid and impressed upon the Lord Himself! (L40,5-6; IC7,2,8) Reflect that you are within, and are one with the Father, the Son and the Holy Spirit, just as Jesus told the apostles that He is in the Father and the Father is in Him. (Jn. 17:21-26) . . . The greatest self-knowledge and understanding of who you really are, and of the riches of your being, are known and proclaimed in this revelation of Christ from John's Gospel. Continue to listen to Christ for any loving inspirations or words, especially the deepest reality and understanding that there is no separation between you and the Divine. . . . You are in the Blessed Trinity and the Blessed Trinity is in you in mutual abiding! You are a tabernacle of the Most Holy Trinity! Ask for understanding and insight into this great gift and mystery that will help you to live the fullest human life possible in God. . . .

"Oh ... how ready this Lord still is to grant us favors just as He granted them to others in the past. And in some ways, He is even more in need that we desire to receive them." (IC5,4,6)

Since my confessors commanded me to write about the favors and kind of prayer the Lord has granted me, I wish they would also have allowed me to tell very clearly and in full detail my great sins and wretched life. (L, Prologue)

MOTHER TERESA of JESUS
"LA MADRE"
Later Adulthood—1567-1582

St. Teresa of Jesus' later adult years were amazingly generative—not only in the writing of her books on prayer and the spiritual life—but also in the founding of many monasteries. In these works she became the Mother of the Discalced Carmelite Order. But she did not set out to make a new religious Order, or to split the Order of Carmel into two branches, which the friars did after her death. The Teresian Reform caused no end of disputes, rancor and division with various friars vying for power in the Order and influence over the charism. Teresa had only been looking to create a situation for herself and her like-minded friends, where she could more authentically live what she felt called to, and share it with her little band which was attracted to her form of religious life.

It was in 1567 with a visit from the Father General of the Carmelite Order—Fr. Rossi—that she was authorized to found other monasteries. This became a new chapter in her life—full of trials—lawsuits, negotiations, money woes, troubles with Ecclesiastical authorities, difficulties within her monasteries, organizing and supervising workmen—along with her usual ill health and the dangerous traveling all over Spain. She wasn't anywhere for very long due to these monastic foundations and came to be called "that gadabout." This is an ironic label for one whose desire was to be a contemplative nun and hermit. By her death some sixteen monasteries had been founded for the nuns.

In 1567 Teresa also met Fr. John of the Cross who became a spiritual director to her nuns and also was instrumental in making foundations of monasteries for the friars. Teresa recognized his talents and holiness, and had great confidence in him.

In 1569 Teresa again took up the pen writing her *Soliloquies*, and once more in 1573 writing *The Book of Foundations* (a history of the founding of her various monasteries). In 1577 she began to write her most mature work, *The Interior Castle*. She could not have written this book until after 1572 when she received the grace of total union with Christ in Spiritual Marriage, gaining the insights she had struggled with earlier.

During these years after the full union of Spiritual Marriage, Teresa was busy with "good works" for the Lord and deeply blended the contemplative and apostolic lives together. She was involved on many fronts all at once—with all her travels and work of setting up new monasteries, with the turmoil of the Reform and its imprisonment of Fr. John of the Cross, with all the manuscript and letter writing, as well as teaching and overseeing the nuns of her monasteries. Unfortunately, she broke her left arm in 1577, which left her incapacitated and requiring help for writing. Her good friend, Sr. Ann of St. Bartholomew, had to help with any writing, but this curtailed Teresa's candidness in some ways. But it didn't stop her writing, or her work and traveling. The last year of her life—in 1582—found her in Avila, Burgos, Palencia, Valladolid, Medina and Alba de Tormes. By the time she reached Alba de Tormes she was exhausted and seriously ill. She took to her bed September 29th due to a severe hemorrhage that left her very weak. Mother Teresa was never to rise from her bed again.

Some of Teresa's last words included: "*Lord, I am a daughter of the Church. I die a daughter of the Church*" (which because of the Inquisition had no doubt been a concern of hers), and "*Sisters, keep our Rule well. Pray for me. Pardon my offences. A humble contrite spirit You will not spurn. O, my Lord and my spouse, now the desired hour has come. Now is the time for us to set forth together. Now is this exile ending, and my soul rejoices at one with You whom I have so desired."*

As she was dying, she appeared to be in the Prayer of Union—motionless and ecstatic until about 9:00 in the evening, when she showed signs of speaking ardently with Someone. She slipped away October 4, 1582 in the arms of her nurse and friend, Sr. Ann of St. Bartholomew. It was fitting for Teresa, who knew from her prayer experiences with the Lord that time was an illusion, that it leapt forward that night. October 4th became October 15th because the Julian calendar changed to the Gregorian calendar the night of Mother Teresa of Jesus' death. It was the work of God that from desiring always to be faithful and to die a daughter of the Church, that Mother Teresa of Jesus became Saint Teresa of Avila—Doctor of the Church.

"Through the strong desire I have to play some part in helping you to serve my God and Lord, I ask that each time you read my work you, in my name, praise His Majesty fervently and ask for the increase of His Church ..." (IC Epilogue 4)

SUPPLEMENTAL MATERIAL

This supplemental material provides additional information of various types and categories. Some of it is spiritual in nature in view of a retreat, and for spiritual guidance and direction. Some of it is technical, pedagogical information. Thus, this material is meant for different audiences with different purposes. Some of it is not suited for beginners and would only mire them in more complexity than they need to know. Some of it is meant for the proficient in prayer, or for students and academics, or for spiritual directors and Carmelites. Readers will have to decide for themselves which material is suited to them.

SUPPLMENTAL MATERIAL

- Absorption and False Mystical Prayer — 227
- Apophatic and Kataphatic Journeys to God — 231
- Centering Prayer — 235
- Consolations vs. Spiritual Delights — 241
- Dark Night and Purification Trials — 243
    - ❖ Passive Dark Night of Spirit Experience (Chart) — 254
- Discursive Meditation and Simple Meditation — 255
- Dispositions for Prayer — 259
- Distractions in Prayer — 263
- Faculties or Powers of the Soul — 269
    - ❖ Faculties of the Soul (Diagram) — 274
- Lectio Divina Recollection — 275
- Passive Recollection or Infused Recollection — 279
- Practical Preparations for Prayer — 281
- Prayer of Recollection—St. Teresa's Way of Praying — 285
- Prayer—Key Teresian Understandings — 291
- Prayer—Types and Categories — 295
    - ❖ Prayer—Stages of Active and Passive Prayer (Chart) — 308
- Praying through the Humanity of Christ — 309
- Soul and Spirit — 311
    - ❖ The Soul (Diagram) — 318
- Spiritual Direction According to St. Teresa — 319
- Spiritual Direction in the Passive Dark Nights — 325
- Union—Types of — 329

- **Various Mystical Favors—Introduction** — **333**
    - ➢ Attribute or Quality of God Revealed — 335
    - ➢ Delightful Wounds (Transverberation), Enkindlings — 337
    - ➢ Locutions — 341
    - ➢ Prayer of Jubilation or Prayer of Joy — 345
    - ➢ Suspensions: Rapture, Ecstasy, Transport, Levitation, Flight of the Spirit — 347
    - ➢ Vehement Desires — 357
    - ➢ Visions—Imaginative — 361
    - ➢ Visions—Intellectual — 365

ABSORPTION AND FALSE MYSTICAL PRAYER
(IC4,3,11-14; 6,7,13-15; F6-7)
(Melancholia and Neurotic "Prayer")

Absorption is St. Teresa's word for a blank, empty state of mind or consciousness. It is the mind, consciousness and interiority lacking thought or images and floating in a languid, impassive, inert or stupefied kind of inner spaced-out zone. It is not Teresian prayer which is an alert attention and connection within a relationship to Someone—God.

Melancholia is Teresa's descriptive word not only for a depressive personality, but for neurosis and various kinds of mental instability or illness for which the sixteenth century did not have well-developed understandings or labels.

Teresa seems to have been caught in the languishing, spaced-out, floating nowhere of Absorption for a couple of years in her prayer journey, until one of her spiritual directors pointed this out to her. Thus, she knew the waste of time and danger of Absorption. She may have gotten pulled into Absorption while she was debating with herself, and trying to discern whether it was a better and higher form of prayer to leave any images and concepts of the Lord behind, so as to attain the so-called "highest" forms of prayer and union with God. It appears that for a while she thought she should block all images. In the end, however, through discernment and attention to her own experience, she decided that it was best to pray and relate to Christ through His humanness, and let the Lord bring her into contemplation with or without concepts or images—as He desires. She wrote that one could reach contemplation more quickly through the humanity of Christ. (L4,7) She discovered that if the faculties of her Intellect/mind, Memory/imagination and Will, seat of her affectivity, were not occupied and focused concretely on Someone to relate to and love, they were left in a nowhere wasteland, and without support. This could lead to difficulty in solitude with languishing and impassivity, or to aridity and trouble with the mind battling the distraction of many thoughts. She is strong in warning against Absorption, as well as melancholia. And if she had known about self-hypnosis as something that could also happen in some techniques of active mindfulness or meditation, she would probably have warned spiritual directors about the possibility of this, too. For her, this would be a waste of time and a hindrance to true prayer as a love relationship with God.

- Absorption is a kind of "zoning out" or "spacing out" of the mind—neither sleep nor prayer.
  - Though it is pleasurable, Absorption is not prayer for St. Teresa, because prayer is a relationship with a person—Christ.
  - Absorption wastes a lot of time, hinders progress in virtue, the strengthening of prayer, and weakens a person.
  - It is a mistake to go along in a languid and pleasurable Absorption waiting for spiritual delights, rather than in a thought, image or feeling about the Lord, or the awareness of the simple loving gaze of Jesus on us, and our returned gaze upon Him.
  - Continual Absorption is extremely dangerous and one should get help with it from a spiritual director if needed.
  - Transcendental Meditation, and some Eastern meditation practices are more like Absorption than Teresian prayer.
- Melancholia is St. Teresa's "psychiatric" word for neurosis.
  - There is exterior languishing, weakness, stupor, listlessness, and inertia in both the psychic illness of Melancholia, as well as Absorption.
  - There are people with weak constitutions and imaginations, unbalanced psyches or personalities, who are unconsciously both easily deceived and deceptive.
  - Some people become weakened by their neurotic prayer or by Absorption and seem to see whatever they can imagine.
  - Unhealthy prayer can be brought on by too much penance, intense solitude or separation from others, unbalanced psyches, Melancholia/depression, too much exhausting prayer, lack of sleep (excessive vigils), or lack of nutrition (severe fasting).

Spiritual Direction for Absorption

- Contemplative prayer and life are not healthy for some people unless they have done any needed psychological work of self-knowledge and healing. If necessary, a competent therapist could be suggested for a directee.
- Usually a good, discerning and competent director can spot shortcomings due to depression or an unbalanced psyche, as well as natural consolations stemming from a directees' own feelings or passions, or extreme or unhealthy prayer and devotional practices.
- The following are some directives for those in Absorption, or unhealthy prayer:

Absorption and False Mystical Prayer 229

- Directees should be reminded that their prayer should always be grounded in the humanity of Christ—His mind and actions.
- If Absorption, or neurosis, or some forms of melancholic behavior are chronic character weaknesses, such persons should be steered away from too much solitude, or from striving for recollection and contemplative prayer.
- It is better that these people are distracted away from a focus on the self and introspection.
- Vocal prayer, and direction more towards an active or apostolic life in the Corporal Works of Mercy would be healthier for them.
- They should be counseled to exercise, eat and sleep well, call off harmful penance, or long periods of prayer, fasting or vigils.

APOPHATIC AND KATAPHATIC JOURNEYS TO GOD

In theology the Greek derived words apophatic and kataphatic refer to different ways of describing and "knowing" something about God—either through negation or affirmation.

The apophatic manner of referring to God is through negation—or what cannot be said, thought, or known about God, because God is invisible, ineffable, and God's essence is unknowable. So, whatever can be said or thought about God is beyond human language and reason. This way of speaking about God would emphasize God's radical *transcendence*. It is sometimes called the *via negativa*, describing what God is not—God is not finite, God is not mortal, etc.

The kataphatic use of language and thought describing God uses actual positive and assertive language and ideas to describe and "know" something about God. This way of referring to God would emphasize God's *immanence* and presence. It involves God's desire to be known through God's Self-revelation in Jesus Christ in His Incarnation. It is sometimes called the *via positiva*, describing what God is—God is loving, merciful, good, etc.

There is debate as to which of these two ways of "knowing" and describing God is the more accurate. As regards the apophatic side, some claim that this way makes God more abstract and depersonalized, though limitless. On the other hand, it is argued that the kataphatic way makes God more anthropomorphic, and personal, but limited by human language, understanding and intelligence. Because of Teresa's experience and description of the Lord in Transforming Union, her advice and sensibilities would be that you will know (something about the answer) when you experience the Lord for yourself!

Be that debate as it may, our concern is focused on how God wants to be known and revealed, and personally acts within an individual life using both favors and trials. These two aspects and means of growth and purification are usually interwoven in a person's life. The apophatic journey is explored here because many people think that if they are in the apophatic darker aspect of the journey that something has gone wrong or they are failing in their response to the Lord. That is not generally the case, but rather a matter of God's choice for them. God uses both of these two basic and different mystical paths or means to transform and acclimate the various levels of our human selves to God. These parts of ourselves include our more *exterior* selves—the five senses, our ego, persona and conscious level, as well as our *interior* selves—the faculties of Intellect/mind, Memory/imagination, Will, our unconscious depths, and our spirit self.

The Apophatic Experience

(see: "Dark Night and Purification Trials" in **Supplemental Material**)

- This journey to God and purification path has fewer experiences of the *presence* of God, or of unusual mystical favors or experiences.
- It is the purification of the dark nights of sense and spirit that St. John of the Cross describes, or the trial purification aspects particularly of St. Teresa's sixth dwelling places.
- This path is less about the nearness and immanence of God and more about the transcendence, incomprehensibility, darkness, Holy Mystery and Otherness of God.
- The qualities of this darker experience of God feel more intangible and harder to understand or explain to anyone else.
- The person is generally aware of desiring the Lord in some unknown manner, and God is primarily experienced as absent, or paradoxically, feels absent and present at the same time.
  - But usually the person is so aware of an experienced or felt absence of God that the desire for God to be present dominates consciousness.
- This apophatic way is usually dry, constricted, barren of images, ideas, or affective emotions and feelings about God.
- The prayer of this way often feels like an arid void with nothing happening.
- It requires radical surrender in dark faith, hope and love without the supports of consolation or the mystical favors of the more kataphatic way. Here persons must go against themselves in choosing to be faithful to prayer in dark silence and attention to God for the sake of love of God alone, and nothing else. It is to choose to love God, not counting the cost.
- There is some light within the apophatic experience of God from time to time.
- It appears that the faith journeys of St. John of the Cross, St. Therese of Lisieux and St. Teresa of Calcutta leaned more to the apophatic way.

The Kataphatic Experience

- This journey of purification has more reported experiences of the felt activity and presence of the Lord in spiritual delights and various other mystical favors.
- It often feels very intense and passionate—something like a kind of "romantic" love—with amorous, ardent, lovesick, burning love and desire in the soul for the Lord.
  - The Lord arouses the desires of the human beloved and engages in a Divine wooing, courtship, and overflowing lovemaking in the deepest *interior* of the human soul. This can affect and flow into the *exterior* body and senses, with extreme pain that is also somehow pleasurable. The effect on the body can be so overwhelming and disjointing that the body malfunctions in various ways, and can feel that it is close to death. (L20)
- This Divine wooing and overflowing love in the deepest interior of the soul is a process which transforms and refines human passion and love in an ongoing and ever deepening love and intimacy with God, and also in genuine love relationships with all others.
- The process generally takes place through a purifying *alternation* of the experienced activity and felt *presence* of God, along with experiences of the felt *absence* of God. This increases longing and desire for complete union with God.
- The process of being purified for this deepening desire for God involves these works of God:
  - Human beings must first be awakened to the reality that the Lord is in love with them, and desires to be loved in return.
  - This love is deeply personal for each human person and God desires that this be known.
  - The love relationship with the Lord can't be deeply entered into without a purification and conditioning to the ways and desires of God in virtue and love patterned on Christ's life. This is a joint work, but primarily the Lord's.
  - It requires surrender on the part of the human person into the desires and shaping of the Lover, God, and the demands of virtue, love and purification.
  - For the deepest and most intimate human/Divine love relationship, persons must be purified and transformed into the likeness of God in Christ.

- Just as there is some light in the apophatic way to God, there is darkness, suffering and trials in the kataphatic way. But this journey is not as stark and dark as the apophatic path.
  o St. Teresa of Avila's journey, because of her many attested to mystical experiences, appears to be more kataphatic.

CENTERING PRAYER

1. **CHOOSE A SACRED WORD:**
   - In advance of your prayer period, choose a sacred word/s (monologistos), preferably one or two syllables meaningful to you, that symbolize your intention to be present and open to God—to use during your prayer when distractions arise. It could be God, Lord, Father, Christ, love, Jesus, Spirit, or Beloved. It could be a sacred word from another language that you know the meaning of as: Abba, Kyrie, Sanctus, Fiat, Domine, Hosanna, Christe, Yeshua, etc. Or, as St. Teresa, you could choose a short meaningful aspiratory prayer that stirs you to love God as: "My Lord and my God," "I love you, Jesus," "Lord Jesus Christ, Son of God, have mercy on me," "Jesus my all," "Lord, I adore you," etc. Or, you can use a word or phrase from a Psalm or the Our Father as Teresa suggests. Do not change your sacred word/s during your time of prayer.
   - It should be a word that has the meaning that you've personally invested in it.
   - You can ask the Holy Spirit to guide you in suggesting a word or prayer.
   - You can experiment for a few days with different words or short prayers that appeal to you, but once you settle on something, do not change it. Changing it during prayer will lead to more distraction.

2. **FIND A QUIET PLACE TO SIT AND STAY:**
   - Sit in a quiet space in a comfortable chair. Take time to close your eyes, get settled and calm—perhaps take a few deep, calming breaths to rest in God. Breathe upwards from your stomach to your chest, or put your attention on the breath at your nostrils.
   - In your prayer space you might have some Christian symbols—candle, icon or crucifix.
   - You may set a timer (that has a *quiet* alerting ring) for the duration of 20, 30, or 60 minutes—or whatever length of time you choose for Centering Prayer.
   - Centering Prayer suggests 20 minutes twice a day. Traditional Christianity 60 minutes.

3. **SET YOUR MOTIVATION AND INTENTION:**
   - Your intention to be present and open to God is what makes this time prayer!
   - Take a few minutes to set your motivation for your prayer. That is, why did you come to pray? Are you coming to give time to the Lord; to clear a space for Him; to listen to Him; to deepen your intimacy and friendship with Him; to express love to Him in this time given to Him? Be very clear with yourself about your intention and motivation, saying it both to yourself and to God, so that you know what it is you truly value and desire as you begin to enter into prayer.

4. **ACKNOWLEDGE WHO THE LORD IS FOR YOU:**
   - So as to fix your attention, and know your intention in praying, and to Whom you are entering into a relationship with, make the sign of the cross and pray a doxology: "Glory to the Father, Son and Holy Spirit," "All praise to you Source of all Being, Eternal Word and Holy Spirit," or in your own words acknowledge in Whose presence you are, and who you are: "Here I am Lord, the one you love," or, "O God, come to my assistance, Lord make haste to help me," etc.

5. **BEGIN PAYING ATTENTION TO YOUR BREATH AND WORD:**
   - Generally, initial calming inhalation and expiration breaths are breathed to about 4 counts in and 8 counts out.
   - Once you have started calming yourself by attention to your breath, begin gently, quietly and calmly to introduce your sacred word/s which will further slow and empty your busy mind. Say your sacred word/s with attention, and try to align it to your peaceful breathing.
   - Use only about 5% of your inner voice energy to interiorly and quietly repeat your sacred word, while leaving the other 95% of your interiority to observe your breath, to be aware of your intention and desire for God, to interiorly gaze at Jesus, or be attentive to the silence and space within you.
   - You need not continually repeat your sacred word/s like a mantra, but only when you notice your mind has become distracted.
   - Teresa recommended to say your sacred word as a gentle puff on the flame of a candle.
     - Say your word as gently as a feather landing on something.
   - As time goes on you will become calm and your breathing slower and shallower.

- Actually, shallow breath is more associated with being calm than big, deep breaths.

6. **CONTINUE FOCUSING YOUR LOVE AND DESIRE ON CHRIST:**
   - Once you are calm and recollected, you can continue focusing on your breath, your gaze and love towards Jesus, and the quiet of your interior space.
   - If distractions arise you may gently reintroduce your sacred word/s, or a momentary picture of a scene of Jesus from His life to stir love for Him.
   - DO NOT keep saying your sacred word/s if you are recollected, calm and thinking has stopped. Only return to your sacred word/s if you become distracted.

7. **WHEN DISTRACTIONS ARISE:**
   - In this form of Active Recollection, you may try several things to turn away from distracting thoughts:
     1) Observe your breath.
     2) Gently repeat your sacred word/s from time to time, but not over and over as a mantra.
     3) Or, if some image of Jesus or His life comes to mind, cast your interior gaze of love towards Him who is with you in your inner sanctum.
   - This image could be drawn from a scripture passage, but is not meant to be an involved reconstruction of a scene or a Discursive Meditation. The image you pick of a situation in Jesus' life may match your own emotions or experience of the moment.
   - Whenever distracting thoughts arise, if you can, just quietly return your attention to your breath, sacred word/s or image, and especially your *desire for God*, letting bodily sensations, feelings, or distracting images and reflections arise and flow away. All things are passing!
   - DO NOT STRUGGLE with thoughts, or perceptions that distract because *resistance* will come with charged emotions that will distract your prayer even more!
   - Distractions and thoughts are inevitable, normal, and often integral to your prayer.
   - Have a tolerant and friendly attitude towards distractions. Lightheartedly say to yourself: "Here they go again."
   - Most of these distractions are easily disregarded by returning to your sacred word/s and breath.

- - Centering Prayer is non-violent prayer. You add disturbance by fighting distractions.
  - Constant thinking is often a defense against painful feelings or memories.
- But if disturbing material arises, do not disregard it, but go to the place that is bothering you and quietly be there with compassion for yourself. Something may need to come to light for your healing.
- N.B. This kind of prayer can raise up painful deep emotions, which need to be recognized, honored and healed.
- These unprocessed emotions, memories and pains are generally gently healed by a light touch of God through Centering Prayer.
- Some people suggest that when you become aware of a thought, you can label it. For example: "I am planning, arguing, judging, daydreaming," etc. But you don't have to. Sometimes this recognition and stepping back from a thought as the observer of it stops it and keeps you from following it.
- Whenever you find yourself following distractions or thoughts, just gently return your attention to your gaze at Jesus, to your breath, or sacred word/s. Even if you are distracted hundreds of times, returning each time to Jesus is good prayer and pleasing to Him.
- If you find yourself nodding off and falling asleep, don't continue in sleepiness. Stop your word/s and attention to your breath if it is putting you to sleep, open your eyes and look at your crucifix or icon or something till you wake up so that you can return to Centering Prayer with the intention to be *lovingly present* to Christ.
- You may not want to do Centering Prayer after a heavy meal, or late at night as it can be too refreshing and disturb your sleep.
- If you are abiding in God and recollected and calm you don't need to repeat your word/s. You need only return to it when you realize you are distracted with other thoughts you have begun to follow.

8. **IF OR WHEN YOU ARE DRAWN INTO CONTEMPLATION:**
   - If your mind should become quiet, emptied, or stilled—of thoughts, feelings or even attention to your breath, sacred word/s, or gaze at Jesus—*let it be so, and just remain in quiet emptiness and non-conceptual loving attention to God,* who is No-Thing.
   - Don't do anything if God draws you into passive contemplative prayer. Don't think you have to be saying vocal prayers or starting a meditation. Let the Lord take the lead, and do as He desires in this intimacy of prayer. There is no need for you to do anything, or even

understand what is happening. Just remain in your response of loving desire towards the Lord.

9. **ENDING YOUR PRAYER PERIOD:**
    - When the period of prayer has ended and your quiet timer goes off, spend a few more minutes with your eyes closed as you slowly bring your consciousness back to awareness of your body and surroundings, so as to readjust your senses. It's too jarring to the system just to jump up from recollection or contemplation.
    - End your recollection with a doxology, the Our Father, or favorite prayer said slowly, or a spontaneous prayer made in your own words—a prayer to Christ of love, thanksgiving, adoration or praise. Then slowly stir, opening your eyes to end your prayer period.
    - Make another sacred gesture before you leave your sacred space.

o After practicing this prayer for some months, you might want to do a follow up with a spiritual director.

CONSOLATIONS vs. SPIRITUAL DELIGHTS

In the fourth dwelling places (IC4,1,4-6; 4,2,1-6) St. Teresa distinguishes between **consolations** (contentos) and **spiritual delights** (gustos).

Consolations
(IC4,1,4-6)

Consolations are the "feel good" feelings and emotions in prayer that are more connected to active Discursive Meditation than to the various stages of contemplation. They are associated with the second degree of prayer in the *Life* chapters 1-4, and with the first three dwelling places of *The Interior Castle*. These are experiences we can arouse within ourselves through our own pious memories and thoughts, and active meditation prayer. They proceed from our own nature, natural capacities, and brain chemicals, though God can have a hand in them. Generally, they are devout feelings mixed with our passions and emotions. They are like any other happy, consoling, or joyful feeling we experience that releases brain endorphins into the body when we are contented or happy about something. Since they are mixed up with our feelings and emotions, they can be deceptive or even wear us out (e.g. the gift of tears), and we aren't necessarily changed or holier for experiencing them.

Spiritual Delights
(IC4,2,1-6)

Spiritual delights—the spring, or rain water of contemplation of the fourth waters of prayer of the *Life* in chapter18, or of the fourth through seventh dwelling places of *The Interior Castle*—begin and end in God. Spiritual delights can accompany contemplative prayer when God gives them, and are much more enjoyable than consolations, usually without taking energy from us. They expand the heart and soul in a different way from consolations and are generally inexpressible. These cause a great sense of gratitude, well-being, joy, confidence and peace. They are known without doubt not to be caused by us, but to come from the Lord. He can give spiritual delights at any time—even in the midst of trials. These favors do bring changes for deepening healing, love and virtue.

DARK NIGHT AND PURIFICATION TRIALS
(IC6; L20,9-16; 30,8f; 40,21)

St. Teresa speaks of the *trials* of purification from selfishness and sinfulness, to growth in virtue in the sixth dwelling places and also in the book of her *Life*. (L20,9-16; 30,12; 40,21) These trials are called the Dark Night in St. John of the Cross. However, Teresa's experience of trials or Dark Night is not everyone's experience. She had more kataphatic experiences, that is, more reported events of the experienced, *felt presence* and *immanence* of the Lord throughout her purification trials. (see: "Apophatic and Kataphatic Journeys to God" in **Supplemental Material**) These included many mystical favors, unusual graced "coincidences," and special understandings of the qualities and mysteries of God. These were intermixed with periods of intense, severe trials and interior darkness.

But many people do not have these more marked positive experiences of the *felt presence* of God intermixed with their great trials, and have the darker, apophatic type of experience of the *felt absence* of God in their purification process. This purification path has fewer reported events of the *presence* of God, or of mystical favors. This purification is more obscure and harder to describe. Since there are typically fewer experiences of the Lord's presence, the mystery, otherness, transcendence, and darkness of God predominate. Paradoxically, the Lord can feel absent and somehow also present at the same time within the felt absence of God. The felt absence of God is the chief experience. In this purification the person has to pray and live surrendered in dryness and darkness in a radical faith, hope and love without much consolation or experienced supports.

Basically, the most purifying aspects of the Dark Night are movements out of our customary finite ways of relating to God through our own limited ideas about Him, as well as our attachments to our spiritual consolations and devotions, and our imperfect and inadequate efforts to grow in virtue. Our little ways of relating cannot satisfy the infinite longings of our hearts. God has much more love for us than we can understand. The Lord has always been with us, but we have not always been with Him—and certainly not in His infinite mode, which if surrendered to, brings the fulfillment of all our desires. However, it will affect us in our most vulnerable places and be purifyingly painful. There are actually three Dark Night journeys: the Dark Night of faith, of hope and of love. In the beginning of the relationship with the Lord, He relates to us in our finite ways so we know that it is He who is relating to us. But there comes a time when He asks us to relate to Him in His infinite mode, which feels like darkness and powerlessness to us, and is beyond our comprehension and thus a dark night of faith.

It is St. John of the Cross who best describes the apophatic Dark Night experience of purification and transformation. Since John's apophatic experience is probably more common than Teresa's more kataphatic journey, it will be helpful to know John's teaching on the Dark Night experience to augment Teresa's, and for a fuller picture of this *essential* part of the spiritual life. To reach union with God, everyone has to pass through the purification trials, or Dark Night. It is part of, and in imitation of, the pattern of Jesus' life. Though one can initiate some aspects of the Dark Night (A1,1,13-14), no one can negotiate on their own the *passive Dark Night of Spirit*. Only God can do this work. But persons can make themselves more disposed for God's work in the Night of Spirit by serious practice of the virtues (in the Active Nights of Sense and Spirit)—particularly through the theological virtues of faith, hope and love—and by a true and humble desire in prayer for transformation.

Reading St. John of the Cross on the Dark Night experience can be confusing, because John writes of one night, two nights, three nights and four nights. However, there is actually only one night of ever deepening purification. For a more helpful elucidation of the spiritual life, John divides the one night into two divisions which relate to two parts of the human person—the more *exterior* senses—the physical, material, bodily self, and the *interior* faculties of the spiritual, immaterial soul and spirit self. These two divisions or two nights he names: Night of Sense and Night of Spirit. These two divisions or two nights he further delineates into two phases for each night. These he calls the Active and Passive Night of Sense and the Active and Passive Night of Spirit. Thus, he can speak of four Nights—the Active Night of Sense, the Active Night of Spirit, the Passive Night of Sense, and the Passive Night of Spirit.

Though the four nights do not follow in chronological order one after another in the spiritual life, as another way of delineating them, John divides them into a temporal scheme of images persons know from experience—the three parts of the night—called twilight, midnight and dawn. We would know these as the commencing darkness of evening, increasing deeper darkness of midnight, and then a darkness lightening into dawn. These three temporal or chronological progressions of darkness related to the images of twilight, midnight and dawn, John also calls the Night of Sense, Night of Spirit, and Night of God. Using Scholastic terminology, he also refers to the three in terms of *persons* in their *progress* towards union with God—Night of the Beginner, Night of the Proficient, and Night of the Perfect, also known in spiritual theology as the Nights or Ways of the Purgative, the

Illuminative, and the Unitive. Now knowing all the names for the Nights, what do they mean? And what are they purifying?

Active Night of Sense
(A1; DN1,1-8)

The active phase of the Night of Sense refers to *our work* in choosing to imitate Christ in our spiritual journey. It is *what we do* to be more like Him when we practice any asceticism in detachment, or self-sacrifice from anything on the *sensual* level that separates us from Christ. It is to make choices that are freely patterned on Christ's life, rather than on what feels good or doesn't. John is only asking us to re-direct habitual, voluntary, destructive desires and appetites that *harm* or *detain* us, or *block* our movement to God. (A1,11,1-3) The ascetical choice is between our relationship with the Lord and anything else that gets in the way of our relationship and union with Him. In St. John of the Cross, the Night of Sense affects the lower part of the soul—the five senses, and the imagination and phantasy. Its purpose is to prepare these *material senses* for the life and control of the *immaterial spirit*. It is a helpful preparation for entering the Active Night of Spirit and also for surrendering to the Passive Night of Sense and the Passive Night of Spirit. Such asceticism would include various forms of fasting or detachment from whatever we are unfreely attached to— such exterior things as food, alcohol, computer, phone, TV, or hidden interior sins of selfishness, judgmentalness or negative thinking. Or, our asceticism could include some new positive habits added to our lives, as getting up earlier to pray, or choosing to volunteer for some good work every week—choices that are moving us out of our comfort zone and bringing us to give up our own will and desires for the good of others. This would be in imitation of Jesus' own Active Night of Sense and suffering purification in *deliberately choosing* to go to Jerusalem and hand Himself over to betrayal and arrest by enemies, with the recognition of the real possibility of looming physical mistreatment and death.

Active Night of Spirit
(A2-3)

The Active Night of Spirit flows from, and continues to build on, the disciplined choices of the Active Night of Sense—on the serious choices we make to choose God above all things—not only on the *exterior* level of sense in the Active Night of Sense, but also at the *interior* level of spirit. This includes not only detachment from exterior goods, but in this night, also to *interior* and spiritual goods and consolations. It includes *our part* in enduring with patience any lack of sustenance from previous spiritual supports and consolations, as well as aridity and darkness in prayer. Our part is still to imitate Christ, be faithful to being there at prayer, and to growing into deeper understandings of the life of the spirit, and living out of faith, hope and love. The Active Night of Spirit demands actively choosing in *perseverance* to imitate Christ and be present for prayer even if God decides not to give consolations or the gift of passive contemplation. This active purification is a progressively more *interior and spiritual deprivation* in the choices to give up a spiritual life that is centered on the sweetness of devotions and consolations. This includes a surrender of how we feel when we pray, as well as spiritual goods we have clung to and depended upon—devotions, ideals, supports, favors and consolations—as the *motivation* for our relationship with God, rather than on love of God alone. More conscious and serious choices will have to be made in the growing awareness of the subtleties of our attachments and sinfulness beyond what we were aware of in the previous choices of the Active Night of Sense. Not even former spiritual things and devotions can be allowed to compete with the love of God! The spiritual life becomes quieter here, and less dramatic or ostentatious in outward appearances or performance, but is becoming more genuine. It is becoming less focused on thoughts and ideas *about* the Lord and more centered on our personal relationship *with* Him. Only the love relationship with God in Christ, and the Divine will matters, not the pleasures of spiritual goods.

As part of His letting go of spiritual goods, Jesus chose at the Last Supper to let go of the disciples He loved and also of his very mission, which He knew they still didn't understand. He chose to let Judas go, whom He also loved, which pierced His spirit. He witnessed to His supreme detachment and surrender in the Garden of Gethsemane from the spiritual goods He had known in His miracles, healings, teaching and spiritual ministry. His choice was to go forward with His self-emptying—His arrest and crucifixion—which was surrendered in trust to God.

John marks a shift from Active to Passive Nights in his Transition Signs (A2,13-15; DN1,9) earlier referred to in material given in the third dwelling places. Many people stop short of disposing themselves, or welcoming, or even allowing the purification of the Passive Dark Nights.

Passive Night of Sense
(DN1,1-14; A2,12-14)

The Passive Night of Sense encompasses all that we undergo and suffer that is not of our choice or arrangement. If we allow these purifications to do their work in us they are safer and more efficacious than the ascetical ones we *choose* for ourselves in the Active Night of Sense. They tend to cut us more deeply and are therefore more transforming. They are helping us transfer the control of our lives from our illusory, exterior self and ego to God alone, and help to put the lower, exterior part of the soul under the control of the higher, interior parts of the soul. This Night can include such stripping as illness, loss of a job, betrayal, financial setbacks, divorce, opposition, broken relationships, loss of reputation, deaths—all manner of exterior trials and sufferings that also spill into our psychological and spiritual interior makeup to destabilize and undo it for a remaking in Christ's image. It also takes what happens to our prayer out of our hands, and is a time when even the spiritual goods and practices we depended on lose their satisfaction, appeal and consolation. From the prayer that we were doing that was in our control, planned, said, and carried out with self-satisfaction, instead, comes a dry, arid, dissatisfying and confusing experience of prayer that will move us from our vocal prayer, meditation, the work of recollection—any prayer we do ourselves—into the passive prayer of recollection or contemplation that we do not understand or control. The shocks, losses and failures take us out of our well-ordered, conventional Christian lives and reveal roots of sinfulness and selfishness beyond what we imagined of ourselves. Previous spiritual activities and zeal have dried up, or become boring. Glib faith explanations cease to help, console, or even seem believable. Former devotions, faith supports, or spiritual insights are no longer helpful, and fidelity to prayer and a true spiritual life become a challenge with our sense of a weakened faith, ambivalent hope, and love that feels or is lukewarm, if even that. God is remaking an authentic and divinized faith, hope and love in us.

The Passive Night of Sense for Jesus was what he physically surrendered to in undergoing all that was out of His control—loss of his ministry, betrayal, the suffering of scourging, crowning of thorns, carrying of the cross, the falling, stripping, nailing, and hanging on the cross. In obedience and trust Jesus gave over His whole self to God alone.

Passive Night of Spirit
(DN2,15-24)

In the Passive Night of Spirit, God is transforming the person into the image of God's Son, Jesus, and preparing the person for union with God. This Night is so passive—so God's work—that the person has little or no role to play in it, except to assent to undergoing it in a dark faith, hope and love and lived virtue. This transformation on the level of spirit is to be undergone—not interfered with—within a hidden darkness and lack of understanding. The person will not experience this process or think that it is the tremendous gift that it is—a gift not given or assented to by many. In the previous Nights, the exterior senses were being acclimatized and *oriented to the control of the higher, interior part of the soul*. Here, all parts of the exterior and interior soul are being acclimatized and *oriented to God and the direction of the Holy Spirit*. So, all ideas, images, projections of God, which are not God—but actually idolatrous—will be dismantled. Whatever was the support within an immature faith, hope and love will come to seem illusory and will be sundered for a surrender and reliance on God alone. The person cannot control the process or length of duration of this work of God. The Passive Dark Night of Spirit is the most painful process anyone can undergo. It will feel very much like any of the following: constricted, meaningless, incoherent, bleak, frightening, unintelligible, sorrowful, alienating, or contradictory. It will seem like there is no way back or forward, that life is out of control with no relief in sight, like the unraveling of all that one had relied upon, needed, thought and cherished, or even as the end of goodness, truth, and beauty itself—like the death of everything. It can come with a sense that one has lost God, been abandoned by God who now seems like an enemy, or that there is no God. (DN2,13,5) This is the Night of God through a dark infused contemplation, that is, God so close and flowing into the soul with blinding light that God is experienced as overwhelming deepest darkness. The felt absence of God in the Dark Night of Spirit is actually a form of mystical union. Since it involves the uncovering and healing of the sickness of the soul, it is qualitatively different than depression from a neurotic or sick psyche.

Jesus' Passive Night of Spirit as He hung on the cross, led to His own experience of shock and confusion about Himself, His mission and God. His Dark Night of Spirit also included the betrayals of friends and the mocking of onlookers who called: "You saved others. Save yourself. Come down from that cross." (Mk. 15:29-32) He prayed as others have in the Passive Dark Night of Spirit: "My God, my God, why have you abandoned me?" (Mk. 15:34) Not knowing what would become of His mission and those He loved He could only surrender His life and utter: "It is finished." We know that Jesus' self-emptying Dark Night led to His resurrection in glory and to a new power and reality for Himself and all humankind.

As the Dark Night worked tremendous transformation for Jesus, so too, will it for us. God is working transformation in the soul in a hidden way that cannot be manipulated or tampered with by anyone, and so it is totally safe. Any efforts on the part of the person to regain their previous spiritual life, images of God, prayer, religious convictions, or affective relationship with God will be useless.

What is God purifying in Dark Night?

God is transforming the whole person into someone who is, as closely as possible, receptive to and capable of the deepest intimacy of love with God. St. John of the Cross links this purification to the three human faculties as they interconnect to the three theological virtues. The Intellect/mind is linked to purification of faith, the Memory/imagination to the purification of hope, and the Will to the purification of love and the affective energies.

- God is darkening the Intellect so it cannot understand the things of God as it formerly and incorrectly had. And the Dark Night is purifying the Intellect from the presumption that God can be manipulated and known by the human Intellect/mind, or is merely one object among others. Faith will not be an assent to glib and conventional ideas about God, but a radical trusting relationship with God in God's Self no matter what is happening or how it seems.
- God is purifying the Memory/imagination from its former function of creating a coherent sense of life based on a *dead* past or *imagined* future, for a new freedom to be open to an *unimagined* future that is in God's hands for all good. God is undoing the memories that underpinned the former understanding of faith, hope and love. Hope will not be reliance on positive thinking, optimism, or consoling God experiences of the past, but in true confidence in God and the things of God unseen and not understood.
- And God is undoing the Will to love from a "love" founded on self-centered needs based on feeling, affect, delight and satisfaction, to the outpoured, self-sacrificial, divinized Trinitarian Love of God, Christ and the Holy Spirit. So that the "love with which the Father loved Christ may be in them." (Jn. 17:26)

If anyone is *sure* they are in the Passive Dark Night of Spirit, they most likely are not. And the Passive Dark Night of Spirit cannot be explained by a spiritual director in such a way that it will seem intelligible, be consoling, or in any manner be convincing that the purifying situation one is in is a tremendous gift, that things are not what they appear to be, and that the Passive Dark Night of Spirit is leading to transformation for deeper *love and union* with God. Even the Prayer of Union will appear to be lost. It is the dying of the former man or woman, the "I live now not I, but Christ lives in me" transformation. (Gal. 2:20)

The four Nights of the Active Nights of Sense and Spirit and the Passive Nights of Sense and Spirit are John's logical progression, though they do not necessarily follow one after another in a linear series. That is, the Active Nights of Sense and Spirit can be happening on their own with or without the Passive Nights of Sense and Spirit. In the Passive Night of Spirit all four Nights would be part of the purification trial.

Sometimes during, or towards the end of the purification of the Passive Dark Night of Spirit, there are also dimly sensed *illuminative aspects,* or some new inchoate understandings of God and Divine love and action—even if they are perhaps not well understood and can't be put into words. And without knowing what or how the grace is happening, the person perseveres and does remain faithful to prayer, virtue, and to new understandings of faith, hope and love. The peace that surpasses understanding is beginning, and a new loving attention to God, that is mainly not a felt love, is also happening.

TEMPORAL DESCRIPTIONS OF THE DARK NIGHT

The Nights or Ways of:

1. 1) Beginner, 2) Proficient, 3) Perfect

2. 1) Purgative, 2) Illuminative, 3) Unitive

3. 1) Night of Sense, 2) Night of Spirit, 3) Night of God

4. 1) Twilight, 2) Midnight, 3) Dawn

1. Nights or Ways of the: 1) Beginner, 2) Proficient, 3) Perfect

1) Night of the Beginner / Way of the Beginner

In John's theology a beginner is one who has begun to practice a spiritual life of detachment and prayer. A beginner is one who is preparing to experience, or begins to experience the beginnings of passive prayer—the gift of Infused Recollection or perhaps even the Prayer of Quiet. This Night is generally more a part of the Active Night of Sense and Spirit.

2) Night of the Proficient / Way of the Proficient

This is the stage in which persons more generally experience God in a contemplative manner. Typically, this stage lasts through much of the contemplative life. It is equivalent to the Illuminative way. It would include the Active Night of Sense and Spirit and also the Passive Night of Sense, and perhaps beginnings of the Passive Night of Spirit. These Nights would be preparation for the gift of the Passive Night of Spirit.

3) Night of the Perfect / Way of the Perfect

This stage of the spiritual life would have included the Active Night of Sense and Spirit, and the Passive Night of Sense, and taken the person into the great purification of the Passive Night of Spirit for union with God. When purification has reached the level desired by God it can become the life described as divinized Transforming Union (also known as True Union, Union of Likeness to Christ, or Spiritual Marriage) in which persons remain in union with the Lord, and consciously know this whenever they turn their attention towards Him.

2. Nights or Ways of the: 1) Purgative, 2) Illuminative, 3) Unitive

1) Purgative Way

Traditionally in Mystical Theology, the Purgative Way describes the beginning of the interior life. It is the life of active choices for virtue and love of God and neighbor—asceticism—and corresponds to the Way of the Beginner.

2) Illuminative Way

The Illuminative Way describes the effects of infused grace and passive or contemplative prayer and life. It is the longest part of the spiritual journey and is equivalent to the Way of the Proficient. It would include the Active Night of Sense and Spirit and the Passive Night of Sense in preparation for the full-blown Passive Night of Spirit or a beginning movement into it.

3) Unitive Way

The Unitive Way has included the purification stages of all the Active and Passive Nights. When God has achieved the purification desired, the actual life of perfect union with God in this life takes place. It is equivalent to the divinization of True Union—Transforming Union, Conformity of Wills, and Spiritual Marriage—or the Way of the Perfect.

3. 1) Night of Sense, 2) Night of Spirit, 3) Night of God

1) <u>Night of Sense</u>

This Night would include the Active and Passive Night of Sense as explained above.

2) <u>Night of Spirit</u>

This Night would refer to the Active and Passive of Night of Spirit as also described above.

3) <u>Night of God</u>

The Night of God would be the Passive Night of Spirit in which the purification and choice is radically for God alone, and not for the understandings, consolations, delights and favors from the relationship with God. It is to love God for God's Self, not counting the cost.

4. Nights of: 1) Twilight, 2) Midnight, 3) Dawn

1) <u>Twilight</u>

This would be the way of the beginning purifications of the Active Nights of Sense and Spirit—some darkness beginning.

2) <u>Midnight</u>

This would include some of the darkest aspects of the purifying Dark Night—the Passive Night of Sense and especially of Spirit or the Night of God as described above.

3) <u>Dawn</u>

This stage would occur towards the end of the Dark Night of Spirit, or Night of God, when the person has become more conditioned to the love, ways, and things of God. It would include some incipient illuminative aspects of God and God's love and action. Having lived through a midnight darkness of God, now in this semi-darkness without knowing what or how the grace is happening, the person will remain faithful to prayer, virtue, and to new ways of believing, hoping and loving. Union with God and the peace that surpasses understanding is beginning. An unfelt loving attention to God is also happening. There is some light breaking through for a new dawn of life in God, and one is becoming more acclimatized to the darkness and otherness of God.

Passive Dark Night of Spirit Experience (chart)

Spiritual State	Thoughts	Feelings	Relationships	Spirituality	Behavior	Responses
Intense soul and spirit suffering	Neither rational nor irrational; no logical escape is visible, and no programs of any kind help	Lack of desire or energy; longing for the spirituality and God of the past; fear a point of no return	No props or support systems, or relationships experienced as reliable or trustworthy	Contemplative passivity to God in prayer and reflection	Signs of disintegration, human fragility, sinfulness and brokenness in behavior	Powerlessness and ambiguity are acknowledged and accepted in resignation
Crisis, collapse, chaos; and undoing transition time	Thoughts of emptiness, meaninglessness and the absurdity of life and former beliefs	Joylessness, boredom, failure, weakness, impotency, disillusionment, deprivation	Rejection by God; and abandonment by God and others	Death and breakdown of former God images and self images	Lassitude, fatigue, ennui, depression; behavior is lacking fervor	Continues as able, to do the work of God in ministry, family, religious life, etc.
Not essentially a brain state, but a spiritual state; in the center of the soul	Can't remember former relationship to God; no affect for spiritual life	Chaotic, sinful, confused, unintegrated, disordered, feeling of self-worthlessness	God, people, career, projects, spiritual life, and prayer do not satisfy	Dry and dark, with no spiritual insight or consolation, or fervor	Restless, impatient, ineffective; no way seen ahead and no way back	Eventual surrender and reliance on God alone
God secretly acclimatizing the person to the life of the Holy Spirit	Former core beliefs and categories are broken down; former comprehension of them is gone	Experience of limits, failure, constriction, mistakes, shock, trauma, outrage, annihilation	Experience of abandonment, loneliness, betrayal, opposition, and alienation	Loss of religious ground; feeling one's spiritual life and progress is over, never to return again	Crying, sorrow, breakdown, burnout, going in circles, resistant and subdued	Keeps praying despite a felt lack of peace, joy or faith, hope and love; Simplified prayer
Unconscious psychological material is exposed, found deficient; true motivations are revealed	Planning, and plausible explanations and spiritual programs do not work	No pleasure or interest in anything or anyone; fear of God's overwhelming awesomeness and strangeness	No one seems to understand or be able to help or relieve the situation and suffering	No feeling of satisfaction in one's spiritual life, prayer, ministry, or in any diversions	Working harder, seeking escapes in diversions, keeping busy; can't think or spiritualize any way out of the situation	One's life surrendered in darkness and radical unknowing of who God and the self are
God is freeing the person from ideas, feelings and projections about God	What should not be happening is happening—back to front; fear and anxiety	Impatience, futility, anger, regret, fear that all is lost, no livable future ahead	Affectivity feels broken in need of reformation and transformation	Self-doubt, impatience and regret over one's own failures and shortcomings	Attempts to return to former devotions, or relationship to God that don't work	Acceptance of suffering, cross and Paschal Mystery
God's work in the soul is hidden and safe from human meddling and manipulation	Contradictory, dead-ends; Reality/Truth experienced as unintelligible	No feelings of security or success for the present life, or of Eternal Life to come; heaven may not exist	Dis-ease in the relationship with God, with an unknown, new relationship to the Mystery of God developing	God is experienced as absent and as mysterious, as totally Other, or Enemy	A fall back to more right brain perceptions for moving more deeply into a new experience of God	As able, fidelity in trying to respond to invitations, will, and desires of God when discerned
God is transforming the human person for preparation for complete union with God	One can't think or imagine a path to a consistent theology or spirituality	Faith, hope, love feel weak, lukewarm, non-existent, and are not experienced on the feeling level	Relationships and affectivity are put in right order in God and in relation to God	An experience that even the spiritual goods and spiritual life cannot compete with the primacy of the love of God	A dialectic of resistance and acceptance in making choices; responses for God can't be made on the feeling level	Surrendered choices for the radical, dark, God-defined understanding of faith, hope and love

DISCURSIVE MEDITATION AND SIMPLE MEDITATION
(Active or Acquired Recollection)

Acquired Recollection

- Acquired Recollection is the *active prayer* we do ourselves in raising the heart and mind to the Lord, and in quieting and calming the mind to listen to Him. This can be through Discursive Meditation with *thoughts about* God and Jesus, or through an *image connected to Him made in the imagination* in Simple Meditation. Vocal prayer, such as, the rosary, Lectio Divina, Divine Office, Stations of the Cross, and Centering Prayer are all forms of active Acquired Recollection.

Discursive Meditation
(IC4,3,4-7; 6,7,7-9; L13,11-13)

- Discursive Meditation is a method of reflection that proceeds from one thought point to another thought point through the work of the faculties or powers and natural abilities of the Intellect/mind or the Memory/imagination.
  - The ideas or reflection moving from one idea to another can be about God, or attributes of Christ, a Gospel scene and its place, situation and characters, or a doctrine of Christianity.
  - For St. Teresa, Discursive Meditation is a form of Acquired Recollection—a form of active prayer that we do ourselves.
    - Centering Prayer is not passive contemplative prayer, but rather active prayer, and thus another form of Acquired Recollection.
- The effort of doing Discursive Meditation in seeking the Lord isn't needed once He takes over in passive contemplative prayer.
  - The Intellect/mind and Memory/imagination become less capable of Discursive Meditation once contemplation is given.
  - Discursive Meditation would be a hindrance to contemplation and simpler forms of prayer.
  - Once God takes over prayer, the work of love in the Will comes to the forefront, and the soul doesn't need or want to tire itself by working with the Intellect/mind or Memory/imagination.

- When love in the Will is not yet enflamed or stirred up for the Lord, and His presence is not sensed, nor the mind quieted, it is necessary that one seek His presence by actively trying to stir affection or devotion for Him in some kind of spiritual thought, reflection, or spiritual image.
- If desire and affection in the Will is already enflamed with love and desire for God, which is the goal, prayer will be simpler and less work.
  - But if not, the Will needs the help of the Intellect/mind and Memory/imagination for reflections or images on the life, work and love of Christ to enkindle love and desire for God. This is particularly so before the soul reaches the fourth through seventh dwellings.
- Until the fourth dwelling places are reached, one will need the Intellect/mind and Memory/imagination to fan the fire of love in the affective Will.
- Discursive Meditation or discursive thinking with the Intellect/mind and Memory/imagination is different from what Teresa calls Simple Meditation, or the momentary, quick and simple representation of an image in the mind by means of the Memory or imagination.

Simple Meditation
(IC6,7,10-12; W26,3; 28-29)

- Simple Meditation is an uncomplicated, *momentary loving look* at Christ, or a momentary gaze at a scene, or picture from the Gospel, a mystery of Christ's life, or a simple truth or idea, about the Lord represented to the Intellect/mind by a construction of the Memory/imagination.
- Teresa also calls Simple Meditation a *brief affective understanding or image* in the Memory presented by the imagination.
- Discursive Meditation or thinking and reflection with the Intellect or mind is very different and much more work than representing a simple affective and momentary image, scene or truth to the Intellect/mind by means of the Memory/imagination.
  - However, Discursive Meditation could be a good preparation for Simple Meditation because the Memory/imagination will already have formed some picture or image stored in the Memory to imaginatively use for a momentary gaze of love at Christ.
- This quick and simple representation of a scene or picture from the Gospel, or a simple truth, or idea about God or Jesus to the mind by means of the Memory or imagination does not hinder contemplative prayer.

- For example, one could cast a quick glance at Jesus in the Garden of Gethsemane, on the cross, embracing children, asleep in the boat, at the Last Supper, praying or teaching, walking on water, healing, etc. One could also add oneself to the quick, imagined picture or Gospel scene.
- Or it could be a momentary image of Jesus near you, cupping your face in His hands, you bathing His feet with your tears, your head in His lap, Him walking with you—or whatever fosters loving affection for Him.
  - These simple gazes help spark and enkindle love for Christ, just as thinking about or imagining any loved one.
  - Simple Meditation could also counter distraction during Centering Prayer with a quick, loving gaze at Jesus taking the place of the sacred word/s.
  - Teresa writes that even in the more enjoyable forms of prayer—as the Prayer of Quiet—there is still time for this Simple Meditation of the loving gaze at Christ, and it is good to do so.
  - Teresa's experience was that the mere sight of an event from Christ's life in the imagination can be enough to occupy the Intellect/mind and Memory/imagination not only for an hour, but for many days.
    - This simple gaze will not impede even the most sublime prayer.
    - Discursive Meditation will be a hindrance if not discontinued when passive contemplative prayer begins.
  - The Lord can suspend the Intellect/mind, Memory/imagination and Will including the simple gaze if or whenever He wants to.
  - Delight in contemplative prayer, as the Prayer of Quiet, is not continual, and one may need to return to the prayer of Simple Meditation, or even Discursive Meditation.
  - The loving gaze at Christ with a simple imagined image of Him from His life was a favorite way of becoming calm and recollected for Teresa.

DISPOSITIONS FOR PRAYER

- Methods of prayer are not emphasized in Carmelite spirituality. But dispositions and attitudes of love for the *relationship* with God in prayer are emphasized.
  - Relationships, and certainly the relationship with God, can't be manipulated by methods.
  - Personal relationships are dynamic, not scripted.
- If you are not attracted to prayer, pray to desire it.
  - It's true that while *"... not all imaginations are capable of meditation, all souls are capable of loving."* (F5,2)
- Prayer doesn't go on in the head but in the heart and spirit—no matter how it seems or what it feels like. Prayer is presence, friendship and intimacy with the One present within us.
  - *"Prayer is like the experience of two persons here on earth who love each other deeply and understand each other well; even without words, just by a glance, it seems, they understand each other."* (L27,10)
- If you are convinced that God is all love, mercy and compassion, you will be confident that God's work of prayer is going on no matter what is happening in your consciousness, mind, or feelings.
  - Thus, you can and should let go of too much concern about just what is happening in your prayer.
- Don't be unduly concerned about distractions, or aridity and dryness in prayer.
- Don't give in to discouragement and keep your eyes, mind and heart focused on the Beloved's eyes, mind and heart.
  - *"... the true lover loves everywhere and is always thinking of the beloved! It would be a thing hard to bear if we were only able to pray when off in some corner."* (F5,16)

False Dispositions for Prayer

- It is a lie and harmful to believe that your weaknesses and sins are stronger than God's strength.
- It is a waste of time and harmful to put an emphasis on your performance in prayer.

- How you feel or experience prayer is no indication of whether or not it was true or "successful."
- It is a false belief that prayer is your work and offering to the Lord, or that you are master and entirely in charge of your prayer.
- There will be no progress in your spiritual life if you think that the way you live has nothing to do with your prayer.
- It is false to think that God only calls saints to intimacy, or that passive contemplative prayer is esoteric and only for special persons or saints.

True Dispositions for Prayer

- Believe that the Lord is in love with you and desires intimacy with you.
  - *"O love that loves me more than I can love myself or understand!"* (S,XVII,1)
- Generally, your primary conversion will be believing the love that the Lord has for you.
  - Jesus entreats: "Abide in Me." (Jn. 15:4) "Apart from Me you can do nothing." (Jn. 15:5) "I want you with Me where I am." (Jn. 17:24)
- You must have a healthy and true image of the Lord as outpoured love, generosity, mercy, tenderness, compassion and desirous of all good for you.
- Be bold, and in faith and confidence, capture God's heart by your own heart of love.
  - St. Therese of Lisieux taught that confidence in the Lord's love is irresistible to Him.
- When it comes to prayer, the awareness that prayer is primarily a deepening *relationship* with Christ is paramount.
- Prayer is not about your performance, but is about the Lord's work and favors.
- Prayer is not about your success. God's work is always efficacious. Thus, God is always successful.
- The efficacy of your prayer has nothing to do with how you feel or experience it.
- God is always doing something within you, whether you are conscious of it or not.
- Your part is to be there, "show up," love the Lord, and let Him direct your prayer.

Those Who Can't Meditate

- Teresa did think that "... *not all who practice prayer are called to be contemplatives.*" (W17,2)
  - God doesn't demand this, and contemplation is a gift from God.
- If you can only pray vocally, so be it. God knows what is suitable for each person.
- If humble, loving and detached, you will receive as much as others, or perhaps more.
- Try to be attentive to those thoughts and words that stir up love for God, but without tiring your mind.
  - Notice and attend to the *affective,* or love-sense, of any word or thought that stirs in you.
- Slowly recite a vocal prayer that has meaning for you, or use a sacred word/s or inspiring book.
- Try, if possible, to form an image of Christ as in a Simple Meditation like Teresa teaches. Then express any affections of your heart for Him from that.
- If you are faithful and generous, despite dryness or inability to meditate, you will arrive at contemplation, if and when God wants to give it to you.
- Some who have much dryness in prayer, but are faithful to prayer, arrive at contemplative prayer sooner.

DISTRACTIONS IN PRAYER

- The constant chatter and conversation in the head are part of being human. It is the mind *"like wild horses"* of St. Teresa, the "jumping bean mind," or the "monkey mind" of Buddhists.
- Distractions do not mean that you do not love the Lord, or desire to love God, or pray.
- Distractions can be harmful or helpful, trivial and bothersome, or something significant trying to get your attention during prayer.
  - They are harmful if they completely derail your prayer with unwanted thoughts, emotions or images. They are also harmful if they separate you from love of God or neighbor, or cause you to give up prayer, or throw you into either self-aggrandizement or self-deprecation.
  - They are a blessing and helpful if they are about some deep issue for self-knowledge that will be beneficial for growth in prayer and Christian life.
- You must listen carefully to any persistent concerns or thoughts for helpful insights and self-knowledge.
  - Genuine life concerns are part of the context of prayer, and generally arise to be surrendered, transformed and healed. They reveal attachments or what has become important.
  - They can help reveal where you are at the present moment of your life.
  - Just trying to ignore *persistent* concerns arising in prayer would make prayer shallow and unhelpful.
  - Also, someone or some happening or event may come to mind that is in need of your intercessory prayer.
- Significant distractions should be reflected upon, and shared with a spiritual director for discernment as to how you should respond to them.
- Depending on where you are in your prayer journey, distractions may be different in cause or purpose for different dwelling places, and need varying or different responses.
- Those who have been seriously practicing prayer for many years need to pay even more attention to significant distractions that may be a call from the Holy Spirit for deeper self-knowledge and conversion—especially of what may lie in the unconscious realm of the self.
- Distractions can arise from fatigue, hunger, sleepiness, illness, being too cold or too hot, being uncomfortable, depression, complacency, lack of seriousness about your relationship with the Lord, or even be a kind of pleasurable staring into space and languishing. You may really only need

to feel better and have more energy—by exercising, getting more rest, recreating, laughing, or relaxing.
- o The faculty of the Will (seat of the propensity, energy and tendency of desires/resistances, affections/aversions, attractions/repulsions, as well as choice) governs Intellect/mind and Memory/imagination, and thus has a part to play in managing distractions.
- o In later stages of prayer, as the Prayer of the Sleep of the Faculties and Prayer of Union, distractions are not as great an issue during passive contemplative prayer, but distractions from thoughts and feelings that cause disruptions in the accompanying contemplative *life* may be a further call for attention and change.

Some Causes of Distractions

- o Lack of careful preparation or intention concerning prayer, and also drifting attention during prayer, can leave the door open to distractions.
  - Failure to guard the five senses during prayer from noise, people, or temptations—as electronic gadgets—can disrupt prayer.
  - An overly busy life with a failure to pay attention to how you come to prayer—rushed or calmly—can carry distractions into prayer.
  - Looking around, or failing to check and stop curiosity in the outer or inner world will cause distractions.
- o Not all thoughts or emotions are voluntary, but you have some control over what you do with them.
- o Not avoiding occasions of sin and indulging in addictive attachments in your life choices can lead to distraction by recalling images of them during prayer.
- o Inattention and laxity in reciting vocal formulary prayers *is distraction.*
  - It is mindless rattling off by rote without awareness of what you are saying, or to *Whom* you are speaking.
  - Mindlessly addressing your prayer words to God while you are thinking of someone or something else is to be distracted.
  - Attention deliberately given to preoccupations outside of the prayer time as well as judging, arguing, rehearsing, recalling annoyances or slights, following daydreams, self-pity, criticalness, fantasies, and "to do" lists, etc. distract prayer.
- o Being irritated or complaining to God about aridity or dryness in prayer is a distraction.
  - Aridity or dryness in prayer can have different causes or purposes according to the stage of prayer you are in.

- It can be caused by inattention and not settling down seriously to prayer.
- It can be a trial for exercising faith, patience, trust, and the depth of love and commitment.
- Dryness and aridity in later stages of prayer may reveal that a deepening of contemplative prayer is occurring in the silent, emptiness and darkness of God's felt "absent presence," which is dryness for the senses and the ego self. However, the spirit may be being nourished in hidden, unknown ways.

o Trying to *forcefully* suspend all thought by any harsh effort, causes resistance—in itself a distracting emotion—that can lead to more distracting emotions or thoughts.

o An unhelpful director can cause feelings of guilt concerning prayer—a pressure to pray in a certain way that the director likes. No one has to pray in the director's way, and you should consider changing directors if you continue to experience pressure.

o Offer to God whatever condition you find yourself in.

Some Sources of Distracting Thoughts, Feelings and Images

o It is important to discern where thoughts or feelings are coming from to know how to respond to them.

o Some distractions are harmful, while others are inspired by the Holy Spirit for deepening self-knowledge.

o Distractions can come from several sources:

1. From the Self:
    - Generally, thoughts and feelings, and their interconnection, coming from one's self are ordinary and neutral, or even revelatory of helpful self-knowledge.
    - Such thoughts include: interior planning, arguing, rehearsing, futuring, or trivia from incidents, TV, books, dreams, or unsolicited memories or feelings—past or present.

2. From the World and its systems, values, spirit and energies:
    - These thoughts come from the unreflective and unexamined conventional thinking of your peer group, culture, country, or world view—materialism, individualism, the throw away culture, nationalism, racism, sexism, narcissism, gossip, judgmentalness, violence for solving disputes, etc.
    - Or, such thoughts as:

- "Someone else will do it." "Live and let live. It's not my concern."
        - "I'm not hurting anyone by doing this." "Everybody else is doing it."
        - "I need to take care of number one." "It's a dog-eat-dog world."
        - "I have to keep up with the Joneses."
        - "I need and deserve the latest technological gadget, fashion, car, size of house, etc."
        - "It's a free country. It is my *right* to _____ as I see fit."
3. From the Holy Spirit:
    - These thoughts are more subtle, quiet, delicate, and perhaps novel and new.
    - They can inspire you to change, to transformation, and to more self-knowledge.
    - Some inspirations are for suffering individuals, suffering humanity or situations needing prayer.
4. From Evil Spirits, Powers—the Enemy—or the apathetic or un-transformed unconscious:
    - These thoughts are more intrusive and disturbing—noisier, rude, accusing, obnoxious, twisted, grotesque, discouraging, judgmental, warring, festering, annoying, or obsessive.
    - They take away peace and bring uncomfortable feelings along with them.
    - They include false images of God, and suggestions that any sinful thoughts and actions are not really that important or serious.
    - Often these thoughts are self-condemning, causing self-hatred, and bring despair.

In Dealing with Ordinary Distractions

o A loving, sincere intention to be with, give time to, and listen to the Lord within at the beginning of your prayer is an important way to curtail many distractions.
    - Closing your eyes and making little acts of love in your own words will stir your affection for the Lord.
o Avoid any criticalness of yourself or others during prayer.
o Set a quiet timer for the amount of time you are giving to prayer.
    - This could be a quiet chime or bell on an electronic device. This will help prevent the distraction of looking at a clock, or feelings of anxiety or of wanting and waiting for the time to be over, or of missing any necessary commitment or appointment.

- After distractions are noticed, return your attention to the Lord's presence—over and over. That is a good prayer in itself!
- Recall that the Holy Spirit is helping you and praying in you, even when you are unaware of it. And the saints are there for help, too, so call on favorite saints for help.
- Avoid judging the success or failure of your prayer, or where you are in the stages of prayer.
- Try to befriend, accept or endure distractions, avoiding becoming upset, exasperated or condemning of them. That will only cause further emotional distractions. Just note or recognize distractions—as either trivial or significant. Return to your loving gaze of Christ and your breath, sacred image, word/s, or prayer.
- It can be helpful to note distractions in passing by giving a name to a distracting thought, feeling or emotion, and then letting it go. Do not go off on a long psychological explanation for the cause of the thought or feeling. The feeling or issue underneath can be brought up later with a spiritual director for more light and understanding.
- Do not deliberately let your mind wander, or follow either painful or pleasurable thoughts or feelings.
- If you don't focus a lot of energy on distractions, generally they will recede to the background of your mind.
- Know that distractions and genuine prayer can go on at the same time. Sometimes distracting thoughts are quieter and off away in some more distant place in your mind.
- Try to practice detachment from distractions and the emotions connected to them. You may have a preference about what you might desire in prayer or your life, but not an addiction or demand for anything. Hold what is with gratitude, reverence, or lightly as needed.
- Pray as you can, in any mode that you can.
- Recall and trust that the Lord knows where you are at, what your needs are, and despite your failures, He desires your company and wants to be with you and hear from you.

What to Do if Distractions Appear Evil, Negative or Harmful

- Leave such distractions alone for the time being and return to prayer at another time when you perhaps have more physical, psychic and emotional energy to deal with any extreme darkness.

- With as much attentiveness as possible, begin to read a spiritual book, Gospel passage, or psalm that relates to your situation, or say a rosary or other formulary prayer to take your mind off of something negative.
- Journal about the situation to get it out of your mind. This distraction then is expressed and surrendered to God on paper. Perhaps you can bring it later to a spiritual director.
- Do something physical. Take a walk, exercise, play a musical instrument, sing or dance, watch a humorous show.
- Get busy with some good work for others.
- Get help from a spiritual director if these harmful distractions persist.

FACULTIES OR POWERS OF THE SOUL
(IC1,2,4 &15; 4,1,6-8; W31,5-10; A2,6)

The three faculties of the soul are Intellect/mind, Memory/imagination and Will. While there was not agreement among medieval philosophers and theologians about the structure and anthropology of the human soul, or how each of the three faculties or powers (abilities) of the soul were related to the others, St. Teresa and St. John of the Cross used the terminology of Intellect, Memory and Will in their spiritual writings. St. John of the Cross as a trained theologian was more thorough and nuanced in his use of the terminology. Teresa was not a trained philosopher or theologian, but she used the concept of the faculties of Intellect, Memory and Will, which belong to the soul, as she understood them for her own purposes. Neither Teresa nor John knew of Freud's or Jung's concepts of ego, super-ego, id, subconscious or unconscious for saying something about the operations in the soul in relation to the transcendent. It doesn't seem that modern psychology or science has done better than St. Teresa and St. John of the Cross at explaining what is occurring in mystical experiences, or the capacities of a soul that is operating beyond "normal" human abilities.

Whatever the argued subtleties of Scholastic anthropology, the three faculties of the soul are a useful schema for understanding something about what happens in various stages of contemplative prayer and life. It names three powers or abilities of the soul for mental and internal processes that understand, form, recall, attract and direct thoughts, beliefs, attitudes, choices and behavior. The three faculties of the soul include and govern such movements and operations as understanding, imagining and remembering, as well as inclinations, attractions, aversions, impulses, and choices.

There is a sense in which understanding something about these operations, powers and abilities of the soul contributes to a genuine source of self-knowledge.

o The three faculties or powers of the soul are:
1. **INTELLECT**/mind is the power for knowing and understanding. This faculty can know things naturally, but also supernaturally.
2. **MEMORY**/imagination is the power for remembering and also constructing images and ideas through using the imagination. It carries consciousness of the past that can extrapolate to the present or future. It also contains consciousness in the sense of self-awareness and self-possession.

- Memory loss—whether from Alzheimer's, or vascular, as strokes, or from traumatic brain injuries and coma—includes a loss of self-consciousness, self-possession, and aspects of one's past.
3. **WILL** has an affective, emotional, or experiential quality in its power concerning allurement, desiring and loving (or their opposites) which is involved with attraction or repulsion, and thus influences intention, deliberation, decision making and, ultimately, choices that affect behavior.
   - Though Intellect, Memory and Will are delineated, they are not three disconnected faculties or powers of the human person or soul, but all are part of one collective whole of the soul's interior operating system under three aspects which work together in an extremely complex set of reciprocating interconnections.
   - The faculties of Intellect, Memory and Will are able to operate on *both a natural and* a *supernatural level* for understanding, recalling experiences or imagining something, and in making choices leading to actions. But only when the faculties have been purified and acclimatized to the supernatural can they be vehicles for union with God, in both experiencing and understanding something on the level of the transcendent. The faculties operating on the ordinary, conventional and natural level cannot attain union or understand the supernatural.
   - In some later intense stages of prayer—as Suspensions—Intellect, Memory and Will can all be shut down completely from operating on the conventional, ordinary and natural level.
     - In prayer, Teresa experienced the Will as the first faculty to be drawn into union with the Lord in loving attention and fascination with Him.
     - In the earlier stages of union, the natural interior faculties of Intellect/mind and Memory/imagination are free to wander and operate normally.
     - Will and Intellect can also be in union while Memory/imagination is free to wander.

INTELLECT/Mind

- Intellect/mind is the interior faculty or power for knowing and understanding. In Teresa's thinking, it also operates on both the ordinary and *natural* level of understanding, as well as on the spiritual and *supernatural* level of understanding and knowing.
- In its ordinary functioning it receives input from the external five senses and the internal senses of Intellect/mind, Memory/imagination and Will.

- Teresa makes a distinction between the faculty of the Intellect and the mind. The mind is a component or part of the faculty of the Intellect. Intellect is capable of *more* "knowing" than mind is.
  - The faculty of the Intellect can be in union with God in prayer, while the mind wanders.
- Teresa discovered that the Intellect had two parts to it: an *exterior part or ability,* the mind, with thinking and natural understanding and apprehension; and an *interior part or ability,* the power of the Intellect that is capable of receiving supernatural understanding, and of knowing the three Persons of the Trinity.
- Teresa also seems to make a distinction between *understanding* and *knowing* in the Intellect.
  - *Understanding* by the Intellect is the comprehension of truths, intellectual content, and information about something or someone as an object of understanding.
  - *Knowing* in the Intellect is intimate experience of someone, subject to Subject, encountering another in a relational intimacy person to Person. It is more like the understanding of the verb of intimacy, "to know," from scripture. (see: Lk. 1:34; Gen. 4:1; Ps.139:15; Jn. 14:7)
- In various stages of prayer, Intellect can be working and operating, or not, off-line from its ordinary function, that is, knowing without knowing exactly what/Who it knows, or receiving information it can't explain or put into words, but knows that something real has been conveyed.
- Only the supernatural faculty of Intellect can attain union with God, while the natural thinking mind cannot attain union, and may still wander or be recollected in prayer.
- St. John of the Cross speaks of the natural and supernatural capacities of the faculty of the Intellect by postulating that there is an Active Intellect and a Passive Intellect.
  - The <u>Active Intellect</u> is what is involved in ordinary knowing through the five senses and internal senses of Intellect, Memory/phantasy/imagination and Will. The natural, Active Intellect is not capable of union with God.
  - The <u>Passive Intellect</u> is a function within the faculty of the Intellect that is involved in supernatural understandings revealed to it by God directly, and is capable of union with God in this life.
  - For St. John of the Cross the theological virtue of FAITH informs and expands the capacity of Intellect for union.

MEMORY/Imagination

- Memory is the interior faculty or power of overall consciousness, of remembering, of constructing through imagination, and of giving consciousness and a sense of the self or persona to a person. It also has both a natural and a supernatural capacity.
- It gathers and stores past experiences and applies them to present and future situations. This influences motives and inclinations towards pleasure or away from pain—of attraction or repulsion—which affects the operations and choices of the Will. In seeing the present moment through the lens of the past, Memory can distort and block a genuine experience of the present or possible future that is different from the past.
- Teresa distinguished the *natural* function of the imagination—which is part of the natural operation of the faculty of Memory—from the *supernatural* operation of the faculty of Memory. Except for the mystical favor of an Imaginative Vision (see: "Imaginative Visions" in **Supplemental Material**) the supernatural operations of the imagination exclude the natural operation of imagination. That is, one cannot make up or imagine *authentic supernatural* persons, things, ideas or understandings through the *natural* imagination.
- During later intense forms of union while Will and Intellect are in union, the faculty of Memory/imagination is also usually not operating. While the natural and supernatural faculty of Memory can be lost during some intense forms of union, in other earlier stages of union the *natural* aspect of Memory/imagination could still be wandering, and the *supernatural* aspect not yet well-developed or operational.
- St. John of the Cross connects phantasy/imagination to Memory.
  - For John, the theological virtue of HOPE can heal the Memory and imagination for the freedom of persons, by unhooking them from both the dead past and imagined, not yet, future expectations, and ease the mind of whatever agitates, attracts, or frightens it.

WILL

- The faculty of Will is the seat of the propensity, energy, or tendency towards disinterest or repulsions on the one hand—or towards affections, attractions, desires and loves on the other. As such, it influences and takes charge, by choices and decisions, of the other faculties of Intellect/mind and Memory/imagination.

- Will is the affective internal faculty involved with desire and attraction, or repulsion, which pushes the soul to the decisions and choices for actions that a person takes.
- Intellect/mind, Memory/imagination and the five senses supply *input and motives* to the Will's desires and affections—or distastes—for determination, choices and behavior. But the Will can work and choose even if the Intellect is unable to understand something. And it can make choices that would not be self-serving. That is, Will can make choices that are not based on natural pleasures or self-gain. It can choose to disregard uncomfortable or pleasurable emotions or experiences that produce joy, or pain in making decisions. It also has the freedom to cut off its nose despite its face.
- In a wholesome spiritual life, the faculty of the Will motivates and directs the other faculties and, indeed, the whole person towards good, right and virtuous functioning. It brings order, unity and purpose to the life of a person.
- The objects of love and desire in the Will make persons as big or as limited as the objects of their love and desire.
- The faculty of the Will should not be thought of solely as "will-power" though it does include the power to choose. It is connected to desires, love, and affections—ordered or disordered—that can give the energy that may tip a choice in one direction or another. Even so, Will can choose against the apparent good or apparent evil, or what is not clearly understood.
  - Sixteenth century theologians would not have known about brain physiology that also affects behavior and choices. They would not have known the physical brain's various centers, nor of the peptides or hormones that release pleasant or unpleasant chemicals that are now known to influence choices and addictive behaviors.
- For St. John of the Cross, it is the theological virtue of LOVE that purifies the Will of lesser or destructive attractions and desires, or apathies. It unites the soul with God through love, through the uniting of human desires and loves with God's desires and love.

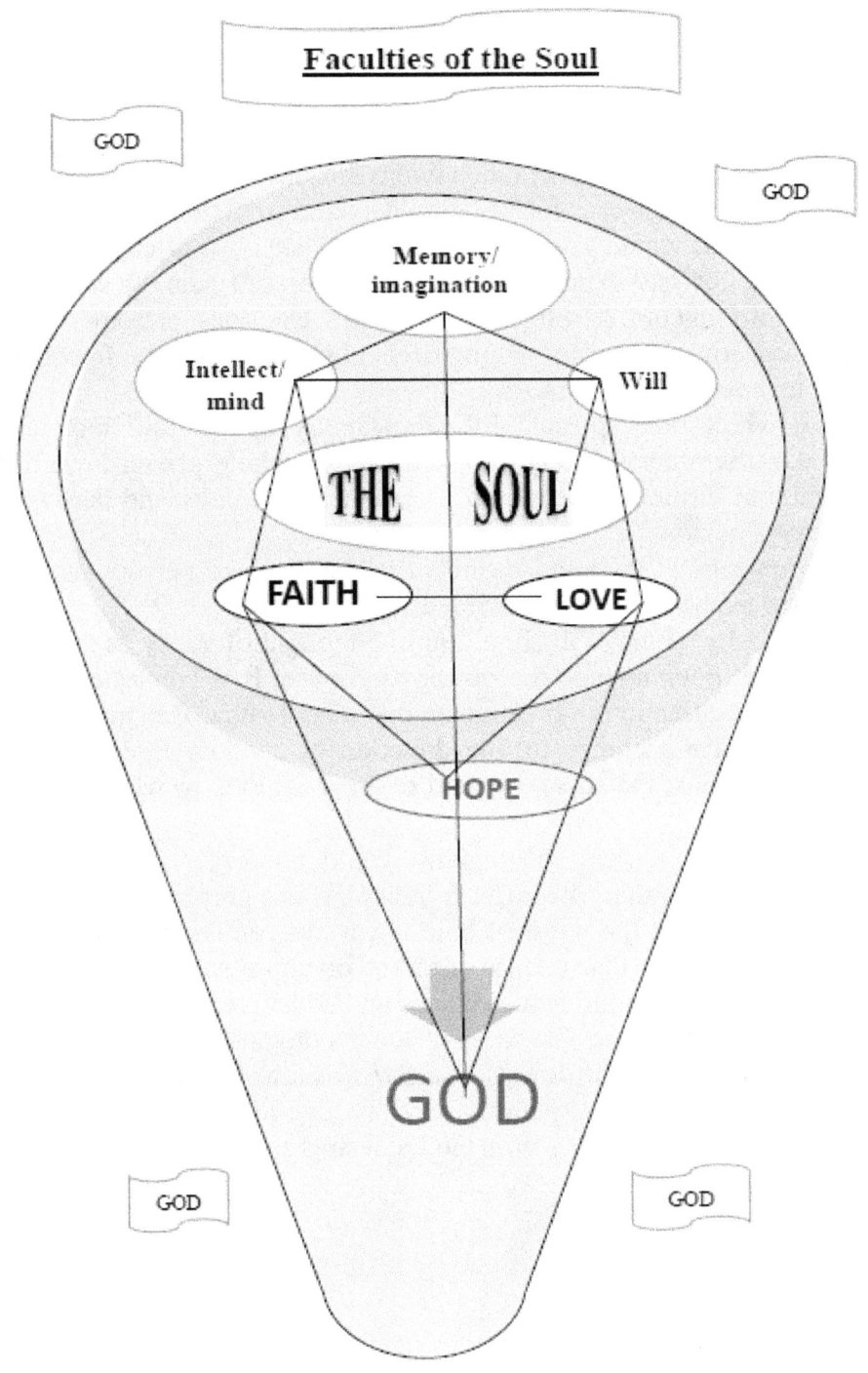

LECTIO DIVINA RECOLLECTION
(Praying with Scripture: (Lectio, Meditatio, Oratio, [Contemplatio]))

St. Teresa would have known the following from the *Carmelite Rule*: "Each one of you is to stay in his own cell or nearby, pondering the law of the Lord day and night and keeping watch at his prayers, unless attending to some other duty." (*Carmelite Rule* #8) And St. John of the Cross wrote: "Seek in reading and you will find in meditation; knock in prayer and it will be opened to you in contemplation." (SLL #158)

However, though the *Carmelite Rule* prescribed pondering scripture, during St. Teresa's lifetime due to a reaction to the Protestant Reformation's emphasis on scripture alone, the Spanish Inquisition in 1559 banned, and put on the *Index* of forbidden books, the Bible and other spiritual books in the vernacular for reading and study! So, except for those readings from scripture at Mass and in the Divine Office (which were in Latin) she could not, at will, read and ponder all of scripture. She found this very difficult until she had the locution from Christ of: "Do not be distressed, for I will give you a living book." (L26,5) At first, she didn't understand what this meant, but shortly afterwards she began to experience that Christ was teaching her about Himself and His truths directly through her prayer relationship with Him. This is an important understanding about prayer. Prayer itself is a self-revelation of Christ, of God the Father, and the Holy Spirit, and of their eternal mysteries, reality, love and being. Experientially, Teresa had a profound education in the Word of God directly from Christ Himself.

Reading, studying, listening and pondering scripture is essential to understanding Christ, His life, actions, consciousness and values and for bringing these into daily life. But contemplative prayer adds another dimension with a direct and recognized involvement and guidance of Christ in the present moment in the particularity of our own lives and transformation needs within the times in which we live. Both Lectio Divina and mystical contemplative prayer experiences can be more than knowing *about* Christ, and bring us to a genuinely profound personal and living *experience* of the person of Christ in His relationship to us in the immediate present.

Lectio Divina as a help to, and method of, recollection is comprised of *Lectio* (a reading of and listening to scripture); of *Meditatio* (meditating and pondering on the scripture); of *Oratio* (prayer that comes forth from the reading and meditation); and *Contemplatio* (contemplative prayer if God draws and gives it).

Suggestions for Lectio Divina Meditation and Recollection

PREPARATION:
o Arrange an atmosphere and setting suitable for Lectio Divina prayer.
- Get yourself away from noise, the phone, TV, iphones, computers, tablets, etc.
- Choose a comfortable chair, or pillows on the floor. Choose low lights, or a candle for lighting. Have any icons or sacred objects in your prayer space that are meaningful to you.
- Set a quiet timer for the amount of time you are giving to this prayer period.

o Set aside ½ hour or more, at the time of day that is freest for you.

o In advance, select a short passage from the Bible—5 to 10 verses—from a psalm or Gospel scene from Jesus' life. It could be one of the readings of the day for Mass.

o Begin to get comfortable and relaxed. Try to get in touch with your inner self, paying attention to your calm, slow breathing. Become more aware of yourself and the presence of God.
- Make the sign of the cross, and pray a Doxology—as the "Glory be …"
- Recall in *Whose* presence you are by addressing the Lord by the name that expresses who He is personally for you. You can use a formulary prayer or one in your own words.
- Speak what comes from your heart, from your needs and desires. Ask the Lord to speak to you through the scripture passage, and help you to listen to His response.
- If there is any uneasiness, anxiety, or fear, call on the name of Jesus to remove it.

LECTIO:
o When you are calm and recollected, begin to read the passage you have chosen for prayer.
- Read the passage slowly. This is mindful, attentive reading—not scripture study.
- This is not reading entire chapters of scripture or very long passages. It is not goal oriented.
- Linger over any word, phrase, sentence or image that speaks to you, *taking time for silent listening*. Remain in stillness and silence and let

the passage settle in you. Memorize the word or verse to take with you.

MEDITATIO:
- Begin to be aware of what you might have heard when you read the passage, how you felt, or what images came to mind that struck you.
  - Gently meditate or reflect on what you became aware of, and attend to this, *taking time for silent listening*. Remain in stillness and silence and let the passage settle in you.
- Slowly re-read the passage a second time. If something strikes you, stop and gently reflect on it till you are moved to silence again.
- Slowly re-read the passage for a third time to see if there is anything further that has struck you or has built on what you have already noticed in the previous readings. There may or may not be more to ponder. *Taking time for silent listening*, remain for a few more moments in stillness and silence, and let the passage do its work in you.

ORATIO:
- Now make any spontaneous prayers that arise in you—prayers of gratitude, need for healing, expressions of contrition, desire for change, for more willingness for service, acts of faith, hope and love, desire to be more faithful to prayer, or petitions for the needs of others that come to mind because of the passage. *Return to the silence in quiet listening and calm.*

CONTEMPLATIO:
- This is not an aspect of prayer that you can achieve because it is passive prayer, but if you are led into a deep, quiet silence with no particular thoughts or images, remain there until it ends.
- When your quiet timer rings, and the prayer period ends, pay attention to what you have heard and what it calls for in your life.
  - Commit to responding to or acting on what you may have understood.
  - Close Lectio Divina with spontaneous prayers of gratitude, praise and adoration, or a favorite vocal prayer.
  - Stir gently and slowly before opening your eyes.
  - Make the sign of the cross, or a reverent bow or action that marks the end of your prayer period.

PASSIVE RECOLLECTION OR INFUSED RECOLLECTION

The terms Passive Recollection and Infused Recollection can be used interchangeably in speaking about what begins to happen in the fourth dwelling places of *The Interior Castle*. It is a degree of prayer that lies between active vocal prayer and devotions on the one hand, and the contemplative prayer of the Prayer of Quiet on the other. The five external senses of sight, hearing, touch, taste and smell, as well as some of the interior faculties of Intellect/mind, Memory/imagination and Will, begin to be loosened from their ordinary functions and begin to be drawn inward, stilled, or captured during the prayer of Passive or Infused Recollection. St. Teresa also uses the terminology of absorbed, captive, tied and even suspended when speaking of what begins to happen to the senses and faculties of the soul with the start of the passive Prayer of Recollection, and even more so in deeper stages of contemplative prayer.

The Spanish words that Teresa uses to convey a sense of what starts to happen in passive prayer include the following:

- **Recollected** (recoger, recogerse, recogido, recogimiento): has the sense of withdraw, take out of use, become quieted, stilled, calm, composed, peaceful, drawn inward, or engrossed.
- **Absorbed** (absorto): has the meaning of being engrossed, with the attention being fully occupied, or fascinated.
- **Captive** or **Tied** (atada): carries the sense of restrained, controlled, bound, fastened, tied, stilled, or stopped.
- **Enraptured** (embeber) and **Suspended** (suspender): has the sense of the faculties being so enraptured or suspended that the senses and faculties are temporarily stilled, interrupted, ineffective, stopped, off-line, and have ceased from their natural functioning. Teresa speaks of these in the later dwelling places—especially in the sixth dwelling places.

PRACTICAL PREPARATIONS FOR PRAYER

Remote Preparations—Initial Preparations for Prayer

- Make a general but deliberate and resolute intention to pray daily—no matter what!
- Give attention to purity and truth of conscience, and consciousness by daily self-examinations and the pursuit of self-knowledge.
- Practice the virtues which support prayer. St. Teresa recommends as key to the spiritual life: love, humility and detachment.
- *"Do not think, my friends and daughters, that I shall burden you with many things; please God, we should do what our holy fathers established and observed ... three things ... love for one another ... detachment (especially from ourselves) ... and true humility, which, even though I speak of it last, is the main practice and embraces all the others."* (W4,4)
    - <u>Love</u> is the first and greatest commandment—love of God and love of neighbor. (IC5,3,7-12; W6-7)
    - <u>Detachment</u> follows because it involves *choices* about what your heart loves, what your heart is centered on, and what you choose to desire and love. (W10-15)
    - <u>Humility</u> entails being in the center of truth about yourself—neither self-aggrandizement nor self-denigration. Your authentic self is the only one who can truly love and give of itself.
        - Such deliberately cultivated attitudes as gratitude, generosity, confidence, forgiveness (of self as well as others), kindness, patience, goodness and empathy are all helpful.
        - Examine areas of needed repentance—especially any primary or serious sin failures. (W16-17)
- Watch with awareness for what is in your Memory and imagination, which influences your emotional life and triggers feelings and reactions.
    - Emotions are stirred when we recall the memory of a loved one. And this also includes remembering the Beloved, the Lord.
- Keep the Memory, imagination and affections focused on love of Christ.
    - Practice maintaining a connection to Christ no matter what you are doing.
    - Take time to frequently look at Christ during the day—as Teresa's *miradas*/glances at Jesus.
    - Dedicate your day's work to Christ, and later reflect on how He has been blessing your day.

- Have short conversations with Christ. Make little short prayers, outbursts or aspirations of love to Christ.
- Prayer doesn't go on in the head, but in the heart—no matter what it *feels* like.
- Avoid foolish or harmful fantasies.
- Watch out for peer pressure. Allow no one and nothing to take away your peace and center in Christ.
  - Your center is always who you are—in and for Christ—not the approval or disapproval of others.
- If attraction and fervor for prayer is lacking, offer this condition to the Lord, and pray for the fervor and desire to pray.
- Aridity and dryness will come in prayer as a natural part of prayer.
  - Difficulty in prayer can also come from a poor state of health, lack of exercise or lack of mindful, mental prayer in thought and affection.
- A short mid-day examination of conscience, journaling, poetry, sacred music, or walks in nature can keep the mind quieted and focused on Christ.
- All the good things of our world are a means to an end, but not an end in themselves. Your end is God. Whatever does not draw you away from God, but closer to Him is good.

Proximate Preparations—Entering into Prayer

- Prepare for entering into prayer by going to your chosen place of prayer, getting situated in a comfortable but alert body posture for prayer, closing your eyes, letting go of any distracting thoughts or external situations in your life, and remembering that you are always in the presence of the Lord.
- As desired, have ready something about Jesus' life from scripture or a spiritual book that fits your life circumstance, temperament or emotion at the time of prayer.
  - A single image or truth about Jesus, His life, teachings and example of love can provoke love and gratitude to draw you closer to Him. The Christian mystics always teach that Christians should pray through the humanity of Christ. (IC6,7,5-15; W29,2-7)
  - Be aware, if you can, of what stories, thoughts, feelings and prejudices you are bringing to prayer with you. Let go of any that are a distraction.
- Continue to try to quiet and recollect yourself with attention to breath and a sacred word, or the name of Jesus, moving your focus inward to the presence of Christ.

- Recall who He is, to elicit responses of reverence, adoration, awe, love and gratitude.
- You may want to change body language and posture during prayer to fit various responses—of adoration: prostration, kneeling or bowing; of gratitude: with open hands; of sorrow: hands striking the breast or covering the face; of joy: hands and arms reaching upwards, etc.
- An examination of conscience, consciousness and behavior is also a good preparation for prayer.
    - A prayer response to your examination of conscience, consciousness and behavior may be appropriate: as the Confiteor (I confess …), Our Father, or a psalm (as 51). It could also be a paragraph or two from an inspirational book.
- If you are in a rut or discouragement about your prayer, it may be good to vary your preparation to keep prayer fresh and avoid stagnation.
    - Don't let prayer become careless, routine, or inattentive.
- Do something different for prayer if you are stuck and not wanting to persevere.
    - Try a different posture, time of day, or a very slow, meditative walk, or some journaling. Sing a hymn, listen to prayerful music, read a poem with a religious theme, try a psalm or different formulary prayer, read a paragraph or two from a spiritual book, gaze with attention at the cross or an icon.

PRAYER OF RECOLLECTION—ST. TERESA'S WAY OF PRAYING
A Teresian "Method" (L9,4)

St. Teresa doesn't really have a method of prayer, and she doesn't direct anyone to pray according to her way of praying. She did pay attention to her own experiences in prayer and spoke about them with her spiritual directors and confessors, when she discovered what was and wasn't helpful for her. She doesn't write that anyone taught her how to pray in her novitiate beyond the Divine Office and formulary prayers. However, she did find help from the book, *The Third Spiritual Alphabet,* by the Franciscan, Francisco de Osuna. Generally, Carmelite novice directors don't impose a method of prayer on novices about how to pray and become recollected beyond giving them St. Teresa's writings to read, and telling them they must spend two hours a day at mindful, mental prayer as St. Teresa recommended and practiced herself.

Teresa doesn't give a lot of instruction about what to do with the body during prayer, though she suggests closing the eyes so as to turn the gaze inward towards Christ and to one's own interior. However, her body did come into her prayer, for example, with tears, or with throwing herself on the ground at the feet of Christ represented by a statue of Him that moved her. Sometimes she would sing. She was also aware that prayer was harder for her when her body was sick. (L11,15) Some Carmelites—perhaps younger ones—still pray on the floor sitting back on their heels. Using a prayer bench to pray this way would keep one alert and be less uncomfortable.

As with many people who begin to pray, St. Teresa first found the prayer of Infused Recollection to be rather easy and pleasurable and to come with some consolations. But in time, as is the case generally with the progress of prayer, it became harder to pray because of dryness and restlessness in prayer. She eventually came to realize that this was a natural development in prayer for God's purposes—perhaps to develop patience, growth in virtue, and fidelity to prayer in loving the Lord for His sake, rather than for the rewards, pleasures or consolations in prayer.

When Teresa's prayer came up against the arid and restless times, she began to have a hard time quieting her mind for recollection. She said she had a mind like *"wild horses"* and was not good at controlling distracting thoughts. (W19,2) Her remedy was to bring a good spiritual book or a passage of scripture to prayer and to read a few sentences to get her mind focused on something other than her busy mind. Teresa wrote she spent fourteen years not being able to practice meditation without reading. (W17,3) If her prayer time was dry, she would remind herself that God was in charge of her prayer and that the Lord could be trusted with what was best for her, and this would bring her to a peaceful confidence in Him and the patience needed to endure the aridity.

She wrote that she couldn't make up long involved meditations about God, or Christ's life with her mind. And her imagination wouldn't work to construct elaborate scenes with many scripture personages or situations from Christ's life. But she did discover that she could do a simple, momentary picture of a scene from Christ's life with her imagination. This she called Simple Meditation. She especially found her imaginary scene of Jesus praying alone in the Garden of Gethsemane helpful for calming her mind for recollection. (IC6,7,11) If Teresa has a method of prayer, it is to enter within her own interior and picture Christ within her, and especially in a simple scene where He is alone and distressed. These simple, created scenes of her imagination tended to melt her heart and stir up love and tenderness for Him. (L9,4) Teresa's prayer was always centered on Jesus, His presence, who He is, and how she was made in His image and likeness. She liked to have a picture of Jesus before her at prayer. Teresa especially liked to be alone with Jesus when He was alone. Lovers like to be alone together, and physical aloneness with the beloved deepens intimacy. Teresa also used a single, loving and gentle word from time to time, said like *"a puff on a candle"* to stir up the flame that can enkindle love for Christ in prayer. (W31,7,13)

Teresa became aware that she could more closely unite herself to Christ if she paid attention to her own emotions and moods. Awareness of self and awakened self-knowledge was always key for Teresa for deepening the relationship with Christ in prayer. If she could match her feelings and moods with those of Christ's in the Gospels, this caused her to feel closer to Him, stirred up love in her, and helped her to know Him more intimately. If she was feeling lonely, betrayed or misunderstood she could be alone with Jesus in the Garden of Gethsemane, or alone at prayer, or in other ways in the Gospels, and the two could comfort one another and share these experiences which strengthened their bond of love. (L9)

Another way that Teresa stirred herself to love for Christ was with holy aspiratory prayers—or expressions of outpoured love. She had made such prayers since she was a child when she would repeat her wonder at the Lord and heavenly life with *"forever and ever and ever."* Teresa gives examples of holy exclamations, aspirations or loving expressions (also known as holy ejaculations) that she prayed as: *"O Life of my life!" "O Sustenance that sustains me!"* (IC7,2,6) St. Teresa's writings are full of outbursts of praise, thanksgiving, amazement and joy at God and the works of the Lord. And these aroused love in her. These are intimate expressions of love and desire between lovers.

Teresa's way of praying always moves away from the head towards the heart—from being *about* Jesus to being *with* Jesus. The energy of ardor, passion and desire is a power for love and the deepening and strengthening of a love relationship. So, remaining in Jesus' company was all important to Teresa and was her manner of "praying always." She recalled Him to herself in the kitchen among *"the pots and pans"* (F5,8) or before going to bed when she would intentionally entrust herself to Him—as any lover recalls a beloved before sleep. (L9,4) "On my bed at night I sought Him whom my heart loves." (Sg. 3,1) Prayer for Teresa is a frequent conversation and intimate sharing between two friends or lovers, and she never let herself be far from His presence in her thoughts, words, actions and awareness of Him. Remaining in Jesus' presence was crucial to the relationship for Teresa and she never began prayer without recalling who He is and in whose presence she lived. Lovers know how to silently gaze in love at one another. This was her practice to look within at Jesus with the loving eyes of her soul. Teresa's way of praying is not complex. Any lover knows how to think of the beloved, imagine being with the beloved, increase desire and love with whispered words of love, and make the beloved present in heart and mind. This was Teresa's manner of being with Christ which led her to a constant recollection of His presence with her and in her, which in time was no longer a huge effort, but second nature to her—a way of living. And Jesus responded to her constant desire for Him by making His loving presence known to her.

In her book *The Interior Castle*, Teresa treats the fourth dwelling places as the places where two friends meet and exchange gifts. In the fifth dwelling places of prayer they begin to fall in love and share signs of affection, as holding hands. In the sixth dwelling places the two become betrothed to one another. And in the seventh dwelling places of prayer they are permanently united in Spiritual Marriage. Teresa came to know and to teach what most people have yet to realize, that God is everyone's "most significant Other"—their true Lover—and the only One who can satisfy all their needs for love and bring to fulfillment all their desires. So Teresian prayer is always in the context of spousal love—of Lover and beloved—deeply including the human longing for union in passion and desire.

St. Teresa's Way of Recollection
(W26)

- If you have had a busy or distracted day, bring a spiritual book or a passage of scripture with you to your quiet place of prayer where you can be alone with the Lord. The cross or an icon or picture of Jesus is also helpful to have at your sacred space.
- Close your eyes. Make the sign of the cross, and put yourself in the presence of Christ, remembering who He is and how you are made in His image. In gratitude remind yourself of how much He loves you and has given to you.
- Begin to fasten your inward gaze in a loving manner on Jesus and try to sense His loving gaze returned to you. Remind yourself that He is not only with you, but also abiding within you, which is the deepest intimacy.
- Turn your attention within yourself, to your desires and intentions for your prayer period.
- Speak to Jesus as to your most loving friend and lover. Let all the desires, grief or joy of your heart be spoken to Him. You can say anything, and you will be unconditionally received.
- Tune into yourself and see if there is any particular feeling you bring to prayer that will affect your prayer. Tell these feelings and emotions to Jesus also, and ask if there was any time in His life that He had similar feelings.
- If a Gospel scene comes to mind that fits with your feelings, just gaze at it momentarily with your imagination and unite yourself to Jesus who has had similar human experiences and emotions as you have. This will more closely unite you to Him in your relationship.
- Try to lovingly gaze at Jesus with your energy of love and desire flowing out from your heart towards His. Speak any outpoured words or phrases of love that you want to say. These can chase away distracting thoughts and refocus your heart on Jesus.
- If you continue to have distracting thoughts, return to the Gospel scene with a quick glance if you can, or if your mind has begun to race, read a few sentences from the scripture passage or spiritual book that you brought with you. This should help refocus your mind and heart on Christ.
- If your prayer is dry and arid, remind yourself that God is in charge of your prayer and what happens during that time. This will give you peaceful confidence that all is well. You can again speak your loving words to Jesus to stir up your love and desire for Him and His presence.

- But always return as you can to your gaze of love at Jesus, with any outpoured expressions of love, or of needs, or sorrows. Say in your own words what you want to speak to Him.
- Always end your prayer with anything that is important for you to share—as your hopes and needs, and words of love and desire for continued presence to one another.

PRAYER—KEY TERESIAN UNDERSTANDINGS

- There is nothing that can compare with the beauty, dignity and magnificence of the human soul made in the image and likeness of God. St. Teresa encourages everyone to enter their own soul by the door of prayer to begin to discover the riches and secrets that are within, and to discover the One who dwells there. (IC1,1,1-5; 7,1,1,5)
- All prayer—including all forms of vocal prayer and devotions, Discursive Meditation, Simple Meditation, Centering Prayer, Lectio Divina, and contemplative prayer—must entail the *mental prayer* that is *mindful* of and *lovingly present to* the One whom we are addressing, seeking and petitioning, as well as to what is being asked, and who is doing the asking. Without this context what we are saying or doing is not *relational* prayer.
  - In vocal prayer the mind and heart must be attentive to the Lord and to what is said, and not mere words thrown into space.
  - To pray properly you must think about *Who* you are speaking with, and also who you are. (W22,3)
  - The best place to look for Christ is within yourself. You don't need to go to heaven to find Him or look any farther than within your own self. (L40,6) The King of heaven is in your very soul! (IC1,1,1; W28,5)
- Most people only think of prayer as a natural activity that we ourselves do in communicating with the Lord, without knowing that there is another supernatural kind of prayer that He does in communicating in return to us. (IC1,2,7)
  - Prayer is not just speaking or thinking words said to the Lord, but includes silent listening in attentive awareness of His returned communication to us. (IC4,3,4)
- Prayer is relationship with the Lord. It is an intimate sharing between two friends or lovers. It requires making time frequently to be alone together for the relationship to grow and deepen in mutuality of love and desires. (L8,5)
- The essence of prayer is not in the mind or thinking a lot about the Lord, but is in the heart and is about loving Him truly. The important thing in prayer is not to have a lot of thoughts about the Lord, but to please and love Him deeply, and do whatever arouses more love for God and neighbor. (IC4,1,7)

- It is not with a lot of words or sound that Christ hears you, but more with the longing, desire and love of your heart that He hears you. (L15,7; 34,9; W26,3)
- Prayer is like two persons in this life who love each other dearly and seem to understand each other even without making any signs to each other, but just with a look. The prayer relationship with Christ is like lovers who look at each other face to Face in love. (L27,10)
- Making Christ present to yourself is what you can do in prayer. (L12,3)
  - In prayer Jesus never takes His eyes off of us and He is waiting for us to turn the eyes of our soul inward and look at Him with love. (W26,3)
- A single, loving and gentle word from time to time in prayer, like a puff on a candle to stir up the flame, can enkindle love for Christ in prayer. (W31,7)
- Do not bypass the humanity of Christ to connect to the Divinity of Christ in prayer. (L22; IC6,7,5)
- The deepening of prayer goes hand in hand with developing humble, unreserved and honest self-knowledge. The most profound union with God cannot be reached without humility. (IC1,2,9-11)
  - Prayer always begins and ends with truthful self-knowledge—especially illusions concerning sinfulness or imagined holiness. (W39,5)
  - Teresa considered one day of humbling self-knowledge more beneficial than many days of prayer. (F5,16)
  - It is God's prerogative to give contemplative prayer to some in one year and others after twenty years or more. (L34,11)
  - Anyone who takes pride in the number of years they have practiced prayer and thinks they deserve spiritual consolations and delights in prayer is not humble and will not make progress in the spiritual life. (W17-18)
- A true prayer relationship requires much courage, determination and perseverance both in the fidelity to prayer, and in serious, sustained effort to avoid sin and grow in virtue and so become a true image of Christ in heart, consciousness and action. (IC2,1,1-11)
  - In the journey of prayer and the spiritual life with the Lord, be determined to die rather than give up prayer and quit the journey. (W20,2; 23,1)
- Dryness in prayer fosters humility. (IC3,1,9) It also raises up unconscious faults that need attention and change, and tests and reveals the seriousness of the desire to love God and align the will to God's without rewards—to love God for God's sake alone. (IC3,1,9; 3,2,1-12)

- Teresa's writings reveal the various degrees of ever deepening prayer and union with God that are possible. (IC4-7)
  - Though the journey of prayer includes struggle and suffering, Teresa emphasizes how wondrous, awesome and beyond comprehension are the joys from the gifts, marvels and outpoured love of God for us in union with Him in prayer.
- Union with God in contemplative prayer begins to put love in order in us. Both love of God and love of neighbor deepen. This love is revealed in good works. (IC5,3,7-12)
- Teresa advises us to be available for the practice of mental prayer and the gift of contemplation, but if you can't do that, turn to vocal prayer, spiritual reading and your own heartfelt words to Christ. (W18,4)
- Prayer itself is an apostolate—for the needs of the Church and the world.
  - Your prayer must not be for yourself alone but also for the good of others. (W20,3)
  - The purpose of union with God in prayer is for good works. (IC7,4,6)
- The deepest levels of the Prayer of Union with God bring wholeness, freedom, healing and integration to the soul. Contemplative life and the apostolic life are integrated here and working most efficaciously and harmoniously together under the direction of the Holy Spirit. (IC7,4)

Summary of Key Teresian Teachings on Prayer

1. Prayer reveals to us who we truly are, and our dignity as images of God. We come to know who we are through our relationship with Christ in prayer.
2. Prayer is relationship—a relationship of love, friendship and intimacy with the Lord. It is a reciprocal interchange of mutual love, friendship, and the intermingling of lives.
3. Teresian prayer is focused on the humanity of Jesus Christ as friend, lover and the model on whom we are to pattern our Christian lives. He is the most "significant Other" who is always with us, and journeys with us in our lives. No matter what is happening, or how it feels or seems to us, we are never alone, and can count on that relationship.
4. Teresian prayer is affective, full of desire, and calls for the intentional cultivating of desire and love for Christ. Desire is the energy that fuels the perseverance and fidelity needed for prayer.
5. Teresian prayer always calls for deliberate intention and attention—the awareness of *Who* we are addressing, seeking and encountering in prayer. This includes serious attention to the presence of the Lord as well

as presence to ourselves, bringing the whole of ourselves into the relationship of prayer.
6. Besides love, Teresian prayer is underpinned by determination, detachment or freedom—especially from ourselves—and humility. Humility as continuing self-knowledge is essential, as no genuine relationship can be based on a false and illusory self.
7. Teresian prayer is apostolic and for the concerns and needs of the whole Church and world. It is to bring forth the birth of good works. It is not a private cozy merely for enjoyment of the Lord, nor solely for our own perfection.
8. St. Teresa views all forms of prayer through the perspective and experience of mindful mental prayer and passive prayer. Though she knows that passive prayer is a pure gift of the Lord, she wants everyone to desire it, and is generous in her teaching of how to prepare for the gift, if and when God desires to give it. It is prayer that fosters our wholeness, integration and glorious potential in God.

PRAYER—TYPES AND CATEGORIES
(St. Teresa's teachings on prayer are all throughout her works, but see also: ST59)

Communal Prayer and Personal Prayer

All Christians are called to both personal and communal practices of prayer.

- **Communal Prayer** calls us to pray with others. This would include participation at Mass, Divine Office, Benediction, Taize Prayer, Charismatic or other prayer groups, etc.
- **Personal Prayer** calls us to our own personal intimacy with Christ—one on One.
  - "When you pray, go into your room, shut the door and pray in secret." (Mt. 6:6)

Active Prayer and Passive Prayer

- **Active Prayer** is prayer that we do by our own efforts, with the help of God. This includes formulary prayer or prayer in our own words, and various devotions as the Divine Office, Stations of the Cross, Adoration and Benediction, Lectio Divina, Centering Prayer, litanies, the rosary, various formulary prayers, etc.
- **Passive Prayer** is prayer at the Lord's timing and calling, which He initiates and takes over. It includes Infused Recollection, and the contemplative prayer of Prayer of Quiet, Prayer of the Sleep of the Faculties, and the various degrees of Prayer of Union. It is God's work and gift of praying and communicating more intimately with and in us.
  - It is the beginning of a new stage of life in Christ.
  - St. Teresa believed God desires to give contemplation to everyone, though not all are ready for it.

Vocal Prayer and Mental (Mindful) Prayer

- **Vocal Prayer** is a form of active prayer that we do by our own efforts, or participate in with others. The words of vocal prayer can be said out loud or interiorly within.
    - Vocal prayer can be in our own words, or in the form of pre-established words or devotions like the Our Father, the Hail Mary, the Divine Office, Stations of the Cross, Mass prayers, psalms, formulary prayers, rosaries or litanies, etc.
    - St. Teresa taught that all prayer must be *mental prayer*, that is, one must say the words of any vocal prayer with *mindfulness*—the recognition of *Who* one is addressing and what one is actually saying. Persons must pray saying the words attentively, and with care and affection, because the primary reason for praying is for building a loving relationship with the Lord.
    - Therefore, for Teresa all authentic prayer must also be *mental prayer*—or raising the mind and heart to God.

- **Mental Prayer** is mindful and heart-full prayer. It can be active or passive prayer, and is prayer that both we and God enter into together. There are qualities to this prayer that are more deeply inward, spontaneous, personal, affective and attentive to God. It is usually less concentrated on our own particular needs and concerns, and is more about the mutuality of being together in a friendship and love relationship with the Lord. Teresa describes it as *"nothing else but a mutually intimate conversation, and frequent solitary time spent together with this Friend, who we know loves us."* (L8,5)

- St. Teresa taught that the qualities of mental prayer—centering the mind and heart on God—are more than saying words or moving the lips in silent prayer. Mental prayer is generally less focused on particular words or formulaic prayers, and is more personal. But the qualities of mental prayer should also be part of vocal prayer and liturgical prayer in the sense that these must be said with attention to the mutual love relationship between the person and Christ, with the affective energy of longing desire for Him that is part of any personal and intimate relationship. It is not, as Jesus said: "to babble on like the pagans who think they will win a hearing by the sheer multiplication of words." (Mt. 6:6-8)

- For the one praying, mental prayer is a response in love to the One whose love is already given.

- It is loving attention and a sharing in friendship with Christ—giving and receiving—not just speaking at, or reciting rote prayers. It includes an attentive listening in return to Christ.
- According to St. Teresa the more this prayer is entered into, the more it becomes an ever-deepening intimate sharing between the soul and the Lord. This prayer grows the relationship.
- It includes time set aside to frequently be alone with Christ, and to include this Friend and Beloved in our lives with a *deliberate* and *leisurely presence* to Him who we know loves us.
- The important thing in this prayer is not speaking or thinking much, but loving much—spending time together, enjoying and appreciating one another's company and sharing in mutual love.
- Lectio Divina, Infused Recollection, Prayer of Quiet, Prayer of the Sleep of the Faculties, Prayer of Union, Spiritual Betrothal and Spiritual Marriage are all forms of mental prayer. But authentic vocal prayer must also include the qualities of mindful, relational mental prayer.
- Centering Prayer would also be a form of mental prayer with the concentration on breath and a sacred word/s, or, a short prayer repeated interiorly with a loving gaze or focus on Christ.
  - Breath is ancient in the Judeo-Christian tradition—the *ruah*, or breath of God. And concentration on breathing is also a form of prayer from the Christian Near East—Coptic, Syrian, Greek, and Russian.
  - Examples of Christian sacred words would include: Abba, Jesus, Domine, Shalom, Hosanna, "O God, I trust in you," "I love you, Lord," "I adore you, O Jesus," "My God and my all," or the Jesus Prayer: "Lord Jesus Christ, Son of God, have mercy on me."

<u>Meditation (Two Types)</u>

1. **Discursive Meditation**
2. **Simple Meditation**

- **Meditation** is an active form of prayer that we do ourselves that includes various forms of reflection or imagining that go on with the help of the mind and imagination—particularly any reflections about God or Jesus. These reflections can involve more or less work for the Intellect/mind or Memory/imagination.
  - Generally, meditation is an active ascetical work of prayer—including the type of meditation that involves more effort (Discursive Meditation), or a meditation that involves less effort (Simple Meditation). It is what we do to stir up more love for the Lord by

trying to get to know Him better and by forming the habit of always keeping Him present.
- This is a category of prayer that is not passive or contemplative prayer, but it can prepare the way for it and bring persons to Acquired Recollection or to the threshold of God-given passive Infused Recollection or contemplative prayer, and so can be very helpful.

1. **Discursive Meditation** that can lead to Acquired Recollection is a form of active mental prayer—prayer that we do ourselves in order to know Christ better, and to calm and recollect the mind and imagination.
   - Discursive Meditation, or thinking about spiritual things, is working with the Intellect/mind or Memory/imagination moving from point to point in a reflection about God, the life and attributes of Christ, a Gospel scene, place, situation or character, or of a doctrine of Christianity. It could be about what we owe the Lord, how we are responding to His love, etc. This could include reflections from homilies, sermons, or spiritual reading.

2. **Simple Meditation** is a form of prayer that Teresa taught and recommended. It can lead to either Acquired Recollection, or the semi-passive Infused Recollection that God gives. It is a form of mental prayer that begins actively with us and our *little bit* of effort, but can end with God's work of passive prayer and quiet Infused Recollection in us. It is using the imagination in a *brief* gaze at Jesus Christ or some scene from His life or teaching, in conjunction with an affective emotion of loving desire for Him. Its purpose is to foster recollection in calming the mind, and to stir up love and desire for the Lord. (IC6,7,10-12; W26,3)
   - Simple Meditation (also called Simple Affective Prayer) is an uncomplicated, *momentary, loving* gaze at Christ, or a simple, momentary gaze at a mystery or scene from Christ's life represented to the imagination or mind by a construction of the imagination.
     - This is a quick and simple representation—not a long drawn out work of the mind or imagination as in Discursive Meditation.
     - This Simple Meditation does not block even the most sublime prayer.
     - The momentary gaze at Jesus could be a scene or simple picture from a Gospel, brought to mind by means of the imagination in the Memory. For example, one could cast a quick glance at Jesus in the garden, on the cross, embracing children, asleep in the boat, at the Last Supper, praying or teaching, walking on water, healing, etc. Any of these or others, with the energy of loving desire for Him can

recollect the mind, strengthen the habit of prayer, increase love for the Lord, and help prepare for passive contemplative prayer.
- These simple gazes of love involving the humanity of Christ help spark and enkindle love for Him, just as imagining and thinking about any loved one increases love.
  - Persons could also add themselves to the picture or Gospel scene in their imagination.
  - Teresa teaches that even in the more enjoyable forms of prayer—as the Prayer of Quiet—there is still time for this simple loving gaze at Christ, at any time of day, and in any activity—even *"among the pots and pans."* (F5,8)
  - Teresa says the mere sight of an event from Christ's life can be enough to occupy the mind and imagination not only for an hour but many days.
  - Over and above one's own efforts at recollection, God can quiet, still or suspend the Intellect, Memory and Will, including the Simple Meditation prayer and gaze, whenever God chooses. One can peacefully surrender to whatever God does during this prayer.
  - Teresa herself found a simple gaze at something from the Passion of Christ particularly helpful in stirring love in her.
  - If given, Infused Recollection or the Prayer of Quiet is not continual, and one may need to return to the prayer of Simple Meditation, or vocal formulary prayer, or spiritual reading.
  - Centering Prayer in attention to breath, with a sacred word/s or image from the Lord's life, or of one of Jesus' attributes—along with a loving gaze at Him—could also be included here.
  - Teresa warns against both Absorption and Melancholia. Absorption is a kind of dreamy, spacing out in prayer—a pleasurable wasting of time. Melancholia can be another inattention to Christ due to depression, apathy, or ennui. Melancholia is Teresa's word for neurosis, depression, and various forms of mental illness. (see: "Absorption and False Prayer" in **Supplemental Material**)

Prayer of Recollection

1. **Acquired Recollection Prayer**
2. **Infused Recollection Prayer**

1. **Acquired Recollection** is our activity in trying to calm and quiet the mind towards a still and quiet inwardness. It is an interior recollection that we achieve on our own.
    - It can be brought about through reflection in Discursive Meditation, Centering Prayer, Simple Meditation, sacred music, the rosary, gazing inwardly at Christ, adoration before the Blessed Sacrament, the cross, or a sacred icon, etc. It will be brief in duration and often move on to other thoughts and affections, since in this form of prayer we cannot keep the mind quiet for long, unless God intervenes and stills it through passive Infused Recollection or various forms of contemplative prayer.

2. **Infused Recollection** is a form of recollection that begins with our activity of trying to become quiet and inwardly still, but ends in a passive recollection that God brings about.
    - It is described as semi-passive prayer—somewhere between Acquired Recollection and the contemplative prayer of the Prayer of Quiet.
    - It is less intense and passive than the Prayer of Quiet, or the Prayer of the Sleep of the Faculties, or the Prayer of Union of later dwelling places. (IC4,3,8) But Infused Recollection is already a tremendous grace.
    - By our own efforts we cannot attain this prayer, because here the soul begins to touch the supernatural which is God's domain.
    - The distinguishing characteristic of this prayer is that the senses and inner powers of the faculties are quieted and drawn within through God's call and work—sometimes even before the person begins to think of God or even tries to become recollected.
    - The Intellect is often stunned and amazed by the first experience or touch of Infused Recollection prayer which quiets, stills, darkens, or stops its natural activity.
    - It is God who draws the senses and faculties into passive Infused Recollection and this can last for a few moments or for some time.
    - Here the faculties or powers of Intellect, Memory and Will are not really as captive and stilled as they will be in later, more intense forms of passive contemplative prayer—as in the Prayer of Quiet, Prayer of the Sleep of the Faculties, or Prayer of Union.
        - Gradually Intellect/mind is more and more purified by the light of faith, Will by love, and Memory/imagination transformed by hope until all the faculties become free, captive and capable of loving union with God.
    - Discursive Meditation and reciting a lot of vocal prayers and devotions usually lack appeal at some point in the prayer journey, and are typically

experienced as wearisome. This is generally because the Lord is preparing the person for the passive prayer of Infused Recollection.
- There can be arid, dry beginnings while the person is practicing any of the various forms of active recollection prayer before the person is drawn into the passive, calm, Infused Recollection by God's allurement. (IC4,3,8)
  - Persons may not be able to get recollected on first sitting down to pray, and may have to start with some work at Acquired Recollection—with a spiritual book, vocal prayers and devotions, scripture, Discursive Meditation, Simple Meditation, or Centering Prayer—before God steps in with the gift of passive Infused Recollection.
  - It can be more helpful to work with the Intellect/mind or Memory/imagination for a while by trying to focus it on *simple gazes and affection* for the Lord rather than on ideas about Him.
- In being drawn into this more passive Infused Recollection, the person should proceed with a simple loving attention to the Lord, without a specific work of active prayer or other activities.
  - However, the prayer of affective Simple Meditation, or of Centering Prayer—with a loving gaze at Christ or sacred word/s of affection—aren't necessarily set aside and aren't wearying.
  - During Infused Recollection, if it is given, one should certainly try to stop such activities of the mind as rehearsing, lecturing, solving, day dreaming, planning, arguing, etc.
  - In passive prayer a person has to deliberately choose not to interfere with it by returning to the work of active prayer—of reading, reciting vocal prayers, rosaries, Discursive Meditation, etc.
- Sometimes, before the person realizes it, the Lord gives the prayer of passive Infused Recollection—an experience of captivated love, and deep rest in God.
  - Though it doesn't know how, the faculty of the Will becomes fastened on God and captive in love—stilled, quieted, and not functioning in its ordinary mode. (IC4,3,3-8) In time, the Will becomes more and more inflamed with holy love and desires for God's glory, and for pleasing Him alone, and becomes captivated from within and without by God.
  - The other faculties of Intellect/mind and Memory/imagination may or may not be quietly recollected—depending on the degree of intensity in this prayer.

- The five senses are also quietly recollected, gently drawn inward, though they are still operating normally, and free to wander. Persons are able to see, hear, smell, etc. (L14-15; ST59#3; A2,12,6-9)
  - During prayer, persons should direct their inner gaze to the Lord without trying to discover which kind of prayer they are in.
  - An account of the prayer can later be shared with a spiritual director who should tell the directee that they have been given a great favor in receiving the prayer of Infused Recollection, and call the directee to deep gratitude and love for Christ, and to a more determined response in aligning mind, heart and actions to Christ's.

Contemplative Prayer

- Contemplation is a new kind of communication of God in the soul, and a totally passive prayer that God guides and controls, not what anyone can achieve or do on their own. (L14-16) It is a peaceful, loving and secret inflow of God. (DN1,10,6) It is also called Infused Contemplation by St. John of the Cross.
- It is a general loving attention and a peaceful, calm glance toward God in gratitude and joy, and can include consciousness of the grace received, or a sense of delight, but not always. The communication can be felt and recognized, or unfelt and unrecognized, and some never know God is gracing them. (L14-16; A2,14-15)
- Contemplation is not necessarily, or even essentially an *experience* of God.
  - It is not tied to the five senses or emotions, or to the ordinary operations of Intellect/mind or Memory/imagination, or anything in particular. (DN1,9,8)
  - Contemplation produces in the soul an inexpressible love that fixes the attention and interior gaze on God, even when the person doesn't rationally know through the Intellect/mind what is happening. It replaces any consolations or satisfactions of Discursive Meditation prayer.
  - Contemplation can include a sense or intuition from the faculty of Intellect of the presence of God, or of some spiritual truth beyond what persons are capable of producing for themselves by the Intellect/mind.
- It can be with or without the extraordinary mystical phenomena that St. Teresa describes in later dwelling places. Generally, it comes without it.

- Persons can only dispose themselves for contemplation by the faithful practice of prayer and recollection animated by the Holy Spirit, and by cultivating the virtues in imitation of Christ.
- Contemplation is a gift of God and given only in the mode, manner and timing that God knows is best for each person.
- If anyone thinks contemplative prayer is what they can accomplish whenever desired on their own without God, problems, confusion and discouragement in prayer will arise.
  - Persons will wonder why they experienced contemplation before, but can't make it happen again.
  - Or, they will try some former technique that they think brought them to contemplative prayer, but it won't work.
  - They may think that they are not praying, that nothing is going on in Infused Recollection or in the various forms of contemplative prayer, and that they are just wasting time. They may think that God has left them, is absent, and have the temptation to abandon prayer or return to earlier stages of prayer that they can control and do themselves.
  - The ego self can feel more secure and more self-congratulatory in doing devotions and reciting prayers on its own, but these are not as efficacious for the soul, nor as beneficial for the Church and world, as passive prayer.
- Contemplative prayer is a *new stage of prayer* as well as a *new stage of life*.
  - The active and contemplative life become more united with the prayer of contemplation. These communications of the Lord deepen the love relationship with Him and give energy and motivation for good works and deeper life-transformation.
  - As contemplative *life*, this begins the process of transformation and divinization into Christ-likeness, and is the beginning of the Life of Resurrection.
  - It is the Paschal Mystery lived in the interior of the soul in conversation and relationship with God, spirit to Spirit. It becomes the deepest Baptismal life in Christ, lifted up to the conscious level, inspired and enlivened by the Trinity, for transformation of the person and for good works.
- It is the Holy Spirit in communication with our spirit. With contemplative prayer persons become more receptive to the influence, and Gifts and Fruits of the Holy Spirit, to be moved in love and virtue.

Three States of Contemplation

Three types of contemplation according to St. John of the Cross (SC Theme)

1. **Purgative Contemplation** [Beginner] (SC1-5; DN1 & 2)
2. **Illuminative Contemplation** [Proficient] (SC6-12; DN2)
3. **Unitive Contemplation** [Perfect] (SC13-15; DN2,23,14; LF)

- Contemplation is only and always received passively by the soul and spirit in an attitude of faith, hope and love.
- Any of these three states of contemplation are given according to the Lord's purposes—His willed effect and actions for a soul. (DN2,7,3-4)
- Purgative Contemplation and Illuminative Contemplation can either be given separately, sequentially, or intermingled.
- One way of explaining the three states of contemplative prayer is that in Purgative Contemplation persons aren't generally conscious of knowing anything during the prayer of contemplation, and may even be unaware that they have been given contemplative prayer. Therefore, there is nothing that they can articulate. In Illuminative Contemplation, persons may consciously know something about their experience during contemplation, or that it is happening, but still aren't able to articulate it very well. In Unitive Contemplation they do know some things about their prayer experience, and some things concerning God, but can share these only somewhat with others.

1. **Purgative Contemplation** is experienced as a darker form of contemplative prayer. It has the label of apophatic. (see: "Apophatic and Kataphatic Journeys to God" in **Supplemental Material**) This is a contemplation in which there are fewer reported occurrences of any experience of God, especially in consolations or spiritual delights. The experience is more of the absence of God and generally lacks any recognition of God's presence. However, there is a way that someone can be present to us precisely because of their absence. The purifying aspect of Purgative Contemplation refers to transformation—especially of darker unconscious elements of the self. These elements aren't generally experienced in the midst of consolations and delights, but when the person has these delights and gifts withdrawn and falls back on the self alone, unconscious elements can rise up and come to the fore.

- This God-given inner passive prayer of Purgative Contemplation with darkness, quiet and a seeming inactivity is for transformation in Christ-likeness and greater union in God.
- This dry, dark contemplation is a form in which the person experiences God as absent, though God is never absent, and is instead closer than ever. But so close that the light of God is like a blinding darkness to the soul.
- In dark contemplation, a person's work would include radical trust in God, deeper faith, hope and love, fidelity to prayer and penance, and zealous commitment to the imitation of Christ.
- In this darkened, obscured and incomprehensible contemplation, scrupulosity can arise as attention is drawn to sin situations in need of reformation. The remedy lies precisely in deepening faith, hope, love, and radical trust in what God is doing. This is the way to genuine humility which is neither self-denigration nor self-aggrandizement, neither judgmental nor self-righteous.
  - God is doing the root work of Christification in the impenetrable experience of the dark, purifying, transforming prayer of purgative contemplation.
- The temptation to turn back from this more difficult form of contemplation caused by feelings of wasting time, dryness and aversion to the things of God, can be strong, yet should never be yielded to. (A2,13-15; DN1,9; LF3,27-67)
  - What is needed is the effort to keep a solicitous, if painful, love and care about serving God despite *feeling* that God is absent.
- In dark contemplation God is breaking self-centeredness and the pleasure or pain influences that have been *foundational motives* for choices and actions. Love will become the sole foundational motive—not what is pleasurable or unpleasurable.
  - One should work at remaining centered and quiet, without anxiety, in unconditional faith, hope and love.
- Transformation will generally be a spiraling process of letting go and taking back, but always moving towards the Lord who is doing this drawing and depth level transformational work.
- Here the Holy Spirit's gifts of fortitude, counsel and fear of the Lord or awe would be operative.

2. **Illuminative Contemplation** is contemplation that is somewhat experienced by the person, and gives some enlightenment about the Lord. It has the technical label of kataphatic. (see: "Apophatic and Kataphatic Journeys to God" in **Supplemental Material**) This is

contemplation that includes more felt and sensed experiences of God's presence and actions.
- These are often sweet, consoling, or delightful—but not always—and may be a Divine sort of seduction to initially interest and attract the person to desire to know God, and to be energized for the journey. Some kataphatic contemplative experiences can even feel like romantic love.

o Illuminative Contemplation can be given as a support that God knows the person's needs at various points along the journey.
- St. Teresa thought that Illuminative Contemplation is usually given to weaker souls who need more tangible support for living the demands of self-emptying, for following Christ, and carrying their crosses. Teresa included herself in the group of weaker people who needed more tangible loving support from the Lord to keep moving forward without discouragement or giving up prayer.

o These God-given, generally more consoling experiences, are for conversion, transformation and for deepening union in God.
- This would include accepting life on its own terms, learning how to live and accept what is—in both the felt presence or felt absence of God. It is to surrender to God's ways for us, trusting God's choices for our transformation. This is another form of interior dying to the ego self. Here we can learn obedience and discernment concerning appropriate responses to the imperative of the moment, which can begin to help break old patterns and sinful habits.

o Usually there is a process or dialectic back and forth between the felt presence and the unfelt presence (felt absence) of God. This may be a process that strengthens faith and trust over time.

o Illuminative Contemplation might be experienced under the Holy Spirit's gifts of wisdom and understanding.

3. **Unitive Contemplation** is the Prayer of Union, or contemplative prayer at the deepest level of union of the soul with God. St. Teresa calls the most profound unitive contemplation Spiritual Marriage.

o In certain earlier stages of the contemplative Prayer of Union there will be Suspensions of various activities of the five senses or faculties of Intellect/mind, Memory/imagination and Will. But in the deepest form of Unitive Contemplation, the exterior senses are purified and operating freely under the guidance of the Holy Spirit, and the faculties of Intellect, Memory and Will are also transformed in God through purified faith, hope and love. This is a permanent state of contemplative life in which the five senses and all the faculties are in union with God and operating

under the direction of the Holy Spirit for deeper enjoyment of God, full imitation of Christ in Christian life, and for good works directed and inspired by the Holy Spirit.
- Unitive Contemplation causes a deeper shifting of balance of the self from ego control to God direction.
  - The ego self is not annihilated, but transformed for a more mutual and true love relationship of Lover (God) and beloved (person).
- In contemplative prayer as both prayer and lived-life, persons are more conscious that their actions and choices manifestly reveal that it is the Lord inspiring and working through them, rather than it being merely their own ordinary practice of virtue. This is cause of great gratitude and praise!
- At the deepest levels of Unitive Contemplation there is *integration of the whole person!*
- There will always be labor, suffering and adversity, but with the gift of contemplative prayer and contemplative life, there will be more acceptance and trust in God's love and care.
- Contemplative prayer and contemplative life for active married persons and lay persons, through the gifts of the Holy Spirit might take different forms than for contemplatives.
  - Parents might exhibit the fruits of contemplation in the endurance of fortitude for their family in love, service and duty; or as inspired wisdom and understanding shown in wise discernment of what their spouse or child needs; or for explaining the truths of faith to a child; or in the gift of piety seen as devotion and services of love for God within the context of service and love for spouse, family, neighbor, community and church.

PRAYER – STAGES OF ACTIVE AND PASSIVE PRAYER
(Chart)

Dwelling Places: **ACTIVE PRAYER**

1 Beginnings of occasional prayer	Vocal, formulary, petitionary prayer
2 Developing practice of prayer	Vocal, formulary, devotions, liturgical prayer
3 Developing habit of prayer and Acquired Recollection	Vocal, formulary, devotions, liturgy, Lectio Divina, Discursive Meditation, Centering Prayer, St. Teresa's Affective and Simple Meditation

TRANSITION from ACTIVE PRAYER
to GOD-INITIATED and GUIDED PASSIVE PRAYER
(Active Prayer will also always be part of any prayer life)

SEMI-PASSIVE PRAYER

4 Passive or Infused Recollection	Can be experienced in arid beginnings. Will is quieted, Intellect/mind and Memory/imagination may be quieted, or wander. Senses operate freely.

INTENSIFYING PASSIVE PRAYER

4 Prayer of Quiet (or Spiritual Delights)	Will, Intellect/mind and Memory/imagination are quieted. The five senses are also quieted, but operate freely.
4 Prayer of the Sleep of the Faculties	Similar to Simple Union (below) but less intense. The five senses are quieted, but operate freely.

FULLY PASSIVE PRAYER

5 Prayer of Union – Simple Union	Will and Intellect/mind are captive. Memory/imagination may be quieted or wander
6 Spiritual Betrothal – Intense Union (Suspensions: Rapture, Ecstasy, Transport, Levitation, Flight of the Spirit)	All interior and exterior faculties can be captive and suspended by God.
7 Spiritual Marriage – Transforming Union, True Union, Participation in God, Union of Likeness	All faculties are habitually and sweetly burning in God in loving communion with the Holy Trinity. The faculties and exterior senses operate freely for imitation of Christ Jesus and good works.

PRAYING THROUGH THE HUMANITY OF CHRIST
(IC6,7,1-15; L22; W26,1-6; 29,2-7)

At one point in St. Teresa's life, she was conflicted about whether it was better to pray through the humanity of Christ, or if it was a higher, more sublime form of prayer to leave behind all images. From experience, Teresa came to know that no matter how lofty our Christian prayer, we still need to recall the teachings, and pattern of life of the sacred humanity of Jesus Christ. Praying through the humanity of Jesus and understanding His Paschal Mystery and teachings was part of Teresa's entry into more understanding of Christ as the Second Person of the Trinity, and of the Holy Trinity itself. Teresa advises emphatically not to believe anyone who tells you to abandon the humanness of Christ in prayer!

- It would be foolish in the midst of any spiritual experience to withdraw from all your good—Jesus Christ—who is the guide in the spiritual life, the Way to God, the Truth and the Life. (IC6,7,1-15) Whoever sees Christ, sees the Father. (Jn. 8:12; 14:6-9)
  - Teresa's experience was that Jesus is too good a companion in prayer for us to turn away from Him.
- No matter how spiritual you are, you will not advance by turning away from Jesus and the mysteries and example of His life.
  - The further a soul advances in the dwelling places the more it is accompanied by Jesus.
- Human beings are not angels or pure spirits, but rather are spirits with bodies of flesh. Human beings need to relate to someone "with skin on," and relating to Jesus—one who has also lived a human life like us—is a helpful support. As a human person, Jesus is ever our companion and desires to be with us always in a relationship, and in ways that we can relate to and understand.
  - The resurrected Jesus deliberately appeared to the apostles and His disciples in His glorified humanity—something they recognized and could understand. He wanted them to be able to relate to Him in His humanity and not be frightened. (Mt. 28; Mk. 16; Lk. 24; Jn. 20-21)
  - Jesus asked Thomas to put his hands in the marks of the nails and sword. (Jn. 20:27)
  - He said to the apostles: "Touch me. Ghosts don't have flesh and bones as I have." (Lk. 24:39)
- In Jesus, the human and Divine are joined and reveal that pattern for all human beings.

- The humanity of Jesus is now forever united to the Second Person of the Blessed Trinity.
- Humanity, therefore, has great dignity and is taken into and forever a part of the Trinity in and with and through the humanity of Christ.

o It is not true that once contemplation has been given, persons never need to engage in Discursive Meditation on the human life of Jesus in all the richness of the Paschal Mystery. Though once souls have encountered the Lord, Spirit to spirit, *during* contemplative prayer itself, they can let go of seeking Him with the Intellect, that is, with thinking about Christ. Instead, they can relate to Him who is experienced in the *now*, directly with the Will stirred and enflamed in love.

- There is human presence to Divine Presence in contemplative prayer with an exchange of love, and no need for the work of trying to *think* about the Lord. Lovers prefer to be present to one another, rather than merely think about one another.
- The soul in contemplation only wants to be occupied with the mutual exchange of love, and nothing else—especially not with thinking up meditations about the One who is already present.
- However, whenever the Lord's presence is not felt, and love in the Will is not enkindled for Him, then it is helpful to seek His presence in some form of Active Recollection. This can be by Discursive Meditation, Simple Meditation, or, by Centering Prayer, Lectio Divina, adoration of the Blessed Sacrament, or other devotions. Reflecting on the human life of Christ underpins all prayer and is necessary, and will not impede contemplative prayer. God can and will suspend the Intellect/mind and Memory/imagination from even these holy reflections if and when He desires.

o It is also potentially dangerous to pray ignoring the humanity of Jesus Christ and His example of selfless love, because it can also lead to false prayer or what Teresa calls Absorption—the dreamy, wasting of time and non-relational languishing. Waiting solely for enjoyment in prayer—rather than the work of Acquired Recollection, or sacrificial love and good deeds—is a serious mistake. (see: "Absorption and False Mystical Prayer" in **Supplemental Material**)

o No one can enter into Spiritual Betrothal or Spiritual Marriage outside of an intimate prayer relationship with the human/Divine person, Jesus Christ. (IC6,7,6)

o It is also a support to meditate on the human lives of the Virgin Mary and the saints. (IC6,7,6)

SOUL AND SPIRIT

The spirit is the human soul's deepest center, and is more than we can speak about or understand. It is the place of hidden emptiness *and* fullness that transcends all feeling and language. A name for this meeting "place" between human spirit and God Spirit is faith. Faith is the secret and mystery of this final dwelling at the center of the soul that opens up to the vastness hidden within each person who is one with God and all that is. (SC1,7-10) It is the unfathomable immensity within our very selves that opens up to infinitude—to God, to ourselves and all Reality.

St. Teresa uses the word "soul" in two ways. She uses soul to refer to an individual person and she uses soul to designate the spiritual part of persons that is the "place" where God enters into the deepest communication and intimacy with them. She believed that we do not prize our souls and their infinite capacities enough, which are made in the image of God, nor have we understood the deep secrets that lie within them, which she tried to describe in her writings. In her opinion there is a difference between soul and spirit, but they are sometimes used interchangeably. (IC7,1-4)

Teresa discovered the soul to be one composite whole, and was able to transcend the earlier bifurcation that she experienced in her journey of prayer. She definitely experienced a division in herself between the *world* and *natural* functions on the one hand, and *God* and *supernatural* functions that were only united for her in the seventh dwelling places. (IC7,1,10; 7,2,10-11) It is only in being brought to the center of the soul in Spiritual Marriage that the two regions of the soul are united in working together. In this unification the soul knows, sees, and acts from God's perspective, because the center of the soul is the place of the intimate and direct relationship with the Trinity.

- Teresa experienced that the soul is not something static, but rather, its powers can be expanded in abilities, receptivity, functions and capacities for knowing and loving God and being in union with God. (IC4,2,6; 7,2,9-11)
- Teresa struggled to try to explain the delicate division she clearly recognized between various faculties of the soul, and the center of the soul, and spirit. (IC7,1,11; 7,2,10)
- She experienced that the soul has wondrous interior light from God, and should not be thought of as something dark unless it is not in the state of grace.
  - Those persons who are not in grace have shackled their souls as though in prison—bound hand and foot—and are blind and deaf as to who they really are.

- We should never cease praying for sinners who are losing all their good from not being near God in their soul's center.
- Scholastic theology speaks of the soul as comprised of two main parts: sense and spirit.
  - The sensory part of the soul—seeing, hearing, smelling, tasting and touching—as well as the *natural* powers and faculties of Intellect/mind, Memory/imagination and Will are in contradistinction to a higher or deeper, most secret and interior place in the soul—the center of the soul—or the spirit.
  - The three faculties of Intellect/mind, Memory/imagination and Will are underpinned by the five senses that provide input to them.
    - St. John of the Cross' opinion was that the human spirit is not the same as the soul, but is a secret inner room *within* the soul that can be in union with God. (SC1,9)
- Intellect/mind, Memory/imagination and Will and the five senses can operate on both a natural and exterior level, but also on a supernatural interior level.
- The three faculties, as well as the five senses, have different functions and capacities depending on which part of the soul they are operating from—either the lower sensory part or the higher spiritual part.
- Beginning with the fourth dwelling places with passive contemplative prayer, the soul is being expanded and acclimatized gradually for union with God. Its faculties of Intellect/mind, Memory/imagination and Will are also being developed in supernatural capacities for God.
- Each of the faculties of the soul and the five senses has two domains and two types of powers for experiencing, sensing, knowing, understanding, remembering, imagining, hoping, believing, loving, and choosing. One operates *naturally and materially*, and the other *supernaturally and immaterially*. The two levels are analogous to one another in capacities and functions, but one operates on the ordinary, natural, bodily level, and the other on the supernatural spiritual level.
- On the <u>exterior material level,</u> the three faculties operate naturally—in thinking, hoping, understanding, remembering, imagining, choosing, believing, loving, experiencing, etc.
  - On the natural exterior level, the five senses feel, see, hear, smell and taste what is presented to them in the material world.
- On the <u>interior spiritual level,</u> the three faculties operate supernaturally, but analogously to how they operate in the material world.
  - It is the interior spiritual part of the soul that is in communication and union with God.

- Here the Intellect "knows" and "understands" something of supernatural things—of God, of Christ, of heaven, of the Trinity—that cannot be known by the natural faculty of the Intellect/mind.
- The Memory or imagination can be given supernatural "images"—of Christ, Mary, the saints, heavenly realities—that cannot come through the operations of the ordinary and natural Memory and imagination. The Will here operates in union with God's Will and desires, and beyond a person's natural choices and affections which are based solely on desire for gratification or avoidance of suffering.
- Likewise, the five interior senses have spiritual capacities analogous to what they have on the natural level.
  - Supernatural experiences are beyond mere physical sensations and can include hearing locutions that no one else can hear; of seeing supernatural visions that no one else can see; of having feelings of desire, love, warmth, or the nearness of Christ, that are spiritual and felt in the soul; or of smelling fragrant Divine aromas; or, of somehow tasting God. "Taste and see the goodness of the Lord." (Ps. 34:9)

Center of the Soul

- In the seventh dwelling places Teresa writes that the soul is all one, but not always experienced as one or unified till the seventh dwelling places. She says that the "center of the soul"—or spirit—is difficult to describe, but that there is some kind of intangible, subtle differentiation between various interior aspects of the soul and the center of the soul or spirit.
  - The center of the soul, or spirit, *differs in function* from other, lower natural regions of the soul, and from lesser interior regions and unions between the soul and God.
  - The faculties, senses, and various other rooms of the soul can have trials and afflictions in union with God, but in the center of the soul—the spirit—there is only peace.
  - And the enjoyment of the Lord in other rooms of the soul also differs in degree and kind from enjoyment in the center of the soul and spirit. (IC7,1,11)
- When the soul's center, the spirit, is drawn into union with God—spirit to Spirit—this is where the deepest union with God occurs. And none of the natural faculties, senses or rooms of the soul outside the "center of the soul" or spirit, can interfere with this, or know exactly what is happening in this union of human spirit to Holy Spirit, or even when it happened. (IC7,2,7-9)

- St. Teresa uses the analogy of the differing functions of Martha and Mary from scripture (Lk.10:38-42), to further describe the two dissimilar operating *functions* of the soul that are happening simultaneously. (IC7,1,10-11)
  - When Teresa turned her attention to it, she experienced a passive, supernatural, contemplative (Mary) part of her life and soul, that was always enjoying the quietude and pleasure of the Lord's company at the center of her soul—spirit to Spirit.
  - But she also experienced the more ordinary, active, natural, apostolic and service oriented (Martha) part of her life and self that was dealing with exterior trials, occupations, and good works, and couldn't continually keep company with the Lord.
  - And the struggles, or delight and enjoyment, which the Lord gave each of these "parts" seemed different to her.
  - The two parts were united in the seventh dwelling places, with the apostolic function completely under the Holy Spirit's direction within the contemplative dimension. This became genuine contemplation in action.

Superior Part of the Soul

- Besides Teresa's understanding of the parts of the soul that are comprised of the faculties of Intellect, Memory and Will and the five senses, she also refers to what she calls the *"superior part of the soul"* which seemed to her to be in the *"upper part of the head."* (IC4,1,10-11; 6,3,1; 7,1,5; L20)
  - She's not sure how to describe this experienced "superior" part of the soul that she has had in her mystical experiences.
  - By "superior" she seems to mean "higher-up" in the soul, rather than greater, surpassing or more important.
  - This part of the soul seems to lie "somewhere" outside of the most *interior* senses, faculties, and functions of the soul, and is somehow another part or degree of the *external* faculties and senses of the soul. Or, it is in a region between the two.
  - It seemed to Teresa to be an experience of being somehow in God, but an experience that happened neither in the deepest center of the soul, nor in the normal exterior experience of being in the world.
  - Here her sense was that the soul was as though incapacitated and unable to act naturally as it would in the world on the one hand, or as it can and may eventually supernaturally act in God.

- Generally, this experience that happened in the upper part of the soul for Teresa seemed to be connected to some mystical phenomena experienced—as Suspension favor experiences.
- Full union for Teresa included not just all the elements of the soul, but also included the body, and spilled into the body with physical effects.
- In being brought into intimacy with God in the center of the soul of the seventh dwelling, the soul becomes more than a mere reflection or image of God, but has become transformed, perfected, and divinized to the level of likeness to God through the mutual indwelling and similarity in mind, heart and action to Christ. This is St. John of the Cross' "Participation in God" declaration: "The soul becomes God from God through participation in God and His attributes…" (LF3,8; A2,5,5-7; SC39,4-6)

INTERIOR PART of the Soul (Mary)	**EXTERIOR PART** of the Soul (Martha)
+Supernatural understanding and sensation reside here	-Natural, ordinary understanding and sensation reside here
+Has supernatural knowledge of the things of God	-Has ordinary natural knowledge and ideas about the world and God
+Includes the faculties of Intellect/mind, Memory/imagination and Will operating on the supernatural level	-Has faculties of Intellect/mind, Memory/imagination and Will operating on the natural level
+Intellect, Memory and Will are capable of union	-Lower faculties can only attend to external, material things
+The Intellect can join in union	-Intellect only operates naturally outside of union
+Has a new kind of supernatural knowing	-Has ordinary knowing, reasoning and thinking only
+Will & Intellect are involved in union, Memory is lost	-Ordinary use of Intellect, Memory and Will are here
+Has spiritual senses analogous to the five senses	-Includes 5 senses, Intellect/mind & Memory/imagination; any 6th sense or any other of the 5 sensory senses have no abilities for union
+In the interior senses is where spiritual activity occurs	-Through the 5 senses and faculties worldly, natural activity occurs
+Person remains in God	-Person remains in the world
+Nothing is felt here according to ordinary sense	-Experiences here are according to ordinary sense

INTERIOR PART of the Soul (Mary) – continued	**EXTERIOR PART** of the Soul (Martha) – continued
+Interior senses operate exclusive of exterior senses	-The 5 senses have no ability to sense the supernatural
+Persons are outside their natural operations and control	-Persons act under their own control and decisions
+Delights (gustos) begin and end in God	-Consolations (contentos) are from self and more natural causes
+This is the life of spirit—spiritual life	-This is life of sense—worldly life
+Joy and peace come from the things of God	-Pleasures come from the world and appetites
+A part within the soul belonging only to God is here	-Parts of the soul related to the worldly and superficial are here
+Freedom in intimate friendship with God	-Unfree and limited human life
+Mutuality of love; God is known intimately within	-God sought outside the self, often in futile ways
+Wholeness is found in the journey's goal to God and self	-There is an unintegrated and dissipated self
+True knowledge of God and self are discovered here	-There is lack of true knowledge of self and God
+Has clear comprehension	-There is ignorance, dissipation, and confusion
+Spiritual knowledge is given passively by God	-Worldly knowledge is gained by active human effort
+This is where true union with God occurs (in the deepest center of the interior part)	-This is where Suspensions and Raptures can occur (in the superior or "higher" part of the soul)
+In Union of Wills with God the deepest self is known	-There is experience of God, but more outside of the true self
+The deepest center of the soul is here	-The natural faculties, senses, and superior (upper) part of soul are here

o The understanding of who we really are, as well as the apex of our perfection and transformation in God, (whereby all parts of a human being that are experienced as separate are made whole and one), is in a transformation and unification that comes only through our relationship and union with God in Christ in the center of the soul—spirit to Spirit.

Here the soul is drawn into the life of the Trinity itself in, with, and through Christ. This is a kind of union of all aspects of the human with the Divine, and is analogous to Jesus' own union in His personhood of the Divine and human natures within Himself.

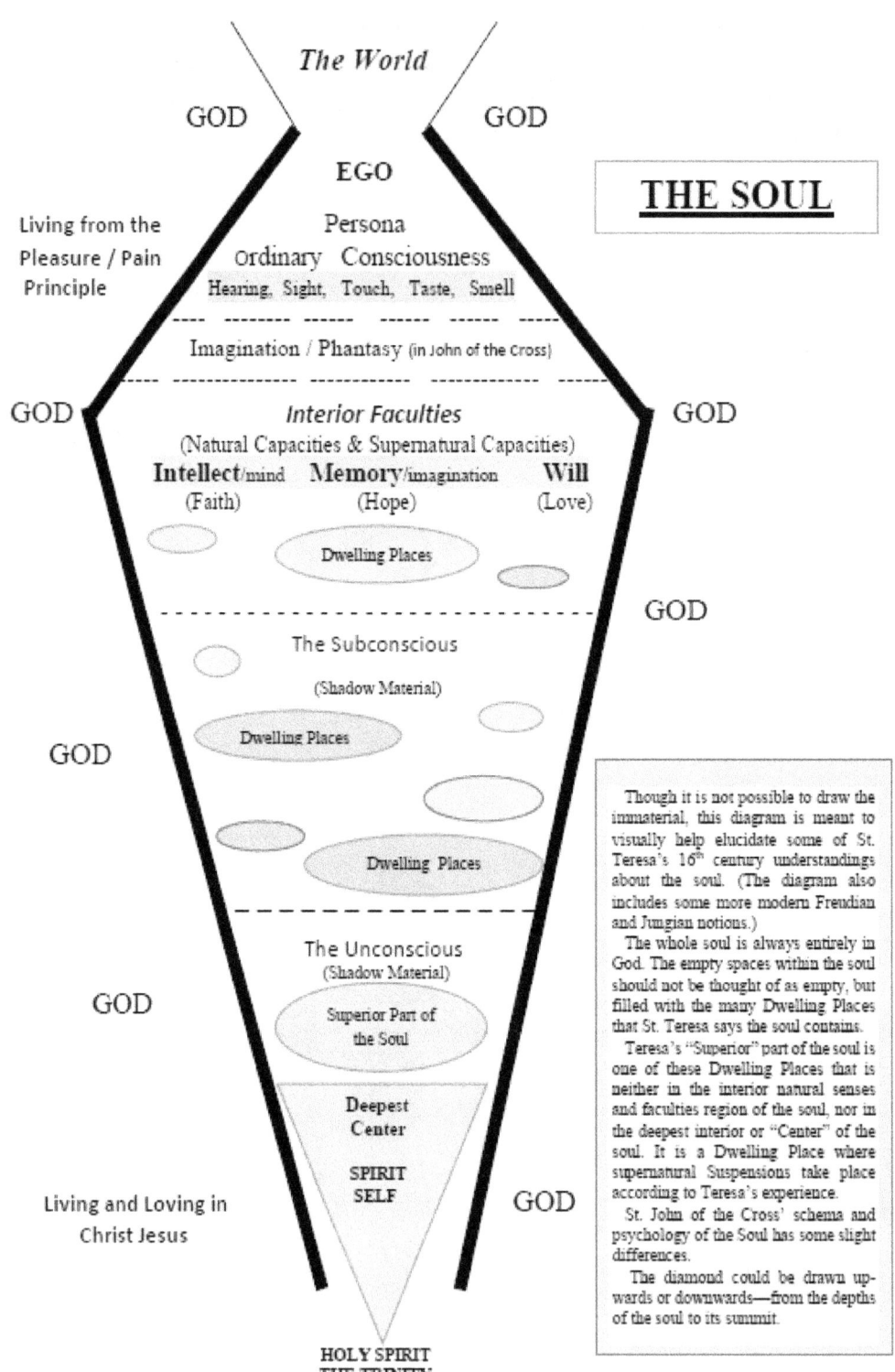

SPIRITUAL DIRECTION ACCORDING TO ST. TERESA
(IC6,1,8-9; L13; 23,8-18; 28,12-18; L40,8)

St. Teresa writes in her autobiography, *Life*, of the suffering and troubles she experienced from having spiritual directors not competent enough to direct her. They caused her no end of self-doubt, suffering, fear and anxiety and some even refused to hear her confession! She was tied up in knots and confusion for quite some time because of these spiritual directors who made her feel that she was under the influence of something evil in her prayer and experiences. (L23,8-12) So it is no wonder that she has definite ideas about what is helpful in a spiritual director and confessor.

Teresa's earlier directors and confessors were not bad men with harmful intentions towards her. They were pious, sincere religious men, but some were younger than Teresa and thus were lacking in experience, learning and judgment. They didn't really know how to direct someone like Teresa who had more experience of prayer and the spiritual life than they had. Plus, the religious climate of Spain and the Inquisition made them fearful of the charismatic, mystical prayer experiences of Teresa. They could neither be good spiritual companions for her nor helpful spiritual directors. It wasn't until Teresa received experienced, learned and judicial direction from her Franciscan, Jesuit and Dominican directors—as St. Peter of Alcántara, ofm, St. Francis Borgia, sj and Dominican Fathers García de Toledo, Pedro Ibáñez, and Domingo Báñez that she could start to more deeply trust her experiences and prayer.

A major mismatch between a spiritual director and a directee as regards the depth of spiritual wisdom and development of a prayer life—as well as extraordinary spiritual gifts and favors as in Teresa's case—is one of the first difficulties that Teresa experienced and writes about. If a directee surpasses the spiritual director in depth and experience of prayer, wisdom and growth in the spiritual life, and human development and maturation, that director will not be a useful guide, and may not understand or be able to give much help to the directee concerning situations or experiences the director has not experienced. Such a director may even be detrimental as some were for Teresa.

A trend these days has often been towards considering spiritual directors generally as spiritual companions. And for those who do not have a genuine Christian community or spiritual community of support to share with, this is a great service. Teresa and Carmelite spirituality would also say that while spiritual directors are also spiritual companions, they are more than that. In the Carmelite tradition spiritual direction would be more directive than perhaps some other traditions. Certainly St. Teresa would be the first to say that it is the Holy Spirit who is the true companion, guide and director of the soul, and the spiritual director must humbly never forget this. The Holy Spirit knows human souls intimately, understands them, and works with persons where they are in their spiritual journey to God. A good spiritual director must also know directees well, strive to understand them, and work with them where they are in their journey, and not impose "one plan fits all" spirituality.

There are three qualities that St. Teresa requires of good spiritual directors: spiritual experience, learning, and discerning judgment. (W4,13-16; W5; IC6,1,8-9) She often spoke of the necessity of learned confessors and directors. Of the three qualities, it's hard to know if she thought *experience* in prayer and spiritual life was most important, or if *learning* and *knowledge* concerning prayer and spiritual life was more important for directors. Substantial knowledge of spiritual traditions and prayer, with spiritual experience and a well-developed prayer life would prevent a mismatch, and hopefully keep a spiritual director some steps ahead of a directee for guidance. But even if a director does not personally have vast experience of prayer and the spiritual life, if they are learned and knowledgeable in scripture, stages of prayer, human maturation, and the spiritual and mystical traditions, they can be of great help to a directee. (L13,16-20) But the director who has also had experiences of contemplative prayer—Prayer of Quiet, Prayer of the Sleep of the Faculties, the Prayer of Union, or favors and mystical experiences of God in prayer will be more able to understand and help any directee who has also been gifted with these astonishing experiences. Learning, as well as discretion in spiritual judgment are needed, and the three qualities form a necessary and holistic triad for the most efficacious spiritual direction.

While it is possible, and has been recognized as a special charism in some of the saints down through the ages to have a gift for discernment and reading hearts—a kind of divine spiritual ESP given by the Holy Spirit for seeing into a person's interiority—most directors do not have this pronounced charism. Most spiritual directors even when gifted by the Holy Spirit with some degree of the gifts of wisdom, understanding, knowledge, counsel and piety must take seriously the responsibility for growing in learning, experience and judgment.

What do these three qualities encompass for spiritual direction? They certainly have fuller meanings than they would have had in the 16th century. Teresa and her directors would not have understood all that we do today about stages of maturation and psychological and brain or chemical aspects (in addiction) for the human person. The three qualities that Teresa advises overlap in various ways, both then and now.

When it comes to the important characteristic of a good spiritual director—of learning or knowledge—this is more than university degrees, book learning, or spiritual direction programs. And this quality overlaps with the attributes of experience and prudent discernment and discretion. For being learned or knowledgeable in spiritual direction includes knowledge in the sense of life experience, familiarity of stages of maturation and human development, understandings of scripture—Biblical interpretation (letter and spirit)—of Christian prayer, theology and values, spirituality, and mystical traditions, as well as experience in directing others. It would involve knowing how the Gospel may be distinct from a particular nation or culture's values, or even of a particular religious denomination's culture. Psychological understandings are also needed as regards human nature, development, motivations, emotions, perceptions, physical and emotional aspects of attachment and addiction, and the ability to discern the uniqueness of each person and how God has been acting in that particular life.

Experience in spiritual direction overlaps with the qualities of spiritual knowledge and prudent discernment. Experience not only includes role-play practicums in a spiritual direction program, and penetrating self-knowledge concerning one's own sinfulness, prayer life and spirituality, or even years of being a spiritual director. It includes all of a person's life experiences and education—particularly as taught by the saints and mystics of the Church—and a deep personal relationship with God, fidelity to prayer, and a spiritual life based on the pattern of Christ's life. Fidelity to prayer and a commitment to following Christ are essential for being a true spiritual director. If directors are not persons of prayer, or engaging Christian life sincerely, they will not be helpful.

An experienced director knows how to provide a safe and welcoming space for a relationship with the directee that allows for honest sharing—of joys, hopes and successes, as well as sorrows, failures, humiliations, and fantasies—what is comfortable to share and what is difficult. Experienced directors can recognize the clues behind words—the affect and body language that reveal a directee's interior. They are wise in discerning the movements of darkness and light, confidence and discouragement, consolation and dryness, or depression. They have the knowledge and experience of Christian wisdom from the holy ones down through the ages, as well as their own experience of living a Christ-centered Gospel life, to offer a directee.

When Teresa speaks of discretion, or prudent judgment, as a quality of a good spiritual director, she means a director who keeps confidences, and is wise, astute, circumspect and discerning of any observed interior or exterior spiritual content of the directee—especially as regards prayer and the spiritual and contemplative life. This discretion and discernment are based upon the other two qualities of knowledge and experience. This wise discretion would apply both to discerning and understanding what is going on in the directee, and to any accountability regarding what the directee is ready to receive, face and change. The astute and judicious director can discern the degree of self-motivation of a directee for growth, transformation, and seriousness of desire for union with God. The wise director recognizes the sacredness and uniqueness of the directee's life in Christ and journey to God, and discerns when to step in and when to step back in allowing the Holy Spirit's lead. They can discern when to prod and challenge, and when to support and console. Certainly, they know if the directee should be referred to another director with more experience, or to a counselor or psychological care giver.

Discretion and wisdom would include the modern psychological and humanistic aspects of spiritual direction generally taught in spiritual direction programs. Teresa would not have known our modern terminology, but most of these qualities would have been operating in her experience of spiritual direction—both as a directee and as a director of souls. These would include the qualities of caring respect and unconditional positive regard and support for the directee. It would involve attentive presence, compassion, empathy, understandings of confidentiality, non-judgmentalness, and commitment to prayer, self-knowledge, and a life patterned on Christ's. Needed also in the director would be developed listening skills enabling open-ended questioning, flexibility, competence in reading emotions and body language, recognizing avoidance tactics and resistance, judicious raising of discrepancies, as well as discerning accurate, tangible, and solid information given by the directee—rather than vague generalities. Today's spiritual directors also recognize other psychological aspects of spiritual direction that Teresa would not have known, but perhaps intuited, as interchangeability, transference, counter-transference and collusion. Healthy spiritual directors do not try to hold on to directees for the sake of their ego and saving face, but are instead detached from any who decide to find another director. Spiritual direction is not about the director, but is God's work in the soul, and the director is only a facilitator not the creator and artist of the soul.

No spiritual director can be helpful to the directee who is not humbly honest and attentive to the discipline and progression of self-knowledge (IC4,1,9; L13,15-16) and who does not disclose their true self and state of soul to the director. Humility, as truthful self-knowledge, is necessary for prayer, and is one of the three pillars of Teresian spirituality along with detachment—freedom from the self and harmful appetites and addictions—and love. There is no progress in prayer and the spiritual life without truthful self-knowledge—acknowledged by the directee and shared with the director. If this self-knowledge is not shared with the director, the director cannot guide or make a discerning, helpful judgment, or spiritual recommendation to the directee that is beneficial. Inexperienced, imprudent, and unknowledgeable directors are dangerous to the soul and often retard the directee's growth. But likewise, directees who hide their true selves and try to save face and protect the ego self from the director only harm themselves. The directee also owes serious consideration to the director's discernment and advice, as well as obedience to any genuine and holy recommendations.

There are certain periods in a person's faith life when a spiritual director is particularly helpful. Beginners who essentially know little or nothing about the spiritual life and prayer, but have a desire to grow, can benefit. Persons who feel stuck in their prayer life, having come up against the dryness, restlessness or joylessness of the third dwelling places, and are primed for making the transition to passive contemplative prayer of the fourth dwelling places need a knowledgeable and experienced director to move forward. And anyone who has been placed in the passive Dark Night of Spirit must have a knowledgeable spiritual director for this bewildering stage of the journey!

SPIRITUAL DIRECTION IN THE PASSIVE DARK NIGHTS
(see: "Dark Night and Purification Trials" in **Supplemental Material**)

Those rare directees who are given the gift of purgative contemplation and the Passive Dark Night of Spirit need a specialized spiritual director who is even more discerning, knowledgeable and experienced in mystical theology than the average spiritual director. Directors will need to give more guidance and be more directive in this night. The Dark Night of Spirit affects not only the spirit and soul of the person, but also their psyche and physical self. The guidance for the Passive Dark Night of Spirit can also be used for the Passive Night of Sense which can trigger the Passive Night of Spirit and spill into it.

Since the Passive Dark Night of Spirit discloses unknown and undealt with unconscious material, the spiritual director may also need to be aware of the importance of psychological elements for the directee's guidance and transformation, or ask the directee to also see a therapist or psychologist along with their spiritual direction. The directee should be encouraged as part of ongoing self-knowledge to share whatever dark and repugnant thoughts and feelings arise from the unconscious that were never known or acknowledged before. These are some of the contents of the human psyche that are in need of God's healing and transformation. The director should not in any way show or indicate shock or condemnation. The experienced and mature director will know they have had similar contents in their own unconscious material.

Since directees will be experiencing all sorts of confusing and negative thoughts and feelings, they are very much in need of the support of the spiritual director to be faithful and to persevere through the trials and Dark Night and not try to escape it. The Passive Dark Night of Spirit is more than Ignatian desolation, and is a form of passive, and dark purgative contemplative prayer. It is a great gift, not given to many, or assented to, and is for the sake of purification of the appetites, self-centeredness and unconscious material, for a deeper love union with God. If there are times that the directee feels unable to cope and has a "melt-down," the director should be readily available to provide some strength and support that the directee may need to get through the episode. However, the spiritual director, though giving hope-filled, faith-filled reassurances, cannot be the one who is the true anchor and ground of support, and must counsel and help the directee to remember the mercy and love of God, and to trust and rely on God above all.

The desperation and panic experience of sinfulness, failure, self-loathing and fear of the loss of God in the Passive Dark Night of Spirit can be so severe that it can be paralyzing, or even lead to thoughts of suicide, as St. Therese of Lisieux was tempted. The spiritual director will need to monitor directees' emotional and physical well-being by reminding them that they are not their thoughts or feelings, and that they need not believe what they are feeling or thinking. They should be reminded that feelings are no indication of God's nearness or distance, and union with God is not based on thoughts and feelings. If self-harm appears possible, the director must refer the directee to a therapist. There may be points in the Dark Night journey when the director would need to advise for a time some entertainment or distraction, in order to dissipate destructive energies. The perceptive director must also discern any emotions the directee may be trying to hide, repress, or ignore that need to come to light. This will require skillful and sensitive questioning. On the physical level the director can ask about the directee's sleeping, eating, socializing, recreating, and exercise habits and make recommendations where necessary. Sometimes directees are numb and don't know what they are feeling. Again, insightful questions can help directees uncover some of their feelings and thoughts. There is useful information contained in emotions, though they should not be the only source for gaining clarity.

The director should advise directees not to put the focus on themselves, but to keep their eyes on Christ and His promises. They can be reminded that their Dark Night is the same journey of Jesus' own passion and death on the cross. If directees continually share the same laments and fears in each meeting, the director must listen patiently with acceptance, and continue to offer encouraging support. These persons need an outlet for their feelings and fears and what they cannot understand, and don't feel safe to share with anyone else. However, if there is continuing self-pity, this can be pointed out as unhelpful to the directee. Any non-life threatening and non-violent acting out or emotional release by these persons in the safety of the presence of the spiritual director should be non-judgmentally accepted and encouraged as a healthy outlet for destructive energy. Directees must also be helped to accept themselves and their failure and brokenness.

The director should share some encouraging perspectives on aspects of the great gift of purgative contemplation, and the Passive Dark Night of Spirit—particularly from the theology of St. John of the Cross—but with a recognition that it probably won't feel encouraging to the directee. Most of the encouraging and comforting words, or theological and mystical explanations won't seem true or possible, and directees will feel that the disintegration, mess and failure they are in is all their fault. The director should encourage the directee not to try to escape the Passive Dark Night of Spirit, for the darkness is a form of purgative and apophatic contemplation, and is itself the overwhelming nearness of God—God who is No-Thing and can't be grasped by thoughts or feelings—God coming so close that He is blinding light in the soul causing darkness. The directee will be incredulous, but the director should keep reminding the directee that this is so! A director can also remind directees of all the strength they have gained, and how far they have already come in their journey through the virtuous and difficult choices they have made in patterning their life on Christ's, and through their perseverance in prayer, faith, hope and love, humility and detachment.

Neither the director nor directee should try to fix things, or make plans of action for dealing with the Passive Dark Night, or for ending it before its work of purification is completed. Nor is it a time to be making any major discernments, decisions or life changes. The Passive Dark Night of Spirit is to be undergone, surrendered to, and cooperated with as best the directee can. The director can suggest to the directee that their primary cooperation involves fidelity to prayer and virtue through hard choices—and especially in surrender under the theological virtues of an obscure, unintelligible dark faith, dark hope and unfelt love. Persons should be reminded to pray as they can—though the simple prayer of the quiet, loving gaze towards Christ should be encouraged, rather than a lot of words or devotions. But be that as it may, each will have to pray in whatever way they are able.

It is not likely that most directees will have St. Teresa's supportive kataphatic, unusual and mystical prayer experiences alternating with darkness within their Dark Night experience, but if they do, they should be reminded that these are not needed for union with God. For they can lead to exceptionalism and pride. Most pleasing to God is the prayer that is the simple, quiet, and loving gaze and yearning for God, along with the desire to align one's will to God's Will.

UNION—TYPES OF

Various types of union are spoken of in Carmelite spirituality that come from Scholastic theology. Some of the forms of union have several names. Generally, the following are the forms of union that need explanation.

1. **NATURAL UNION** or **ESSENTIAL UNION** is that union by which God is present to all beings and creation, keeping and preserving everything in existence. Everyone and everything is in Essential Union with God or would go out of existence. God dwells in all souls—even the greatest sinners. (A2,5,3)

2. **TRANSITORY UNION, DELIGHTFUL UNION,** or **ACTUAL UNION** for St. Teresa involves temporary union in the "superior" part of the soul as well as in the three faculties—Intellect, Memory and Will—which can temporarily be stopped and placed in union with God. These come with Spiritual Delights (gustos) such as Suspensions. For St. John of the Cross Transitory, Delightful, or Actual Union is in the "Substance of the Soul." (A2,24,4; 26,5-6)
    - This union tends to involve briefer, more intense, passionate moments of Suspension in Rapture, Ecstasy, and Transport in which the faculties are caught up in a kind of Divine Passion, with attraction and love for God, and in the delightful inflamed favors of God.
    - These union encounters are not lasting, but transitory. (IC6,4-6; SC26,11)
    - They can include union in the Will, or union in the Intellect, or union in the Memory.
    - Transitory Union in the faculties can occur singly in one of the faculties, or two together as in Intellect and Will, or all three united together, caught up, and absorbed in God.
    - These are also termed Substantial Touches in St. John of the Cross, because the Divine "Substance" touches the substance of the human soul.

3. **TRUE UNION, UNION OF LIKENESS, SUPERNATURAL UNION, CONFORMITY OF WILLS, TRANSFORMATION IN GOD,** or **PARTICIPATION IN GOD** is brought about through mutual

love and the union of Wills between the soul and God, and includes the likeness of the soul to God in Divine qualities.
- This divinization of the human person is the goal of Christian life and involves hard, sacrificial choices aligned to the actions, mind and heart of Jesus. (A2,5,3-4)
- Here persons in their consciousness, and all cognitive, sensitive and affective activities bear a full likeness to Christ's activity, mind, will and life, with nothing contrary to it. (LF2,34-36; A2,5,3-4)
- This is the safest type of union—the true following of Jesus and imitation of His life.
- This complete divinization and transformation of a person's activities and qualities is through likeness to Christ in mind, virtue and actions, and by the means of the theological virtues of faith, hope and love.
- In this union, persons are habitually and continuously moved by the Holy Spirit in their interior life and exterior actions. (LF1,3-4) These persons live the life of the scripture passage: "I live now not I, but Christ lives in me." (Gal. 2:20)

4. **HABITUAL UNION, PERMANENT UNION,** or **SUBSTANTIAL UNION** is union with God in the deepest center of the soul, or in the soul's substance, and can also include the faculties of Intellect, Memory and Will. (IC7)
   - It is a less disruptive or intense state, and more subdued than Transitory, Delightful, or Actual Union.
   - Habitual Union is Permanent Union or Substantial Union, in which the soul in Spiritual Marriage is always in permanent union with God in the deepest center of the soul—Substance to substance. For St. John of the Cross, it is the union of the Substance, Inner Nature and Essence of God with the substance, inner nature and essence of the human soul.
   - Transitory experiences of Suspensions such as Rapture, Ecstasy, or Transport—the disruptions of Actual Union or Transitory Union—can occur along with this Habitual Union.
   - In order to be given the favor of Habitual Union in the center of the soul, or the substance of the soul, and in the faculties, persons must be purified and transformed through the hard choices and purification trials of Teresa, or the Dark Nights of St. John of the Cross.
   - This final Habitual Union on earth joins good works and contemplation together, such that the works of God and the soul are united as one, and are not merely the good works of the person acting alone on the natural level.

5. **UNION OF GLORY, TOTAL UNION,** or the **BEATIFIC VISION** is the union with God after death in the perfect state of the Beatific Vision and eternal life in the Trinity.

VARIOUS MYSTICAL FAVORS—INTRODUCTION
(IC6)

In the Carmelite Order, mystical favors are rarely, if ever, spoken about, and St. Teresa herself downplays the importance of mystical favors and unusual phenomena. But she does include descriptions of them in her writings because they happened to her and because she knows they can and do happen to others. She thought that she partly received them because she was weaker in faith and in need of the support of favors, while others of much stronger faith than hers would not need them. "Blessed are those who have not seen and yet believe." (Jn. 20:29) The view of the Carmelite Order and the Church is that she was given these mystical favors by God to confirm her teachings on prayer and the spiritual life, and to enhance her authority as a Doctor of the Church in Mystical Theology, supernatural prayer, and the spiritual life.

Favors may not come up often in spiritual direction to be dealt with, but some form or another of the ones St. Teresa describes do happen to people of prayer—maybe not as spectacularly—but various mystical favors are given by God. The favors will do whatever work in the person that God intends, and need not, and should not be overly focused on or stressed.

- There are many ways the Lord can communicate Himself in prayer. (IC6,10,1)
    - Some communications and favors are granted when a person is afflicted.
    - Some favors are given to strengthen a person when a great trial is about to come.
    - Other favors come so that His Majesty might delight in the soul, give joy to the person and stir up love.
- Teresa wanted to explain mystical favors so that persons would know that they are possible in prayer, and also so that they wouldn't be worried and disturbed about their sanity. And she also wanted to give advice that would help distinguish false experiences from true ones.
- Some of the communications are more sublime than others, and therefore less dangerous because they can't be counterfeited by the faculties of the Intellect/mind, Memory/imagination, evil spirits, or a neurotic psyche.
- St. Teresa's mystical favors included:
    - Attribute or Quality of God Revealed
    - Delightful Wounds (Transverberation), Enkindlings
    - Locutions
    - Prayer of Jubilation or Prayer of Joy

- Suspensions: Rapture, Ecstasy, Transport, Levitation, Flight of the Spirit
- Vehement Desires
- Visions—Imaginative
- Visions—Intellectual

ATTRIBUTE OR QUALITY OF GOD REVEALED
The Showing of an Attribute, Quality, or Truth that is within God
(IC6,10,5-8)

- This favor is sometimes granted to some who have entered the sixth dwelling places, received the Prayer of Union in betrothal to God, and who are determined to do God's will in all things.
- God can grant the favor of showing a truth, or a grandeur about Himself from within Himself.
- The understanding from the experience of being shown an attribute or quality of God is not that God *has* a particular quality, but that God *is* that quality and attribute. That is, God is Being, God is Love, God is Mercy, God is Beauty, God is Justice, God is Goodness, God is Joy, God is Truth, etc.
- The experience of a quality or attribute of God is ineffable and unexplainable.
- This favor leaves the soul in profound peace and satisfaction, and the Lord should be praised for it.
- There is nothing to fear in receiving this favor. Neither the imagination nor anything evil can cause this favor.
  - As an example, being shown the quality of truth in God brings a new understanding of *supernatural truth* itself, and causes the person to be diligent in walking in this truth, which is beyond ordinary, natural truth or falsehoods, just as being shown other attributes of God bring new understandings of such qualities as love, being, beauty, mercy, joy, etc.
  - Being shown the quality of truth in God brings an understanding that God alone is everlasting truth and unable to lie.
  - This ineffable truth seems to leave in obscurity all other so-called earthly "truths."
  - In comparison, the world of human beings and earthly concerns are seen to be illusions or lies. (IC6,10,5; Ps. 116:11)
  - God is SUPREME TRUTH and to be humble is to walk in truthful self-knowledge. Of ourselves, we have nothing good apart from God, and in imitation of God, one should never leave the path of truthful self-knowledge, which is participation in God's own truth.
- If any are given this favor they should not desire that others consider them better than they are. It is not about their worth, but rather God's holiness, beauty, magnificence, sovereignty and being.

- The favor makes clear what works we attribute to God, what is His part, and what is ours.

DELIGHTFUL WOUNDS (TRANSVERBERATION), ENKINDLINGS
(IC6,2; L29,13-14)

Delightful Wounds (Transverberation)

- St. Teresa speaks of the Delightful Wounds and Enkindlings as touches and anointings of love.
  - They are part of the courtship, seduction and wooing of the soul by God. The description is of a kind of Divine "foreplay" of God.
  - God is a fire of love and it seems like a *spark* of His love leaps forth and strikes the soul making His fire of love felt. The pain of love and desire is great, but delightful and sweet.
  - The wound of love doesn't set the soul all on fire, for just as the fire from the encounter seems about to start, the *spark* goes out and the soul is left with the desire to suffer again this loving pain. If the Divine Spark had not left the soul, the person would have died.
- These wounds of love are an exquisite, delightful, desire-filled touch of arousal, heightening desire within the beloved's soul in yearning love for God, the Lover.
  - What does the soul desire? What pains the soul? It doesn't know, except it seems like desire and longing for fulfillment of love, from and with God.
  - The *"soul dissolves with desire, and yet it doesn't know what to ask for since clearly it thinks that God is with it."* (IC6,2,4)
  - The wound is experienced as something precious from which the person would never want to be cured.
- Delightful Wounds are not like the peaceful, or quiet prayer of most of the other dwellings.
  - The wound of love satisfies much more than the enjoyable and painless experience of being engrossed in the Prayer of Quiet or the Prayer of the Sleep of the Faculties, which is a gentle resting in the Lover's arms.
- Before belonging to God completely in Spiritual Marriage, God makes the soul desire Him vehemently by certain loving favors or wounds of love that the soul itself doesn't understand.
- The favor and wound of love proceed from the most interior part of the soul, from the higher "superior part" of the soul, or some secret place in the substance of the soul.

- In the center of the soul, God is communicating and communing, and neither the senses nor Intellect/mind, Memory/imagination or Will stir. The faculties and senses are caught up in longing desire and love in Suspension, and are "off line."
- This Delightful Wound or Enkindling can come at an inconvenient time, though it is a pain that the person would not want to be rid of. It can happen suddenly and unexpectedly when one isn't even thinking about God.
  - One can neither increase nor take away this Delightful Wound or Enkindling pain of love.
- It is not continuous, although sometimes it lasts a long while. At other times it goes away quickly. It comes and goes and is not permanent.
- There's no doubt about the experience. It is so intense and penetrating that the soul has no doubt about its impact. These delights are distinct and clear, and felt as clearly as a loud voice is heard. They leave a clear understanding that the favor comes from the Lord.
- The experience cannot be imagined or counterfeited.
  - Evil powers can never give delightful pain and cannot meddle in the deep interior of the soul.
- Generally, a spiritual director can discern if the experience is from a weak nature or neurosis operating in the directee.

Transverberation
(L29,13-14; IC6,2,4)

- Transverberation is a wounding of the *heart* in love, and a particular favor and form of a Delightful Wound, as well as an Ecstasy which may occur during the period of betrothal, but must not be confused with Spiritual Betrothal itself.
- It is a dart, or rapid shaft of fiery love felt as plunged into the deepest part of the heart or the soul to purify it, enlarge it, and increase its hunger for complete union with God. (L29,13)
  - When God draws out the fiery arrow, it feels like God is drawing out the very depths of the soul after Him.
- It leaves the soul inflamed with great love for God, and carries the soul away and places it in an ecstatic state with painful love and longing. The soul is no longer content with anything less than God.
- It can also occur before, or simultaneously with, the great trials of purification and Dark Night of the Spirit.

- St. Teresa describes her experience of Transverberation within the religious and psychic categories of her time as an angel plunging the dart of love into her heart.
  - The great pain of the shaft of love made Teresa moan with the sweetness and intensity of the love experienced.

Enkindlings
(IC6,2,8)

- Enkindlings are also experienced in the substance of the soul.
- They come unexpectedly upon the soul: *"as though the soul was suddenly assailed by a fragrance so powerful that it spread through all the senses."* (IC6,2,8)
- These Enkindlings make a person feel the Lord's presence in such a way that the soul is moved with a delightful desire just to enjoy Him!
- There is nothing of fear in these favors, and there is not the same pain of longing, unfulfilled desire and love as in Delightful Wounds—only overflowing elation and joy.
- These favors should be received with gratitude and thanksgiving.
- The person is moved to make intense acts of love, and to give praise and glory to the Lord.

Benefits of Delightful Wounds (Transverberation), Enkindlings

- These favors bring wonderful benefits to the soul, preparing it for the deeper union of Spiritual Marriage.
- With these favors there is strong determination to suffer for God, with the desire to have trials so as to show and prove love for God. (IC6,2,6)
- The determination to forego earthly satisfactions is strengthened.
- Love and desire for complete union and happiness with God is increased almost beyond what the person can bear.

LOCUTIONS
(IC6,3; L25)

Locutions are words or utterances of the Lord, which persons can "hear." God uses them to awaken, teach, warn, strengthen, or inspire. God speaks and is heard in various ways, and many Christians have Locutions in the sense of hearing something strongly that remains with them—perhaps for a life time—from scripture, something spoken by another, but heard deeply internally, or from thoughts that impress themselves from a homily or good book. Some of St. Teresa's Locutions may be more impressive or dramatically supernatural—because God intended her teaching authority in Mystical Theology and prayer to be recognized and listened to—but ordinary Locutions specific for an individual happen and are important for inspiration, support and growth.

- Locutions are not essential to the service of God—everything needed is already revealed in scripture—but they are a support and guidance in particular circumstances.
- St. Teresa believed that Locutions can come from the Lord, Mary, angels, saints, the imagination, fantasy, or an evil presence or spirit.
- Some are exterior, from outside oneself, and heard through the sense of hearing.
- Some are interior, from either deep within the soul, or from the superior part of the soul.
- True Locutions are often a consolation, source of support, or spiritual advice about a specific fault that needs attention for growth.
- Locutions can be of great benefit, or very dangerous if they are false or misunderstood.
  - They are beneficial if they lead someone closer to Christ and support the Christian in a life of love, virtue, transformation and good works.
  - It isn't necessary to know the source of beneficial Locutions if they have a good effect.
  - Locutions are harmful or dangerous if they lead a person away from Christ and virtue, puff up the ego in a pride that one is holier or more special, or if they become a preoccupying focus away from what should be more serious concerns in the spiritual life.
  - Illusory "locutions" can come to psychically ill persons, who are neurotic with weak imaginations that can fabricate them.
- Spiritual directors need to know directees and their spirit and psyche well to discern genuine Locutions if the need arises.

Imaginative Locutions

- Locutions that come from the imagination do not carry the intensity of certitude, peace, or interior delight that Divine Locutions carry.
  - These can happen, especially if one slides into the relaxation of natural recollection, rest or sleep, so that the mind begins to think, imagine, or dream. In such cases someone may hear nothing important, but could also hear something significantly helpful.
- These "locutions" can have more the quality of being composed about something the person wants to hear, rather than something unexpectedly received and heard.

Intellectual Locutions

- Intellectual Locutions are truly supernatural and take place in the intimate depths of the soul and are heard with the "ears" of the soul.
- These words have a different quality from others. Unexpected things are known from these Locutions which may also be connected to an Intellectual Vision. (see: "Visions—Intellectual" in **Supplemental Material**)
- One has no control over Locutions from God. Much more comes to be understood than what the person thought possible from the words alone.
- They have the quality of being suddenly heard and not gradually composed. The Intellect could not compose them so quickly.
  - They can come unexpectedly, even in the midst of a conversation, concerning things the person wasn't even thinking about.
- They are so secret and clear that every syllable and the way in which it was said is remembered. There is certitude about what was heard, and they produce wonderful spiritual effects.
- The evil spirits cannot meddle in these Locutions. The Holy Spirit puts a stop to all other thoughts so that attention will be given to what is said.
- These Locutions can refer to things about the future that have never entered the mind before, or concern things never before desired, wanted or thought, so they could not be fabricated.

Genuine Locutions—Effects

- If a Locution comes from God it will effect what it says with power and authority.
- The words will remain in the memory a long time, and some are never forgotten.

- Even if it takes a long time, there is certitude that God will find a means to accomplish the words that were heard.
- Any genuine Locution will bring confidence in the mercy of God, God's fidelity and particular love and guidance. So, the person should remain in an attitude of faith and trust.
- True Locutions bring greater awareness of failures, as well as suggestions for growth.
- True Locutions bring great quiet, devotion, peace, and readiness to praise and serve God.
- Genuine Locutions should cause the person to become self-forgetful and concerned for the honor and service of God.

False and Destructive Locutions—Effects

- Rather than the holy awe of God, there is a more sinister quality of fear attached to false "locutions." The evil spirit knows tricks to counterfeit the Spirit of Light.
- These can come with a kind of spurious certitude, and some peace or pleasure, but evil presences cannot counterfeit the effects of an Intellectual Locution.
- In the end, the person will be left in restlessness and disturbance from destructive "locutions."
- Persons must beware if a "locution" concerning something *serious* that instructs them to carry out a deed, in spiritual or worldly affairs that includes a third party who could be harmed.
- In doubtful locutions do not do anything without the discernment of a knowledgeable director.

Responses to Locutions

- It is generally not as important where Locutions *originate*. Rather than giving too much importance or credence to them, look for their *effects*.
- Beware of pride, thinking you are better than others if you have received a Locution. The favor of a Locution should leave you more humbled and grateful.

PRAYER OF JUBILATION or PRAYER OF JOY
(IC6,6,10-13)

- In the sixth dwelling places St. Teresa writes that in the midst of experiences that are both painful and delightful, the Lord sometimes gives a strange Prayer of Jubilation that the soul doesn't understand.
- This may be an outpouring of the Holy Spirit and similar to an intense kind of "Slain in the Spirit" experience, perhaps including the "Speaking in Tongues" experience of glossolalia. (Acts 2)
- It is a kind of blessed madness, which sometimes causes others to think the person is crazy. (IC6,6,11; 1Cor. 14:23)
  - These persons go about as those who seem drunk, but not so much as to be completely drawn out of their senses. (IC6,6,10,13; Acts 2:12-15)
- This is a safe and beneficial prayer experience.
- It is a prayer of deep union of the faculties and senses in God, though these are left free to delight in the joy of this prayer.
- The soul doesn't know what it is enjoying or how it is enjoying.
- The joy is excessive, and all the soul's activity is directed to the praise of God.
- The joy is in the interior part of the soul and gives much peace and happiness during the experience.
- The soul has the desire to tell everyone about this joy in God, so that others might help the soul praise God, too. The person would like to prepare festivals inviting all to praise God.
  - Attempting to conceal this great joy is no small pain in itself and generally not possible.
- It is impossible to acquire the supernatural Prayer of Jubilation ourselves.
- The prayer may last a whole day.
- The Prayer of Jubilation or Joy is precious, and makes one forgetful of self and anything else except the joyful praises of God.

SUSPENSIONS: RAPTURE, ECSTASY, TRANSPORT, LEVITATION AND FLIGHT OF THE SPIRIT
(IC6,4-6; L20; ST59,7-13)

Suspensions

- St. Teresa uses the term Suspension to cover a variety of mystical prayer experiences—as Rapture, Ecstasy, Transport, Levitation and Flight of the Spirit. These are a class of supernatural interruptions to normal or natural human experiences in prayer that cannot be withstood or stopped by the person.
  - These take away one's own natural operations from their control by drawing them nearer into God and deeper within their own interior.
  - The powerlessness or interruption of a Suspension affects the *soul and body*. It generally happens because the body is very weak and not acclimatized to the favors and visits of God. It can happen because the capacities of the innermost soul have not been expanded to accommodate God and God's overwhelming love and favors. As a disruptive effect on the body, it can prevent physical activity—including good works!
- They are *not essential* for True Union/Union of Likeness of the human will with the Will of God. And they are not Full Union—not permanent—but only transitory.
- This favor brings the soul into deeper union with God within His Kingdom which is already interiorly within the soul.
  - Here, God carries off the entire soul for Himself, as one who is His own, and begins showing the soul part of the Kingdom that He wants to share with the soul.
  - The soul "sees" that the palace in which it lives is God, Himself—the King.
  - God closes the doors of the faculties and senses and the other dwelling places in the soul, so that only the door to His dwelling place remains open for the soul to enter.
- Suspensions produce greater effects in the soul than the Prayer of Union, increase desire for the Lord, and awaken the person to the things of God with some enlightenment and knowledge about God.
- Courage is needed to be joined to the Lord as spouse, and affliction and suffering build the strength of soul needed to be joined to Him. It takes more courage than one can imagine! If God did not give the courage and

strength for the Suspension of the faculties and senses in drawing the soul nearer to Himself, the person would die.
- True Suspensions are supernatural, and not to be confused by the unusual manifestations of "high strung" people with weak constitutions, who faint, swoon or have convulsions easily.
- While at prayer and while a person is very much in their natural senses, the astonishing interruption of a Suspension—in a short interval of time, or pause—can suddenly be experienced. This favor passes in a moment.
- Suspension is not an imaginative vision of the humanity of Christ, but very much an Intellectual Vision, which reveals Divine secrets, and how things are known in God.
  - Here, nothing is seen, but the soul interiorly senses deep secrets in God Himself.
  - In them is revealed how things are seen in God, and how God has all things in Himself, in the unity of being and creation.
- The understanding and secrets revealed in a Suspension are deeply engraved in the soul.
- The experience causes great confusion and discomfort, with a profound experience of any past evil in offending God in whom we live, move and have our being.
  - This favor reveals that within God Himself, who is all goodness, we commit our sinful actions!
  - The Creator suffers so many evil things from His creatures who live within His very Self, while at the same time they cannot endure even the minor injuries they experience from each other.
- Even though a Suspension is the experience of a higher inner state, the soul feels completely outside itself interiorly and exteriorly. It feels separate, in that it knows nothing through its natural senses and faculties, and is also separate from its own interior while caught up in God, even though it senses something supernatural and wonderful in being caught up so near in God.
  - St. Teresa explains that Suspensions do not occur in the deepest *center of the soul*, but in the *superior part of the soul*. This seems to be a region of the soul—not the most interior—but some inner region that is "higher or deeper" than the exterior and natural parts of the soul, and is somewhere between those and the most interior region that is the deepest center of the soul. (IC7,1,5)
- St. Teresa says that Spiritual Betrothal comes about when God *"gives the soul raptures that draw it out of its senses."* (IC6,4,2)

Effects of Suspensions
(IC6,4,14-17)

- It is of great benefit to the soul to keep the remembrance of a Suspension habitually present and called to mind.
- The realization that whatever anyone does is encompassed within God's very own Being brings sorrow and shame for sinfulness committed within God!
  - Persons have shame that they have ever felt resentment about anything that has been said or done against them by others.
  - They will have a great sense of their presumption, audaciousness, and lack of comprehension about their sinfulness. With this comes a deep realization of the mercy and compassion of God.
- There is an eagerness to imitate God's love, pardon and patience towards others.

Raptures, Ecstasy, Transport
(IC6,4; L20; ST59,7-12)

- St. Teresa describes two kinds of Rapture: 1) Rapture Sparked by a Word, 2) Extreme Rapture.
  - The first type of Rapture is less extreme in display, and does not have the outward appearance of Rapture that manifests in fainting or convulsions. It is known and experienced between God and the soul, but others do not know it. The second is visible to others.

Rapture Sparked by a Word
(IC6,4,3-11)

- In Rapture sparked by a word, the soul—either in or outside of prayer—is touched by some word about God, remembered or heard, that causes suspension of the faculties and senses.
- God is moved with compassion for the soul that has been suffering extreme desire for Him, and undergoing purification. But God chooses the mode and timing to join the soul to Himself, without anyone understanding what is happening except Himself and the soul. And the soul can't understand or explain the experience in words, though it has some interior understanding.
- This Rapture experience is different from ordinary fainting or convulsion in which consciousness is lost and nothing is understood inwardly or outwardly.

- It increases the spark of the fire of love and renews the person from within. (IC6,2,4; 4,3)
- The soul was never so awake to the things of God with such deep enlightenment and knowledge of God as in this Rapture.
○ While in a Suspension of Rapture, the soul is shown some secrets about heaven, in Imaginative or Intellectual Visions.
- The person is able to speak of Imaginative Visions afterward because these are vividly impressed on the memory. They are never forgotten.
- Intellectual Visions—visions with no images—are so sublime that they are harder to understand or convey.
○ Sometimes the Rapture decreases enough for a soul to see what is in this interior room where God dwells. And when the soul returns to itself, the representation of the grandeurs it saw remains.
- This experience is of an Intellectual Vision, not an Imaginative Vision.
- If a person in Rapture doesn't understand that these secrets are revealed by God, the Rapture is not given by God, but caused by a weak constitution, being prone to suggestibility, or to some naturally caused fainting spells or swoons.
- *"Though the Lord gives blessings to whomever He wills, His Majesty would give them all to us if we loved Him as He loves us. He doesn't desire anything else than to have those to whom to give."* (IC6,4,12)

Effects of Rapture, Ecstasy, Transport—Sparked by a Word
(IC6,4,3-11)

○ The benefits of Rapture, Ecstasy, Transport, are so great that they cannot be exaggerated.
○ They are unexplainable truths about the grandeurs of God that are inscribed in the very interior part of the soul and are never forgotten.
○ The experience brings the person to deep adoration of God.
○ God begins showing the betrothed some little part of His Kingdom that the soul has gained in being espoused to Him.
○ God closes the doors of the faculties and senses and other dwelling places, and only the door to His dwelling place remains open for the soul to enter.
○ The soul sees the nothingness of everything in comparison to the grandeurs of God's Kingdom.
- *"And if we hope even in this life of enjoying this good, what are we doing? What is causing us to delay?"* (IC6,4,10)

Extreme Rapture, Ecstasy, Transport
(IC6,4,13-14)

- The second type of Rapture—Extreme Rapture—is a kind of Rapture, Ecstasy, or Transport, which involves an *extreme* Suspension of the faculties and senses that is visible to others.
- Sometimes when God carries the soul off, He takes away the breath, and the person cannot speak at all. The other senses sometimes function a little longer.
  - The senses can be taken away gradually or all at once.
  - The hands and the body appear to grow cold and sometimes no breathing is discerned, and the person appears to be without life.
- This Extreme Rapture, Ecstasy or Transport cannot be disguised and would be very noticeable to anyone who was in the presence of a person in Extreme Rapture.
- Extreme Rapture or Ecstasy lasts only a short while.
  - Even though Extreme Rapture, Ecstasy or Transport ends, the Will remains so absorbed and the Intellect so withdrawn, that for a day or even a few days, the Intellect/mind seems incapable of understanding anything except what leads to awakening the Will to love.
  - The Will is wide awake to love, while asleep to attachment to anything material or created.

Effects of Rapture, Ecstasy, Transport
(IC6,4,15-17)

- After the favor of Rapture, Ecstasy or Transport there is bewilderment and an intense desire to be occupied in God in every kind of way God might want!
- The soul desires to have a thousand lives so as to use them all for God.
- The soul desires that everything on earth be a tongue to help the soul praise God.
- There is a desire for penance, and suffering becomes easy. Anything the person does for God does not seem like anything much at all.
- These persons complain to God when there is no opportunity for self-sacrificing love for God.
- When the favor of Rapture is granted in secret, the person values it more highly.
- But when the favor of Rapture is in the presence of others, the embarrassment and shame is so great that it takes away some of the experience of enjoyment.

- This reveals more need for humility due to the shame of being talked about or judged by others.
- If others gossip and criticize the person, or if the person praises God for this Suspension favor, either way the soul will have a gain.
○ When the favor of Rapture, Ecstasy or Transport is visible to others, it is as though the Lord wishes everyone to understand that this person is now His, and no one should bother this soul.

Levitation (Elevation)
(L20,5-8)

○ St. Teresa described a prayer favor of a great Divine power that raised her body into the air.
○ The power of the Levitation is very great, the struggle to resist it of little or no avail, and thus very exhausting for the body.
○ The lack of control over one's body and the experienced power and awesomeness of God, is frightening, and parts of consciousness are lost—especially of feeling.

Effects of Levitation (Elevation)
(L20,6-8)

○ These favors reveal the tremendous power of God, and how God is Master of both the soul and the body when God desires. There is fear of offending One so awesome.
- This manifestation of God's power deepens humility in the soul as regards human frailty and littleness. The experience leaves the person tired and exhausted.
○ The experience makes clear that God desires the whole person, with a desire to draw the soul as well as the body to Himself.
○ The experience brings a new level of detachment or freedom of the spirit from the body and material earthly things.

Flight of the Spirit (Out of Body Experience)
(IC6,5-6; L20,1-4; ST59,11-12)

○ This is substantially the same as other Suspensions, but interiorly experienced very differently.
○ It's a sudden movement of the soul so quick that it seems the spirit is swiftly carried off from the body. The experience cannot be resisted and is not in the person's control.

- For some moments the person can't say if they are in the body or not. There is uncertainty in knowing if the soul is still in the body, or if the body is without the soul.
- It could be that the soul remains in the body, but the spirit rises above the soul and goes somewhere unknown.
- The spirit truly seems to leave the body, but it is clear that the person is not dead.
○ At the beginning of Flight of the Spirit there is not as much certainty that the experience is from God, and so there is some fear.
- The experience is frightening and requires strong courage, though it happens so unexpectedly and quickly that there isn't even time to muster that.
- Courage is necessary for this knowledge of one's own littleness, powerlessness and weakness. It seems God gives the courage for it in the surrender to it.
- Persons can only surrender and abandon themselves to the One who is all powerful, and make virtue of necessity.
○ Persons still have their senses and faculties and begin to realize the soul/spirit is leaving the body, though they don't know how, who's doing this, or where it is going.
○ It seems that the spirit or soul goes to another region or reality different from the one in which they live—with different lights, sounds and other things—which are so different from earth's that these can't be imagined.
○ The experience is clearly felt as a movement, and not the work of the imagination. Instantly many things are taught that the person cannot re-create with their imagination.
○ This is not an Intellectual but an Imaginative Vision, in which the eyes of the soul see without words, and some understanding of things is given to it of another region, of a saint, angels, or of the Lord, etc.
○ The Flight of the Spirit is an experience which remains engraved in the memory.

Effects of Flight of the Spirit
(IC6,5,7-12)

○ The benefits are remarkable. The person understands many ineffable things.
- Earthly things and goods by comparison pale, and life on earth seems small and painful.
- The experience leaves more peace, calm and improvement in virtue.
○ Three kinds of sublime knowledge are imparted to the soul:

1. There is knowledge of the grandeur of God and the vastness of the regions of the Kingdom of God.
2. Self-knowledge and humility increase at seeing the self so small in comparison with God.
3. There's less esteem of earthly things except for those that can be used for the service of God.

- The soul is left full of longings to enjoy God completely, lives in a delightful torment, and must sometimes distract itself if possible. The suffering of longing for God becomes continual or habitual.
  - The person is full of tender love, which enkindled can send the soul into more Suspensions.
- The person is led to ask for prayers from others, and to ask God to lead it by another path.
- There is great affliction over personal imperfections. Any good the soul sees in itself is seen to come from God.
- There is a desire to die and be out of this earthly exile, with the inability to find a lasting place of rest. At the same time there are desires to delve into the world, to do good works, and to get others to know and praise God more.
- During Flight of the Spirit the interior part of the soul can't choose to stay where it wants, or make its senses or faculties do other than what they are made to do by God. And the soul ceases caring about what happens in the exterior senses.
- Flight of the Spirit may or may not be common in these sixth dwelling places. If they occur in public, they can lead to criticisms, investigations and persecution.

Gift of Tears
(IC6,6,7-10)

- There are a lot of emotions in the sixth dwelling places—as timidity, fear, or longing—all manner of authentic and inauthentic desires, joys, and tears.
- Though Teresa writes about the Gift of Tears in the sixth dwellings of *The Interior* Castle, it is a grace that can be given in any of the dwelling places. (IC4,1,4-6; L12,1; SS2,22)
- Discernment with a spiritual director is needed concerning emotions, desires, false tears, or the genuine Gift of Tears.
  - The true Gift of Tears is comforting and brings peace—not turbulence or harm—and produces fruit.

- Emotional persons of weak constitutions cry over every little thing and are not necessarily weeping for God or their sinfulness.
- False tears weaken a person. They should get busy strengthening virtue and doing good works.

VEHEMENT DESIRES
(IC6,11; ST59,13-15)

- The mystical favor of Vehement Desires is an *affliction* of extreme longing and desire—the overwhelming desire for the complete union of love with God.
- In this gift from God, the favors granted to the soul do not satisfy the soul—but rather leave it with *intensified desire* for God, and thus in a greater pain of love and desire for complete union with the Beloved Lover. The soul is afire with thirst for God.
  - The more the soul knows of the grandeurs and wonders of God, and the more it sees itself unlike God, and distant from God, the more the pain intensifies from being unable to enjoy God fully.
  - Love increases in the measure the soul discovers how much this great God deserves to be loved.
  - Over the years the love grows so intense that it reaches a point of almost unbearable and tremendous suffering of love sickness.
- However, limits can't be put on God, who can in a moment, bring a person to the lofty experience of Spiritual Betrothal union.
- The desires, anxious longings, delightful wounds, tears and sighs mentioned earlier from the Suspensions of Ecstasy and Rapture, are nothing in comparison with this more extreme experience of desire for a permanent, consummated union with God.
- Here, the soul burning up within itself, experiences a sudden blow (golpe)—a sharp wound, stroke, touch, or rush from somewhere—from Someone. The soul doesn't understand from where, or how this is happening.
  - The feeling is not in the body, but in the very deep, interior and intimate part of the soul.
  - It feels like a sharp pierce of a burning shaft or arrow—though it is not literally a blow or an arrow.
  - The person comes to know how much more severe and profound the desires and feelings of the soul are compared to those of the body!
  - The touch or blow can come through a sudden thought or word about a delay of union that is put off until death.
  - It is like a flash of lightening that reduces to dust everything found in human earthly nature.
  - While the experience is taking place, nothing can be remembered, even about the person's own existence.

- St. Teresa wrote that it gave her an understanding of the suffering possible in purgatory.
- In an instant, the experience so blinds and suspends the faculties and senses that they have no freedom for anything except those things that make this pain of desire and love increase all the more.
- The experience lasts only a short while, fifteen minutes to, at most, three or four hours.
- The favor of Vehement Desires is an enrapturing of the faculties and senses away from anything that is not part of this affliction of desire.
- The faculty of the Intellect is alert in understanding the reason why the soul feels far from the Lord, for He helps the soul at that time with vivid knowledge of Himself in such a way that the pain of love is increased.
- Here, persons see what they could have, but do not have, and the pain of the desire of love makes those who experience this, moan or cry out loud.
  - Even though persons in these sixth dwelling places have been used to great suffering, in this pain of extreme desire they can't help but cry out. The fire of desire-love is so intense that with a little more intensity, God would fulfill the soul's desire to die of love.
  - Only God can take away this desire to die by a great Rapture or some vision and understanding of the Lord and His presence that supports the soul.
- The person feels they are dying—a dying from a desire to die—and it is so extreme that there is danger of death. (Poem #1: " ... *I die because I do not die.*")
  - This favor cannot be resisted or hidden from others who witness the possible danger of death.
- The favor of Vehement Desires puts the person in danger of death in two ways:
1. There is danger of death in the extreme pain and disjointing effects on the body.
   - The experience leaves the body cold, and very disjointed, dislocated, displaced—as though the body is coming apart.
   - While this favor is happening, heartbeats are so slow it seems the person will die. Little is keeping the soul in the body in these unbearable desires.
   - For three or four days afterwards, the body feels weak and without strength to do anything.
2. The overwhelming joy and delight also puts the person in danger of death, because these cause the person to swoon in an oblivion of joy to the point that the soul is hardly kept from leaving the body.

Vehement Desires **359**

- Any pain in the body is not much felt, because the pain in the interior feeling of the soul is so much greater than the body's pain, that it isn't noticed.
  - All previous bodily afflictions and spiritual pains seem as nothing compared with this soul-suffering of desire.
- The person wonders if these intense feelings are an imperfection from not conforming to the Will of God.
  - The soul has always tried to surrender to the Will of God, but now in this favor, the reasoning faculty is in no condition even to think. The soul is not the master of the Intellect or mind, nor can the soul think of anything else than its grief of being absent from its Beloved Lord, and its desire to die so as to be with Him in the union of love forever. But God strengthens the soul to desire to live as God wills.
- However, the pain is seen to be precious and undeserved, and suffered willingly out of love for God. *"Ah, God, help me, how you afflict your lovers."* (IC6,11,6)
- This experience cannot be exaggerated and is unexplainable. It is unendurable thirst for God.
- The suffering is to purify the soul for entering the seventh dwelling places—for Spiritual Marriage.

Effects of Vehement Desires
(IC6,10)

- Though the Vehement Desires favor is painful, the soul is left with the most beneficial effects.
- The soul experiences a strange solitude following this favor, because afterwards nothing on earth provides the company it seeks.
- Everything on earth is a kind of torment, and the person hangs as though between heaven and earth.
- In comparison to the painful experience of the soul here, trials don't seem to amount to anything.
  - All fears of trials that could come in the future are lost.
  - Now the person is happy to suffer any pain for love of God.
- There is an even greater fear of ever offending God.
  - With this favor there is even greater care needed in virtue.
- There is a greater sense of the illusion of the world in comparison to the Kingdom of God, and a disregard for the charms and allurements of earthly things.
  - The soul knows with certainty that only God can console and satisfy all desires.

- Much *courage* is necessary to be joined to God in Spiritual Betrothal union.
  - God gives the strength needed to those called to this union. "Can you drink the chalice?" (Mt. 20:22)
- God defends these persons in all things when they are persecuted and criticized—if not in words, then through deeds that show His love and favor towards them.
- God will pay for everything suffered all at once in the seventh dwelling places of the Spiritual Marriage.

VISIONS—IMAGINATIVE
(IC6,9; L28-29)

- St. Teresa states that she never had a *bodily* vision—a corporeal, physical vision. That is, she never had a vision that came through the *exterior senses* of sight or hearing, and wouldn't know how to speak of them. She also wrote that there are no visions comparable to the Intellectual Visions of the seventh dwelling places.
- Teresa uses the term Imaginative Vision not because they are manufactured by fantasy or the imagination—though they can be—but because these visions are represented to the faculty of the imagination in ways and categories that are understandable or comparable to actual natural human experience.
- The *inner eye of the soul*, not the physical eye, is what "sees" in the Imaginative Vision. (IC6,9,4)
- The "image" or what is seen is not like a static painting, but something alive.
- Sometimes an image comes with the Lord speaking to the soul and even revealing great secrets.
- Because these visions are in keeping with human nature and what people have experienced, or are related to religious categories they are familiar with, they are more agreeable, and in some ways more beneficial, than Intellectual Visions.
- Interiorly seen or heard experiences or apparitions of the Blessed Virgin, the saints, or the Lord down through the centuries could be these kinds of Imaginative Visions. They could be seen or heard solely by one individual as St. Paul (Acts 9:3-4), or by several, as the children at Fatima, or perhaps by many at a time, as the five hundred mentioned in 1Cor. 15:6.
- These visions are not as safe from error as Intellectual Visions, and evil spirits and neurotic imagination can meddle more in these Imaginative Visions making them false and dangerous.
- Of great benefit is the vision when Christ wants to give the soul more delight and show it His most sacred humanity in some way—either as He was on earth or after His resurrection.
- An Imaginative Vision passes quickly—like a streak of lightening, though the soul can be detained by this kind of vision for some while. Because of the brilliance of the image, the soul can't fix its inner gaze on the vision for long.

- The brilliance of the vision is like that of an infused light, coming from a sun covered or filtered through something transparent like a well-cut diamond.
- The image remains engraved on the imagination and does not fade.
- These visions can come unexpectedly and unconnected to whatever the person was doing or thinking.
- The Imaginative Vision of Christ usually causes a Rapture (a suspension of faculties and senses) because Christ's extraordinary majesty is so awesome or frightening to the soul. Suspension is to help the soul endure coming closer to the Divine. It is a support in human weakness in being joined to God's greatness and God's sublime communication.
- These visions come with such power that they cause a kind of a stirring up, tumult, or disturbance for the faculties and senses all at once, though later all remains calm.
  - *"Almost invariably the soul on which God bestows this favor remains in rapture, because its unworthiness cannot endure so terrible a sight."* (IC6,9,4)
- The vision is frightening—though the Lord's presence is beautiful and delightful—because the Lord's Majesty is a revelation surpassing human imagination. The soul knows this is the awesome Lord of heaven and earth!
- Teresa says that: *"If the soul can remain for a long time looking upon the Lord, I do not think it can be a vision at all. It must rather be that some striking idea creates a picture in the imagination, but this will be a dead image by comparison with the other [real] one."* (IC6,9,8)
- The vision surpasses the limitations of human imagination and intellect and carries certitude from the awe of the vision that makes the soul certain that the vision is of the One who is Lord of heaven and earth.
- Evil spirits and neurotic imaginations can present a vision, but not with the truth and majesty of genuine Imaginative Visions.
- Directors need to be wise in discernment of spirits, and are right to question and caution someone who has had a vision, and wait to see if the apparitions bear fruit in humility and fortitude in virtue and good works.
  - A confessor or director can put fear and doubt into a directee, who can waver in certitude, but the blessings and wisdom from the vision make the person more certain it was from God.
  - The directee should proceed very openly and truthfully with the confessor or director about any such experiences.
  - The person should give a full account of his or her prayer and deeds to help discernment and guidance.

- If a full account is not given, the person is not proceeding well, and the vision may not be from God.
  - If the full account is given, even if the vision is not from God, it will do no harm to those who have humility and a good conscience. Then God will draw good out of the deceptive vision.
  - The favor of visions is not given continually, and usually when they are given they come with many trials.
  - Remembering these visions of Christ's meek and beautiful countenance is a great consolation and can support growth in virtue.
  - These visions are to be highly esteemed and reverenced, but desiring them is inappropriate.
    - Desiring these visions that are not deserved shows a lack of humility.
    - It is presumption to desire the path of visions without knowing what suits one's soul. Only God knows what is needed.
    - Desiring visions plays into the hands of evil spirits or of the tricks of an over active imagination. Or the person can begin to dream things at rest or in sleep that flow over into the imagination.
    - The trials that come with visions are extraordinary, and the person may not be able to bear them.
    - Though a soul may think it will gain by having visions, it may well lose.
  - These visions are generally not given to those who desire them but to those with a deep self-knowledge and attention to virtue.
    - Some who receive these visions are not holy, while others who do not receive them are.
    - Some holy persons ask God not to send them these favors, because they do not want God to think they serve God for pay or reward. They want to love God for God's sake alone.
  - The safest way for persons to journey with God is to want only what God wants for them and to desire to serve Him without rewards, but only for the sake of love.
  - The person who receives more is obliged to serve more. The Lord does not take away from us what is in our power to do for Him. God loves and is pleased by our selflessness, generosity and loving service.

Effects of Imaginative Visions
(IC6,9,10-18)

- Many are the blessings from visions, but as well many are the purifying trials that accompany them.
- The soul is left well instructed about great truths concerning the Lord through visions.
  - Without effort, true wisdom about God has filled the mind.
- Certitude that the favor was from God remains and lasts for some time.
- When it is a vision of Christ, His meek and beautiful countenance later recalled is a support and a great consolation.
- These visions are a powerful help towards possessing the virtues with greater perfection.

Neurotic Imaginations

- St. Teresa had experiences of dealing with lay persons and nuns who were neurotics. These were individuals with weak, neurotic or overactive imaginations and intellects, or perhaps schizophrenic or disconnected from reality. She didn't exactly know what to call the problem. Sometimes she used the word "melancholia" to describe them.
  - She experienced these people as very suggestible or absorbed in their own imaginations to the extent that everything they thought about seemed to become something they said they saw clearly.
  - Sometimes, something can go wrong in the psyche, and these people somehow "see" what their imaginations have composed.
  - No attention should be given to these, and they should be discouraged.
  - Persons should be reminded that the safest way to union with God is to want only what God desires for them.
  - If these persons were to see a real vision, they would have no doubt about the difference.
- These false imagined visions need discernment concerning good or lasting effects, or harmful ones.

VISIONS—INTELLECTUAL
(IC6,8; 6,3,12; 6,4,5-6; 6,5,8-10)

- God can communicate through apparitions and visions, and St. Teresa describes these because she doesn't want anyone to be afraid if they are given.
- The favors are not granted to many and should be highly esteemed, though not sought.
- Intellectual Visions give a particular knowledge of God, or the Blessed Virgin, or a saint, and are wonderful and valuable for the soul.
- It can happen that without a thought or any notion that one is at all deserving of a vision, that a vision is given. And the person will feel with certainty the presence of Jesus Christ nearby, though unseen with the eyes of the body, or of the soul.
  - The experience does not come through the senses, which can be deceived.
  - This is an unsought experience of Jesus Christ being beside the person, and of His continual presence.
  - Persons experience that Christ is always looking at them, and walking beside them.
  - They come with a constant feeling that Christ was so near that He couldn't fail to hear them.
- Intellectual Visions are interior, unexplainable, and more delicate than Imaginative Visions.
- They cannot be produced whenever desired by any human effort.
- Unlike Imaginative Visions, Intellectual Visions last many days and sometimes more than a year.
- Sometimes, when God chooses, words (Locutions) accompany the vision which gives them added power.
- The experience isn't caused by the senses, and can't be caused by neurosis, active imaginations, or evil spirits and influences.
- It is good to speak with a learned director or confessor from the beginning about any such experiences.
  - Directors may be frightened, judgmental, or condemning if not trained in these matters.
  - Director and directee should pay close attention to growth in virtue, love, mortification, humility and purity of conscience.
  - Persons should not speak of visions with others, and use discretion to avoid misunderstanding.

- Sometimes God leads the weakest along this path, so there is nothing to approve or condemn.
- If the vision is merely fantasy—but still an experience of Christ—it can do little good or evil.
- If a person is overly self-confident or careless in virtue, it is a sign the favor is not from God.
- This favor along with a person's cooperation, may be preparation for becoming a very good servant of God.

Effects of Intellectual Visions
(IC6,8,3-8)

- These favors can cause various emotions, especially awe and confusion, as well as humility.
- They require great self-knowledge, purity of conscience and service.
  - There are even greater desires to surrender oneself totally to God's service.
- The person is left with a great concern about avoiding anything displeasing to God.
- The soul is left with peace and a continual desire to please God.
- Because Christ's continual presence makes the soul pay closer attention to everything, there is greater purity of conscience and presence to what one is doing or thinking.
- Intellectual Visions are a great help for remaining with a continual remembrance of God.
  - Though the Lord is always present—due to human nature—the person can become preoccupied with other things and forget. But when recalled, His presence cannot be forgotten.
  - The person is left very happy over the good company of Jesus or the saints, as well as greatly strengthened.
  - This favor carries with it a particular knowledge of God, of Christ, Our Lady, or a saint.
  - Sometimes the vision is of Mary or some saint, as a help and companion to the person in need.
  - It can't be explained how persons know if it is Christ, Our Lady, or a saint beside them, but they have certitude about who is with them.
- The soul has no interest in anything that doesn't bring the Lord closer.
  - The continual companionship of the Lord gives rise to a tender love for Christ.

- The person goes about with more attachment to and love for the Holy One beside them, whom they "see," and now better understand. Their thoughts are occupied in Him.
  - When the vision is withdrawn, these souls feel very alone.
  - These persons do not consider themselves better than others, but more obligated to God due to the favor.

How late have my desires been enkindled and how early, Lord, were You seeking and calling that I might be totally taken up with You! What need is there for my love? Why do you want it, my God, or what do You gain? O my delight, Lord of all created things and my God! How long must I wait to see You? What remedy can you provide for one who finds so little on earth that might give some rest apart from You? ... Behold, we don't understand or know what we desire. ... O long life! O painful life! O life that is not lived! Oh, what lonely solitude! How incurable! How long! What shall I do my God, what shall I do? Should I desire not to desire You? Here, in this, my God is where You must show Your power; here Your mercy. (Soliloquies VI, VII, VIII)

SAINT TERESA of JESUS
ST. TERESA of AVILA
"LA SANTA"
DOCTOR OF THE CHURCH
1515-2015

At Mother Teresa's death, her nuns who were present with her reported that her face was gloriously young and beautiful and a sweet fragrance emanated from her body which was incorrupt nine months later when it was exhumed and taken secretly to Avila for reburial. Later, what was left of her body, was returned to Alba de Tormes. Much of Teresa's body was distributed around the world as relics! Unusual occurrences and many miracles were attributed to Teresa's intercession after her death.

April 24, 1614 Teresa was beatified by Pope Paul V, and March 12, 1622 she was canonized a saint by Pope Gregory XV, along with St. Ignatius of Loyola, St. Francis Xavier, St. Philip Neri and St. Isidore the Laborer—illustrious company indeed!

September 27, 1970 St. Teresa of Jesus was declared the first woman Doctor of the Church by Pope Paul VI, who declared her "The Teacher of Prayer."

In 2015 the 500th birthday of Saint Teresa of Avila was commemorated, and remembered with celebrations all over the world. Her writings have never gone out of print and enjoy great popularity to this day. St. Teresa of Jesus is an authoritative guide for anyone wanting to know more about prayer and to grow in their relationship with Christ. In her own weaknesses and struggles she lived a very human life and so has perceptive understanding of the human condition. She is a consummate guide for the peak experiences and the lowest points of prayer and the spiritual life, as well as the resting and resistant places in between. If you continually read St. Teresa of Jesus you will have the best of spiritual directors, and discover profound wisdom for your own life.

AFTERWORD

The reflections here primarily concern Carmelite spirituality as distinct in some ways from that of others, but particularly perhaps from Jesuit spirituality. After my own Carmelite formation, Ignatian spirituality is the one I have more knowledge of than any other Catholic spirituality. I offer these reflections especially for consecrated Religious women and lay people, who seem to have been greatly influenced—and admittedly for tremendous good—by Jesuit spirituality, but haven't yet been exposed as much to Carmelite spirituality. That is partly the fault of Carmelites who tend to have more an ethos of hiddenness, enclosure, and even some exceptionalism. They haven't shared the riches of St. Teresa of Avila and St. John of the Cross as much as they could have. Pope Francis has recently mandated in *Vultum Dei Quaerere* that contemplative nuns share their contemplative charism more widely. I do think Carmelite spirituality may better fit women's spirits in some ways than Ignatian. So, I offer this book and these reflections as an invitation particularly to women to look more closely at St. Teresa for guidance in their own lives.

    I have a Jesuit education—an M.A. in Religious Studies from a Jesuit University which I treasure. Jesuit spiritual directors I have had were helpful to me at various times in my life. (Rarely do even the Carmelite nuns have access to a Carmelite confessor or spiritual director, even though it was St. Teresa's initial desire to have Carmelite friars as confessors and spiritual directors for the nuns. None were stationed near my monastery.) My courses on St. Ignatius and Ignatian spirituality—especially discernment, and consolation and desolation wisdom were very useful in certain situations. However, at the same time as I was learning Ignatian spirituality in courses at Gonzaga University, I was also taking a course on the mystics—St. John of the Cross and St. Teresa of Avila, and was more drawn to that spirituality. This may have something to do with the mysteries of personality and preference, but to me, the teachings on prayer of Teresa and John seemed to go deeper. And though I know St. Ignatius to also be a mystic, I did not find that *The Spiritual Exercises* took persons much beyond the initial beginnings of contemplation, nor described the *more* that is possible that St. John of the Cross and St. Teresa of Avila described of contemplative prayer. I discovered and understood contemplative prayer better from St. Teresa. I also discovered that the Ignatian way of praying—often in elaborate Discursive Meditation in a detailed use of the imagination and thought—didn't come naturally to me, tired me, wasn't appealing, and was not my way of praying. Perhaps what St. Teresa offers will also appeal to others as it has to me, which is a purpose of this book.

I have four different translations of *The Spiritual Exercises* in my personal library collection (Fleming, Puhl, Savary, and Dyckman, Garvin, Liebert) but every time I've ever tried to use any of them for prayer, I've felt resistance and mental and spiritual exhaustion in praying that way. Reading an intricate program of what I was supposed to do felt like a lot of work, and more complicated than my prayer seemed to need to be. I don't find that those methods attract me or figure prominently in my personal love relationship with Christ. I have come to realize that such methods and ways are not a good fit for me, or many others. Thus, I have arrived at the conclusion that there are different prayer paths for different personality types. And to me, *The Spiritual Exercises* have more of a male, hierarchical or military orientation to them, and a kind of underlying feel of a "can do" spirit or more will power type of self-rehabilitation. That doesn't fit all women well (nor a lot of men either) though there is a version revised and offered for women with a feminine spirit to it from Holy Names Sisters I've personally known (Dyckman, Garvin, and Liebert). So presumably they also must have experienced Ignatian spirituality as a more masculine approach in relating to God. Carmelite prayer and spirituality have offerings from both men and women—St. John of the Cross, Brother Lawrence, or St. Raphael Kalinowski, but also from St. Teresa of Avila, St. Therese of Lisieux (Doctors of the Church), St. Edith Stein, St. Elisabeth of the Trinity, St. Teresa Margaret Redi, St. Teresa of the Andes and others.

Both Ignatian and Carmelite prayer and spirituality are grounded in a deep allegiance to Christ. A "life of allegiance to Jesus Christ" is part of the *Carmelite Rule* #2. But Carmelite prayer is simpler, and preeminently focused on the *energy of love and desire* for Christ/God, in its emphasis on affective love and desire as the *intimacy of spousal union* with Christ/God, which is not the same as a Jesuit emphasis on *companionship* with Christ (or, "The Company/Society" as partner, auxiliary, friend, confederate, accompanier, or the comradeship of a brotherhood of Spanish Knights for God). Even though in the relationship with God the soul is the one that surrenders, perhaps because Jesuit spirituality is more out of masculine energy, there is a discomfort to the more "anima/feminine" energy of surrendered submission to God required to be a *spouse* of one who is Lord. Some people will be resistant and unable to relate to the spousal desire that God has for human beings, even though it is in scripture. (Is. 62:4-5; Ho. 2:18,22) Teresian spirituality may meet the needs of personality types that don't experience an affinity with masculine friendships, or the masculine energy of the *The Spiritual Exercises*, but are more desirous of complete spousal intimacy with God as the fulfillment of all desires of love. [As an aside, I have to say that I have always been impressed and inspired by the level of unity of mind, commitment, love and friendship of Ignatius and his first little band of companions for one another! I recommend the book, *Impelling Spirit*, by Father Joseph F. Conwell, sj from Loyola Press, 1997.]

In keeping with my interest, and in my relationships with people of various spiritual charisms and traditions, I have come to think that different personalities need different spiritual paths or even different emphases within a religious tradition. As an example, I think of Hinduism and four yogas that it includes. Briefly, these would include *Jnana Yoga* (the way and prayer of knowledge and wisdom); *Raja Yoga* (the way of devotions and rituals); *Karma Yoga* (the way of work and service in the world); and *Bhakti Yoga* (the way of the heart and affective love for the Divine). This led me to wonder if Ignatian prayer and spirituality is more the way of spiritual knowledge and wisdom, while Carmelite prayer and spirituality is more the way of the heart and affective desire and love. Certainly, elements from the other three paths enter into both traditions, and into all authentic spiritual paths, even though there is a particular emphasis within each of the paths. In Christianity, for example, along with love and spiritual knowledge and wisdom, would also be devotions, rituals, training, discipline, and good works in the world.

I know that *The Spiritual Exercises* have helped and energized many people in their spiritual lives, and could be a good place to start for anyone who doesn't know Christ well, and hasn't made a clear choice to follow Him. However, many people do have a deep personal love relationship already with Christ and don't need to do *The Spiritual Exercises* to get to that point. A professor who taught the class on Teresa and John at my Jesuit University once said that many Christians don't need to do a lot of Discursive Meditation because they've been doing it in many ways already—in spiritual reading, retreats and decades of hearing the scriptures and thinking about them for their own lives, and hearing (hopefully) good meditations and reflections by homilists.

I have made a thirty-day retreat (not Jesuit) and afterwards wondered if it would really fundamentally matter which of the Christian traditions one used as the inspirational guide. Desert Spirituality, Benedictine, Franciscan, Dominican, Carmelite, Ignatian, Salesian, Vincentian, Passionist, etc. all have much of the same basic Christian wisdom, though some of it is time bound and not helpful. I think thirty days of silence, solitude and time given to God in loving, listening prayer, and hopefully receiving the gift of passive contemplation, would draw one closer to God no matter the particular Christian charism of the retreat. I do know apostolic Sisters and contemplative nuns who have made *The Spiritual Exercises*, or given them for years to retreatants. Some, as young Sisters, first encountered Jesus personally through them, and this was a significant spiritual experience in their faith journey, though they are not attracted to that way of praying now as more elderly, or mature Religious. Others feel they have outgrown *The Spiritual Exercises*—including some Jesuits I've known—and have gone on to explore and use Teresa's (or other mystics') teachings in making or giving retreats. For some Carmelites who were already deeply in love with God and who have made a thirty-day Ignatian retreat, there were some new insights and renewal, though for others it didn't add much more to what they already had. The discipline that *The Spiritual Exercises* demands in doing the exercises, praying many hours a day, and giving an account of one's time and prayer is a helpful asceticism—especially for anyone who has no habit of prayer. No matter which Christian charism, fidelity to prayer reveals what is possible when serious commitment and time are given over to God. However, retreatants have reported that not all directors are equally skilled at guiding *The Spiritual Exercises*, nor can most people afford the cost of such a retreat, or find the time for an intensive Thirty Day Retreat. Most people are probably incapable of devoting many hours a day to prayer and could never do *The Spiritual Exercises*. And some directors report that many modern people are not even capable of the discipline of extended prayer, quiet and solitude, and can't really deeply enter into *The Spiritual Exercises*—not even *The Spiritual Exercises in Everyday Life* (SEEL). Carmelite prayer may allow for more individuality and freedom in prayer, and perhaps be a gentler way of entering into a deeper relationship with Christ that evolves over time into a solid commitment to prayer and virtue, and the relationship with Christ. Carmelite prayer and spirituality is not directed so much towards guiding and confirming the making of an initial *choice* for Christ as it is towards purifying and deepening the love relationship and commitment to Christ and His people which has already been made, and is still in the process of being deepened. Carmelite prayer may better conform to the pace, mode and capacities of some persons and allow them to start from where they actually are in their lives. It is reasonable to say that most people would not be making *The Spiritual Exercises* unless they had already made some kind of a choice for getting to know Jesus Christ, otherwise who would be going through the trouble, time and expense to make *The Spiritual Exercises*. However, in the hands of a skilled director for those attracted to *The Spiritual Exercises* deeper levels of commitment and knowledge of Jesus would enrich the person's life. Certainly, Teresa also offers a lot of advice—even for "beginners"—but even more so for the genuinely serious—the "proficient," and all the way forward to the "perfect," for deepening the choice and desire to love Christ above all. St. Teresa recognizes that not all are called to wordless contemplative prayer, or the work of Discursive Meditation, and some attain great holiness in their vocal formulary prayers, and some are even drawn into contemplation through their vocal prayer.

I would say that Ignatian, and some of Teresian spirituality would be helpful for beginners in the spiritual life. It is generally thought that Ignatian spirituality and prayer takes one up to contemplation, but doesn't provide a teaching on the subtleties or what is possible in later stages of contemplation. St. Teresa is the Master, a Doctor of Prayer for the Church. Though St. Ignatius was a mystic and contemplative, he didn't write as much as St. Teresa in that regard. Carmelite spiritualty and prayer mainly begins, and focuses, on *passive prayer*, beginning with Infused Recollection, and going on from there to a description of deeper forms of contemplation, and the complete transformation of the person, what that looks like—and if God wills, and the person cooperates—to the full True Union or Union of Likeness of Spiritual Marriage. This is Transforming Union that is permanent, where Christians live now not just in their own lives doing good works through their *natural* lives and best-guessed choices, but live and act through a supernatural life in the union and constant guidance of the Blessed Trinity within the life of Christ who lives in them. (Gal. 2:20)

Teresa's contemplative prayer focus is union with God in passionate *spousal* love—loving God with all one's heart, soul, mind, will, strength and desire. Her discovery was that *within this love* persons are the most efficacious they can be in service and love of others. Both Ignatian and Carmelite prayer and spirituality share a similar goal. St. Ignatius called it contemplation in action—being immersed in prayer and in the world in apostolic service, doing good for others. And St. Teresa said the purpose of contemplative union was the *"birth of good works, good works,"* in a complementarity and union of Martha and Mary. For St. Teresa, any contemplative who lives in an airy-fairy world of a self-centered, cozy prayer relationship only with God, without doing good works is stunted. Teresa's good works wouldn't necessarily be as far afield as Jesuit good works, but more confined to whatever good works were needed that came across her path and life. This would be the same for any contemplative life in the world. However, she did think that she and all contemplatives have access to affecting the good of the whole world through contemplative prayer. Or, as St. John of the Cross taught—even a few minutes of the contemplative prayer in God does more for the world than anything else one could do! (SC29,2-3)

The most emphasized Carmelite goal is intimate spousal union with God in a Lover and beloved relationship. This is primarily an affective union of the will with God's Will—*not mystical, supernatural experiences*. This is the absolute love of God for God's own sake, that is, not for any gifts, consolations or blessings from God. This is like St. Ignatius' question asking: "Can you work without pay?" Certainly, both traditions call for the love of others within that primary love of God which includes the self-sacrifices that love demands, and also the desire that everyone love God as God deserves. Carmelite spirituality and prayer is less a method and more about a thorough shaping and purification of desire and love, which is intimately linked to contemplative life. This is *not monastic contemplative life*—but any style of life that is underpinned by contemplative prayer—which again is not a prayer that we do, but that God does in us and is therefore more efficacious in fruits for the sake of others. Carmelite spirituality is also universal in that it can be lived in any Christian life-style—just as the Carmelite Order has friars, monastic nuns, apostolic Carmelites, lay men and women, married Carmelites, and hermit Carmelites. Women Jesuits have not been allowed, even though there have been women who desired this as a charism that fits them.

While both Ignatian and Carmelite discernment is towards what furthers union with God and communion with neighbor through faith, hope and love—which flows into service—Ignatian discernment is perhaps more oriented towards a greater variety of worldly apostolic service, while St. Teresa's primary apostolate was prayer itself. Also, Carmelite spirituality in later stages of prayer and union wouldn't have as much need for discernment for this or that decision, because once a person has attained True Union with God, their will is in union with God's Will. They live in the presence of the Holy Trinity and in the flow of that Divine life. There's nothing generally to discern. What God wants, the person wants, and what the person wants, God wants, and that is quite clear in Teresian Carmelite spirituality. (IC7)

I found spiritual wisdom from my Jesuit directors in our discussions on St. Ignatius' observations concerning desolation and consolation and the Rules for Discernment of Spirits. St. Teresa has these same observations, scattered throughout her writings for *specific stages of prayer*. It is helpful that Ignatius pulled these together in a compact and useful form. However, the Rules for Discernment of Spirits don't seem to operate in the same way that St. Ignatius generally describes when it comes to the Passive Dark Night of Spirit, or the later forms of contemplative prayer, especially in the Prayer of the Sleep of the Faculties or in the Prayer of Union—stages of contemplation in St. Teresa's writings. When it comes to the radical purification of the Dark Night of the Spirit (St. John of the Cross) there is little that is "sensible" or understandable to be aware of, that can be explained in order to apply some of the discernment principles. And major decisions would not be made in the Passive Dark Night of Spirit. It is a time of unknowing, non-knowing impasse. Also, some prayer experiences of contemplative union come with a seal of *certainty* about them such that no discernment is necessary about where they come from, or what is understood or expected. And too, in some of the deeper forms of contemplation, feelings or movements of any kind, whether consolation or desolation are not always experienced, *nor are they reliable indicators* of progress or union. Only radical faith, hope and love, and fruits and works are indicators in these unknowable regions, and St. Ignatius would agree about fruits revealing progress in the spiritual life. For me, Ignatian teachings on consolation and desolation don't go far enough for dealing with the darkest, deepest purifications of the Passive Dark Night of Spirit. The Passive Dark Night of Spirit is actually a *form of contemplative prayer* within a serious spiritual life. *The Spiritual Exercises* do not describe this radical purification, and Ignatian desolation isn't a description that exactly fits this spiritual state, form of prayer, or work of God in the soul. The Rules for Discernment in consolation and desolation would be helpful within some earlier parts of the Dark Night, and intellectually give some support by way of what to do or not do, and offer some consoling explanations within feelings of desolation, but these Rules cannot be an explanation or comfort for the Passive Dark Night of Spirit. They won't ease or take away the dark, *felt* absence and abandonment of God experience of the Passive Dark Night of Spirit. St. Teresa experienced her deep purification in alternating more consoling experiences of Christ's presence (kataphatic), along with her darker, unknowing purifying experiences of God in contemplation (apophatic). But there isn't generally any consolation in the apophatic Passive Dark Night of Spirit as St. John of the Cross describes. I haven't found any spiritual wisdom that goes as far as St. John of the Cross for the darkest purifications and the most interior, spiritual and incomprehensible sufferings of human experience—or the Passive Dark Night of Spirit. For some understanding of what is happening at this level of transformation and purification, especially as regards the purification of unconscious materials, St. John of the Cross is master. But it certainly needs to be acknowledged that not many people allow God to give them the *gift* of putting them in this incomprehensible transforming Passive Dark Night of Spirit, and so this Carmelite wisdom is really for the "Proficient" who allow God to move them more deeply towards likeness to Christ—towards Spiritual Marriage and the state of the "Perfect"—to use Scholastic theological terms for stages of spiritual development.

Both John and Teresa uniquely offer signs for *discerning the transition* from active prayer and Discursive Meditation to Passive Recollection and later stages of contemplative prayer. This is extremely helpful for discernment concerning prayer itself, for understanding what is happening, and how to move forward when the discomfort and block of dryness and aridity come up into prayer. John's and Teresa's teachings are very helpful here. Ignatian wisdom concerning consolation and desolation and discernment could also be a helpful support in the earlier dwelling places of *The Interior Castle*, and in supporting the movement to the fourth dwelling places of passive Infused Recollection and contemplation. But for the deepest stages of contemplative prayer and Prayer of Union, *The Spiritual Exercises* don't go far enough in giving descriptions and teachings for what is happening and what is possible in the later stages of Christification transformation and contemplative prayer.

St. Teresa in her time admired and consulted Jesuits and Dominicans whenever she could as experts and "learned men." However, generally these men reported that they learned more from Teresa, because they hadn't experienced in prayer what she had. At first, some of the "learned men" were skeptical of her and her experiences. But in time she helped guide some of them into the contemplative prayer she was trying to explain. And when they experienced it for themselves, they knew she was their teacher and speaking the truth concerning the riches of God in prayer. *The Spiritual Exercises* can be used for the benefit of many, and are very useful for Christians who want to know Christ better and deepen that relationship through prayer and good works. But so can the writings of St. Teresa—and perhaps better for some people. It could be said that not all Carmelite spirituality and direction is suitable for beginners—except perhaps for the beginners in the first three dwelling places of *The Interior Castle*. After those early dwelling places, the presumption of St. Teresa is that persons have already moved more seriously to a choice for Christ. The fourth dwelling places onward are for Christians who are already becoming more "proficient" and moving more and more towards the way of the mind, heart and actions of Christ. Though Teresa describes what beginners look like in the first three dwelling places of *The Interior Castle*, she is *anxious* that persons move quickly beyond those and get prepared for the gift of contemplation and the contemplative life that accompanies it. She wants to reveal what is possible in the relationship with Christ *in this life on earth* that most people never imagine! God wants the complete wholeness and integration of the entire person—soul and body—which can only happen in True Union—the Union of Likeness of the soul in God through Christ. The Lord desires everyone to know that He is their Most Significant Other—their ultimate, True Lover—and that He wants everyone to have the love relationship with Him that fulfills all their desires to love and be loved!

BIBLIOGRAPHY

PRIMARY SOURCES

John of the Cross, Saint. *The Collected Works of St. John of the Cross.* Translated by Kieran Kavanaugh, ocd and Otilio Rodriguez, ocd. With Revisions and Introductions by Kieran Kavanaugh, ocd. Rev. ed. Washington, D.C.: ICS Publications, 1991.

Teresa de Jesús. *Obras Completas.* Rev. por Fr. Tomas de la Cruz, (Alvarez) DC. (Archivo Silveriano, De Historia y Espiritualidad Carmelitana, 1) Burgos, España: Monte Carmelo, 1977.

Teresa of Jesus. *The Collected Letters of St. Teresa of Avila.* Translated by Kieran Kavanaugh, ocd. (Vol. 1: 1546-1577) Washington, D.C.: ICS Publications, 2001.

_____. *The Collected Letters of Saint Teresa of Avila.* Translated by Kieran Kavanaugh, ocd. (Vol. 2: 1578-1582) Washington, D.C.: ICS Publications, 2007.

_____. *The Collected Works of Saint Teresa of Avila.* Translated by Kieran Kavanaugh, ocd and Otilio Rodriguez, ocd. (Vol. 1: "The Book of Her Life," "Spiritual Testimonies," "Soliloquies") Washington, D.C.: ICS Publications, 1976.

_____. *The Collected Works of Saint Teresa of Avila.* Translated by Kieran Kavanaugh, ocd and Otilio Rodriguez, ocd. (Vol. 2: "The Way of Perfection," "Meditations on the Song of Songs," "The Interior Castle") Washington, D.C.: ICS Publications, 1976.

_____. *The Collected Works of Saint Teresa of Avila.* Translated by Kieran Kavanaugh, ocd and Otilio Rodriguez, ocd. (Vol. 3: "The Book of Her Foundations," "Minor Works") Washington, D.C.: ICS Publications, 1985.

_____. *The Complete Works of Saint Teresa of Jesus.* Translated and edited by E. Allison Peers. (Vol. 1: "Life," "Spiritual Relations") New York: Sheed and Ward, 1946.

_____. *The Complete Works of Saint Teresa of Jesus.* Translated and edited by E. Allison Peers. (Vol. 2: "Book Called Way of Perfection," "Interior Castle," "Conceptions of the Love of God," "Exclamation of the Soul to God") New York: Sheed and Ward, 1946.

_____. *The Complete Works of Saint Teresa of Jesus.* Translated and edited by E. Allison Peers. (Vol. 3: "Book of the Foundations," "Minor Prose Works," "Poems") New York: Sheed and Ward, 1946.

_____. *The Letters of Saint Teresa of Jesus.* Vols. 1 & 2. Translated and edited by E. Allison Peers. Westminster, MD: Newman Press, 1950.

_____.*The Prayers of Saint Teresa of Avila.* Compiled by Thomas Alvarez, ocd. New York: New City Press, 1991.

_____.*Saint Teresa of Avila: Way of Perfection, A Study Edition.* Translated by Kieran Kavanaugh, ocd and Otilio Rodriguez, ocd. Washington, D.C.: ICS Publications, 2000.

SECONDARY SOURCES

Ahlgren, Gillian T. W. *Entering Teresa of Avila's Interior Castle: A Reader's Companion.* Paulist Press, N.Y.: Mahwah, NJ, 2005.

Alvarez, Tomas, ocd. *The Mind of Our Holy Mother Saint Teresa as to the Essentials of the Carmelite Life.* Darlington Carmel, n.d.

Alvarez, Tomas, ocd. *St. Teresa of Avila: A Spiritual Adventure.* Washington, D.C.: ICS Publications, 1982.

Alvarez, Tomas, ocd, compiler. *The Prayers of Saint Teresa of Avila.* Brooklyn, NY: New City Press, 1990.

Alvarez, Tomas, ocd and Domingo, Fernando, ocd. *The Divine Adventure: Saint Teresa of Avila's Journeys and Foundations.* Washington, D.C.: ICS Publications, 2015.

Auclair, Marcelle. *Saint Teresa of Avila: A Spiritual Adventure.* Translated by Kathleen Pond. Petersham, MA: St. Bede's Publications, 1988.

Burke, Daniel and Lilles, Anthony. (Introduction and Reflections). *30 Days with Teresa of Avila.* (Navigating the Interior Life Series) Steubenville, OH: Emmaus Road Publishing, 2015.

Burrows, Ruth, ocd. *Essence of Prayer.* Paulist Press, Mahwah, NJ, 2006.

_____. *Interior Castle Explored.* London, England: Sheed and Ward, 1981.

Clissold, Stephen. *St. Teresa of Avila.* New York, NY: Seabury, 1982.

Crisogono de Jesus, ocd. *Teresa of Jesus, Her Life and Her Doctrine.* India: Alwaye, 1939.

Culligan, Kevin, ocd and O'Donoghue, Noel Dermot, ocd. *Your Servant, Teresa: St. Teresa of Jesus and Her Letters.* (The Living Flame Series, vol. 32) Dublin, Ireland: Carmelite Centre of Spirituality, 1988.

Dicken, E. W. Truman. *The Crucible of Love.* New York, NY: Sheed and Ward, 1963.

Doohan, Leonard. *The Contemporary Challenge of St. Teresa of Avila.* Amazon.com., 2016.
DuBoulay, Shirley. *Teresa of Avila: Her Story.* Ann Arbor, MI: Servant Publications, 1995.
Eileen Mary, Sr. SLG. *Pilgrimage and Possession.* Fairacres, Oxford: Convent of the Incarnation, SLG Press, 1983.
Elliott, J. H. *Imperial Spain, 1469-1716.* New York: NY, St. Martin's Press, 1966.
Glynn, Joseph. *The Eternal Mystic.* New York, NY: Vantage Press, 1982.
Hamilton, Elizabeth. *The Great Teresa.* London, England: Burns & Oates, 1960.
Howells, Edward. *John of the Cross and Teresa of Avila: Mystical Knowing and Selfhood.* New York, NY: Crossroads Publishing Co., 2002.
Humphreys, Carolyn, ocds. *From Ash to Fire: An Odyssey in Prayer: A Contemporary Journey Through the Interior Castle of Teresa of Avila.* New York, NY: New City Press, 1993.
Lincoln, Victoria. *Teresa: A Woman: A Biography of Teresa of Avila.* Albany, NY: State University of New York, 1984.
Lund, Leslie, Sr. ocd. "Carmel and World Transformation." *Spiritual Life* 30, no. 2. (Summer 1984): 97-105.
_____. "Desire in St. John of the Cross." *Spiritual Life* 31, no. 2. (Summer 1985): 83-100.
_____. "Dread (the Dark Night) and Christian Transformation." *Review for Religious* 36, no. 6. (November 1977): 824-832.
_____. "Holy Seduction and Divine Passion." *Sisters Today* 72, no. 6. (November 2000): 479-483.
_____. "Teresa of Avila's Prayer of Quiet—1978" *Spiritual Life* 24, no. 2. (Summer 1978): 79-84.
Madeleine of St. Joseph, ocd. *Within the Castle with St. Teresa of Avila.* Chicago, IL: Franciscan Herald Press, 1982.
Marie-Eugene, P. (Giralou), ocd. *I Am a Daughter of the Church: A Practical Synthesis of Carmelite Spirituality.* Vol. 2. Trans. Sr. M. Verda Clare, csc. Chicago, IL: Fides, 1955.
_____. *I Want to See God: A Practical Synthesis of Carmelite Spirituality.* Trans. Sr. M. Verda Clare, csc. Chicago, IL: Fides, 1953.
Medwick, Kathleen. *Teresa of Avila: Progress of the Soul.* New York, NY: Doubleday, 1999.
Melia, Norah. *Saint Teresa and Friendship.* Melbourne, Australia: Carmelite Communications, 1988.
Morello, Sam Anthony, ocd. *Lectio Divina and the Practice of Teresian Prayer.* Washington, D.C.: ICS Publications, 1995.

Myss, Caroline. *Entering the Castle.* New York, NY: Free Press, 2008.

Muto, Susan. *Where Lovers Meet: Inside the Interior Castle.* Washington, D.C.: ICS Publications, 2008.

Nevin, Winifred. *Teresa of Avila.* Milwaukee, WI: The Bruce Publishing Co., 1956.

Peers, E. Allison. *Handbook of the Life and Times of St. Teresa and St. John of the Cross.* Westminster, MD: Newman Press, 1954.

Rodriguez, Ortilio, ocd, et al. *Word & Spirit: A Monastic Review (Dedicated to St. Teresa of Avila, 1582-1982).* Still River, MA: St. Bede's Publications, c1983.

Rohrbach, Peter Thomas. *Conversation with Christ: The Teaching of St. Teresa of Avila about Personal Prayer.* Rockford, IL: TAN Books and Publishers, 1982.

_____. *Mother of Carmel: A Portrait of St. Teresa of Jesus.* New York, NY: Morehouse-Gorham and Co., 1946.

Seelaus, Vilma, Sr., ocd. *Distractions in Prayer: Blessing or Curse? Saint Teresa of Avila's Teachings in the Interior Castle.* Staten Island, NY: Alba House, 2005.

Simsic, Wayne. *The Inward Path to God: A Prayer Journey with Saint Teresa of Avila.* Frederick, MD: The Word Among Us Press, 2015.

Steggink, Otger, o.carm. *Tiempo y Vida de Santa Teresa.* Madrid, España: Biblioteca de Autores Cristianos, 1968.

Stein, Edith, St. *The Science of the Cross.* Translated by Josephine Koeppel, ocd. Washington, D.C.: ICS Publications, 2002.

Sullivan, John, ocd. *Carmelite Studies: Centenary of St. Teresa.* (Vol. 3) Washington, D.C.: ICS Publications, 1984.

_____. *Teresa: The Life and Message of the First Woman Declared a Doctor of the Church.* Pasay City, St. Paul's Publications, 1970.

Walsh, William. *Saint Teresa of Avila: A Biography.* Milwaukee, WI: Bruce Publishing, 1943.

Welch, John, o.carm. *Spiritual Pilgrims: Carl Jung and Teresa of Avila.* New York, NY: Paulist Press, 1982.

SONG:
"Nada Te Turbe" (Let Nothing Disturb You)

Mandala of the Interior Castle by Sr. Vilma Seelaus, ocd

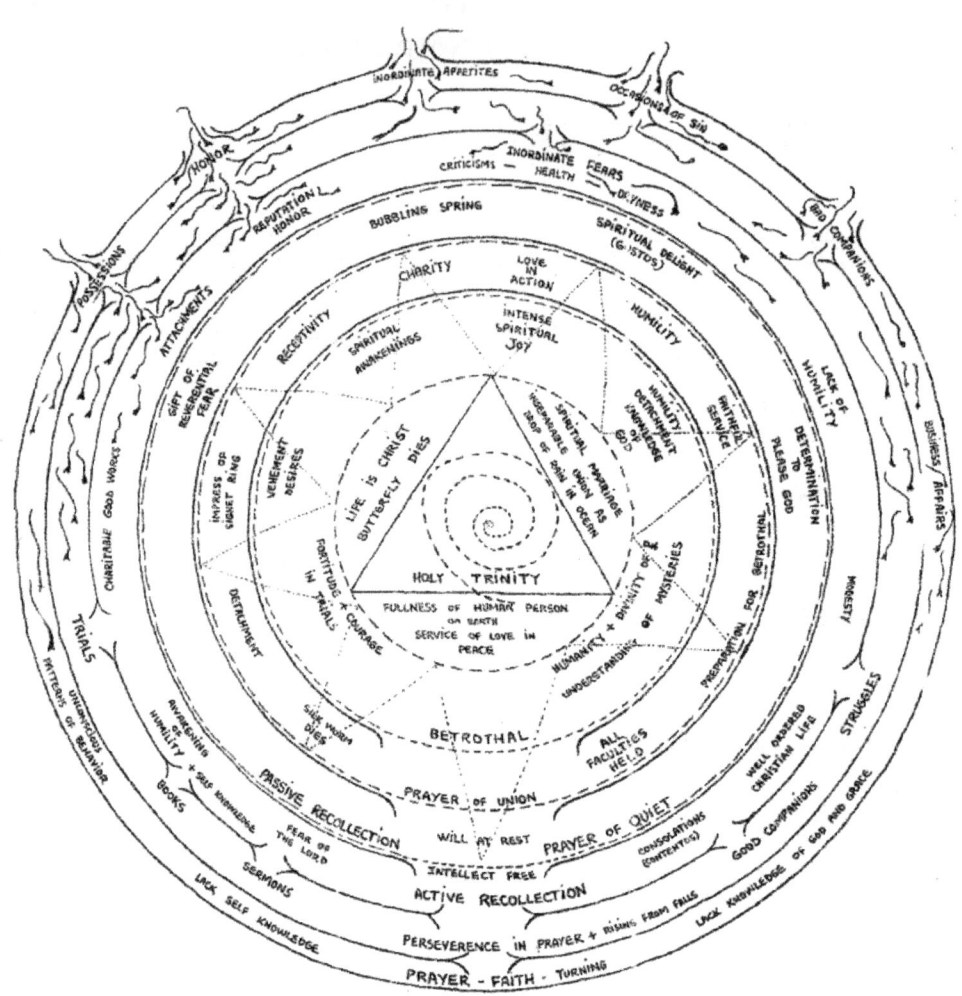

Drawing by Sr. Berenice Casale, ocd

Another Book of Interest in Carmelite Spirituality

By Sister Leslie Lund, ocdh

Journey with St. John of the Cross through the Dark Night to Divine Intimacy:

A Spiritual Direction Guide, and Study Resource

Journey with St. John of the Cross through the Dark Night to Divine Intimacy is a guide for the stages of the spiritual life, based on St. John of the Cross' masterpieces on contemplative prayer and the spiritual journey: *Ascent of Mt. Carmel* and *Dark Night*. It is an introduction as well as an academic teaching for those who want to better understand their reading of St. John of the Cross. This book can be for beginners on the journey, those in stalemate, or those proficient in prayer and the spiritual life. It would be of great value to Clergy, Apostolic Religious, lay Associates, Carmelites and anyone interested in the stages of the spiritual life and its difficult passages, prayer and spirituality. This book also offers helpful suggestions for prayer, explanations of Sanjuanist terminology, and the spiritual direction guidance of St. John of the Cross. Unique to this book is also practical suggestions of a psychological and neurological nature that underpin and can support the teaching and counsels of John of the Cross for transformation.

"This is a wonderful study on the Dark Night in John of the Cross. Sister Leslie Lund has given to all scholars, researchers, and students of St. John of the Cross both a detailed study and an exceptionally useful reference book for all the components of John's understanding of the Dark Night. This is Sister Leslie's second book, following the well-received and appreciated study of St. Teresa of Avila—*Journey into Divine Intimacy with St. Teresa of Avila: A Retreat, Spiritual Direction Guide, and Study Resource.* Like her first book, this current one is a gift not only to scholars and serious students of spirituality, but also a companion to disciples who seek to journey to God along the path of the great Carmelite spiritual guides. The book will be particularly helpful for spiritual directors and formation personnel."

Professor Leonard Doohan, PhD, Teresianum
Professor Emeritus, Gonzaga University, and Teresian and Sanjuanist Scholar

"Anyone involved in researching or teaching John of the Cross, anyone serious about their own prayer and spiritual growth or guiding another in prayer and formation, anyone involved with John in any way, would be denying themselves a major asset in not having a copy of this extraordinary book at hand. This is a comprehensive, readable, unbelievably thorough work that is not only informative and helpful, but fully engaging, while going beneath any superficial ideas of how John has been interpreted. One would be hard put to find an area of John's spirituality that is not thoroughly and intelligently treated. The work is arranged so that a particular area can be easily accessed. However, once the needed information is located and read, it is difficult to put the book down. It is not an exaggeration to say that this engaging encounter with Jesus, through the teachings of John of the Cross, is a work of genius. I can only express gratitude to Sr. Leslie for the work, love, and knowledge of John, that she has poured into this *Journey with St. John of the Cross through the Dark Night to Divine Intimacy"*.

Sister Mary Clare Doherty, ocd
Boston Carmel

"*Journey with St. John of the Cross through the Dark Night to Divine Intimacy* is a wonderful guide for beginners and proficients in the spiritual life, and an excellent resource for spiritual direction for those entering the active and passive dark nights of sense and spirit. The book is well-written and a pleasure to read, and Sr. Leslie does a marvelous job unpacking what is sometimes difficult reading in St. John's Dark Night. The book contains a comprehensive review of various "prayer paths" that include Lectio Divina, Centering Prayer, St. John's Simple Gaze, St. Teresa's Simple Recollection, and Eastern and Christian Western meditation. Furthermore, the impact of body/brain, mind/psyche dynamics on spiritual growth and development is explored and very interesting. This book has been particularly helpful to me in my own personal dark night journey, and I highly recommend it for anyone wishing to go deeper in their relationship with God."

Sister Susan Elisabeth Labyak, ocd—Seattle Carmel

"This is not a book that will be read through once, closed and then seem digested. Sr. Leslie's book is a comprehensive teaching companion to the reading and study of *The Ascent of Mt. Carmel* and *The Dark Night* works of St. John of the Cross. It is also a supportive spiritual direction companion for the reader's daily life. This book makes John's teaching on the Christian life in imitation of Jesus more accessible to any seeker of a committed, intimate relationship with God in each moment of every day through contemplative life and prayer. Practical suggestions are offered to move the reader from moments of prayer into a life lived to the full in the unwavering faith, joyful hope and self-giving love of intimacy with Jesus Christ."
Sister Nancy Casale, ocdh--Carmelite Sisters of Mary

Available on Amazon.com Fall 2023

www.ingramcontent.com/pod-product-compliance
Lightning Source LLC
Chambersburg PA
CBHW080528170426
43195CB00016B/2498